AA Book of Driving

AA Book of Driving

The Automobile Association

Produced by the Publications Division of the
Automobile Association

Phototypeset, printed and bound by
Sir Joseph Causton Limited London and Eastleigh

© Copyright The Automobile Association 1980   55819

ISBN 0 86145 021 3

Published by the
Automobile Association,
Fanum House Basingstoke
Hampshire RG21 2EA

Consultant Editor
Marcus Jacobson DipAM(Sheff) CEng FIMechE MSAE(USA) MIProdE FIMI MInstCTech
Chief Engineer of the Automobile Association

Editor
Michael Buttler

Assistant Editor
Rebecca King

Associate Editor
Douglas Mitchell

Design Consultant
David Playne NDD MSIAD MSTD

Contributors

Adrian Ball
Ivan Brown
Andrew Clayton
Bill Degenhardt
Mike Franey
Richard Hudson-Evans
Joss Jocelyn
Roy Johnstone

John C Kennedy
Murray Mackay
Martin Morris
Ian Morton
H P C Murphy
Ken Rogers
John Vann

Designers, photographers, illustrators and researchers

Robert Ayliffe
Roland B Berry
Simon Borrough
Laurie Clark
Jonathan Chapman
Mark Huggett

Tony Jenkins
Nick Jones
Chris Norman
David Playne
Craig Warwick (Linden Artists)
Lois Wigens

Contents

Introduction

For most car owners driving has become a tedious chore, to be endured rather than enjoyed, and to be completed as soon as possible. To travel (hopefully or otherwise) is no longer better than to arrive. This book has been prepared in order to awaken and develop interest in all aspects of driving. One of its objects is to rekindle the pleasure of motoring.

Driving is a skill which takes time to acquire and practice to perfect. Like all skills, doing it well is a source of satisfaction in itself, but in the case of driving, a high degree of skill could result in possible saving of lives or, at the very least, a saving in money. The latter can come about through economising on fuel, but also by avoiding accidents and the consequent repair bills.

The subject of driving standards is frequently surrounded by heated debate and it is right that this should be so. Every driver should care personally about the way he or she drives. Standards, in general, are good, although this is not to say there is no room for improvement. One of the aims of this book is to point the way to where such improvements could lie. The general purpose of this book, however, is to inform, stimulate and entertain everyone who drives or is interested in driving. Every subject which bears upon the task of driving is explored and discussed here in a way which is authoritative yet never dull.

Clear and ingenious diagrams explain what can be complex to describe, while most aspects of driving are illustrated with photographs taken from the driver's viewpoint. These all help to bring the subject alive and relate it to what actually happens on the road. Every reader will find in this book echoes of his or her own experience on the road.

There are many ways to use this book. The subject matter is presented in a logical order as described on the contents page. Each topic discussed is generally allocated and contained within a double spread of two facing pages. Many readers, however, may not wish to read the book from beginning to end, but might prefer to dip into particular parts. For them, a quick guide to selected aspects of the book's contents is provided on pages 10 and 11. Here, individual topics can be picked up and traced to their respective places in the book. A special section at the end of the book has been devised for those who are learning to drive.

The contents of this book are serious subjects, yet there is a risk of becoming too solemn. A change of pace is provided from time to time by the appearance of a quiz or test-your-knowledge feature. These are intended to be an opportunity for readers to compare their own knowledge and experience with what is contained in this book.

Almost every aspect of owning and using a car is described in these pages, with the exception of technical description and servicing and maintenance information. As a work of reference it can be consulted whenever an experience on the road makes you question who was right. Its general purpose will have been achieved, however, if it brings more pleasure into a driver's life and, because of that, brings greater safety and courtesy to the roads.

How to use this book

Driving is a very personal and individual activity. No two drivers are the same and we must all co-exist with everyone else. This book is designed to show how varied and interesting driving can be, bringing together as many different aspects of the subject as possible. To help each reader find those aspects of the subject which have most appeal, this page and the facing page pose a number of questions or challenges. Your responses to these questions lead to suggestions as to where to turn first.

This book contains a wide diversity of material. It is split up into 120 individual topic spreads, each of them self-contained. It is not a book to be read straight through from the first page to the last. It is a book to be used, to be dipped into, and to be referred to constantly. It can be opened at random, but it can also be approached in a planned way.

If the questions posed on these pages start you wondering and questioning your own knowledge and attitudes, they will have met their purpose. In most cases, however, the answers to them will be found on the pages referred to.

The second part of this quiz, 'Do you enjoy driving?' is slightly more challenging as it questions some deeply held attitudes. On the basis of this quiz, which should not be taken too seriously, you can also start to find your way around the book, as each answer you give is linked to a suggestion about the section you should read as a result.

Have you wondered which are the best towing techniques? Do you know how to load your caravan correctly? Would you know how to control a snaking movement if it developed? Would you know how to prevent it happening in the first place?

Pages 182–187

Is your car costing too much to run? Do you know just how much it does cost? Can you save money by driving in a different style? Is your car wasting your money by poor tuning or through leaks? Do you regularly monitor your motoring costs?

Pages 162–167, 244–249

Do you always wear a seat belt? Do you have doubts about their usefulness? Do all the members of your family use safety belts or restraints? Should pregnant women wear seat belts?

Pages 132–135, 168–173

Would the idea of driving in a foreign country worry you? Are you familiar with the preparations you should make and the documents you need? Are you prepared for driving on the right hand side of the road?

Pages 74–81

Do you think motorways are dangerous or do you enjoy the opportunities they present? Would you know what to do if you broke down on a motorway? Do you know what all the light signals mean?

Pages 60–65, 148–149

Does heavy traffic make driving difficult for you? Do you tend to avoid the cut and thrust of town centre driving? Do you take advantage of small gaps in the traffic stream or do you wait for others to give way to you?

Pages 18–29, 66–71

Do you know how much you can drink before it affects your driving? Do you know the effects of alcohol on any drugs you may be taking? Do you know the legal limit of alcohol in the blood? What happens if you mix your drinks?

Pages 150–153

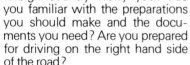

How well do you read the road ahead of you? How often do you look in your mirrors? How far ahead of your car do you normally look? Are you often taken by surprise when driving? Do your eyes sometimes feel strained when driving?

Pages 34–41, 72–73, 88–93

Do you try to avoid driving in wintry weather? Are you confident your car will not let you down in bad weather? If you get stuck in the snow would you know how to get out? Do you know where to fit any extra lights you may buy?

Pages 100–113, 176–177, 252–257

Is someone in your family learning to drive? Have you considered teaching them yourself? What will you do if you are asked to help them practise what they have been taught? Have you looked at the Highway Code recently?

Pages 196–239

Do you enjoy driving?

Many people claim that most of the pleasure has now been removed from driving. This is not true for everybody and it is usually the case that the more interest you take in your driving the more enjoyable it will be.

This short quiz will give you an opportunity to assess your attitudes to driving and to other motorists, and it will also guide to certain parts of this book, depending on the answers you give. In this way you will be directed straight to the section which you will find of interest or will help to resolve some of your doubts.

1 Do you find driving:
a is often terrifying?
b is just a convenient way of getting about?
c gives you pleasure and satisfaction?

2 When driving do you:
a concentrate on driving your own car and let other people sort themselves out?
b adapt your driving to keep everyone moving?

3 The thing that makes a good driver is mostly:
a fast reactions
b good anticipation

4 Knowing what goes on under the car's bonnet is:
a essential for good driving
b useful but not essential
c irrelevant to good driving

5 Accidents happen mostly because:
a the driver is not skilful enough
b the driver is unlucky

6 The people who cause most accidents are:
a young and reckless
b old and overcautious
c pedestrians and cyclists

7 The Highway Code is:
a just to help new drivers
b to be followed by everyone

8 Seat belts:
a are dangerous
b should be compulsory
c should be worn only if people want to

9 Driving long distances:
a is best done at night when traffic is light
b is best done during the day

10 Do you drive:
a only in this country?
b abroad occasionally?
c abroad quite a lot

Your answers to these questions can be scored as follows: According to which answer you selected, certain parts of this book will be found particularly interesting or relevant, and you will be able to find out from reading these sections whether you were right.

Use the table below to score your answers and see which parts of the book to read first.

Under 20
You probably do not have a great deal of experience on the road, being either a newly-qualified driver or someone who makes only short, very local journeys. Even though you have passed the driving test, Section 7, on learning to drive (pages 194–239) will undoubtedly contain much of interest and be a good jumping off point to the rest of the book.

21–30
You may regard motoring as mainly a method of getting from A to B, and perhaps your work involves a great deal of driving. Section 2, On the Road (pages 46–83) could be particularly valuable and interesting for you.

31–40
You have probably acquired considerable driving experience over the years and you should find Section 1, Better Driving (pages 12–45) the best place to start reading this book.

41–50
You undoubtedly have great interest in the subject of driving and probably drive with skill. All parts of this book should interest you, particularly Section 6, Living with the Car (pages 156–193).

1	2	3	4	5	6	7	8	9	10	Question
b	a	b						b	a b c	**Section 1** Better Driving, pages 12–45
a		a b a b						b	a b	**Section 2** On the road, pages 46–83
		a b						b	c	**Section 3** All weather driving, pages 84–113
			b c a b a	c		b c				**Section 4** Emergencies, pages 114–139
		a b			b			a		**Section 5** Fit to drive, pages 140–155
c		a				a b c				**Section 6** Living with the car, pages 156–193
						a				**Section 7** Learning to drive, pages 194–239
						a b				**Section 8** Useful information, pages 240–264
0 3 5	0 5	1 5 5 4 0	5 1 5 1 3	0 5	0 3 5	1 5	1 3 5			Score

1 Better driving

Better driving

For most drivers, however good their performance, there is seldom room for complacency. There is always the possibility of a situation arising, which makes you think, afterwards, that you did not handle it quite as well as you might have done, or that it could have been avoided by advance planning.

Everyone who takes an interest in his driving will find many echoes of his own experience in this section of the book. The basis of it is an imaginary route to be followed through photographs, commentary and a route map, in which many familiar situations occur. The reader has the opportunity to compare what he would have done with what is described here. The situations are arranged so that almost all aspects of everyday driving occur at one time or another.

The dominant theme underlying this section is the importance of careful observation and good anticipation. The section ends with details of how to develop your driving skill through advanced driving courses and tests.

Acceleration
pages 18–19

Acceleration is a more subtle and versatile form of car control than simply making the car go faster. Careful use of the throttle can help you drive more safely and also more economically.

Steering
pages 20–21

Gentle but firm steering control is one key to driving safety and economy. The steering procedures for different situations are described here as well as the best ways of holding the steering wheel.

Gear changing
pages 22–23

One of the most common driving faults is being in the wrong gear for a particular situation. Planning ahead and changing gear at the right time results in a safer and smoother journey.

Cornering
pages 24–25

The safest approaches to different types of corners including the best ways to increase your vision are described here, as well as the ways in which the cornering forces affect the car's stability.

Driving with consideration
pages 34–35

Thoughtfulness and consideration towards other road users makes a great deal of difference to the safety of any particular situation. Many road users are pedestrians or riders of two-wheeled vehicles. These people are most vulnerable and need extra consideration.

Observation
pages 36–37

Good observation is the foundation of better driving. By looking well ahead as well as to the sides and the rear, you can ensure that you will hardly ever be taken unawares by any road situation. You will also give yourself plenty of time to react well in advance.

Pre-start routine
pages 16–17

It is of great benefit to develop a regular routine which you carry out before getting into the car. It is valuable to carry out this routine as a preamble to every occasion when you drive your car. A systematic list of quick checks is suggested, the first part of which is carried out before getting into the car, and the second part when starting up and driving off. Making this series of checks a routine helps to make you a safer driver.

Braking
pages 26–27

Understanding the best and safest ways of slowing down in particular situations can also result in greater fuel economy. Good anticipation and gentle deceleration may often save wear and tear.

Overtaking
pages 28–29

The most dangerous manoeuvre on the road is that of overtaking. It needs to be carried out with great care, planning well ahead to protect the safety of yourself and other road users.

Junctions
pages 30–31

Many unfamiliar junctions can appear to be forbiddingly complex unless you know how to tackle them in simple stages. The procedure for many different types of junction is explained here.

Roundabouts
pages 32–33

Several different kinds of roundabout are encountered on the road today, from mini-roundabouts to extremely complicated traffic schemes. This section explains the right way to treat them all.

Anticipation
pages 38–39

One important object of good observation is to be able to anticipate a development on the road before it takes place. Examples given here illustrate the situations to watch out for and ways of predicting what will happen on the road ahead.

Commentary driving
pages 40–41

A very good way to ensure that you are observing the road adequately and planning your driving accordingly is to keep up a running commentary while driving, including everything you expect to develop as well as the decisions you plan to make.

Advanced driving
pages 42–43

A widely recognised standard of better driving is that laid down by the Institute of Advanced Motorists in their driving test. This spread summarises the general attitudes and approach expected by the Institute and explains how the test is carried out and main faults found.

Skilled driving courses
pages 44–45

Many different kinds of skilled driving courses are available for those who wish to improve their driving to the highest standards. Some courses are about night driving and motorway driving, while others are pitched at a considerably higher standard.

Pre-start routine Better driving

It is unwise to get into your car and drive away immediately without spending a few minutes carrying out some simple checks. A few minutes spent walking round the car will be enough to spot any obvious defects which could turn out to be dangerous.

Wipers

Lift all wiper blades clear of the screen and wipe them with a damp cloth to remove any dried-on grit.

Side and rear windows

The rear and side windows should be wiped clear with a damp cloth for optimum visibility.

Rear lights

Clean the lenses of all the rear lights and check that they are working properly. It will probably be necessary to switch on the ignition to carry out this check.

Windscreen

Use a soft damp cloth to clean the windscreen. This will lessen the chance of scratches being made which then cause dazzle in bright sun or at night.

Tyres

A visual check of all the tyres should be carried out every day by walking round the car. It should not be necessary to check the pressures every day, although this should be done whenever you believe any tyre is not at the right pressure. Look for any damage to the side walls and quickly clear any large objects from the tread. While walking round the car check the road behind and in front of the car to make sure there are no objects which might damage the tyres.

Lights

Dirty lights can be 50% less efficient, so wipe off any grime, using soapy water if necessary. Also clean the sidelights. Check these are working, also the headlights on full and dipped beam.

Mirrors

Align the external mirrors correctly. Clean them if necessary with a damp cloth and then dry them.

Under the bonnet

A few seconds spent checking the oil and coolant levels could save time and money later. This will also be an opportunity to check that the windscreen washer reservoir is topped up. Make sure the bonnet is shut securely.

When the quick visual inspection and cleaning of the exterior is complete, you can then settle yourself inside the car. A few minutes spent getting comfortable, making sure the windows are clean and that your seat belt is adjusted properly will add to your safety. Acquiring a routine which you carry out every time you get into the car will save time and ensure that no items are missed out.

6 Start the engine Before starting the engine check that the handbrake is on and the car is in neutral. Apply the starter motor in bursts of about 5 seconds, with intervals of about 30 seconds. If you have to use the choke push it home as soon as you can to save fuel.

7 Check instruments When the engine is running look briefly over the dashboard instruments. Check that the ignition warning light and oil pressure lights have gone out, and that you have sufficient fuel. If you are in a strange car, be sure you know where all the controls are.

8 Move off After checking all round and in the mirrors that it is safe to do so, you signal and move off. As soon as possible, preferably within the first few yards, and after making quite sure that it is safe, you should reassure yourself that your brakes are working properly.

1 Windows It is just as important to clean the inside of the windows as the outside. Use a dry cloth rather than a damp one.

2 Doors Check that the doors, including the passenger doors, are properly shut before starting up the engine.

3 Seat Adjust your seat to give yourself maximum comfort on every journey.

4 Mirror Ensure the interior mirror is clean and properly adjusted.

5 Seat belt Wearing a seat belt is widely accepted as sensible. Make it a habit to fasten your seat belt before starting.

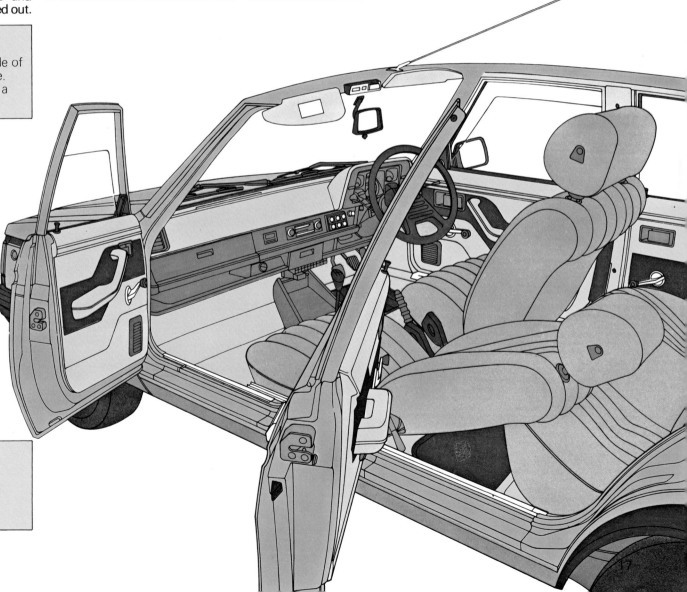

17

Acceleration Better driving

A good way to think of the accelerator is not so much as a device to increase speed but rather as emptying a purse containing the cash equivalent of the petrol in the tank. The more you put your foot down, the more coins are drawn out of it. Accelerate violently and even more money disappears. Just how much more is amply illustrated by a road test in which a family saloon was twice driven over the same 21-mile road route. All speed limits were observed but on the first run the throttle was used harshly. The saving in time was just 4½ minutes but there was a 22½% increase in fuel consumption.

Acceleration and stability

The moral is to drive smoothly and keep a light touch on the controls at all times. Sudden bursts of acceleration puts more strain on steering, tyres and transmission linkages, while equally sudden deceleration hastens brake and tyre wear. Economy is not the only consideration, however. No passenger is going to be comfortable when he

or she is being pushed backwards and forwards like a yo-yo, as well as having to contend with the extra centrifugal forces on bends.

Our journey begins in suburbia and, from the outset, the aim is to drive with modest acceleration, braking and gearchanging. This is only achieved by painstaking observation, anticipation and positioning and not hurrying. We are approaching a right hand bend.

Right hand bend

Although the bend is still some distance away, take the foot off the throttle, brake lightly and change down if necessary.

As we enter, keeping well to the left to improve stability and sight-line, our speed is at its lowest point.

Light, progressive throttle through the bend increases grip and stability. Unless obstructed, never brake as it could induce a skid. Exit speed should generally be slightly higher than on entry. Now, if safe, accelerate smoothly away.

Left hand bend

Views differ on the best position approaching a left hand bend . . .

Some authorities advise keeping well over to the left and reducing speed because of restricted visibility.

Other experts recommend taking a wide course, if safe, to increase vision and stability through the bend, but ensure that

the car doesn't cross the centre road markings.

Hazard ahead

Continuing along the long straight section of road we observe a car parked on the left just before the left turning. The passenger's door is open and someone is standing

beside it. We take care preparing to pass this hazard, as one of the car occupants may walk into the road, a car may emerge from the left turning or opposing traffic may come round the right hand corner ahead, close to or over the centre line. We ease off the power on the approach to the

parked car and check the mirrors to ensure that no one is coming up fast behind. Once we are satisfied that it is safe to pass we accelerate firmly, changing gear to do so if necessary.

18

Normal overtaking

Planned overtaking, should be smooth and calm. There is a slow moving lorry some way in front.

We have now joined a short section of dual carriageway road, and we now start to overtake. All clear behind, so we signal and select our course. We shall take a wider path along the dual carriageway than the other vehicle and, accelerating smoothly, pass it with the central reservation on the offside, returning to the nearside when safe.

Decelerate—not brake

Observing the 'dual carriageway ends' sign, we adjust our speed to the speed limit without braking.

The road is level and clear: so power off in good time to ensure correct speed when we reach the single carriageway.

Anticipate

Traffic lights ahead so ease off the power now and check the mirrors (braking lightly and changing down) to avoid a rapid stop.

Junction

Decelerate before the bend approaching the junction. Check mirrors (braking lightly and changing low gear and turn.

Gear changing

For economy, comfort and safety, build up speed with correct gear changing and smooth acceleration. The owner's handbook will give figures for the maximum speeds in each gear, and it is commonly recommended that by halving these figures, the appropriate speeds for normal gear changes will be obtained. Most people, however, rely on the note of the engine to guide them when to change gear. Never allow the engine to labour, however.

Forces of acceleration

Rapid acceleration and fast cornering exert considerable forces. When accelerating hard from rest in first gear these forces reach their peak. In a typical saloon, occupants will be pressed back as if someone about one-fifth of their weight were leaning on them. Fast cornering generates harsher pressures on drivers and passengers. These can be so great that it feels as if someone of half their weight or more is leaning on them sideways.

Research into car handling has shown that new cars will achieve a sideways acceleration of 0.6g (0.6 times the force of gravity) at a steady speed in dry weather on a circular steering pad. In real-life traffic conditions when older vehicles are involved, this behaviour cannot always be reproduced, and it has been found that on normal British cross-country roads, forces of the order of 0.3g are usually involved. Those who corner very violently, however, can create forces of around 0.5g.

Acceleration sense

A close understanding of how your car behaves is an important safety factor. In some situations, it is better to accelerate past the hazard and out of harm's way. Knowing what performance you can obtain from your car is crucial to doing this safely. The alternative of braking sharply might result in loss of control and possibly a collision. It is also important to be able to assess the speed of other vehicles accurately.

Steering Better driving

As with everything else connected with driving, the maxim where steering is concerned is to keep it gentle, and keep it smooth. Once again, the key is anticipation, observation and concentration. Just as important is regular maintenance —not only of the steering mechanism, but of the suspension, transmission (especially if front wheel drive) and wheels and tyres. Incorrect and mis-matched tyre pressures can seriously impair the car's handling.

Left hand corner

We now want to turn left. Having taken the usual precautions (especially checking for cyclists and motorcyclists on the nearside), signalled, adjusted speed and selected appropriate gear, we steer round the corner, ensuring that we don't swing out. Don't let the steering wheel spin back on its own: feed it through the hands. And watch out for pedestrians!

Parking

A shopping stop: we shall park at the side of the road. Check mirror, indicate left, and draw abreast of the leading car. Check the mirror again; now reverse carefully. Steer left, aiming for the kerb midway in the space. As our front wing clears the car's rear, steer sharply right, then straighten and park tidily.

Reversing into side road

We have just missed a right turning but a minor road is coming up on the left. We look into it as we pass.

We check mirror, adjust speed with the brake and pull into the kerb just past the opening. If all is clear behind, reverse. As the nearside rear wheel draws abreast of the start of the corner

we steer hard left, making sure that the side turning is clear.

Steering around parked cars

We are now approaching the outskirts of a town and, coming up on the nearside, is a long line of parked cars. We set our course well in advance, first checking the mirror and, after ensuring that all is clear behind, indicating our intention before pulling out.

Beginning the manoeuvre well before the first of the obstructions avoids swerving (always dangerous) and improves visibility.

Steering guidance

● After changing gear or operating the indicator and dashboard controls, return your hand to the steering wheel as quickly as possible.
● The recommended position for the hands on the steering wheel is usually given as 'ten-to-two'. In some cars, to keep to this position can become tiring, and it may be more comfortable to put the hands at 'quarter-to-three'.
● On a long journey requiring little steering variation, such as on an empty motorway, do not allow your arm muscles to become fatigued.
● Keep both hands on the steering wheel. Any sudden need to change course, or any change in the road surface will need quick reactions.

Turning in the road

Reverse towards the car behind and stop. Once the road is clear, move off, steering hard right. Brake a few inches from the opposite kerb changing steering to the left, apply handbrake and, after checking the road, reverse, steering hard left. Stop once the nose is pointing the way we've come and, when safe, proceed forwards and straighten up.

As the car comes round . . .

we keep left lock until the pavement is visible through the rear window. We then steer right and finish close to the kerb.

Right hand turn

Back on the correct road, we must turn right at the T-junction.

Check mirrors and, if clear, signal. Then adjusting speed, we steer gently towards the crown of the road.

Keep the right indicator switched on and, after another mirror check slow down, selecting low gear just before the junction.

Be prepared to stop but, if safe to do so, proceed into the junction, steering right to the line of an imaginary nearside kerb.

Holding the wheel

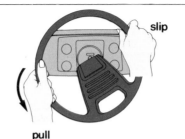

The usual position for the hands when driving straight ahead is at ten-to-two. When turning do not cross hands.

pull

When turning to the left, first pull down with the left hand, allowing the wheel to slide through the right hand. For a right turn, reverse the procedure.

slip · push / slip

If a further turn of the steering wheel is needed, slide the right hand down, in a line with the left, then push up, sliding the rim through the left hand.

Overtaking

Prepare the manoeuvre well ahead.

By giving ourselves plenty of time, we can begin to overtake early. This will enable us to steer out smoothly as opposed to swerving.

Blowout

A blowout in a front tyre does not pose extreme handling problems. Take the feet off all the pedals and steer the car gently to the side.

A blowout in one of the rear tyres is more serious.

When this happens the rear of the car may break away. Avoid panic and do not over-correct the skid. Many blowouts would not occur if tyres were properly maintained.

Right fork

Many road junctions are now planned as forks in the road preceded by well-defined road markings.

The right-turning lane is separated by hatched road markings. Signal in good time and move into the turning lane early.

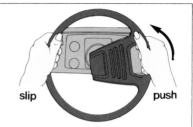

Gear changing Better driving

It is a fact that few people use their car's gears properly. The reason is that they have never become fully aware of their car's all-round performance and handling characteristics. Lack of observation and anticipation are other contributing factors. As a result, many motorists waste fuel by driving in the wrong gear, and a common fault is to use the gears to slow down.

Best methods of gear changing

One of the commonest driving faults is being in the wrong gear—sometimes the result of wayward anticipation, at other times sheer laziness. This is a dangerous and uneconomical shortcoming. It is hazardous because, if you are in too high a gear, it is impossible to escape from situations that demand smart acceleration; it is wasteful because you will use more petrol and put unnecessary strain on the engine and transmission. Experience and 'feel' will tell you when you need to engage a different gear. Do not try to reach the maximum speed in each gear. Listen to the engine note and change gear when the engine labours.

Most cars will apparently start away quite happily in second gear, but you should always use first. It will minimise clutch wear and prevent the engine labouring. If you are in too high a gear, do not take the lazy way out by slipping the clutch. Habits of this kind can lead to rapid wear of the lining and, indeed, of all moving, load-bearing components.

Missing out a gear

Keeping gear changing to a sensible minimum should be the aim. This is only done by reading and assessing the road ahead, with the instinctive knowledge of how the car will behave in every eventuality. Another way, when appropriate, is to miss out a gear. On our journey, the sign tells us that the road is about to narrow; not only that but where the wide stretch ends there is a left hand bend and, immediately beyond a steep upward gradient.

Clearly, we need a low gear before the road swings left. So ease off power in good time, then gentle braking and, mindful of the 1 in 10 climb, change down from 4th to 2nd just before the bend.

Top, 3rd, 2nd

Now let us suppose that instead of changing down we had remained in top gear. The engine, having lost most of its revs through the bend, would labour on the gradient, and might almost stall. Many motorists, to add to the troubles, are in the habit of going right through the box when changing gear.

In consequence, they would select 3rd gear at this point then, finding the engine still labouring, change down again to 2nd gear. By skipping a gear earlier, we can now change up to 3rd gear.

Changing up

To work out the right moment to change up, we must refer to our knowledge of the car's performance. The moment comes in this case when the speed reached in 2nd gear can be maintained in 3rd without increasing pressure on the throttle pedal. The time to change gear is best judged by listening to the engine note.

We stay in 3rd gear until we have negotiated the bends ahead.

Barrier across road

For maximum economy, we should get into top gear whenever possible, providing speed is sufficient, and conditions are suitable. So we change into 4th gear now.

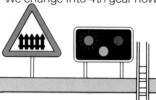

Up ahead, we see flashing red lights on both sides of the highway. These generally mean only one thing: a level crossing barrier across the road and, judging by the small traffic queue, the train is still due. There is no sense in maintaining speed, so save petrol. Ease off the power, check the mirrors and brake gently. By the time we get to the crossing, the barrier may have lifted, enabling us to select the right gear and continue.

Heel and toe

This technique is frowned on by many experts because it invariably means that anticipation has been lacking, or the motorist is in a hurry. It enables you to brake and change down in one smooth movement. On engaging second gear quickly from fourth, say, you blip the accelerator with your heel, at the same time depressing the brake with the ball of the right foot. This action is synchronised to the movement of your left foot as it lets in the clutch, and is designed to eradicate the sharp jerk which would otherwise result. It is far better, however, to give yourself sufficient time to brake first and then change down.

Automatic gear boxes

If you have been taught in and passed your test in a car with automatic transmission, you will break the law if you drive a car fitted with a manual gearbox.

Many owners of cars with automatic gearboxes simply put the selection lever in the 'drive' position and keep it there.

There are some occasions, however, when you need more rapid acceleration. To achieve this with an automatic transmission, you push the accelerator sharply to the floor; assuming that it is within the appropriate speed range, the next lower gear is automatically engaged. It is more economical to use the manual override.

Gear or brakes?

After leaving the level crossing, a sign warns of a steep downhill section. The right hand bend makes it impossible to gauge conditions, so we check the mirrors, brake gently and select the appropriate gear before the hill. To maintain caution and car control, we stay in low gear, adjusting speed with light pressure on the footbrake.

Many drivers remain in top gear when travelling downhill and rely on their brakes to slow their rate of progress. This can be dangerous (and expensive) because the friction caused by constant pressure on the footbrake can result in the brakes becoming glazed and ineffective.

5th gear or overdrive

Having negotiated the downhill stretch, we round a slight left-hander and, changing up to 4th gear and increasing speed, come to a lengthy section of dual carriageway. For economy, this is an ideal opportunity to select 5th gear or overdrive if the car is so equipped. It is all clear ahead, the highway is straight and level, and there are no side roads joining our course in the near future.

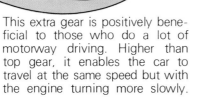

This extra gear is positively beneficial to those who do a lot of motorway driving. Higher than top gear, it enables the car to travel at the same speed but with the engine turning more slowly.

Back to fourth

The end of the dual carriageway section is now in sight

. . . and that means get ready for the change in speed limit. In fact, we shall need to adjust our speed much more than that. Although that bend ahead looks harmless enough, we do not know yet what is around it. If in 5th gear, change down to 4th and take off the power, braking gently if necessary. If in overdrive, disengage the overdrive switch to obtain 4th gear.

Change down to 3rd

It is as well that we took the precaution of slowing before that bend, slight as it was.

The curve hid the road junction ahead, and the straight section leading into it is not very long. If we had simply adjusted to the speed limit, we would have had to brake sharply to reduce our approach speed. As it is, having dropped to 4th gear and taken off the power, we have given ourselves plenty of time. Now we check the mirrors, brake to get the speed right, then change gear, if necessary, in readiness for the junction procedure ahead. When we reach the junction we shall be at the right speed and in the right gear to have time to assess it and stop or proceed as necessary.

Cornering Better driving

A car is at its most stable when travelling in a straight line. Completely different forces come into play on a curved path, pressures that act against a driver's efforts to steer the required course. Assuming that the car is roadworthy and tyre pressures correspond to the manufacturer's recommendations, we are left with the all-important system of approach.

Forces during cornering

When a vehicle is driven round a bend, forces are set up which make it less stable. The main force is centrifugal, tending to push the car towards the outside of the bend. This force acts in addition to the forward momentum of the vehicle.

The tyres are designed so that they maintain their grip on the road during cornering. As the driver steers round a bend, the tyres usually point in a slightly different direction from the one in which the car is moving. The difference in these two angles is called the slip angle. Different kinds of tyres have differing slip angles, radial ply tyres having a smaller slip angle than cross-plies. The cornering force generated by the tyre must be greater than the centrifugal force for the vehicle to travel round the bend successfully.

Although the rear tyres do not steer round the bend, they must generate adequate cornering forces. These forces are generally less than those generated by the front tyres.

Right hand bend

The first step, well before the bend, is to weigh up the layout of the road. Only then can we select our course for correct positioning on entry, and the right speed. We keep to the nearside throughout to improve sightlines and accelerate progressively.

Left hand turn

Well before the 'Stop' sign we check the mirrors, indicate left and ease off the power. We halt at the 'Stop' lines and apply the handbrake. Then we engage first gear while carefully assessing the road we're joining, looking especially for approaching motorcycles and pedestrians about to cross the road. If clear, we move off, keeping to the nearside.

Left hand bend

Like right handers, the approach

is vital. But this time, if safe, steer a

wide course to increase visibility.

Hairpin bend

These are usually a combination of steep gradients and tortuous curves.
Select low gear before the initial bend to assist the brakes.

Keep to the nearside, on left handers too.

Cornering rules

There is a winding stretch ahead and the priority, as with all bends, is to adjust approach speed sufficiently to avoid the need for braking while cornering.

When a car starts to turn, the distribution of weight builds up on the outside wheels.

The car should always be in the right position in the road, travelling at the right speed and with the right gear engaged. To improve stability, accelerate gently through the bend. Speed on exit should generally be higher than on entry.

Sightlines through bends
Position   Vision

Left hand bend

Keeping close to the left restricts vision

Keeping nearer to the centre line improves sightlines

Right hand bend

Keeping close to the left improves sightlines

Braking Better driving

Braking is potentially a hazardous driving procedure. A common mistake is to apply the brakes either too lightly or too late.

There are three methods of reducing speed: braking, changing down, or simply taking the foot off the accelerator. Unfortunately, many motorists do not match speed to road conditions by observation and anticipation. Instead, they rely on harsher braking than necessary when a hazard materialises. This is a practice that wastes fuel, increases wear and tear, and heightens the skid risk. How often, for instance, have you seen drivers approaching a traffic signal at speed and braking hard at the last minute? The safe, economic way to approach red traffic lights is to ease off the power in good time and brake gently after the usual mirror checks, of course.

Emergency braking

Tardy and harsh braking is the hallmark of bad driving. None-the-less, we all come up against the unexpected occasionally when emergency braking is the only option. The car sitting in the side road suddenly moves out directly in front of us, as though he has not seen us. Although we had noted his presence, we were unprepared for this irrational move. Our speed is such that we can stop before hitting him if we brake hard.

We apply the brakes hard, but as soon as we feel the wheels lock, we release the brakes then, re-apply them again. Continuing this process until we come to a halt is the best method of braking under these circumstances where the road is narrow and the surface provides very poor grip. Keeping the brakes hard on

all the time would certainly have resulted in a skid and a collision.

Hazards

Allow a space between vehicles of one foot per mph at speeds below 30 mph, and one yard per mph at speeds over 30 mph.

While being passed, start to hang back, ready to maintain a safe following distance behind the overtaking vehicle once it returns to the nearside.

Exercise caution wherever children are about. An emergency stop might not be enough to prevent an accident. As with all hazards, observation and anticipation will help avoid sudden braking and skid risk.

The 'School' warning sign means ease off the power and extra care.

A good driver is always watchful. He is as alert to the behaviour of all road users around him as he is to his own, alive to everything that's going on, even anticipating the actions of others and reacting accordingly in good time. This, in turn, will enable an adjustment of speed well before any hazard and, just as important, good, progressive braking. The sign coming up tells us that the left-hander we are approaching will become

tighter. We do all our braking on the straight road remaining.

Braking limits

Many drivers brake too lightly and too late in a hazardous situation, often because of poor anticipation and observation. Drivers' habits vary from one country to another. In Britain the average braking force applied is 0.3g to 0.4g, rising to 0.55g in heavy urban traffic.
In North America 0.4g is rarely exceeded, but in Italy that figure is the norm, rising to 0.55g in towns. Very heavy braking is common on congested German motorways. The braking limit depends on the grip of the tyre on the road. Only a very small area of the tyre is in contact with the road at any one time. This area is about as big as a size 9 shoe. Braking can only be effective if the tyre keeps revolving on the road (it must not lock up and skid). Maximum tyre grip is only obtained on a good road surface which is firm and dry. If these conditions hold and the tread on the tyre is good, all should be well.

When these conditions do not hold, as for example when the road is wet or the surface is loose, drivers should allow considerably more room between themselves and other vehicles to give plenty of space for braking in safety while maintaining control.

Cadence braking

This very specialised technique is used mainly by rally drivers and should not be attempted without a great deal of practice. The brakes are applied hard, the front of the car dips, the brakes are released momentarily, the front suspension rises then dips again. When it dips the brakes are reapplied hard.

Approach to a junction

As we near the T-junction we take off the power. We can see

along both carriageways of the main road that nothing is coming in either direction.

Our speed is such that we can change direct from top to second gear. Switch on the right indicator and

look well into the junction before making the right turn.

Covering the brake

We might not have used the brakes at the T-junction just now, but for safety, we kept our right foot covering the brake just in case. We shall do so again shortly as we close on the side turning coming up on the left. Positioned as it is and with a high hedge on our nearside, we notice as we approach that a vehicle is about to join our road. We adjust our speed by taking off the power and, as the car slows, our right foot hovers over the brake pedal. In this situation the other vehicle does not move out, but the precaution was a wise one which most drivers are taught, but regrettably, few keep up. Many situations would be safer if this were done.

Gradients

There is a steep down gradient ahead and, as the second road sign warns, a crossroads at the bottom. Many drivers, judging by the time

their brake lights stay on, would appear to stay in top and keep their foot on the brake pedal for virtually the whole descent. By doing so, however, they are in danger of polishing their linings, and making the brakes less efficient. It is better to take off the power and change to a lower gear in good time. After that, to check speed, brake firmly rather than make prolonged, light, applications.

Handbrake

Our route now climbs steeply. Halfway up the hill, the traffic

ahead of us stops. Once stationary, apply the handbrake and change into neutral. Do

not, as many drivers do, rely on the footbrake even on a slight gradient. The car might roll back when you prepare to get away, or your foot could slip off the pedal.

Overtaking Better driving

It is a sobering thought that when two cars approach one another on a collision course at 60mph, the gap between them closes at the rate of 176ft every second. Overtaking on a single carriageway is, consequently, often a most hazardous manoeuvre, and it is a major cause of fatal and serious injury accidents. It is important to pick exactly the right moment to overtake, ensuring that you can return safely to the nearside without cutting in sharply in front of the vehicle you have just overtaken.

Correct lane for overtaking

With the few exceptions listed in the panel on this page, drivers must overtake on the offside. In practice, however, it is clear that many motorists foolishly ignore this requirement.

A more common fault is to devote all one's concentration on the vehicle to be overtaken and any

oncoming traffic. But in assessing road surface conditions, carriageway width, closing distance, and other potential hazards, essential minor checks and signalling one's intention to pull out can be forgotten. Always check your mirrors for that car which might be about to pass you.

Three-lane road

Particular care is called for if overtaking on a three-lane road like this. Fortunately, there are few such stretches left in which opposing traffic uses the same (centre) lane when passing other vehicles.

These days, the old three-lane system has largely been superseded by road markings that indicate whether or not you can move into the centre lane (on no account enter it if the road marking on your immediate offside is a solid white line). These are usually staggered—first allowing overtaking by one stream and then, farther along, by the other. However, there are still some roads on which the centre lane for both traffic directions is bounded by a broken white line. These are especially hazardous; indeed the centre channel on these remaining examples is often referred to by police as the 'suicide lane' because of the risk of head-on collision.

On such a section, the only safe policy is to treat the centre lane as if it were the opposing stream of a single carriageway road.

No Overtaking

There are a number of situations when you must not overtake.
These are as follows:

if you would cross or straddle double white lines, where the solid white line is nearer to you;

after a 'No Overtaking' sign and before the sign showing the end of the restriction;

within the area marked by zig-zag lines on the approach to a Zebra crossing.

You should not overtake in the following situations:

approaching a pedestrian crossing even when there are no zig-zag lines;

when you would force another vehicle to slow down or swerve;

when approaching a corner or bend, the brow of a hill, a hump-backed bridge, or other place where you cannot see far enough ahead and other places where you might come into conflict with other road users.

If you are in any doubt, do not overtake.

Overtaking a line of traffic

The road narrows now and, ahead of us we see that five vehicles are moving slowly. It is a long, straight section and, with the absence of warning signs, and the presence of double line centre markings, cars

ahead decide to overtake and can do so safely. When the opportunity arises to pass the slow-moving vehicle in front we check our mirrors then signal. Before overtaking we sound the horn or use the headlamp flasher to warn other drivers of our presence. When it is safe to do so we accelerate firmly past.

Hold back positions

It is essential to keep our distance when overtaking—as it is when driving in traffic. From this distance we cannot see to overtake.

Preliminary planning should take place about 90ft behind the truck. From here we have a clear view of the offside and nearside well beyond the lorry.

When it is clear to overtake we note that the carriageway is sufficiently wide, and take a position slightly proud of the lorry, enabling us to see well ahead, and putting us in a good preparatory position.

Do not follow through

Resist blindly following the van in front when it starts to overtake the car.

Cyclists

We are now at the outskirts of a town, and ahead of us on the nearside is a pedal cyclist. After a mirror check and the correct signal, we overtake if safe ahead and behind. When passing powered two-wheelers or bicycles, always give them plenty of

room, at least 6ft. This allows for the contingency of a rider wobbling suddenly, or falling off his machine. If it is impossible to allow a good safety margin because of opposing traffic, we stay back until it is safe.

Stationary vehicles

We must halt before this line of parked vehicles on our nearside, if, by overtaking, we will cause opposing traffic to stop or slow.

Pedestrian crossings

Keep a sharp lookout for pedestrians at all times, but especially at Pelican, Zebra or traffic light controlled crossings. We must

not overtake when approaching a crossing even if the lights are in our favour. In the case of Zebra crossings, we must never overtake in the area marked by zig-zag lines.

Junctions Better driving

The golden rules to be observed at all road junctions are: select the right course, signal your intentions clearly and in good time, look all around you, and proceed only when it is safe and clear to do so.

This T-junction is more straightforward, but like all 'give way' situations, it is vital that we look carefully in all directions, stopping at the junction if necessary for a better view.

The first of these two crossroads may be only a minor junction, but we must still check mirrors and adjust speed to get a right-left-right view of it on the approach.

The second intersection (below left) is guarded by 'Give Way' road markings, so we slow right down, ready to stop if necessary. At the next crossroads, we want to turn right, so, after following the initial 'weighing up' procedure, we check the mirror. It is clear behind, we signal in good time and take up the correct position.

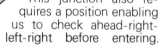

This Y-junction needs particular care. We have followed the routines in the panel below and, in accordance with the road sign, have come to a stop at the junction. We then apply the handbrake. After looking right and left, we check right again; this time we notice that a car has drawn up at the junction in that adjacent turning ready to turn left. Who should go first? There is now a chance that we could cause a dangerous situation by proceeding, so the best course is to give way.

Having joined our new route, we propose to turn left at the crossroads. The broken white lines across the road at the entrance warn that we must give way. As we turn, we watch carefully for any pedestrians who may be crossing the road, unaware of our presence.

This junction also requires a position enabling us to check ahead-right-left-right before entering.

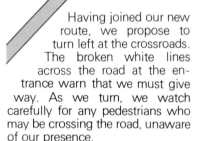

Junction procedure

Whether it is a T- or Y-junction, or a crossroads, the approach routine is the same. Check the mirrors first—then, by observation, find out all you can about the hazard in advance, and work out the position and course required.

Having decided the correct course according to whether you are turning left or right, or driving straight ahead, check the mirrors again. Next, if you are turning, signal in good time. Now adjust your speed and be ready to stop if necessary.

Keep looking into the junction and also into the mirrors to obtain a complete picture of the overall situation. Do not enter the junction until you have assembled all the information you can and have ensured that it is safe and clear to do so.

Once you enter the junction do not hesitate. You should have ascertained which path you would take before entering and, provided the way is clear, you ought not to leave other road-users in any doubt about what your intentions are.

We are now coming to a staggered crossroads and wish to turn right. At the previous intersection, we emerged into the junction at the same time that an oncoming vehicle, also turning right, entered. Both of us passed offside-to-offside before turning, the usual routine unless road markings or

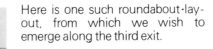

Here is one such roundabout-layout, from which we wish to emerge along the third exit.

Do not be put off by the apparent complications. The roundabout effectively comprises a series of junctions, the approaches to which follow the junction routine featured in the panel on the opposite page. The main difference between this and conventional

roundabouts is that the traffic flows in both directions, clockwise around the outside, anti-clockwise inside. Our course is shown by the dotted line. Thus, the key hazards are the points where opposing flows meet and same-direction traffic joins and leaves it. Roundabouts, including contra-rotating types, are covered comprehensively overleaf.

Do not cut corners!

Avoid a wide course when turning left, and do not cut right hand turns either. Imagine that you are following a kerb on a right hand bend, and keep close to it all the way round. Cutting a corner restricts your vision and causes danger to

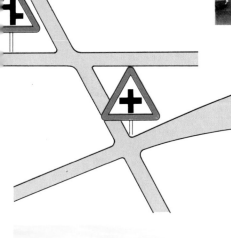

conditions dictate otherwise. A staggered crossroads can be an exception. We shall need to pass oncoming vehicles, also turning right, nearside-to-nearside. Extra care is necessary as our view of opposing traffic will be obstructed. The manoeuvre completed, we check the mirrors then prepare to turn left at the next intersection. Again, we follow the routine, check mirrors, plan ahead, check mirrors again, signal, adjust speed and keep looking before proceeding into the junction.

Some spectacular and complicated roundabout experiments have been devised in recent years.

Like this one, they can seem off-putting and confusing when first encountered. In reality, they are straightforward enough, providing they are approached with care, common sense and good all-round observation. Many other drivers at the roundabout may be even more confused than you are, so exercise even more consideration than usual.

traffic emerging from the road that you are joining.

Turning right

Turning right is one of the most dangerous driving manoeuvres. It is three times more dangerous than turning left. A common error when turning right into a side road is to cut across the mouth of the side road. Be prepared for others to do this as you approach such a junction and slow in good time.

Roundabouts Better driving

Roundabouts are designed to reduce congestion and keep traffic flowing through a road intersection without everything coming to a halt. Unfortunately, not all motorists use them correctly.

The first of four one-lane roundabouts lies ahead, and we want to take the first exit. The approach routine is exactly the same as the junction procedure described on page 30. We enter by filtering in when there is a suitable gap. The left indicator stays on until we reach our turning.

Minor roundabouts

The importance of correct signalling cannot be stressed too much.

The third exit is effectively a right turn, so we signal right on the approach to the roundabout.

Mini roundabouts

Most mini roundabouts have small central islands placed or painted on the road.

Some motorists, consequently, drive right over them when going straight on.

In fact, the rules governing conventional roundabouts also apply to mini roundabouts.

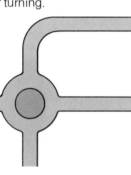

Without signalling, this car turns into the road we are occupying. Believing it was staying on the roundabout, we wait needlessly. We wish to go straight on, so we signal left when passing the first exit.

We keep the indicator flashing until we pass exit 2 when we indicate left. A late signal change causes as much confusion as not signalling at all.

Roundabouts: other points to watch

The normal procedure at roundabouts is to give way to traffic coming from your immediate right.

There is no road sign, but note that a single broken white line road marking across the mouth also means 'give way'.

Once entry onto the roundabout is clear continue after going through the junction procedure.

Take extra care when following long vehicles. They may need to encroach on your course.

Contra-rotation roundabouts

There will undoubtedly be long discussion about the advantages of contra-rotation roundabouts. The end product of breaking with convention by introducing *opposing* traffic streams into a roundabout situation can be confusion to the uninitiated. This example is not so difficult to work out as the one shown on page 31. The traffic flow here is clockwise on the outside of the roundabout system and anti-clockwise round the inside. The incorporation of mini roundabouts keeps all the traffic flowing well, however. Provided you observe the 'Give Way' and arrow markings on the road, you should not get into trouble.

Those who want exits 4 or 5 reap the benefits of this system. Compared with a conventional roundabout, it should be possible to reach them quicker.

Major roundabouts

A major, conventional, two-lane roundabout is coming up with a two-lane approach. We take . . .

A similar roundabout is coming up here and, to complete our journey, we need to take the 2nd exit.

We approach in the left lane, but we can use the offside if conditions dictate. In the roundabout, we keep to the lane by which we enter, signalling (and, if relevant, filtering) left once abreast of exit 1.

the offside lane on approach and, signalling right, move to the lane nearest the island. We keep the indicator on until we're abreast of exit 2 when we signal left and filter left to reach our turning.

Driving with consideration Better driving

Better driving consists of more than merely equipping yourself to handle situations as they arise. The better driver is also a courteous driver who exercises consideration for the particular requirements of different road users. This consideration will usually also result in smoother traffic flow.

Old people should be given extra consideration. Their eyesight may be poor, their movements slow, they may be deaf, and they could be absorbed in their own affairs. Allowing them to cross the road in front of you is a simple courtesy, provided it is safe for them to cross and that other traffic realises what is happening.

Cyclists should be given a wide berth, and if you cannot give them plenty of space when overtaking you should stay behind them until it is safe to do so. When starting off, or on hills, they may wobble from side to side, but do not startle them with a sudden horn blast or there is the risk that they might fall off in your path.

Children are one of the most vulnerable groups of road users. This sign warns, not of a school, but of some other area such as a playground where children will be found. Young children cannot accurately estimate the speeds of approaching traffic and their size often limits what they can see along the road. When they are playing their minds concentrate exclusively on the game and they are oblivious to passing traffic. These are only three reasons why the presence of children near the road requires great caution.

Pedestrians on country lanes must often walk in the road. They should walk so that they face oncoming traffic, but this is sometimes not the case. Drive at such a speed that you do not endanger them should you meet opposing traffic. Especial care is required at night when pedestrians may be wearing dark clothing and are obscured.

Keep a close watch out for motorcyclists. Although they are not very wide they move at least as fast as other traffic and are sometimes barely visible. Many of them use their headlights to make themselves more conspicuous, but this is by no means universal. Give them plenty of room as the slightest touch can overturn them.

Taxis behave unexpectedly from time to time, stopping or turning suddenly in order to pick up or set down fares.

Delivery vans of all kinds can be expected to obstruct traffic from time to time, but milk floats travel extremely slowly. They may turn across the road unexpectedly, and, in residential areas, pedestrians may walk towards them without considering the traffic.

All buses should be treated with care and consideration. Any sign of bus passengers preparing to alight will signal the approach of a bus stop to an observant driver, probably before the bus stop itself is visible. Beware of pedestrians crossing the road to or from the bus when it has stopped and allow the driver to move off and join the traffic stream when he is ready to do so.

Horse riding is an increasingly popular pursuit and horses on the road should be approached with great restraint. Any horn blast could frighten them and make them rear, so pass them quietly without revving the engine.

Emergency vehicles should always be given priority. Any indication of their presence, such as a siren or flashing lights, should prompt you to keep well to the left, preparing to stop if necessary in order to let them through.

Observation Better driving

One of the most important ways to develop better and safer driving is to cultivate the skill of sharp observation. This entails more than just looking at the road in front of you. It involves looking also to the side and rear, and studying the road ahead in a particular way.

The experienced driver will constantly shift his gaze, from side to side and along the road ahead, between a point close to the car right along to the horizon. He will also regularly look in his rear view mirrors. The less experienced driver will tend to concentrate his attention on a point not very far in front of the car. Because of this, every new development will arise very suddenly and will often catch him unprepared to respond.

Maximum information about any road scene is obtained in several ways. Apart from assessing the behaviour of all the vehicles and other road users in sight, additional aspects can sometimes be seen by looking along the nearside or offside of the vehicles in front or, according to the road layout, under them or over them. It is frequently possible to see through the rear and front windows of private cars and passengers can sometimes be seen preparing to alight from a bus. All these methods help the driver find out as much as possible about the road situation ahead.

The road markings provide the observant driver with a great deal of information about the road ahead and any hazards coming up.

The centre line markings change from a short, dashed, white line to a series of longer, white dashes. This warns of the approach to a hazard which is the sharp right-hand bend ahead where the side road joins.

The path of the road ahead, particularly in country areas, can often be inferred from the line of hedges or telegraph poles. At times other traffic can be seen a considerable distance away.

When passing a line of parked cars, always look into each one to see if there is a driver at the wheel or a passenger likely to open a door. Look for signs of exhaust smoke or wheels turning which indicate that a car may be pulling out. In this street, near a school, be prepared for small children, concealed by the cars, to suddenly run into the road right in front of you.

Looking along this line of cars, we see that the driver can be seen in the car just ahead, and that he is beginning to open the driver's door. In view of the oncoming traffic you should slow down before reaching him.

The scene ahead demands great caution. As well as the horses a dog can be seen running loose in the road. Be prepared to find more horses round the left-hand bend, but do not hoot or startle them.

The sight of a play area, especially if it is unfenced, should alert you to the possible presence of children near the road when you get round the corner ahead.

Housing estates require cautious driving and careful observation. A group of children can be seen by looking through the windows of the parked car. Children often play in the road on housing estates so watch carefully for any indication of their presence.

Watch out for the dog off the lead on this busy road. If he were to run into your path, several vehicles could be caught unawares, so ease off the power earlier than you otherwise would when approaching this junction. You should also be checking that the parked van is not likely to move out obstructing your path.

Additional information about the road ahead can be obtained from the reflections in shop windows. This is particularly valuable for obtaining early warning about other traffic at times when your own view is obscured by other vehicles or by a bend in the road.

Anticipation Better driving

The better driver uses the art of good observation by developing a keen sense of anticipation. Not only should you look carefully all round you for any information you can glean about a developing situation, but you should also look for clues which will help you anticipate what will happen next. This awareness will enable you to adjust your driving so that you do not have to take sudden action, possibly endangering other road users as well as yourself.

The road itself will give you several clues as to its likely path. A right-hand bend is coming up ahead, and those skid marks on the approach tell you it must be sharper than it appears. You can thus slow down in good time.

Read the road ahead for any indications of likely hazards. Just before the left-hand bend ahead, a signpost can be seen warning of a turning on the right. You can anticipate that traffic may turn out of it, and this, indeed, proves to be the case.

Due notice should always be taken of road signs, and the flashing amber lights on this school sign warn that children are on their way to and from school. Be prepared to have to stop for them—this is obligatory when a school crossing patrol holds up the sign with the warning 'Stop—Children'.

In winter beware of concealed patches of ice. You can anticipate that they are likely to be present on those portions of the road overhung by branches.

Side turnings, especially farm entrances, are not always signposted on country roads, but their existence can sometimes be anticipated. The road ahead looks clear and free from any side turnings, but the fence visible in the field on the left is, in fact, a warning to the observant driver that a farm entrance is coming up.

This sign announces the presence of roadworks, but none are visible. Anticipate that they could be masked by the parked van and expect to find workmen or lorries obstructing the road just behind it. Adjust your speed as you approach the van in case this happens and give as much clearance as possible.

Always look well ahead of you for advance warning of developing situations. A van can be seen parked on the left side of the road. On the opposite side can be seen a pedestrian. Anticipating that he will walk across the road to the van will prepare you for this situation when it happens.

When driving through a housing estate be prepared for children and animals who will not be expecting much traffic. Small children may suddenly come round a corner on bicycles or chasing a ball. The appearance of one child is often an indication that others are not far behind, so slow down immediately. Children are seldom good at assessing the speed of approaching traffic.

Whenever you see an ice cream van parked anticipate that it will be a magnet for children. In this incident a young girl ran to it, without looking, right across the road in front of the car in order to get her ice cream.

This scene looks quiet and trouble-free. The main road appears to continue down a dip when it is concealed from view and then uphill on the other side. A vehicle can be seen descending the hill before the dip. The edge of a red triangular warning sign can be seen, however, and this should warn us of something unexpected. As we get closer to the dip in the road, we are warned that it con-tains a cross roads, but it is not until we are much closer that we see the signpost indicating that the major road turns right here. Looking well ahead while driving can warn of impending situations such as this. Early anticipation that it is not completely straight-forward should have led you to proceed with caution into the dip, giving you plenty of time to prepare for the junction.

Driving commentary Better driving

The art of better driving is extremely well illustrated by a driving commentary. This consists of a running commentary made while driving, and embraces your observations, present driving behaviour and plans for future tactics. Even when driving on your own, a spoken commentary will confirm that you are putting the principles of better driving into action. A good commentary takes a great deal of practice to perfect, and an example is given here based on a typical cross-country journey involving several different types of road environment.

We are driving along a minor country road. The weather is dry and sunny, casting shadows across the road. There are no central line markings on the stretch in front of us and the nearside edge is badly broken up. We are approaching a sharp right hand bend with hedges concealing any opposing traffic. Looking in our mirror we see there is no traffic behind us and we slow to 25 mph, changing into third gear to negotiate the bend.

The road has widened now with centre line markings and long, straight stretches. Approaching a cross roads the centre line markings become warning lines and we can see a car waiting to emerge from the right. We ease off the power in case he moves out.

We note the staggered cross roads sign, and as we approach the junction we see a parked car blocking a portion of the road just before a left bend. We take up a position just to the left of the centre line in order to see as far as possible into the bend.

At first glance it appears as though the road goes straight on but there is in fact a sharp right hand bend. We have just passed a school sign and now deduce from the existence of the bus shelter that we are on a bus route.

Approaching the brow of a hill with warning line markings and an obscured road sign ahead we check the mirrors and slow, preparing to change down. It turns out to have a steep downhill gradient of 1 in 5.

The road is narrow with straight stretches. Ahead is a long vehicle and two cars are opposing. The centre line markings change to warning line markings so there must be a hazard ahead, perhaps a turning to the farm buildings visible on the right.

Coming up behind this slow-moving tractor we do not try to overtake it. He is signalling left and a car can be seen waiting to emerge from the right. Traffic on this road may include horse riders, so we keep our speed down.

Coming to this parked car we slow right down. There are road works and a petrol station beyond it, but we give a brief horn signal to make the people standing in the road aware of our presence.

We are on the outskirts of a town with cars parked on both sides of the road. Two cars ahead are blocking the left portion of the road as they turn into and out of driveways. We cannot see if any of the other parked cars intend to move and we ease off the power.

We are approaching red traffic lights and note the presence of the right-turning lane. The car in front of us is indicating left, but no left turning can be seen at the traffic lights, so we check in the mirror for traffic behind and prepare for him to stop at the side of the road.

In this side road we give way to an oncoming bus. He flashes his lights at us, but we wait until we are absolutely certain of his meaning before moving. It becomes clear he wishes us to come on, so we check the mirrors, signal and move forward without further delay.

The road is now a dual carriageway and we are approaching the end of it where we can see a petrol station, a shopping area and a set of traffic lights. We prepare for traffic moving into or out of the petrol station.

Driving through a shopping area we take the opportunity to look along the nearside of the van in front for possible hazards. We see a pedestrian waiting at the kerb to cross on the Pelican crossing and prepare to stop.

Leaving the town we approach a cross roads just before the derestriction signs. No traffic is waiting to emerge, but the motorcyclist seems uncertain of his intentions. We slow to allow him plenty of room to manoeuvre.

Continuing towards the town, we pass a zebra crossing and see a car waiting in a side road on the left. The traffic is not heavy, but, out of courtesy, we allow him to feed into the traffic stream in front of us.

At this set of traffic lights a group of pedestrians is waiting on the central island. We check that they have seen us and that no small children are concealed behind the bollards.

The road widens to a dual carriageway; the car in front is turning left and the road ahead appears clear after that.

Advanced driving Better driving

Many people who take a serious interest in driving wish to improve their standard of performance. The basic knowledge required by the driving test is only a starting point. The experience gained by having to deal with varied and complex situations helps to improve the standard, but there is only so much you can usefully learn on your own. For further improvement, expert tuition is the best method.

What is advanced driving?

A number of misapprehensions about advanced driving need to be dispelled. It does not involve very high speed driving nor does it consist of esoteric techniques such as may be used, for example, by a rally or racing driver. It requires developing a sympathy for the car and using careful planning and thought in order to drive safely and make good progress while keeping within the law.

It is sometimes believed that advanced driving techniques mean an increase in fuel consumption, but the reverse is usually the case. Even though achieving higher average speeds between A and B than an ordinary driver, an advanced driver will probably achieve better fuel economy through good planning and driving techniques.

Institute of Advanced Motorists

The aim of the Institute of Advanced Motorists is "skill with responsibility", and it is devoted to the promotion of road safety. All motorists are encouraged to take a pride in their driving. The key to membership lies in passing the advanced driving test and keeping up standards afterwards.

The Institute was founded in 1956 and is a non-profit-earning organisation, registered as a charity. It is run by a Council, the members of which are elected because of their expertise in various spheres of motoring. Their experience ranges from accident prevention, medicine, motor sport, the motor industry and trade, the driving schools, the motoring press, motoring organisations, the legal profession and Parliament.

Advanced driving test

The test lasts for one and a half hours and is conducted by one of the Institute's examiners. Some 95 test routes are located all over Britain and you can select the route most convenient to your home. You have to use your own car for the test. The examiners are all ex-police drivers holding Class I police driving certificates, and of all the motorists taking the test some 60% pass and join the Institute. As many women as men pass the test.

The test route measures about thirty-five to forty miles and incorporates road conditions of all kinds, including main roads, country lanes, urban areas and a short section of motorway where possible. The examiner will want you to drive in a steady, brisk manner, observing speed limits and driving with due regard to road, traffic and weather conditions.

Exaggeratedly slow speeds are not required, nor is excessive signalling. You will be expected to cruise at the legal limit when circumstances permit. Tests of manoeuvring skill such as reversing round a corner, are included and so is a hill start.

Observation forms an important part of the test and there will be one or two spot checks on this aspect during the test. There are no attempts to catch you out, however. You are free to give a running commentary if you wish to demonstrate your ability to read the road, but this is not a test requirement.

At the end of the test the examiner will give you an expert and candid view of your skill and responsibility, telling you whether or not you have reached the required standard. You will not fail for minor faults.

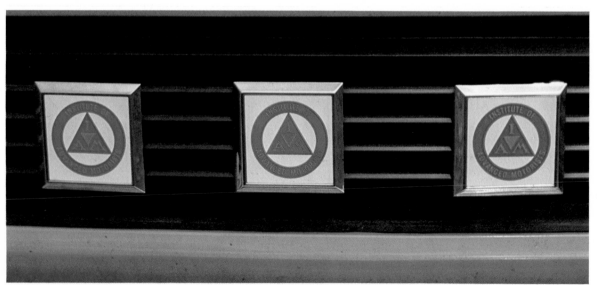

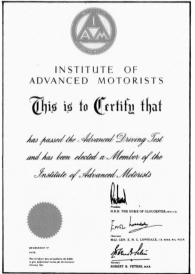

Technique	Assessment	Failure rate	Reasons for failure
Acceleration	Is your acceleration smooth and progressive? Is it excessive or insufficient?	12%	Uneven acceleration. Poor acceleration sense.
Approach	Do you approach traffic signals and other hazards correctly?	48%	Too fast approach. Coasted to compulsory stops.
Braking	Is your braking smooth and progressive? Is it late and fierce?	60%	Late brake application. Harsh handbrake application. Applied brake and changed gear simultaneously.
Car sympathy	Do you treat the car with care or overstress it?	40%	Not expressed in use of clutch, brakes and gears.
Clutch control	Do you co-ordinate your engine and road speeds properly? Do you ride or slip the clutch? Do you coast with the clutch disengaged?	48%	Ride clutch. Clutch slip. Coasting.
Gear changing	Do you change gear without jerking? If you have automatic transmission do you make full use of it?	38%	Harsh selection. Changed down with relaxed accelerator.
Gears, use of	Do you select and use your gears properly? Are you always in the correct gear before reaching a hazard?	72%	Late selection. Intermediate gears not used to advantage.
Hazard procedure and cornering	Do you cope with road and traffic hazards correctly? Do you turn corners properly?	78%	Incorrect assessment. Poor safety margin. Unsystematic procedure.
Horn	Do you use your horn and headlamp flasher according to the recommendations laid out in The Highway Code?	14%	Failed to use when required.
Manoeuvring	Can you reverse smoothly and competently?	28%	Lacked judgement and control.
Observation	Do you read the road ahead and drive accordingly?	58%	Late planning and assessment of traffic conditions.
Obstruction	Are you careful not to obstruct other vehicles—by driving too slowly, taking up the wrong position on the road or failing to anticipate and read correctly the traffic situation ahead?	8%	Loitering at minor hazards. Cutting in.
Overtaking	Do you carry this out safely and decisively, maintaining the correct distance from the other vehicles involved and using your mirror, indicators and gears properly?	38%	Too close prior to overtaking. Overtaking on bends. Overtaking in the face of other traffic. Cutting in after overtaking.
Positioning	Do you keep to the correct part of the road, especially when approaching and negotiating hazards?	70%	Straddling lanes. Incorrect position for right and left turns.
Progress	Do you keep up a reasonable pace and maintain good progress bearing in mind the road, traffic and weather conditions?	14%	Adequate progress not maintained when safe to do so.
Restraint	Do you show reasonable restraint and no indecision at the wheel?	20%	Insufficient restraint demonstrated.
Road signs	Do you observe road signs, approach them correctly and obey them?	36%	Failed to remember signs when asked. Failed to conform to "Stop" signs or "Keep Left" signs.
Signals	Do you give indicator and, where appropriate, hand signals at the right place and in good time?	14%	Late or misleading signals.
Speed	Do you show the ability to judge speed and distance?	26%	Excessive speed in country lanes. Failed to make adequate progress in 70 mph area.
Speed limits	Do you observe them?	22%	Exceeded speed limits.
Steering	Do you hold the steering wheel correctly? Do you pass the steering wheel through your hands?	20%	Released wheel. Crossed hands.
Traffic conditions	Do you observe traffic conditions and demonstrate anticipation?	38%	Poor anticipation. Late reaction.

Skilled driving courses Better driving

A variety of courses is available for all who wish to improve their driving in any way. The test and standards devised by the Institute of Advanced Motorists are explained on pages 42 and 43, and this spread describes what else is currently available.

Night driving course

Drivers who have recently passed the driving test can obtain a grounding in driving at night and the correct use of headlights through this short course run by the British School of Motoring.

Motorway course

In those areas with convenient access to a motorway a short course is available, run by the British School of Motoring, aimed at teaching newly-qualified drivers the rudiments of motorway driving.

Harrow Driving Centre

The Driving Centre at Harrow features a specially devised road layout situated away from public roads. This enables highly realistic experience to be acquired by those learning to drive and by those wishing to practise unfamiliar manoeuvres away from the bustle of everyday traffic. Several courses are available from this centre and include manoeuvrability for those who wish to improve their reversing and parking, caravan towing, Continental driving, car maintenance and advanced driving, which includes some basic skid control techniques.

Local Authority courses

Many Local Authorities run advanced driving and car maintenance courses as evening classes. These are not expensive to attend and generally run for between eight to twelve weeks.

High performance course

This $17\frac{1}{2}$ hour course run by the British School of Motoring is the most advanced driving course currently available. It takes place on a wide variety of normal roads as well as on a race track, although even here two-way traffic rules are applied. The facility is available, however, to learn cornering lines, braking and acceleration under the safest possible conditions and without being a hazard to other traffic. A session on a 'skid road' is also included in the course.

The instructor compiles a detailed report on each pupil throughout the course, and at its conclusion using the report as a guide the committee can elect the pupil to the High Performance Club.

demonstration is also required of car control in a confined area, including a 'wiggle-woggle' through cones.

Those who continue with the advanced test are required to show 'that they are capable of conducting a good, safe, smooth, but brisk drive for about 30 minutes'. This includes smooth acceleration coupled with an awareness of what other road users are doing, and gentle, smooth braking as well as gear changing. Good overtaking procedure must be demonstrated with no evidence of following too closely, the positioning of the car during cornering, correct use of speed, as well as the driver's powers of concentration, anticipation and road observation. His reactions to an unexpected hazard will also be tested, as will his knowledge of the Highway Code and car maintenance.

League of Safe Drivers

The aims of the league are 'to promote road safety by requiring members to reach and maintain a high standard of driving skill and to encourage co-operation among all drivers whether using roads for pleasure or business.'

The league is organised into a number of regional branches, and applicants are required to take an advanced test similar to the IAM test. Having passed the league's test members are allowed to display a badge.

At the end of this test, candidates are given a grading of either first, second or third class. No candidate is failed, but everyone must re-take the test each year, endeavouring to maintain or improve their standard.

Grand touring course

The beginnings of high performance driving are taught in this British School of Motoring course. Three sessions cover driving on country roads, trunk roads and motorways.

Advanced driving course

Advanced driving courses are available through local authorities and the BSM to drivers wishing to polish and re-assess their own performance. These courses can also be tailored to the requirements of the IAM test.

Lectures, models, demonstrations, and simulators are all used in driver education courses.

Part of the test is held off the road and the applicant must demonstrate that he can park parallel to a kerb as well as reverse into an imaginary garage space. A

2 On the road

On the road

Almost any car journey will involve several types of road environment, each of which requires attention to different aspects. Preparation for the likely hazards and problems on each type of road will lead to a smoother and safer journey.

This part of the book takes the different types of road in the sequence in which they might be encountered in a journey which started in a country area and continued along trunk roads and a motorway to end in a town. Each of these areas poses situations for the driver to cope with and the relevant spreads discuss how to resolve these situations. After a discussion of the care to be exercised on different types of road surface, the final sections in this part of the book explain some of the intricacies involved in taking the car abroad to Europe. An amusing quiz rounds off Part Two.

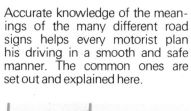

Road signs
pages 50–51

Accurate knowledge of the meanings of the many different road signs helps every motorist plan his driving in a smooth and safe manner. The common ones are set out and explained here.

Country roads
pages 54–55

Although they may seem quieter than other roads, the twisting country lanes can require a greater degree of concentration and alertness from the driver. These pages describe the hazards to beware of.

Trunk roads
pages 58–59

The main arterial roads can be very fast, and anticipation of the movements of other traffic is the key to safe travel. Special problems arise when the trunk road passes through a built up area.

Joining and leaving the motorway
pages 62–63

The special requirements when joining and leaving the motorway are fully explained in this section, together with the driving hazards associated with the service areas.

Navigation
pages 52–53

Advance planning with an appreciation of the national signposting systems can make every journey quicker and more economical. This spread explains how to understand the signposts.

Villages
pages 56–57

The tranquil village scene hides many possible dangers for the unwary motorist, particularly if it is a popular attraction for tourists. Many of these are shown on this double page spread.

Motorways
pages 60–61

Strict regulations apply to motorway driving and these must be obeyed in order to keep these high speed roads as safe as they are. A review of motorway signs and regulations is given here.

Motorway driving
pages 64–65

Motorways put considerable strain both upon the driver and his car, especially when weather conditions are bad. The correct procedures for safe motorway driving are reviewed here.

Town driving
pages 66–69

The complexities and hazards of driving in towns, particularly during heavy traffic, are analysed in detail and many suggestions are given about how to reduce the stress which town driving imposes.

Road surfaces
pages 72–73

The different types of road surface can have important effects on the car's handling and tyre adhesion. Tell tale signs indicate the road surfaces to watch out for and the special driving requirements.

European road signs
pages 76–77

Every European country includes the internationally agreed signs in its road network, but most of them have some individual signs which are harder to understand. These are featured on these pages.

Driving techniques in Europe
pages 80–81

Many driving conventions apply in most European countries although there are a few aspects of European roads which need a completely different approach from that adopted in Britain.

Parking
pages 70–71

Parking can sometimes become a nightmare in highly congested towns. This section describes the main systems of parking control and it also explains the different parking techniques.

Driving in Europe
pages 74–75

Careful preparation is the key to a safe and confident journey when taking the car to Europe. Basic information is provided here about the documentation required and insurance arrangements.

European driving regulations
pages 78–79

Driving regulations vary from one country to another and can become quite complex. A summary is given in this section of a few of the important regulations for every motorist visiting Europe.

Are you a better driver?
pages 82–83

One of several quizzes in this book enables you to pit your wits against some entertaining, but sometimes puzzling questions based on problems and situations commonly met on the road.

Road signs On the road

A set of road signs has been evolved which has become a consistent and comprehensive source of information and warning to the motorist. Attempts have been made to align it to a European system of road signs, but each country still has some signs which are only found in that country.

Attention to and understanding of road signs is a vital part of safe driving. Several surveys have suggested that large numbers of people do not understand the meaning of many common road signs.

With so many signs on the road today, often crowded together in a small space, it is easy to become confused or to miss some vital warning. It is a salutary reminder to ask yourself from time to time while driving along, what was the sign you last passed.

Junctions and roundabouts

Warning signs lead up to the junction or roundabout and provide information about the nature of the junction. They will probably be followed by a Give Way or Stop sign and the European octagonal stop sign is coming into more general use. The road markings at a stop sign consist of solid white lines marking the farthest point you may drive to. It is obligatory to stop and look to see that it is possible to enter the major road in safety.

The Give Way sign has different road markings, and drivers are required to delay joining the main road until it is safe to do so. If the main road is clear, there is no obligation to stop completely. The road markings consist of a pair of dashed white lines.

Cross Roads · Staggered junction · Side Road · T junction

Stop signs · Give way · Roundabout

STOP 100yds Distance to STOP sign · GIVE WAY 50yds Distance to GIVE WAY sign

No vehicles · REDUCE SPEED NOW · No through road · Advance warning of no through road · Countdown markers

Classes of signs

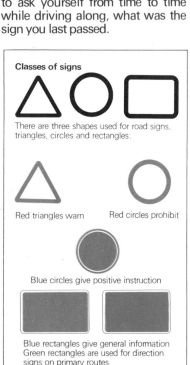

There are three shapes used for road signs, triangles, circles and rectangles:

Red triangles warn · Red circles prohibit

Blue circles give positive instruction

Blue rectangles give general information Green rectangles are used for direction signs on primary routes.

Traffic behaviour

Information, advice or warnings about the way traffic should be organised on the road are given in a series of specific signs. The speed and general approach at any situation is governed by these signs which must all be obeyed.

 No stopping (Clearway)

No overtaking

No U turns

National speed limit applies

Motor vehicles prohibited except for access

Two way traffic

Give priority to vehicles from opposite direction

Turn left ahead

Pass either side to reach same destination

No entry for vehicles

ONE WAY

Turn left

Keep left

Ahead only

No right turn

No left turn

The road ahead

Advance warning of how the road ahead is laid out helps a driver plan his approach to a situation which he cannot see completely. The information is generally precise about which side of the road is affected or which direction the road will take.

The triangular signs give warnings, the circular signs must be obeyed.

 Bend to left

 Double bend first to left

 Traffic merging with equal priority from left

 Road narrows on left

 Bend to right

 Double bend first to right

 Traffic merging with equal priority from right

 Road narrows on right

 Series of bends

 Road narrows on both sides

Dual carriageway ahead

 Dual carriageway ends

 Ford

 2 TONS Axles weight limit

 10% Steep decline

 20% Steep incline

 14'-6" No vehicles over height shown

 7'-6" No vehicles over width shown

 10 TONS No vehicles including load over weight shown

London A3 Dorking (A25) | Town Centre Horsham A281
Lane information sign

  Sharp deviation

Hazards ahead

The signs warning of hazards ahead should never be ignored, and provide valuable information about what is round the next corner.

 Pedestrian crossing ahead

 **Hospital** Hospital, quiet please

 Children

 Wild animals

 Wild horses

 Cattle

School Children going to or from school

Patrol School crossing patrol ahead

Cattle grid

 Cattle grid

 Road works ahead

 Slippery road

STOP CHILDREN School crossing patrol; vehicles must stop

 Uneven road

STOP POLICE Stop at sign

 Traffic signals ahead

 Other danger

 Safe height 16'-6" Overhead electric cable

 Quayside or river bank

Hump bridge

Risk of falling rocks

Opening or swing bridge

Low flying aircraft or sudden aircraft noise

Level crossings

Level crossings are of various kinds and are always preceded by the appropriate signs.

 Stop at amber and flashing red lights

 Level crossing with gate or barrier

 Level crossing without gate or barrier

 Countdown

 Level crossing without gate or barrier

51

Navigation On the road

Careful planning of any journey can assist driving economy by cutting down mileage, and also improve safety by avoiding dangerous hesitations and uncertainties. A short time spent with maps before the start of a journey can save time, petrol and money, and also minimise the frustration, particularly if the journey is at all unfamiliar.

A consistent set of signs has been evolved for Britain's road network, which often relates to the colours used on road maps. Familiarity with the system used will enable the navigator to recognise the various types of information to be found on the different sorts of road signs.

Modern highway engineering has resulted in systems designed for maximum traffic flow. Understanding this will make it evident how important it is to know which route you need to take. It is often difficult or impossible to change your mind in such a complex situation, and hesitation is dangerous. When planning to visit an unfamiliar town, a modern town plan is extremely valuable for trouble-free navigation. Plan your route in detail and keep a note of road names and numbers.

In order to show the importance of preparing a route in advance, and understanding the related direction signs, a specific example has been selected. The principles apply to a route of any kind. This particular route involves a cross-country journey to a motorway, along the motorway, into Birmingham, then out again in a different direction finally joining the M6. All varieties of direction signs will be seen, but those relating to motorways are discussed on pages 58–61.

Into town

The signs found on the approach road to join the motorway have a white background with black lettering. It indicates that this is not

a primary route. The direction for the motorway is clearly indicated by a sign with white letters on a blue background.

Several signs are found on the motorway approach to Birmingham. Only advance planning using a map would have indicated that junction 4 was not the best one to use.

This sign at junction 3 shows the road number and destination needed on the journey into Birmingham.

The green background of these signs indicate that they are primary routes. These primary routes are the main non-motorway road arteries of the country. As well as the destination (in white letters) and road number (in yellow), the signs also carry a yellow symbol. These symbols are used in diversion schemes from motorways (see page 63).

Continuing along A456, the destination becomes 'City Centre'. The diversion indicated by the yellow rectangle turns off left here.

A large city will have a number of ring roads. If it is preferable to use one of these to by-pass the city centre, its road number should be ascertained during the route planning. In our case, we shall follow the signs to the City Centre.

Along the route, local establishments are indicated by signs which have black lettering on a white background, bordered by blue.

Confirmation that you are on the correct route is obtained from road and street names.

At complex junctions, the road signs may move from their usual position by the side of the road to a gantry. In this instance, at Five Ways, the City Centre route uses the underpass, reached from the right hand lane. Careful observation, well in advance, will warn the driver that this development is occurring, and he will be able to move into the right hand lane in plenty of time.

Within the city, a variety of non-standard signs may be encountered. General information about how to get to the city centre is indicated. A special lane, provided for buses, should be avoided.

Ladywood

Calthorpe Fields

At the 3rd exit from this roundabout, a sign to the left indicates the central shopping area. Pre-planning of the route warns to avoid this and continue to the 4th exit, following signs to the West and South West. This shows the value of detailed advance route planning.

At a subsequent roundabout, the 1st exit leads to the Bull Ring Shopping Centre and its car park,

Aston

Digbeth

although this is not evident from the signposting. It is always better to rely on a pre-planned route than to hope that the signing in a strange town or city will be as comprehensive and informative as you would wish.

Careful study of the map will have indicated where the car park is located, allowing it to be approached without fuss.

Out of town

Leave the car park carefully, looking for the signpost to another primary route, the A38(M), North. The direction of the A38(M) is

signposted and the road is followed along Moor Street Queensway to leave the City Centre.

Although the road is wide, do not travel too fast if it is unfamiliar. At Masshouse Circus, the A38(M) follows the underpass, reached from the right hand lane, which must be selected in good time, particularly in busy traffic.

At the next intersection, do not take the underpass. Pre-planning will have indicated that you need to go on to the roundabout and take the 3rd exit. Signs for the M6 appear at this point on the route.

Another variation on the road signs to be found is the illuminated sign on the overhead gantry. This is not always easy to see, but it can be anticipated by looking well ahead. Again, it is important to select the right hand lane in good time in order to follow the A38(M). From this point on, motorway regulations apply.

On this modern expressway, traffic is controlled using a 'tidal flow' system. A set of lights on the overhead gantry indicates which lanes are in use for each direction. The red cross tells you which lane not to use. The lights in the sign also indicate the directions of the different lanes, and, on this journey, you should look out for signs, M6, South.

The approach to M6, South is clearly marked, and early lane selection is, again, essential. Only thorough pre-planning will have forewarned you to follow M6 South to join the M1.

The extensive network of minor roads linking rural communities and the main cross-country routes are seldom as peaceful and relaxing to drive along as they may seem. Agricultural and other country traffic which use them can pose situations requiring degrees of concentration and anticipation every bit as high as driving on more major roads.

Road surfaces

Many country roads have a relatively poor surface, although there are outstanding exceptions. The edges may be crumbling and potholed. The roads will also be susceptible to frost damage.

Farm machinery which has been working in muddy fields will lay a

Visibility

The twists and bends of narrow country roads often restrict long distance visibility. This is made worse by the high hedges which sometimes line the sides of the roads in rural areas.

Drivers should proceed along this type of road at a speed conducive to safety. Slow-moving traffic may be encountered round any corner on a country road. The use of the horn on approaching blind, narrow bends is a wise precaution.

Wherever the road layout permits, try to look over and beyond hedges or any other sight restrictions. This can give an early indication of the path the road will follow, and sometimes high vehicles, such as tractors can be seen well in advance down the road.

trail of mud when it returns to a properly surfaced road. If you see tractors working in a field, expect to find mud on the road ahead of you. This may happen even in dry, sunny weather and the trail may continue for a considerable distance. Any dirt or mud on the road surface could cause a skid in an emergency.

Road works

Because they are so important as links in the rural community, local councils usually carry out maintenance and repair work on country roads a short section at a time. This may involve re-laying the surface of the road, but it can also be hedge-trimming, laying sewerage pipes, or reinforcing the edges. It is sometimes possible to obtain early warning of road works from a glimpse of the metal cab top

of a lorry or the tip of a metal exhaust stack seen over the tops of the hedges.

Hazards on the road

Very narrow roads may not be sufficiently wide for two vehicles to pass each other. These will usually be signed as such on the approach and will have passing places set into them at periodic intervals. On a hill, always allow the traffic going up the hill to have priority, particularly if it is a heavy vehicle.

Occasionally, a road will be found which has a gate across it. This is usually placed there in order to prevent cattle wandering outside the area. The gate should always be closed after you have passed it, even if it was open at the time you approached.

When harvest time is over, farmers frequently burn off the stubble. Although this may seem a dramatic and attractive sight, be prepared for dense smoke reducing visibility down the road.

Driving at night on country roads can be easier than on other roads. The use of headlights is universal and the discipline of the drivers to dip their headlights is usually good, although speeds tend to be slow. Headlights flashed when approaching corners or humps in the road give advance warning of your presence to other traffic. Oncoming traffic can be seen from some distance, as the light from their headlights will be visible above the highest hedge.

Some country roads may be broken by a ford, often near a village. Several of these have a depth

Farm animals

If you see animals grazing in a field, be alert to the possibility that it may be milking time, or that a shepherd might be moving a flock of sheep from one pasture to another. Either of these activities if met with on the road must be faced with patience and the animals allowed to pass safely. Impatience may result in the animals damaging your car.

Cattle and sheep graze wild in moorland countryside for months on end, and it is not uncommon to find animals literally lying in the road. Great care must be exercised in these circumstances.

gauge indicating the danger level. Drive through the ford slowly but steadily, and remember to dry out your brakes afterwards by applying them progressively. A careful check should be made that the road is clear ahead and behind when you do this.

Tractors

Even the best and most modern tractors move at a speed considerably lower than the average family car particularly if they are pulling a trailer.

Tractor drivers may well be oblivious of traffic approaching from behind, particularly if they are wearing ear muffs. Before passing one, signal your presence to the tractor driver with horn and headlights and, preferably, wait for some indication that he has seen

you and is aware of your intentions. You should also check that there are no turn-offs into farmyards or fields, before overtaking the tractor.

Other vehicles

Country roads provide routes for large commercial vehicles collecting or delivering produce, and huge agricultural machinery, such as combine harvesters, may be met from time to time. Due to the high

cost of combine harvesters, they are often used all round the clock at harvest time, so they could be met on the roads between fields at any time of the day or night.

Another common sight at harvest time is the fully-laden hay lorry. Hauliers tend to take on massive loads of hay, and if they are not properly secured, loose straws may whip off the lorry, or complete bales may fall on to the road.

Horses

Horses being ridden on the road should be treated with great caution. Even the best trained horse may shy at a sudden noise or the sound of a car. As you approach, slow right down and be prepared to stop if necessary. If it is not possible to pass the animal safely, stop well behind it until the approaching vehicle is past. Drive past the horse slowly, quietly and giving it as wide a berth as possible.

Villages On the road

Every village has its own community life which the motorist must consider and allow for when driving through it. Some villages also contain historic treasures or beautiful settings which bring great numbers of visitors, and these too call for consideration and anticipation from the driver.

Village life

Although a village may appear to be small and quiet, it should never be forgotten that its facilities serve a wide community and it will attract a wide variety of interests. Always slow down when driving through a village, even if no speed restriction is in force.

Life in general proceeds at a slower pace than in towns. Patience should be exercised when travelling behind a slow moving vehicle, rather than taking unnecessary risks. Bicycles will also be encountered relatively frequently, and these too should be treated with respect.

One of the most common features of village life is the delivery van. In many cases, it will not be possible for the driver to park close to his destination without partially blocking the road. The driver will usually park in the best place from his own point of view, and may then walk into the road without warning. Be prepared for, and tolerant towards any inconvenience caused by this behaviour.

Country buses play an important part in rural life. They may be too large for the small lanes they have to travel down, but they usually expect, and get, priority over other traffic. Around bus stops there may be numbers of pedestrians, especially children, and they will frequently stand in the road if there is no pavement or only a small pull-in.

Another hazardous aspect of village life is the school. From 08.30 to 09.00 and from 15.00 to 16.00 as well as at lunch-time children will be coming and going to and from school. In addition to the extra traffic to be expected near a school at this time where parents collect them, also beware of children rushing into the road. Not all of them may be used to the speeds of non-local traffic.

The population that uses the village shops will probably consist of quite a high proportion of old people, very young children and people with dogs (not always on a lead). Be prepared for them.

Parking in a village calls for consideration for others. Many gateways and openings which may look unused are, in fact, in use. Parking with the wheels on the pavement may contravene local by-laws and should be avoided because of the problems it poses to pedestrians such as mothers with prams, those pushing bicycles, those with dogs on a leash, and old people.

Parking under trees may cause problems since some types of leaf exude a gum which is not only unpleasant but difficult to remove. This, as well as any flower petals and bird-droppings can damage the car's paintwork and should be washed off as soon as possible.

Remember all these possible hazards when approaching a village and reduce speed.

Village attractions

Well-known villages will attract visitors who are paying more attention to the sights than to the traffic. There may also be drivers passing through who are looking around and not at the road in front of them.

In any village with historic or scenic attractions, be prepared to find tourists. Pedestrians may suddenly walk in front of you, or the car in front could stop without warning. Coaches may also be in evidence, either parked, or trying to negotiate a narrow street. Give way to coaches whenever it is possible. If the village holds attractions for you, resist the temptation to look at them while driving through. Find a safe, clear, place to park and explore the village at leisure and on foot. Should you be visiting an historic house or monument, its car park will usually be signposted.

Local events such as a fete are very popular in the locality, and will usually be accompanied by congestion and obstruction near the entrance. Choose a different route if possible, otherwise drive with extra caution and expect problems if you intend to park close by.

The local hunt may be encountered in or near a village between November and April. It will usually be accompanied by many people on foot, intending to follow the hunt, and there may be vehicles and horse boxes parked at inconvenient places. Horses and hounds will be in a particularly excited state, so proceed with extreme caution, being prepared to stop if necessary.

Horses being ridden on the road are increasingly met in country areas. They are easily scared and you should not hoot at them or rev your engine noisily. If you cannot allow plenty of room when passing them, you should wait quietly behind them until it is clear to do so. Horses should be given priority.

Trunk roads On the road

The fast suburban and arterial roads which link the country's towns and cities carry a wide variety of traffic whose speed and density have been increasing year by year.

Road markings

The heavily-used, fast, cross-country routes are usually well marked with advance warning of hazards, and local authorities generally erect warning signs on sharp bends. The more chevrons shown on one of these signs, the sharper will be the bend.

The lines and markings painted in the road also provide a great deal of information. In general, the more white paint that is visible on the road at any given point, the greater will be the degree of hazard there.

Centre lines

The white centre line or lines provide valuable information to the driver on the best use of the road space. A dashed line will have very short dashes if it is a lane marking, longer dashes for the centre line marking and longer still for warning line markings.

The edges of the road at bends or other hazards will be marked with a continuous white line, and with a

dashed white line or no marking at all elsewhere.

Double white lines also carry an important message. Where both lines are unbroken, it is forbidden to cross them. The only exceptions to this are when a stationary vehicle is blocking the road, when a policeman or road work signals direct you across them, or to enter or leave a side road.

A broken line on one side of the solid centre line is to indicate that traffic on the side of that broken line may cross it, when overtaking, for example, provided it is safe to do so.

In some areas the two lines will spread apart, the space between being filled with diagonal solid white lines. No vehicles must drive on this area as it is there to keep traffic streams apart.

Observation

Looking well ahead when driving on trunk roads will give the driver more information as well as more time to react to it. High hedges are not common on cross-country roads, and it is usually possible to look across bends and some way into the distance to spot approaching traffic and other features, such as the next village.

Dual carriageways

Many trunk roads contain sections of dual carriageway, some of which may be wide and of almost motorway standard, and some much narrower and rather short. All dual carriageways are indicated well in advance, and a series of signs and road markings also warn when they will end.

Many dual carriageways are signed as clearways, and no parking is allowed on them at any time. Keep in the left hand lane except when overtaking, although you should not weave in and out of the lanes if there is much traffic moving slower than you are.

Turning right off dual carriageways can be a dangerous manoeuvre. You should be looking sufficiently far ahead to be able to see the turning in good time. Check the mirror and indicate as early as possible, then start to slow down in plenty of time.

Three lane roads

Considerable dangers exist on this type of road, because of the use of the centre lane for traffic going in either direction. Before entering the centre lane, whether to overtake or to turn right, take especial care that the road is clear ahead, and also for a long distance behind. Signal in good time, and keep checking the road ahead and the road behind in your mirrors.

Whenever possible, any overtaking manoeuvre on this type of road should be timed in such a way that you avoid putting your car in a 'sandwich' of the vehicle you are overtaking and a vehicle coming the other way. It is safer to wait until there is a gap in the oncoming traffic, giving yourself extra room in case any dangerous situation arises while you are overtaking.

Suburban areas

Trunk roads frequently pass through villages and small towns, and usually suburban areas. The normal life in all these places may cause problems for the motorist, but suburban areas can be particularly difficult.

A typical stretch of trunk road may pass, in a relatively short space, a shopping precinct, several industrial or business premises, schools, and housing areas. At each point, pedestrians or vehicles may suddenly cross into the path of the oncoming traffic, often without warning.

Shopping areas

Around the shopping area, cars will be found parking, often so that they partially block the road. Alternatively they may be moving off, sometimes without sufficient care or warning.

Pedestrians of all kinds, including children, elderly people, young mothers with prams and shopping, will often be trying to cross the road in these areas. If pedestrian crossings, footbridges or underpasses are not conveniently situated people will often take great risks to cross a busy road, dodging the traffic.

Around bus stops be prepared, not only for the passengers who get off and then dash from behind the bus across the road, but also for people trying to catch the bus who may appear from any direction and run across the road in front of you.

Schools

Take great care in the vicinity of schools, especially at the times they start and finish. Amber warning lights may be seen which flash at these times, and one can also expect to find a school crossing patrol helping the children to cross.

Numbers of parents, frequently with their cars, congregate around the school entrance at the start and finish times, although there are usually markings on the road which forbid parking directly in front of the school premises.

Industrial estates

Heavy goods vehicles make great use of trunk roads, often as a link between the motorway and their destination. This destination is often a factory or part of an industrial estate situated quite close to the road.

Lorries manoeuvring into and out of these areas will probably take up most of the road while they do so. Patience and consideration for the lorry drivers will be appreciated by them. The many people who work in these areas may work shift systems as well as normal working hours, so be prepared for an upsurge of pedestrian, bicycle,

motorcycle, car and bus traffic at unusual times.

Housing estates

Where the roads from a housing estate join a trunk road, one can expect to find volumes of cars trying to enter the main road, especially in the morning rush hour. The roads on housing estates have dangers of their own.

The fact that housing estates tend to be quiet during the day gives children, in particular, a false sense of security. They often play near the road, and sometimes actually on it. When chasing after something, their attention is on the object of the chase.

Frequent visitors to housing estates are ice-cream vans and mobile shops. Pedestrians, especially children, will congregate around these, and may often walk into the road without looking.

The motorway system On the road

In 1956 when the Preston by-pass was opened, it constituted Britain's first motorway. Since then, over 1,500 miles of motorway have been constructed, providing fast, efficient and safe transport to many parts of Britain.

The usual layout of a stretch of motorway is:

Pair of hard shoulders, 10ft wide
Pair of three lane carriageways, 36ft wide
Central reservation, 13ft wide, with safety fence
Bridge clearance, 16' 6" minimum
Marker posts on both sides at 110' intervals
Telephone at one mile intervals opposite each other

Regulations

Motorway regulations apply from the start of motorway to the 'end of motorway' sign. The following are not allowed to use motorways:
pedestrians
animals
learner drivers (except HGV learners)
pedal cycles
motor cycles of less than 50cc
invalid carriages
agricultural vehicles
slow moving vehicles (except by special permission)

No parking on the central reservation
No parking or reversing on the carriageways or the hard shoulder. Parking on the hard shoulder only in an emergency
No walking on the carriageways or central reservation except in an emergency. Buses and coaches and those vehicles over 3 tons laden weight are not permitted to use the right hand lane except in an emergency.

Direction signs

Directional signs and route confirmatory signs are rectangular, with white lettering on a blue background. Details of these signs are given on pages 62 and 63.

Warning signs

Light signals are used to provide motorway warning signs. These are remotely-operated from the motorway control room, and are often switched on in response to a radio call from a motorway police patrol.

The operation of these signals is monitored by a computer, for safety reasons. This prevents a particular light signal from being switched on without the correct sequence of signals leading up to it also being switched on. For example, if a low speed limit is to be imposed, the computer will ensure that this is preceded by one or more further signals, reducing the speed more gradually.

The computer also enables a continuous record to be kept of which signals were in operation, with details of the time and date. This is designed to prevent a signal from being left on inadvertently.

The signals will be found either on pedestal signs situated on the central reservation, or located on an overhead gantry. Warning signs are accompanied by amber lights flashing top and bottom. These lights do not flash for the 'all-clear' sign.

Some of these signals have red stop lights incorporated in them. These flash from side to side, and it is essential to stop when they are switched on. When these stop lights are located on overhead

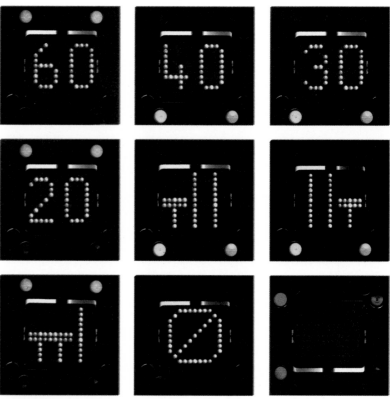

A selection of typical light signals encountered on motorways

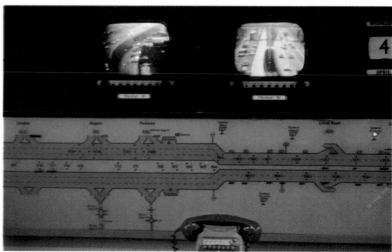

Some motorways are monitored by closed circuit television

gantries, they apply only to the lane directly below them.

The earliest type of signal used was a pair of amber lights, one above the other, mounted to the left of the hard shoulder. When these flash alternately, they give warning of a hazard such as fog. Motorists are advised to slow down to 30 mph at such a signal.

Message signs

Several motorways have message signs located to the left of the hard shoulder. When not in use, these are blank, but they can be switched on to give warnings of fog, slippery road surface or an accident ahead.

Experimental signs

Some motorways have experimental light signals which are designed to convey some of the variety of information contained on the normal road warning signs.

Marker posts

These posts are placed at intervals of 110 feet on the outer edge of each hard shoulder. The sides which face the motorway bear a telephone symbol and an arrow pointing in the direction of the nearest telephone. Each post has a number accompanied by a letter A or B which indicates the carriageway concerned. No telephone is more than ½ mile from any marker post.

Telephones

Situated one mile apart, motorway telephones are placed opposite each other, so there is never any need to cross the carriageways

Examples of motorway telephones

in order to use one. The marker posts will indicate in which direction the nearest telephone may be found.

These telephones are for use in emergencies only. They are connected to the motorway control room, and no other calls can be made from them. They are not locked and no money is needed in order to use them.

Several different styles of telephone are in use, but they all follow the same general principle. The old style telephones work only in one direction to the control room, but with the newer types, it is also possible for the control room to ring back to one of the telephones.

Breakdown

In the unfortunate event of a breakdown, it is permissible to use the hard shoulder. When stationary, the hazard warning lights should be switched on, and a warning triangle placed at least 100 yards behind the car.

Great care should be taken when getting out of the car. The driver's door should not be used as it is

so close to a carriageway of fast-moving traffic. It is preferable to get out of the car through the nearside door.

After walking to the nearest telephone, a phone call can be made to the motorway control room. The police will take details of the telephone number, the registration number, make, model, year and colour of your car, information about the breakdown, your name and address, and your membership number of a motoring organisation. They will then either ask you to ring them back, or they will ring you back to tell you what action they have taken.

If you are a member of a motoring organisation, the police pass details of the breakdown direct to them. If not, it will be necessary to pay the garage sent out by the police.

It is unwise to leave your car on the hard shoulder for more than a few hours. It is a very hazardous position, and the police move vehicles left in such a place as quickly as possible, charging the owners for doing so. They will also remove your car if you have been involved in a collision or are blocking a carriageway.

Joining and leaving the motorway On the road

Joining the motorway

The entry onto a motorway is made along a two-lane slip road which leads into an acceleration lane. Some slip roads have tight corners, so do not speed up too quickly, but do not hesitate either. As you drive down the slip road watch the traffic in the nearside lane of the motorway, looking for gaps. Long before you reach the point of merging with it, check the mirrors and switch on the right indicators. Look over your right shoulder for gaps in the traffic and match your speed to that of the other vehicles. When a suitable gap occurs, move smoothly into the nearside lane, and cancel the right indicators.

Should traffic on the motorway be so dense that you reach the end of the slip road before a suitable gap has presented itself you must be prepared to stop. You should not try to force your way into the traffic stream, nor should you drive on the hard shoulder.

Once safely on the motorway, accustom yourself to motorway speeds before building up to your desired cruising speed.

When overtaking watch carefully for traffic approaching from behind. It may well be going faster than you think.

Leaving the motorway

On the approach to a junction where you intend to turn off, check the mirrors, switch on the left indicators and move into the nearside lane as early as possible, between the half-mile signpost and the 300 yard countdown sign.

The adjustment from motorway speeds to the halt likely to be required at the junction roundabout needs to take place over a relatively short distance. It is better to glance at the speedometer once or twice on the exit slip road than to rely on one's subjective assessment of speed. Even after joining the subsequent non-motorway road, check your speed from time to time, as it takes a short while to recover from the rhythm of high speed motorway driving and adapt to the slower speeds of other roads.

Direction signs

The approach to the motorway is marked by the international symbol for a motorway, together with its number. From this point until the end of the motorway, all motorway regulations apply. A similar sign crossed diagonally with a red bar indicates the end of a motorway and all its regulations.

One mile from each junction, the direction sign shows the junction number and also the number of the most important road number leading away from that junction.

The sign at half a mile from the junction repeats the junction number and gives more information including some of the main destinations reached.

Service areas

Signs indicating service areas are placed one mile before the turn-off. In some areas there are long distances between service areas, and it is preferable to stop at the first convenient one, particularly if you have been driving continuously for over two hours, rather than continue to the next service area.

The approach to a service area needs great care. The precise layout of the parking areas and roads to the fuel pumps will not be clear until the last moment. In the car park vehicles and pedestrians will be moving in all directions. You will need to lose almost all your speed on the approach

slip road, so that you are not going too fast when you enter the car park. Because it is difficult to adjust quickly from the high motorway speeds to the much lower ones required in a service area use your speedometer to get an idea of your speed, rather than rely on your subjective impressions.

From time to time, traffic may have to be diverted off a section of the motorway, to return to it farther along its length. The cause may be roadworks or an accident. A system of signs has been devised in which the diversion route is indicated by a geometric symbol in yellow with a black border.

To keep to a diversion route, all that is necessary is to follow the yellow and black symbols wherever they appear.

The start of the deceleration lane leading to the exit slip road is prefaced by countdown markers at distances of 300 yards, 200 yards and 100 yards.

The slip road itself has a confirmatory direction sign, repeating the junction number, the details of the roads and the destinations reached from that junction.

Road markings on the approach to a junction include large arrows indicating the start of the deceleration lane. That lane is bounded by a dashed white line incorporating green reflective markers. Some junctions also have the junction number painted on the motorway at the approach.

Junctions in urban areas, or where motorways merge and separate are usually heralded by gantry signs. These contain the junction number, direction information relevant to the lanes below them. They also frequently carry flashing light signals, and are sometimes found at distances of $\frac{2}{3}$ mile and $\frac{1}{3}$ mile from the junction.

Motorways have a better safety record than other roads, and provide fast communication links over long distances. Their freedom from interruptions such as roundabouts, traffic lights and sharp bends means that uninterrupted travel is possible for long distances. Large volumes of traffic can be carried provided everyone observes good lane discipline. Long distances on motorways can prove monotonous, so regular breaks for refreshment and exercise should be taken.

When preparing your car for a motorway journey be sure to check tyres, petrol, oil and water

Car preparation

The strains on a car during a motorway journey can be greater than on other journeys because of the higher continuous speeds involved and the longer distances. A breakdown can be an expensive annoyance on a motorway, and reliability is essential.

Lane discipline

This is one of the most crucial aspects of motorway driving. A common but dangerous misconception is that the right hand lane, especially on three lane motorways, is a 'fast' lane. This is not the case, it is an overtaking lane only and is not to be used for continuous motoring at 70 mph.

The left hand lane should normally be used on two and three lane carriageways. Occasionally it is filled with slow, heavy traffic, for example on some hills.

The centre lane (or right hand lane where there are only two) is used for overtaking the traffic in the left hand lane. Where there is a stream of slower traffic in the left hand lane, however, it may be preferable to remain in the centre lane until all the vehicles have been passed, rather than weaving in and out of the lanes. As soon as possible, however, return to the left hand lane. Do not stay in the centre lane if the left hand lane is empty.

All lane changes need to be planned well in advance because of the speeds involved. Always look well ahead so that the need to overtake another vehicle is realised in good time. Carefully check in your mirrors for any traffic approaching from behind. Keep checking this during the overtaking manoeuvre as it is easy to underestimate the speed of following traffic.

Braking distances

A consequence of the fact that speeds are higher on motorways is that braking distances will be greater. It is not always realised just how great these distances become. At 70 mph on a dry road with tyres, car, and driver in first class condition, it takes over 300 feet to stop completely. This is equivalent to about 23 car lengths.

If the roads are wet, the tyres are worn, or the driver's reactions are slow, this distance becomes more than 600 feet, or 46 car lengths. These very long braking distances serve to emphasise the importance of adequate spacing between vehicles on motorways.

Consideration for others

Always try not to baulk other vehicles when driving on a motorway. Before beginning any overtaking manoeuvre, consider whether your car's acceleration is fast enough to take you past the vehicle in front and back into the nearside lane without holding up other, faster traffic wishing to overtake you.

When approaching a motorway junction it is frequently possible to see traffic travelling along the approach slip road intending to join the motorway. It makes their entry on to the motorway simpler if you move from the left hand lane to the centre lane (having checked the mirrors and signalled correctly) well before reaching them.

Lorry drivers are grateful for consideration on motorways. Heavy goods vehicles are forbidden to use the right hand lane on a three lane motorway, and must make the best progress they can on the other two lanes. These heavy vehicles sometimes have a separate 'crawler' lane reserved for them on hills. Cars towing caravans are also banned from using the right hand lane on three lane motorways.

Night driving

Dipped headlights should generally be used when travelling on motorways. In spite of the distance between carriageways, it is still possible to dazzle oncoming motorists if main beam lights are used. Always dip your lights if the possibility of dazzle exists.

The system of reflective studs used on motorways is red for the left hand side, with green at junctions, white along lane markings and amber on the right hand side.

Adverse weather

Whenever visibility is restricted by the weather, switch on dipped headlights and high-intensity rear lights. Even when it is not actually raining, the spray thrown up by motorway traffic from a wet road can reduce visibility considerably.

In heavy rain; it is especially important that speeds should be considerably reduced as visibility will be low and braking distances will be increased. (See pages 94–97).

In fog take especial care. Drive slowly so that you could stop in the distance you can see to be clear. Do not be tempted to speed up in order to keep in sight of the lights of the vehicle in front. Do not also be tempted to believe the fog is thinner than it actually is.

The fog immediately behind a vehicle often looks thinner, but this will be found to be a false impression should you try to overtake. Keep watching your speed and always obey any speed restriction signs. It is easy to unwittingly allow speed to build up to a dangerously high level. (See pages 101–103).

Light snow does not usually block motorways altogether, although it may result in at least one lane being impassable.

Motorways are particularly susceptible to cross-winds. Keep a sharp look out for any stretches which seem as though they may be badly affected, and keep firm steering control of the car when passing high-sided vehicles. (See pages 98–99).

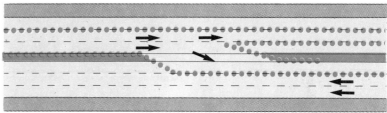

Extensive roadworks schemes can involve directing some traffic on to the opposite carriageway. These changes are given plenty of warning and the correct lane should be selected early

Speed limits should always be obeyed, particularly in bad weather

Roadworks

Most motorways are subject at one time or another to maintenance or improvement works. These can sometimes be substantial undertakings lasting for years.

All roadworks are preceded by sets of warning signs and, sometimes, flashing light signals. In nearly every case high speeds are impossible past roadworks, so you should slow down as soon as the first indication of roadworks is displayed.

When the roadworks are extensive, some lanes of the motorway may be switched on to the other carriageway. This sometimes means you have to make an early decision about the junction at which you need to leave the motorway, since that particular stream may be separated some miles before the junction. This emphasises the importance of planning your route so that you know which junction number you need to take in order to leave the motorway.

Fatigue

Driving for long distances on motorways can be monotonous, and it can lead to drowsiness and fatigue. Try to prevent this from happening by keeping the car well-ventilated, listening to the radio occasionally, checking instruments regularly, and constantly shifting your gaze.

Avoiding heavy meals before or during a journey will lessen the chances of fatigue setting in, as will taking regular breaks, at least every three hours, and more often if you feel like it.

Should you feel yourself becoming drowsy, you should realise that you cannot stop on the hard shoulder and sleep. Get off the motorway at the next exit, however, or at the first service area. Park the car in a safe place off the road, and either sleep there, or take a few minutes' break with some brisk exercise to get the blood circulating again. (See pages 148, 149, 154 and 155).

The majority of motorists spend a large proportion of their time driving in traffic and usually experience some congestion. These delays can be the cause of great irritation among drivers, with a consequent lowering of driving standards.

Driving attitudes

Observation and anticipation of events around you will give time to plan your driving well ahead and to execute the necessary moves without having to interrupt the traffic flow.

Courtesy to other drivers can calm ruffled tempers as well as smooth the traffic flow. Allowing some traffic from a side road to join the main traffic stream will relieve congestion without delaying you a great deal. A sensible system for this kind of situation is for one car from the side road to fit in front of one car in the main stream, the second in front of the one behind, and so on.

A relaxed attitude to the journey will make it considerably pleasanter for you, and probably for other drivers as well. This can be brought about by planning the journey so that you know exactly where to go, and have arranged matters so that you have plenty of time to complete it. Starting earlier or delaying the intended time of arrival will usually help you feel more relaxed. Try to avoid rush hour travel which so greatly increases fuel consumption at slow speed. Try to curb your impatience over other drivers' mistakes or bad driving. Give them enough room to sort themselves out rather than trying to compete with them or forcing them to conform to your own ideas.

Traffic lights

Look well ahead for traffic lights, particularly those with filter lanes. Always try to get into the right lane for your destination as early as possible. A late lane change may be impossible without severely inconveniencing the other traffic and risking an accident. If you find yourself in the wrong lane and cannot easily move to the right one, it will be necessary to continue in the wrong direction until you have an opportunity to turn off, return and try again.

The intention to turn right should be signalled and the move made to the right-turning lane as early as possible. At traffic lights keep the right indicators going for the information of the other traffic. Never leave it until the last minute before switching them on.

Always try to avoid making any congestion worse. At traffic lights in heavy traffic, for example, even if the lights are green, do not cross the junction unless you can see the exit is clear.

In some towns the traffic lights are linked to allow heavy traffic to flow at a steady speed.

All traffic must turn left

Box junctions

A box of yellow crossed lines marked on the road at a junction defines an area which no one should enter unless they can see it is clear on the far side. This practice should always be carried out at junctions, whether marked with a yellow box or not, but where the box is in place it is an offence to block it.

The one exception to this regulation is for drivers intending to turn right. If the road into which they intend to move is clear, it is permissible to wait in the box junction for a gap in the opposing traffic. More than one vehicle intending to turn right may wait in a line (but not a whole column), provided oncoming traffic wishing to turn right is not blocked thereby.

Right turns are banned here

One-way streets

Modern traffic schemes make increasing use of one-way streets in order to speed up traffic flow. Those unfamiliar with town driving may find themselves in situations where the presence or not of a one-way street is uncertain.

When joining a one-way street from a side road, a one-way sign will indicate the direction of traffic flow. If this is obscured, perhaps by a parked van, it is not always easy to tell that it is, in fact, a one-way street. A hint is given by the fact that all the parked vehicles will be facing one way. Vehicles are normally parked facing the same direction as the traffic flow.

One-way street lane markings

Lane discipline in a one-way street is important. Select the lane which will lead to your destination, using either lane markings or direction signs for information, then stay in it. A right hand or left hand lane is preferable to a centre lane, however, because traffic is entitled to overtake on either side in a one-way street.

Side streets leading off the one-way street may also be one-way. You should expect traffic to join the street from either side, and if you are intending to turn off down a side-street, look well ahead to confirm that entry to it is actually allowed. The confusion caused by making a mistake about this can be dangerous.

Bus lanes are sometimes laid down in one-way streets. The correct use of these is explained on pages 68 and 69. The use of contra-flow bus lanes in one-way streets may cause confusion when the situation is first encountered. Look out for the warning signs, and take care not to stray into the bus lane.

Tidal flow traffic working

Some wide two-way streets are adapted for tidal flow traffic working to help avoid peak-time delays.

Light signals on gantries across the road indicate by an arrow or a red cross the direction of flow along each lane. Where a red cross shows you should move out of that lane, as it will be open to traffic from the opposite direction.

Tidal flow lane indicators

Town driving On the road

The task of driving safely in towns is eased by an intelligent anticipation of the behaviour of other road users. Traffic in towns may become very congested, but every driver can minimise his own contribution to any congestion by driving smoothly, and with courtesy and consideration.

Pedestrians

In a busy street pedestrians may spill off the pavement into the road, so you should never drive so close to the kerb that they may be struck by door handles or wing mirrors for example.

An important situation in which to check for pedestrians is when turning left or right. Many people walk across side roads without looking, assuming the traffic on the main road will continue straight on. A gentle sound on the horn will tell them you are there, but remember that the pedestrian has priority and also that some people are deaf.

Pedestrian crossings

Pedestrians have the right of way on these crossings and traffic must stop for them. Drivers should stop at the give way line placed about one yard from the crossing. Within the area defined by the zig-zag road markings, no parking or overtaking is allowed. Some zebra crossings are divided into two parts by a central island.

Look out for pedestrian crossings well ahead of you. This will give plenty of time to slow down gently for any pedestrians, either on the crossing or waiting to cross. Children and old people should be given plenty of time to cross. In heavy traffic, do not stop on the crossing itself, but wait until there is enough space on the other side.

Pelican crossings are controlled by traffic lights activated by the pedestrians. These lights incorporate an amber flashing light, which authorises traffic to proceed only if there is no one on the crossing.

When the amber light flashes . . .

Stop at the Pelican crossing

Cyclists

Cyclists have a particularly difficult time in town traffic, and they should be given plenty of room. They may appear unexpectedly between you and the kerb, and you should always check for them along the nearside before turning left.

On a windy day in a city street, gusts of wind will blow between the buildings, and these could easily blow a cyclist out into the road. A cyclist who looks round and behind him is very likely to turn across your path.

Some towns have set aside reserved lanes for cyclists, where motorists are not allowed to drive.

Motor cyclists

Like cyclists, motor cyclists may also appear unexpectedly, and you should look out for them when turning and at junctions.

Although they are not so easily seen, and sometimes do not use their headlights in towns, they are just as fast as other vehicles and may well be weaving their way quickly through the traffic.

Buses

Wherever you are, always find out if you are on a bus route. In towns most of the busy roads will be bus routes and you should look well ahead to spot the bus stops.

Always give way to buses, provided it is safe to do so, particularly when they are pulling away from a bus stop. In the vicinity of a bus stop be prepared for bus passengers to jump off the bus just before it comes to a halt, and for people crossing the road behind and in front of the bus.

Take extra care near bus stops

When passing a bus at a bus stop check whether there is any movement of its wheels. If this is very slight it is probably safe to pass with caution, but otherwise it is better to let the bus go first.

Bus lanes

In some towns special lanes have been marked out and set aside for the use of buses. They may sometimes also be used by taxis. Signs at the start of the lane indicate which times of the day these lanes operate. These may be during peak hours, or the lane may be in continuous use for 24 hours. During their use, all vehicles are prohibited from driving or parking in them. They may be crossed when turning right or left, although this must be done with great care.

The bus lane may sometimes go in the opposite direction to the traffic in a one-way street.

Contra-flow bus lane

Taxis

In large cities taxis make up a substantial part of the traffic. They are very manoeuvrable and often drive fast. When picking up or setting down fares they are liable to stop suddenly, or to swing right across the road. You should allow room for the taxi to move or stop unexpectedly, without having to brake harshly yourself.

Other vehicle hazards

Delivery vans and milk floats may cause a hazard to the unwary by stopping unexpectedly or blocking the road. Good observation and anticipation should prevent anyone being baulked by them.

The sound of a siren or klaxon warns everyone of the presence of a police car, fire engine or ambulance. If you cannot see a flashing blue light or headlights in front of you, this vehicle is probably approaching from behind or from the side. You should pull well to the side as soon as possible and stop until it has passed. Remember that one emergency vehicle may be closely followed by another, so make sure it is safe before starting off again.

Special consideration should be given to cars carrying L-plates. If the car belongs to a driving school, it is very likely there will be a novice behind the wheel.

Delivery vans may double park and cause obstruction

Parking On the road

Parking, especially in the larger cities, is often so restricted that motorists can spend a large amount of time searching for a space. A variety of different parking control systems is in use, and familiarity with all of them will make life easier and may avoid a parking fine.

Road signs and markings

The general sign indicating the existence of waiting restrictions is circular, with a blue background, a border and a single red bar diagonally across it. Beyond this sign, different restrictions will apply in different areas. The precise details of these restrictions are provided by kerbside signs and yellow lines and markings on the kerb.

Double yellow lines mean that no waiting is allowed (except for loading and unloading) during any working day and at times outside normal working hours.

The yellow sign mounted on the post at the kerbside gives more details of what these times are. It may be a continuous restriction which applies on every day including Sundays and Bank Holidays, or a shorter period.

A single yellow line restricts waiting during every working day, and again, the details of the times when this is in force are given on the kerbside sign.

A dashed yellow line restricts waiting for periods shorter than the working day, details being provided by the kerbside signs.

Restrictions on loading and unloading may be applied in addition to the yellow lines, which do not in themselves limit the loading or unloading period. Three yellow stripes marked on the kerb or the edge of the carriageway mean no loading or unloading for a period longer than any working day.

A white sign on a kerbside post details this more precisely, and it may extend to no loading and unloading at any time.

Two yellow stripes mean no loading and unloading during any working day. Single yellow stripes reduce this restriction to a period shorter than any working day.

Roadside parking areas

Areas of some streets in towns and cities are sometimes set aside for limited short-term free parking. Notices near them detail the period allowed, and they also generally forbid return within a specified time. Some of these roadside parking areas are reserved for the exclusive use of local residents.

Parking meters

Many places charge motorists for parking space on the street by the use of parking meters.

A certain amount of parking time can be bought for a given payment. The rate can vary considerably from one town or area to another,

but is always given on a plate fixed to the side of the meter.

Normally, insertion of the appropriate coin operates the mechanism, but with some types it is necessary to turn a lever as well. You are at liberty to take advantage of any unexpired time remaining on an unoccupied meter.

Where you find the meter does not work, you should attach a note to it stating the fact. You may then park at that spot for the maximum time available on that meter.

A parking meter covered with a transparent plastic bag is one which the traffic warden has discovered as inoperative. All of these and any other meters which do not work are regularly repaired by a

parking meter mechanic.

When the meter has been repaired he will set it to the maximum time available on the meter. Any vehicle remaining there after expiry of that time will be liable to get a parking ticket and may be towed away by the police. Fines imposed for overstaying time at a meter are reviewed constantly and are increased periodically.

Occasionally, a meter may be covered by a red hood. This is the equivalent of converting it to a no-waiting sign, and is an indication that the area must be kept clear. Any vehicle parked there is very likely to be towed away, and the driver charged the recovery fee as well as the fine for illegal parking at that bay.

Pay-and-display car parks

Off-the-road parking is often provided in open-air car parks where certain defined periods of parking time can be bought.

The ticket supplied by the meter in exchange for the correct money must be fixed to one of the car windows, and be visible to the car park attendant. Failure to display a ticket can lead to a parking fine.

Multi-storey car parks

A multi-storey car park is often the most convenient place to park, although these parks are, generally, fairly expensive.

Upon entry to the car park a ticket is issued stating the time and date. When you leave the car take this ticket with you.

Parking techniques

In a car park, it is simpler and saves petrol to reverse into a parking space. The manoeuvring necessary is best done when the engine is warm. When starting from cold, the car can move forward with no interruption, thereby saving fuel. It is also often easier to manoeuvre precisely when driving in reverse. To save possible damage to your car you should park as centrally and as far back as possible in a parking space.

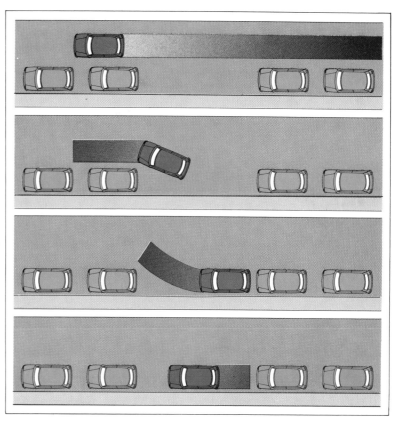

Parking parallel with the kerb is a manoeuvre which many people are hesitant about and consequently avoid. The technique is as follows:

Drive alongside and stop parallel with the vehicle in front of the space in which you intend to park.

Check your mirrors and indicate left (if you are on the left side of the road). When it is safe to do so, reverse very slowly with only slight left lock until your rear wheels are in a line with the rear of that vehicle.

Increase left lock, looking at the far corner of the parking space.

Continue slowly until your front wheels are in a line with the rear of the vehicle in front.

Watching the front of your car now, straighten up until the front nearside corner is past the rear bumper of the vehicle in front.

From this point, watch the rear of your car again, and apply full right lock.

Continue slowly until your car is close to the vehicle behind and is parallel to the kerb.

Drive slowly forwards, straightening up, to position your car midway between the other vehicles.

Most roads in Britain and Western Europe have a permanent covering on them. It is usually either white-topped (concrete cast as a continuous ribbon or in slabs) or black-topped (asphalt-covered). To counteract the effects of frost, ice and snow, many Alpine roads, and some roads in Holland, have stone blocks or even hard brick surfaces, which give a reasonable grip with good drainage.

Stone chips

Black-topped roads usually have small stone chips rolled into them in order to improve their grip under all weather conditions. The asphalt binds these stones, and acts as a cushion, spreading some of the load. The stones take the abrasive wear and crushing loads of the passing traffic.

Because they are generally quarried locally, the stone chips vary in their 'grippiness' from one part of the country to another. The granite chips of the Grampians, for example, are hard, durable, resistant to traffic polish, and give an extremely good wet grip. The gravel stones found near London and the Home Counties give a lower friction grip, are softer and therefore polish more readily, and tend to give less of that distinctive tyre rumble. Economics, however,

guide Local Authorities as to which chips they use, subject to laid-down standards of evenness and surface-grip.

Special surfaces

In a few accident black spot areas, and where the density of heavy goods traffic warrants it, special surface dressings are applied, which give remarkable polish resistance, very good wet grip, and a low maintenance cost. The materials are scientifically designed, and initially more costly, using graded stones and special materials to obtain the desired qualities.

On some elevated sections of roads, where black ice could be a danger, the roadway has electric wires embedded in it. These can be switched on to prevent ice forming, or to melt light snow deposits.

Newly surfaced roads

If the new surface on a road has not hardened, drive slowly over it. The excess stones can be flung up by your own vehicle, as well as by those in front, overtaking or passing in the opposite direction. They can chip off paint, scratch glass and even shatter windscreens. The tar picked up on your tyres is harmful to rubber, but never remove it with a rag dipped in solvent such as petrol, paraffin or

naphtha. These penetrate deep into the rubber, ruining and blistering it. In hot weather, particularly near bends where the stones have been pushed off or into the surface, tar can begin to melt. That wet look on the road can bring trouble to motorists who drive too fast into the bend or brake hard. Tyre grip is reduced and the surface is easily formed into ridges.

Potholes

Badly-maintained roads with deep potholes should be negotiated at a relatively slow speed, dipping into and out of each pothole, and steering round the worst of them. Those with greater experience of rough roads may prefer to drive at a speed high enough for the wheels to bounce from the rim of one pothole to the next.

Camber

Most roads have a certain amount of camber to give rapid drainage of the surface water. By introducing a controlled amount of texture roughness to both white-top and black-top surfaces, more drainage channels can be introduced to cope with heavy rainfall.

A change of camber as the road bends can have a marked effect on the car's handling. The steering response is governed by the design and layout of the suspension and tyres, in relation to the weight distribution of the car. Depending on the tyre-to-road-grip, the nature of the road surface, and the radius of the bend, there is a certain speed for every car

above which it will drift out tangentially on a given bend. Whereas it may be just safe to enter and exit a given bend at 50 mph in good conditions, a summer shower may bring the speed down to 30 mph, and black ice could reduce it to 15 mph.

Surface damage

The most important function of a road is its ability to take the crushing forces exerted by the traffic passing over it. A heavily loaded rolling tyre tends to 'flow' the road surface ahead and to the side of it.

The fact that the track of the wheels does not vary a great deal from one truck or bus to another means that a rhythmic pattern of ripples develop in the road surface, leading to eventual collapse.

This is most pronounced at the

approaches to traffic lights, intersections, roundabouts, or any section of road where inclines cause drivers to shift into lower gears. The loads tend to oscillate on the springs, particularly when braking or taking up a lower gear.

This rabbit-like pounding of the road can result in substantial road deformation. The greater the traffic density and the axle loading, the greater is the resultant damage.

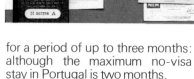

The prospect of driving in Europe is likely to provoke some apprehension, even among those who have been abroad before. There is no mystique about it, however, and no sensible motorist should ever encounter a situation he cannot handle.

Thorough preparation and common sense are all the motorist needs to carry him through the initial stages, and experience will take over from there.

Preparation

Timing

Decide your dates, decide your route, and book your ferries in good time. A longer sea route may not be your first choice, but it could place you hundreds of road miles nearer your ultimate destination and so save time.

If you are travelling during the summer months, book your ferry or hovercraft as far in advance as possible.

It is a good idea to time your ferry so that you have plenty of daylight left on arrival to get you to your first destination.

Checklist

Make a checklist of all the things you need to do and to take. Separate lists are advisable for documentation, car, and personal necessities.

Documentation

Passport

Make sure it will remain valid for at least the length of your stay and preferably longer, in case of delays.

If you need to renew it, apply at least three weeks before departure, and earlier still if the peak holiday season is approaching. Application forms are obtainable from any local post office.

Visas

These are essential for entry into Czechoslovakia, East Germany, Hungary, Poland, Rumania and Russia. A visa is not necessary in Bulgaria, except for those in transit. Application should be to the Embassy concerned.

A visa is not needed when visiting other West European countries on a full United Kingdom passport for a period of up to three months: although the maximum no-visa stay in Portugal is two months.

Personal Insurance

It is advisable to take out special holiday and medical insurance. Within the EEC, Form E111 (issued by the Department of Health and Social Security) and widely known as the Health Passport, will entitle the holder and nominated members of his family to receive the same state medical benefits as a citizen of the country. In some cases this means free treatment, in others a third of the medical fees will be payable. However, the benefits of reciprocal agreements do not extend to the self-employed or non-employed who should carry full medical insurance.

All visitors to non-EEC countries should take out full medical insurance. Outside the EEC, Bulgaria offers free medical care to UK passport holders. Emergency treatment is free in Austria, Norway, Poland, Rumania, Sweden and Yugoslavia. In Switzerland, Spain and Portugal, however, full charges will be levied.

Even EEC agreements do not cover fringe expenses arising from illness or injury, such as ambulance, nursing, extra hotel, extra food, extra travel.

Medical insurance is part of the cover provided by the AA "Five-Star" Travel Service, which also includes Vehicle Security in case of breakdown, Touring Security and Personal Security.

Driving licences

Check when planning a trip that your driving licence will not expire while you are abroad.

The full British licence is acceptable in most European countries, but Italy requires an official translation (obtainable from your motoring organisation). Certain countries demand an International Driving Licence as well (obtainable from your motoring organisation).

Vehicle insurance

EEC agreements entitle you only to the minimum insurance cover operating in each country. So ask your insurance company in good time (minimum three weeks ahead) for a Green Card even though it may not be inspected.

You may also need a Green Card if you are driving in some countries outside the EEC. If you are towing a caravan, make sure the details are on the card.

Caravanners intending to take a caravan to Europe require complex documentation such as a camping carnet.

A Bail Bond will be necessary if you drive in Spain—otherwise you could find your car and possessions impounded as a matter of course after quite a minor traffic incident.

Nationality plate

Your car must have a regulation size GB plate mounted near the rear registration plate. A caravan or trailer needs its own plate.

Vehicle registration book

Always have this with you. A photostat copy will suffice in most cases, but the original is better. If you have borrowed the car, carry a letter of authorisation. If you have hired it, a Vehicle On Hire Certificate should be carried.

On and in the car

Service

Give your car a thorough service at least three weeks before you set off.

Spares

Your motoring organisation will advise you on an essential spares kit and supply it. Obvious items are: a good spare wheel and tyre, fan belt, contact breaker points, plugs, bulbs, cooling system hoses. It is also wise to take a stout and powerful torch with spare battery,

insulating tape, waterproof sheet, and a tow-rope.

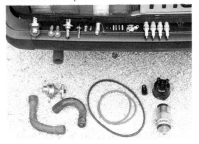

First aid kit

Always carry one. In several countries it is obligatory. A basic kit includes: scissors, cotton wool, safety pins, thermometer, needles, plasters, tweezers, mild antiseptic, sterile gauze dressings, bandages of different widths.

Headlamps

Converters must be used to throw the dipped beam to the right—it is illegal in many countries for headlights to dip to the left. Four-light cars need only convert the outside lights. Remember that rear passengers and a full boot will throw headlight beams high, so adjust the beam alignment before starting the journey.

Adaptation of the headlights for dipping to the right can be simply achieved by blocking off a portion of the beam with a mask.

Warning triangle

Always carry one—many countries now demand it. If you break down you should place it behind your car to warn approaching vehicles. See pages 78 and 79 for the correct distances in each country.

Maps

Cover your entire journey with up-to-date maps. Include a route planning map for general planning; country maps for the particular countries you are visiting; town plans for any major towns you intend to visit.

All maps should be kept together inside the car with a pencil and paper for making a daily itinerary.

Loading

No children should travel in the front seats (this is law in several countries), and you should always wear your seatbelt. In most European countries this is mandatory.

Stow spares, the emergency triangle, the first aid kit and equipment for the journey in an easily accessible place at the side or rear of the boot.

It is always a temptation to take far more things on holidays abroad than you really need, and this can lead to overloading. An overloaded car is likely to handle badly, responding to steering and braking in an unfamiliar way. In many countries it is an offence punishable by an on-the-spot fine. You would also be required to reduce the load to the proper limit before being allowed to drive on. Excess loads also mean extra fuel consumption.

Roof racks

These should not be overloaded. Apart from instability problems due to excessive bulk, a badly packed roof-rack can increase fuel consumption by between 15 and 20 per cent. Keep the lowest possible profile.

A warning triangle should always be carried when driving in Europe. Its use in emergencies is compulsory in most countries.

European road signs On the road

A great many of the road signs used throughout Europe are international and will be familiar to the British driver.

Red triangles mean hazard in every language, and the symbols they contain are usually obvious. Red circles signify restrictions and again the symbols will be familiar in most cases.

Road junctions in Europe may have a yellow diamond inside a white diamond signifying a priority road (a black diagonal line through it shows the end of the priority).

Although road signs are becoming more standardised all the time, most countries retain a few of their own and some examples of these are given here.

Austria

Federal road with priority

Federal road without priority

Bregenz
Beginning of built-up area

Ortsende von Bregenz
End of built-up area

Street lights not on all night

No through road

◀Umleitung
Diversion

◀EINBAHN
One-way road

Tram turns at 'yellow'

Belgium

Two-lane carriageway

D Traffic restricted

EXCEPTE CIRCULATION LOCALE — UITGEZONDERD PLAATSELIJK VERKEER
Local traffic only

Z / **Z**
DISQUE OBLIGATOIRE — SCHIJF VERPLICHT
Beginning of Blue Zone area

Z
End of Blue Zone area

Greece

END
Overtaking allowed

One-way only

X ΚΙΝΔΥΝΟΣ
Danger Yield to Traffic from Right
Danger: give way to right

Denmark

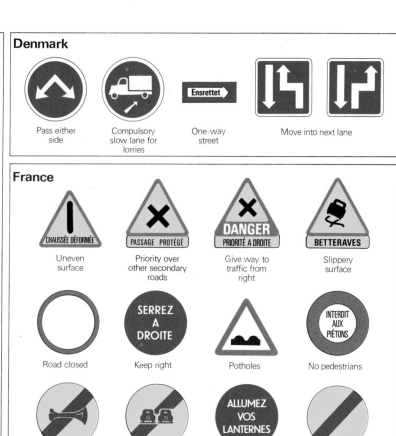

Pass either side

Compulsory slow lane for lorries

Ensrettet ▶
One-way street

Move into next lane

France

Uneven surface (CHAUSSÉE DÉFORMÉE)

Priority over other secondary roads (PASSAGE PROTÉGÉ)

Give way to traffic from right (DANGER PRIORITÉ A DROITE)

Slippery surface (BETTERAVES)

Road closed

Keep right (SERREZ A DROITE)

Potholes

No pedestrians (INTERDIT AUX PIÉTONS)

End of ban on sounding horn

Overtaking allowed

Switch on headlights (ALLUMEZ VOS LANTERNES)

End of all restrictions

No parking between dates shown (INTERDIT 1-15 / INTERDIT 16-31)

Fortnightly parking on alternate sides (STATT-ALTERNÉ SEMI-MENSUEL)

Germany

35 Federal road number

U22 ↑ Emergency diversion

P Parking disc zone

H Tram or bus stop

Stuttgart Diversion ahead

70-110 km Recommended speed

Italy

Road suitable for cars

Two-lane carriageway

Motor cycles only

Give way to post buses

One-way only

No parking left on odd-numbered dates; right on even

No buses

No pedestrians

Stop: police check

Netherlands

Straight ahead only

End of route B

End of built-up area speed limit

Disc parking when indicated

End parking zone

Cycles and mopeds crossing

Cycle track

Norway

Road merges: black priority

Tunnel

Parking permitted for 2 hours between 0800 and 1800 hours

Car park 0.8 kms away

Sightseeing

Layout of priority road

Portugal

Cattle track

Stop: toll road

Spain

No entry

Give way

No motor vehicles

Maximum advisable speed

Taxi rank

Turning permitted

Motor cars only

Take care

Maximum length

Sweden

Stopping place on narrow roads

Stop: customs patrol

Restricted parking zone

Tram crossing

Switzerland

Coaches have priority

Slow lane

Passing place for lorries

Parking disc compulsory

Motorway exit

No motor vehicles

Yugoslavia

No vehicles

Maximum length

77

	Lights	Children	Speed limits
Austria	Dipped headlights obligatory in towns. Parking lights required if street lights are off.	Children under 12 forbidden to travel in the front seats.	Towns: 50kph(31mph); outside towns: 100kph(62mph); motorways: 130kph(81mph), unless shown otherwise. Towing: weight less than 750kg: all roads 100kph (62mph); over 750kg: main road outside towns 80kph(50mph), motorways 100kph(62mph).
Belgium	Between dusk and dawn where visibility restricted to 200m(218yds), use of headlights is obligatory. Headlights must be dipped: where street lighting is continuous, permitting clear vision for 100m(109yds); at approach of oncoming traffic; when following another vehicle; where road is adjacent to water.	Children under 12 forbidden to travel in the front seats.	Towns: 60kph(37mph); outside towns: 90kph(56mph); motorways and dual carriageways: 120kph(75mph). Minimum limit of 70kph (44mph) on straight, level parts of motorways.
Denmark	Left-dipping lights prohibited. Use dipped headlights on roads with ordinary lighting. Sidelights are permitted on well-lit roads. Parking lights obligatory in poorly-lit areas and when visibility is poor. Use dipped headlights when daylight visibility is poor.	No specific regulations.	Towns: 60kph(37mph); outside towns: 90kph(56mph); motorways 110kph(68mph).
France	Headlights must dip to the right and emit a yellow beam. In fog or poor visibility, day or night, two foglights or two dipped heailghts plus two sidelights are obligatory. At night, dipping from two lights to only one is forbidden.	Children under 12 forbidden to travel in the front seats.	Towns: 60kph(37mph); outside towns: 90kph(56mph); dual carriageways and toll-free motorways: 110kph(68mph); toll motorways 130kph(81mph). Those who have held a licence for less than 1 year must not exceed 90kph(56mph).
Germany	Driving on sidelights only is prohibited. When visibility is poor, dipped headlights are compulsory. Foglights can only be used with dipped headlights. Rear foglights may only be used if visibility is less than 50m (55yds).	Children under 12 forbidden to travel in the front seats.	Towns: 50kph(31mph); outside towns: 100kph(62mph) or, if signposted, 120kph(75mph); motorways and dual carriageways 130kph(81mph). Towing: 80kph(50mph).
Greece	Dipped headlights must be used in towns, and also in tunnels. In fog, dipped headlights must be used, with foglights if fitted.	Children under 10 forbidden to travel in the front seats unless a seat belt is worn.	Towns: 50kph(31mph); outside towns: 100kph(62mph); motorways 100kph(62mph). Towing: 100kph(62mph) on open roads.
Italy	Headlights on full beam are only permitted outside towns. Dipped headlights are compulsory in tunnels, even if well lit. Fog lights may be used in pairs when visibility is restricted.	No specific regulations.	Towns: 50kph(31mph); outside towns: 80kph(50mph)—110kph (68mph); motorways: 90kph(56mph)—140kph(87mph), depending on engine capacity.
Netherlands	Dipped headlights must always be used in towns and when meeting oncoming traffic. Foglights should only be used in conjunction with sidelights. Headlights should be flashed at night as a warning signal. Sidelights are compulsory at night if parked farther than 30m(33yds) from a street light.	Children under 6 forbidden to travel in the front seats. Children aged 6–12 may do so, provided a seat belt is worn.	Towns: 50kph(31mph); outside towns: 80kph(50mph); motorways 100kph(62mph). Towing: 80kph(50mph) on all roads.
Norway	Headlights on full beam are only permitted outside towns. Foglights must be used in conjunction with sidelights or headlights.	No specific regulations.	Towns: 50kph(31mph); outside towns: 80kph(50mph); certain motorways 90kph(56mph). Towing: trailers with brakes: 70kph (44mph); those without brakes 60kph(37mph).
Portugal	Headlights on full beam are only permitted outside towns. Parking lights must be used when visibility is poor.	No specific regulations.	Towns: 60kph(37mph); outside towns: 90kph(56mph); motorways 120kph(75mph). Towing: in towns: 60kph (37mph); outside towns 70kph(44mph); motorways: 40kph(25mph) minimum limit unless signposted otherwise.
Spain	Headlights on full beam are only permitted outside towns. Dipped headlights are compulsory on dual carriageways and motorways.	It is recommended, although not obligatory, that children under 14 do not travel in the front seats.	Towns: 60kph(37mph); outside towns: 90kph(56mph); motorway and dual carriageways: 100kph(62mph). Towing in towns: 50kph (31mph); outside towns: 80kph(50mph).
Sweden	Left-dipping lights are prohibited. Headlights are compulsory in fog, snow, heavy rain and at dusk. Parking lights must be used when visibility is poor.	It is recommended, although not obligatory, that children under 12 do not travel in the front seats.	Towns: 50kph(31mph); minor and high-density-traffic roads: 70kph (44mph); all other roads: 90kph(56mph); motorways and trunk roads: 110kph(68mph). Towing: trailers with brakes: 70kph(44mph); those without brakes 40kph(25mph).
Switzerland	Driving on sidelights only is prohibited. Spotlights are forbidden. Foglights must be used in pairs. Dipped headlights must be used: in towns; in tunnels; when waiting at level crossings; traffic lights; or near roadworks; in badly lit areas when visibility is poor; when reversing, travelling in lines of traffic or stopping.	Children under 12 forbidden to travel in the front seats.	Towns: 60kph(37mph); outside towns: 100kph(62mph); motorways 130kph(81mph). Towing: 80kph(50mph) on all roads outside towns.
Yugoslavia	Spotlights are prohibited. In fog, dipped headlights must be used, with foglights if fitted.	No specific regulations.	Towns: 60kph(37mph); outside towns: 80kph(50mph) or 100kph (62mph), according to signs.

Drinking and driving	Warning triangles	On the spot police fines	Tyres
Limit is 80mg of alcohol per 100ml of blood. Above this a fine may be imposed plus withdrawal of licence and/or imprisonment.	Compulsory outside towns. Must be placed behind vehicle and clearly seen from 200m (218 yds).	Not refundable even if later proved unjustified. Refusal to pay results in a court appearance.	Ordinary tyres must show a continuous tread depth of 1·6mm. Police can spot check and halt a vehicle until new tyres are fitted.
Limit is 80mg of alcohol per 100ml of blood. Exceeding it is punishable by a fine and/or a prison sentence, plus possible disqualification.	Compulsory. Must be placed 30m (33yds) behind vehicle on ordinary roads, 100m(109yds) on motorways and visible at 50m (55yds).	Must be paid within 48 hours with special stamps (on sale at post offices).	Spiked tyres are permitted during certain dates in winter. They must not be used on motorways, and maximum speed on other roads is 60kph(37mph).
Limit is 80mg of alcohol per 100ml of blood. Above this prosecution may result in imprisonment of up to 1 year and suspension of licence.	Compulsory.	Not imposed.	Spiked tyres are permitted from Oct 1–Apr 30; must be fitted on all four wheels.
Limit is 80mg of alcohol per 100ml of blood.	Compulsory. Must be placed 30m (33yds) behind vehicle and be visible from 100m (109yds).	Stamps (available at licensed tobacconists) to the value of the fine must be fixed to an official card. A motorist may refuse to pay and go to court, but this is costly.	Spiked or studded tyres are permitted Nov 15–Mar 15 with a speed limit of 90kph (56mph).
Limit is 80mg of alcohol per 100ml of blood. Exceeding it is punishable by withdrawal of licence for a period and a fine. If blood content is more than 130mg per 100ml of blood, punishment is imprisonment, a fine or suspension of licence.	Compulsory. Must be placed 100m (109yds) behind vehicle on ordinary roads, 200m (218yds) on motorways.	Imposed, but the motorist may refuse to pay and request to be tried in court. The police will demand a cash deposit.	Minimum tread depth of 1mm over entire surface compulsory. Chains are not allowed on some roads.
Limit is 50mg of alcohol per 100ml of blood.	Compulsory outside towns. Must be placed 50m (55yds) behind vehicle.	Levied only by senior police officers. A motorist may refuse to pay and the matter will be referred to court.	No special regulations. Spiked tyres may be recommended in mountain areas.
A driver found to be under the influence of alcohol (no specified level) may be sentenced to up to 6 months' imprisonment and fined.	Compulsory outside towns. Must be placed 50m (55yds) behind vehicle and be visible from 100m (109yds).	Speeding and parking offences incur heavy fines.	Snow tyres may be used instead of wheel chains where the latter are required; fixed on all four wheels.
Limit is 50mg of alcohol per 100ml of blood. Those with excess alcohol may be subjected to imprisonment and a driving ban for up to 5 years.	Compulsory. Must be used at night if vehicle's lights fail, and in daylight if the vehicle is not easily visible.	Imposed in certain districts only.	Visitors may use spiked tyres if they are permitted in their native country, with a speed limit of 80kph(50mph).
Those with more than 50mg of alcohol per 100ml of blood may incur a prison sentence and confiscation of driving licence.	Not compulsory but visitors are recommended to use one.	Fixed fines imposed for certain speeding offences up to a level of 20kph(12mph) above limit. Beyond that level, the licence may be impounded, followed by a court case.	Spiked or snow tyres on all four wheels permitted Oct 15–Apr 30. Speed limit 50kph (31mph) on ordinary roads, 80kph(50mph) on motorways. Chains may be necessary in winter.
No regulations apply.	Compulsory. Must be placed 30m (33yds) behind vehicle and be visible from 100m (109yds).	Imposed.	No specific regulations.
Those with more than 80mg of alcohol per 100ml of blood are liable to a heavy fine and withdrawal of the driving licence.	Not compulsory for private cars.	Imposed and must be paid immediately unless a name guaranteeing payment is given. Otherwise, the vehicle will be withheld.	Spikes on tyres must be of 10mm diameter and not more than 2mm long.
According to the level of alcohol in the blood, a fine or prison sentence will be imposed. From 50–150mg of alcohol per 100ml of blood, the penalty depends on whether or not driving was considered dangerous. Above that level, the penalty is automatically applied.	Compulsory.	The police do not impose these. Various fixed fines are imposed for minor offences, and are paid at a post office.	Spiked tyres on all four wheels permitted Oct 1–Apr 30. If towing, the trailer must have them too.
Those with more than 80mg of alcohol per 100ml of blood incur a fine, imprisonment and withdrawal of licence for a minimum of 2 months.	Compulsory. Must be placed 50m (55yds) behind vehicle on ordinary roads, 150m(164yds) on motorways.	In addition to motoring offences, fines can be imposed for displaying an 'L' plate when the learner is not at the wheel, having an illegal number plate and not carrying a licence.	Spiked or studded tyres on all four wheels permitted on light vehicles Nov 1–Mar 31. Speed limit 80kph(50mph). Prohibited on main roads and also on motorways.
Those with more than 50mg of alcohol per 100ml of blood are liable to a fine, prison sentence and, possibly, suspension of licence.	Compulsory if vehicle cannot be seen from 100m(109yds) and at night. Must be placed 30m(33yds) behind vehicle and 1–1½m(3–5ft) from the kerb. If towing, carry two which must be placed side by side.	Imposed. Serious offences incur high fines, imprisonment, and suspension of licence.	Spiked tyres permitted Nov 1–Mar 15. Speed limit 100kph(62mph). Use on snow/ice covered roads only.

Driving techniques in Europe On the road

The fundamental driving techniques are the same in Europe as they are in Britain. Different rules of the road apply, however, and you should find out what these are for the countries you intend to visit. Many situations are treated in very much the same way by drivers in all European countries, and successful driving in Europe consists of an appreciation of what is generally expected.

Priority

In accordance with driving on the right hand side of the road, the general rule in Europe is to give way to traffic approaching from the right. Road signs and markings indicate priority at a given junction and you should watch out for these. Some main roads take priority over side roads but this is not always the case, so do not assume you automatically have the right of way. Make your intentions quite clear at junctions or cross-roads as other motorists may interpret hesitancy as giving way.

Slow moving vehicles will often assume right of way regardless of signs and you should always give way to public service emergency or military vehicles.

Take care when continuing a journey after a break that you drive on the correct side of the road, particularly on dual carriageways when traffic is light.

Roundabouts

Travel round these in an anticlockwise direction and, unless signs indicate otherwise, always give way to traffic entering the roundabout. To make the exit easier, keep to the outside lane.

Priority on roundabouts is given to vehicles entering

Traffic lights

These are not always as obvious as traffic lights in Britain and are often suspended high across the road. Watch out for filter lights as you may obstruct traffic by stopping in the wrong lane. In country districts there may be only one set of lights on the right hand side of the road. In some cities the traffic lights will be linked to help traffic flow. Occasionally, the speed may be indicated which will be needed to catch the next set of traffic lights at green. Many sets of lights have repeater lights at the driver's eye level.

Filter lanes and cycle lanes often have their own set of lights.

Traffic lights in towns are often found high over the road

Overtaking

You will need to take especial care when overtaking on the left. Follow the procedure of checking the mirrors, signalling and then beginning the manoeuvre. A wing mirror on the left-hand side is very useful. The front seat passenger can often help the driver by advising of oncoming traffic, although the driver should always rely on his own assessment.

European drivers tend to use their lights and horn to warn of overtaking, although the use of the horn is restricted in some areas.

Motorways

Continental motorways are longer and the speeds are faster than in Britain. Driving on them is tiring and it is easy to overestimate the distances that can be covered in a given time. A sensible target is no more than 300 miles a day, taking care never to drive for more than three hours without a break.

Services are available at regular intervals and emergency telephones are sited every two kilometres on most motorways.

Trams

These take priority over other vehicles. They usually travel along the middle of the street and you must always give way to passengers getting on or off them. Always overtake trams on the right, except on one-way streets.

Tolls

Tolls are charged on many motorways in France, Italy, Spain and Austria according to distance travelled and the type of vehicle concerned. The methods of payment vary, but for the majority a travel ticket is issued on entry and the toll is paid on leaving the motorway when the ticket is handed in. On some motorways the toll collection is automatic and the correct money is thrown into a basket. If change is required, use the separate marked lane. Toll booths will not exchange travellers cheques.

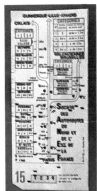

Motorway tolls are collected in many different ways. In some instances payment is made on leaving the motorway. At other times the correct toll must be thrown into a bin. The ticket includes full route detail

Road surfaces

Standards vary considerably in different countries but generally they are not as high as in Britain. Town roads and main routes are usually fairly well maintained but in country regions broken edges and large potholes often occur. Many villages still have cobbled streets.

Mountain roads

Mountain roads can be hazardous with hairpin bends, steep gradients and rough surfaces. It is sometimes necessary to negotiate acute bends by crossing some way over to the other side of the road, but watching out for approaching traffic.

Steep ascents and descents should be taken in a low gear avoiding excessive use of the brakes.

Be prepared for large lorries and coaches which always have priority and give way to all ascending vehicles.

Many mountain roads have snow on them all the year round and surfaces are therefore treacherous. You may need to fit wheel chains to the two driving wheels and sometimes these are compulsory so look out for relevant signposts. Check the regulations regarding their use in different countries. In winter some roads may be impassable and warning notices are displayed if this is the case. It is inadvisable to cross mountain passes at night.

Tunnels

There are many motorway tunnels abroad and they can be up to nine miles long. Various restrictions regarding speed, overtaking and stopping apply to different tunnels so watch carefully for these signs. Dipped headlights should always be switched on when entering the tunnel, and it is advisable to drive cautiously as it takes some time to adjust to the transition from bright sunlight to darkness.

Many of the tunnels exact toll charges which are calculated on the wheelbase of your vehicle. Emergency bays and telephones are situated along the length of the longer tunnels.

Are you a better driver? On the road

Do you think you are a good driver? It is very likely that you are interested in driving, otherwise you would not be reading this book. It is also likely that you will be a good driver. There is a difference, however, between being a good driver and being a better driver. This is not necessarily a question of your own belief in your abilities, but it is rather more a matter of how you behave towards other road users and how safely you handle unexpected situations.

The questions on this spread should set you thinking about your driving. Try to answer as you honestly believe you would have behaved in the situation described, not as you think you ought to have done with hindsight! The answers to the questions are also given on this spread but do not read them until you have answered the questions. They can easily be covered over with a piece of paper while you record your answers.

1 You realise you have just missed a right turning you had intended to take. Do you:
a take the next convenient turning on the right, reverse into the main road, then return to your intended turning?

b stop just past the first convenient left turning, reverse into it, then turn right, back into the main road, and continue to your originally intended turning?
c carry out a U-turn in the main road as soon as it is safe to do so and return to the turning?

2 You are approaching a T-junction with a major road. It is marked with double broken white lines across its mouth. There is no traffic on the major road. Are you obliged to stop before turning into it?
a Yes
b No

3 You are driving round a right hand bend. The road surface is dry and traffic is light. For maximum stability should you:
a keep your speed constant throughout the bend, leaving it at the same speed that you entered it?
b take your foot off the throttle and be prepared to brake if your speed gets too high?
c use light throttle and aim to leave the bend slightly faster than you entered it?

4 You are planning to overtake a lorry on a stretch of dual carriageway. Before starting the manoeuvre should you:
a switch on your right indicators, then check in your mirrors that all is clear behind before starting to overtake?
b check your mirrors before you switch on your right indicators?

5 You are driving along a narrow road with a constant stream of opposing traffic. Suddenly, a car turns out from the left and is proceeding directly in front of you. Your speed is such that you must slow down rapidly to avoid hitting him. Do you:
a change down through the gears as quickly as you can?
b brake hard, then release the brakes, then brake hard again?
c brake hard only once, keeping the brakes on all the time?

6 You are approaching a set of traffic lights which are at red. You are still some distance away from them and can see a small queue of traffic waiting at them. Do you:
a ease off the power to slow the car gently, waiting for the lights to change before you get there?
b change into third gear when you get nearer to the lights?
c brake early so that you can accelerate when the lights change?

hand lane and have just completed overtaking a vehicle in the centre lane. You are about to begin your return to the centre lane when you notice another car has approached very rapidly from behind, and appears to be planning to overtake you on the inside. Do you:

a move as quickly as you can into the centre lane so that he will be able to pass you without breaking the law?

b stay where you are for the time being, allowing him to carry out the dangerous and illegal manoeuvre of overtaking on the wrong side?

7 You are driving along a motorway in light traffic. You are in the right

8 You are driving in a small town approaching a section of road with cars parked on both sides. The road is effectively wide enough for only one vehicle. At the far end of the line of parked cars, another car appears and flashes his headlights. Do you:

a accept his invitation to come on and drive forward immediately?

b stop and wait to see what he does next before placing any interpretation on his signal?

c invite the other driver to come on by flashing your headlights at him?

Answers

1 a Reversing from a side road into a main road is dangerous and should never be done.

b Correct. Make sure the left side road is clear by looking into it as you drive past, preparatory to reversing into it.

c Carrying out a U-turn can be dangerous, particularly if there is much traffic on the main road.

2 a The broken white double lines mean 'Give Way'. There may also be a 'Give Way' sign or a white inverted triangle marked on the road. This means that you should give way to any traffic on the major road, but that if it is clear you may proceed.

b Correct.

3 a You should get your speed right on the approach to a bend, braking or changing gear if necessary. Taking the bend on a trailing throttle does not give you adequate control or the car maximum stability.

b Your speed should never become too high during a bend if you have assessed it correctly during the

approach and slowed if necessary before reaching the bend. You should not take your foot off the throttle, as applying the power helps to give the car stability. Never brake on a bend unless in an emergency and even then do not brake any more harshly than necessary. The tyres, already under cornering forces, may skid.

c Correct. Progressive throttle through the bend increases the car's stability, although the amount of power should be carefully controlled. Once you can see that the exit of the bend is clear, accelerate smoothly, but not too harshly, out of it.

4 a Switching on your right indicators denotes your intention to move to the right. You should have checked in your mirrors that it was safe to do so before indicating your intention to overtake.

b Correct. Once you have decided on your course of action, you should always check in your mirrors before making a signal of any kind.

5 a You should never attempt to slow down suddenly or in an emergency using the gears.

Precious seconds will be lost while the clutch is disengaged and you are changing gear. During this time, no speed will be lost. The brakes are designed to stop the car and should be used for this purpose.

b Correct. This technique of releasing the brakes just before they lock up then quickly re-applying them is the safest way to stop, particularly if the road surface is poor or slippery. The process is repeated as often as necessary to stop the car. You should have spotted the side turning earlier, however, and been prepared for a vehicle to emerge.

c Keeping the brakes hard on could easily lead to the wheels locking up and a resulting skid.

6 a Correct. By looking ahead you will have seen the red traffic lights in good time. You will conserve fuel by staying in top gear for as long as possible.

b Changing gear nearer the lights is unnecessary and wasteful. If you need to slow down nearer the lights, use the brakes.

c Braking now will slow you down more than necessary and the subsequent burst of acceleration will waste fuel.

7 a Changing lanes quickly could be very dangerous. If the other car is moving very fast, he could well have committed himself to overtaking you on the inside before you move, and to do so would be to risk a collision. You should never try to force another driver to do what you want him to do, even if you are trying to stop him breaking the law.

b Correct. If the other driver is intent on breaking the law you should not do anything dangerous to try to stop him.

8 a You would be foolish to automatically assume the other driver's flash on his headlamps was an invitation to come on. He could have meant the opposite, that he intended to "come on". Headlamp signals are very ambiguous and can be easily misinterpreted. The only safe meaning they can have is I am here.

b Correct. You should not assume the other driver's headlamp flash was an invitation until it is confirmed or otherwise by what he does next.

c You should never flash your own lights to convey a signal or a message to another driver.

3 All weather driving

All weather driving

Whatever the weather, the good driver prepares himself for a wide range of likely driving conditions. A central consideration is the question of visibility. Many people are unaware of the effects some slight vision defects can have on their observation of the road scene. Good weather with bright sunlight can pose some visibility difficulties and problems of a different kind arise when driving at night.

Adverse weather conditions are a familiar part of the motoring scene and it is wise to learn to cope.

The problems of driving in rain vary according to its intensity, but both the driver's vision and car control on the road are affected. High winds can be dangerous if drivers do not react to them quickly and a spread in this section shows how to anticipate where conditions will be worst. Winter brings its own driving problems of which the most worrying are fog and falling snow. Snow and ice bring their own problems, many of which are made less serious by adequate preparation of the car and its contents.

Night Driving
pages 92–93

Driving at night is easier in some circumstances than daytime driving because other traffic can often be seen from farther away thanks to its headlights. For the most part, however, restricted visibility makes driving more difficult.

Vision
pages 88–89

Good vision is essential to safe driving. Although a certain minimum standard of eyesight is required, many people may not realise that they suffer from some vision defects. This spread shows the implications for the driver.

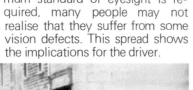

Rain
pages 94–97

Aside from the important visibility restrictions brought about by rain, a wet road surface lowers tyre adhesion and affects handling and braking. How tyres cope, stopping distances, aquaplaning and flooding are all covered here.

Bright sunlight
pages 90–91

The problems of glare and dazzle when driving in bright sunlight can worry many drivers. The choice of sunglasses is important, and the advantages and disadvantages of the various kinds are compared in this section.

Wind
pages 98–99

Keeping control of the car in strong winds, particularly near high-sided vehicles, demands quick and positive reactions. Being able to anticipate when these situations are likely to arise can help a driver prepare for them.

Lights in fog
pages 100–101

The problems of driving in fog are eased by the ability to see as far ahead as possible. The correct use of the car's existing lights is an important first step, but the advantages of different kinds of auxiliary lights are reviewed here.

Fog
pages 102–105

The dangers of fog may not need to be emphasised but it is not commonly realised to what extent the driver's senses can be deceived by it. Understanding this and making allowance for it will help many people adjust to the conditions.

Preparation for winter driving
pages 106–107

The difficulties of motoring during the winter can be minimised by careful preparation. The car itself needs proper maintenance and servicing, while many other items, could be selected from the range of suggestions given here.

Snow and Ice
pages 108–109

Patches of ice, perhaps lying unseen on the road, are treacherous. Being able to anticipate where ice may form and knowing how to control the car if it skids will arm the motorist against the worst dangers.

Snow
pages 110–111

Maintaining mobility in snowy weather is one of the more tiresome problems of driving in winter. This spread includes information on how to get started again after being stuck in the snow, keeping going and coping with blizzards.

Test yourself
pages 112–113

How much do you know about driving in all weathers? Check your knowledge by solving the range of entertaining problems presented on this spread which have to be faced by all motorists sooner or later.

Vision All weather driving

A driver receives most of his information about the road situation through his eyes. Certain minimum vision requirements are laid down before a driver may obtain a licence, but everyone should always remember that their eyesight may slowly get slightly worse as time goes on. Any suspicion of eyesight problems should be followed up without delay because of the serious implications for driving safety.

Legal requirements

In order to obtain a driving licence a motorist must be able to read a number plate from a fixed distance outdoors in bright daylight. The distance is 75 feet for number plate characters of $3\frac{1}{2}$ inches height (as commonly found on motor cars) and 67 feet for number plate characters of $3\frac{1}{8}$ inches height. This eyesight check is normally made at the beginning of the normal driving test.

If glasses are worn for this eyesight test they must be worn all the time when driving. The motorist is legally obliged to ensure that his vision remains up to the standard of this eyesight test.

Vision defects

The British number plate test is one of the most basic to be found anywhere, and is not very exacting. It demands only about one-third normal vision in one eye, in order to pass it.

Few accidents, about 1–5% of the total, are due to vision defects, even in part. Where they are involved, the situation is usually one in which the hazard is difficult to see, because of poor visibility or lighting, for example.

The major aspect of eyesight which is important for driving is the sharpness of the vision. This is checked with a distance test involving reading letters on a chart.

Long sight or short sight produce blurred images, and both these conditions are rectified by the appropriate spectacles, convex (positive) lenses for long sight and concave (negative) lenses for short sight.

Tunnel vision is caused by some eye defects. The normal visual field is about 160° but it can be narrowed to 90° or less in those affected by tunnel vision.

The most serious condition is the inherited defect of retinitis pigmentosa, which gradually restricts the field of vision until almost nothing remains. Sometimes, those affected compensate by moving their head from side to side.

Those afflicted with tunnel vision are not always aware of the fact. If only one eye is affected the other compensates. As peripheral vision is reduced, those with tunnel vision do not see objects such as pedestrians or vehicles outside the narrow field of vision, and this is a potentially dangerous situation. They will also find great difficulty when driving round corners. A similar effect to tunnel vision can be produced by wearing spectacles with broad sides. These are totally unsuitable for motoring.

Associated with tunnel vision is the phenomenon of night blindness. The periphery of the eye is used in night vision, and as this becomes affected in those with tunnel vision, night vision gets very poor indeed.

Colour blindness can have serious implications for motorists, particularly if it is not recognised. Men are more likely to suffer from it than women, and the most common defect is red-green blindness. Many people, however, do not realise they are affected. In many cases, colour blind people can drive satisfactorily, however, provided they are aware of the defect. Traffic signals can usually be interpreted by the position of the lights, and the movement of other traffic usually allows accurate interpretations of other lights.

Colour blindness is usually inherited, but it may be acquired by excessive pipe smoking, especially if coupled with high alcohol intake.

Good vision is absolutely essential for driving. The eyes are the most important of the driver's senses, as he receives 80% of all his information through them.

Many people think their eyesight is better than it actually is. It may have been good once, but it has probably deteriorated over the years. Surveys of large numbers of motorists have found that over 30% failed some aspect of an eyesight test and were advised to have a detailed eye examination.

No one need allow this situation to arise. A free sight test once a year is available to everyone under the National Health Service.

Those with only one eye should not drive until they have had time to adjust to using the single eye. Plenty of time should be allowed after any eye operation. Once the adaptation has been achieved, however, it is normally safe to drive, provided there is a full field of vision in the remaining eye.

Elderly people will probably suffer a deterioration in vision. This may not be recognised or admitted, and, if spectacles are worn, they may have become useless. All elderly drivers should have their vision checked regularly.

Visual field test

A simple test sometimes used by doctors is to face the patient, about 30 inches away; both doctor and patient cover their left eyes, and watch each other with the right. The doctor moves his forefinger steadily in from the right periphery, and then from higher and lower directions. The patient reports when he first sees the finger, and the doctor compares this with his own finding.

Distance test

The usual test for distance is to view a series of letters of carefully calculated sizes. The largest letter represents 1/10 normal vision, and inability to see it results in registration as blind. Can you read the centre row from 10 feet away?

```
          7 5
A  C  E  H
           6
T  L  C  N  O
          4
O  D  E  C  L
```

Normal sight The scene is sharp in the foreground and in the distance, with good peripheral vision and colour.

One-eyed vision The loss of one eye restricts vision on that side and affects distance judgement because stereoscopic vision is impossible.

Colour blindness The dangers of colour blindness are greatest when the defect is unrecognised. Several warning lights on the road may be missed by colour blind drivers.

Tunnel vision This less common defect causes loss of peripheral vision and is potentially very dangerous. The view straight ahead is satisfactory, however.

Short sighted The whole scene is blurred and out of focus, except for very close objects. Concave (negative) lenses are needed.

Long sighted Distant objects are in focus but the foreground is blurred. The eye can correct this, but it causes strain and headaches. Convex (positive) lenses are needed.

Night blindness Those affected by tunnel vision are severely handicapped at night by a further reduction in night vision.

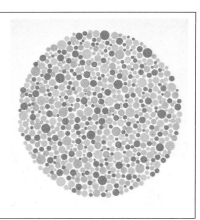

Colour test

The simplest reliable colour test is the Ishihara Colour Plates, designed by a Japanese surgeon. The plates are filled with different coloured spots, some of which, in a contrasting colour, form the shape of a number. Colour blind people have difficulty distinguishing the number from its surroundings, or may be totally unable to recognise the number.

Although bright sunlight is generally welcome, it can bring problems of visibility to the motorist. The human eye is extremely adaptable to a wide range of light intensities, much more so than a camera, but it cannot see comfortably in very intense light or dazzle.

The eye

The normal human eye can see all the colours from violet to red in the visible spectrum, but not ultra-violet or infra-red rays. It can cope with quite high intensities of light, but staring directly at the sun for any length of time can permanently damage the retina and cause a partial or total blindness.

The very bright light reflected from snow on mountain tops can also affect the eye, although not permanently. It may be the cause of the painful external inflammation, conjunctivitis.

Wet roads can cause serious dazzle problems

Windscreen glass

The glass of the windscreen and the other windows absorbs 20% of the light passing through it if it is clean (more if it is dirty). For this reason, if for no other, that part of the windscreen which the eyes regularly look through should be not tinted at all. Night driving, in particular, will be made more difficult. The driver is better advised to use sunglasses in bright sunlight, which can then be removed when visibility is reduced.

The main value of tinting the upper part of the windscreen is in keeping down the temperature of the car interior a little.

Dazzle

Intensely bright spots or shafts of light, such as headlight beams, bright sunlight or reflections off water, can cause dazzle. The pupil reacts quickly, but not instantaneously and there may be a temporary 'blinding' which is a serious hazard. All the softer colours and the objects in partial shade temporarily disappear and contours become indistinct. For the average person in good health, however, the eye makes a partial recovery in a second or so. During the short period of 'blindness' the driver must rely on what he has memorised of the scene ahead and to the side.

The reflected light which causes dazzle is particularly disturbing because it becomes partly or wholly polarised. The eye is extremely sensitive to this polarised light.

A few people, however, suffer from the effects of excessive brightness (photo-phobia).

Sherry-brown tinted sunglasses

Green tinted sunglasses absorb some infra-red light

Sunglasses

Some people manage to drive in bright light without wearing sunglasses. If there are no unpleasant side effects such as headaches, soreness or watering of the eyes, there is probably no need to wear them.

The use of sunglasses when driving at night, in order to avoid dazzle from oncoming headlights is extremely ill-advised for it reduces your ability to pick out poorly-lit objects. In Germany it is illegal to drive at night with glasses of anything more than 15% absorption.

When considering the range of sunglasses available, choose a pair with good lenses. Any waviness on the surface (detected by watching through them something with straight lines, such

as a building, then moving the lenses up and down and from left to right), or prismatic effects (detected by looking through the lens at a fixed point, then rotating the lens round that point, when no movement should be seen) will produce symptoms of fatigue and headaches while driving.

Plastic lenses can be a false economy because some types scratch so easily.

Three basic types of sunglasses are in common use.

Tinted

Deeply-tinted lenses are available to cut down visible and ultraviolet light, and, in some cases, infra-red as well. The colour of the tint is important. Sherry-brown or grey tints are best for preserving colour neutrality, but some green

Photochromic lenses

Polarised lenses

or darker element is necessary to absorb infra-red. Good sunglasses should cut out about 75% of the infra-red radiation.

The better quality sunglasses of this type will bear an indication of the amount of light they absorb. A higher absorption figure, perhaps 85%, may be preferable for tropical wear, use at sea or in high mountains. The general rule is to choose the lightest tint which gives comfortable protection.

Some eye defects aggravate the discomfort caused by sunshine. If you suffer discomfort, even when wearing sunglasses, it is wiser to have your eyes checked, rather than try out darker lenses.

Photochromic

These lenses automatically darken in bright light, and lighten in poor sunlight. They are also affected by the temperature, darkening in low temperatures and lightening in warm ones.

An important factor with this type of lens is the time it takes to darken fully, and, especially, the recovery time (the time to return to the lightest state). The recovery time is longer than the time taken to darken, and this can cause problems when driving in rapidly changing light intensity.

Polarised

This type of lens is particularly effective against the dazzle and glare of light reflected off wet surfaces. No colour distortion is caused, although the overall light reduction is usually less than with other types of sunglasses. They show up the stress pattern on toughened-glass windscreens.

Winter sun

The winter sun brings problems of its own. For most of the day, sunglasses are rarely required, but the effect of driving into the slanting rays of the sun when it is low in the sky is irritating.

Photochromic glasses are less effective in these circumstances. The low ultra-violet content of the sun's rays, combined with the warm temperature of the car's interior, mean that this type of lens may not darken sufficiently. Lowering the sun visor often cuts down the rays adequately but it reduces your field of vision.

A better solution to this problem is to keep a pair of fixed tint sunglasses of, say, 65% absorption in the car and to put them on when you are driving into the setting sun.

Tunnels

The switch from bright light to relative darkness on entering a tunnel causes a potentially dangerous situation. Photochromic sunglasses will not lighten quickly enough; and fixed-tint sunglasses will not lighten at all, of course. If you wear sunglasses when entering a tunnel you will be unable to see for the first few yards. The best solution is to remove any sunglasses before entering the tunnel.

When driving in Europe, a series of short tunnels may have to be negotiated. They often have two lanes in either direction and can have a bend in the middle. Always switch on headlights so that you can see and be seen, even if the tunnel has overhead lighting.

Never change lanes when driving in a tunnel, and do not drive too fast. If you are in any doubt about the tunnel and exit layout, reduce speed gradually. Do not brake sharply or drive very slowly, for the car behind may not have seen you in time and could drive into you.

Slanting sunlight through an avenue of trees requires careful concentration

Amber and blue street lighting produce different effects, particularly on colours

In some circumstances driving at night can be easier than daylight driving. The roads may be clearer of traffic and you can sometimes see approaching vehicles from a greater distance. On the other hand, however, the dazzle from oncoming headlights can be unpleasant and even dangerous. The golden rule is always to drive at such a speed that you can stop within the distance your headlights show to be clear.

Always look carefully into dark areas between street lights

Eyes at night

The eyes react to dim light and darkness by opening the pupil wide. Adaptation from bright light to relative darkness takes several seconds, and some people take longer than others to adapt. Prolonged bouts of cigarette smoking can increase the adaptation time. Some sight deficiencies also become worse at night.

Tinted glasses should never be worn at night, nor should so-called 'night driving' glasses. When it is dark the eye needs to receive as much light as possible through the windscreen glass.

Clean windows

A dirty or scratched windscreen will be very much more likely to provoke dazzle than one that is kept clean. Clean all the windows, inside and out, before driving at night, and also clean your spectacles if you wear them. When cleaning a windscreen at any time take care to avoid scratching it.

Auxiliary lights

Before considering the purchase of auxiliary lights it is worthwhile making sure that the existing lights are functioning as efficiently as possible. Check that the lenses are clean and that the reflectors are in good condition. A straightforward improvement in headlight performance can be achieved by replacement of the tungsten bulbs with quartz-halogen ones. These give a very much more powerful beam. Yellow bulbs give no improvement to the performance of the lights.

Any auxiliary lights must be fitted according to dimensions specified by law. A spotlight mounted on the near-side used to be considered the best way to improve illumination of the kerb, but many of the modern auxiliary driving lights have a wider beam.

White reversing lights are very useful accessories if your car is not fitted with them. These can be connected in such a way that they are switched on when you engage reverse gear.

Use of dipped headlights

Dipped headlights should be switched on as dusk approaches. No economies are made by delaying switching them on as it gets dark, and their use enables other road users to see you. Even if other traffic has not put on its lights, if you believe the visibility is such that it will be safer to use them, do not hesitate to do so.

Dipped headlights should be used unless the street lighting is of a high standard. They should certainly be used when there is no street lighting at all (where the streetlights are farther apart than 200 yards). The lighting, in some places, is uneven, leaving pools of darkness which could conceal a pedestrian or parked vehicle, and dipped headlights would pick these out. They should always be used on motorways at night, even if the motorway is illuminated.

When following another vehicle your lights should always be dipped (you should never turn the headlights off). You should also keep sufficient distance from it that you do not dazzle the driver through the reflections of your lights in his mirrors. (Your dipped beams should fall just short of the rear of the other vehicle). When overtaking, do not switch to main beam until you are at a point where you will not dazzle the driver of the overtaken vehicle. When you are overtaken, dip your lights as soon as the other vehicle is past.

You should always be the first one to dip your headlights when another vehicle is approaching you with his lights on main beam. If he does not dip his lights at all, on no account retaliate by attempting to dazzle him with your lights on main beam. A quick flash of your lights may remind him that he has forgotten to dip. It is courteous to dip your lights for cyclists also.

Dipping your lights for oncoming traffic should be carried out early on left hand bends, because your light beams meet the other driver's eyes before he is very far into the bend. Right hand bends, however, give you slightly more time on main beam before you run the risk of dazzling the other driver.

When it is possible you should quickly return to main beam in order to give yourself the best possible visibility. There is no point keeping on dipped beam when driving on unlit roads where there is little traffic.

Avoiding dazzle

Most people find that their eyes are drawn involuntarily to stare directly at the lights of oncoming vehicles. Firm determination is needed to stop yourself doing this and to force your eyes to look straight in front of you directed at the nearside kerb.

The risks of dazzle are reduced if you keep the windscreen scrupulously clean (as well as your glasses if you wear them for driving). Keeping the lenses of your lights clean and the lights correctly aimed will also minimise the chances of your seriously dazzling other motorists.

When driving on main beam you can prepare yourself for the reduction in visibility which happens when you dip your lights, by carefully studying and remembering as much of the road scene ahead as you can while your lights are still on main beam. Your speed should be such that you can stop within the distance you can see in your dipped beams to be clear. If you are dazzled, or cannot see far enough ahead, you should

slow down, even if you think you will hold up following traffic by doing so.

You may find yourself dazzled by vehicles coming close behind you or not dipping their lights. If you have a dipping mirror, switching it over will help to alleviate the irritation, but do not forget to switch it back again once that other vehicle has gone. When it is in its dipped position, it becomes very difficult to estimate the speed or distance of following traffic. If you do not have a dipping mirror, moving it slightly to one side will divert the reflection, but, again, you should re-align it correctly once the other vehicle has gone.

Driving at night

You should prepare yourself, as well as your car, for any journeys at night. Remember that your judgement of the speeds of other vehicles will be affected since you have only their lights to base your judgements on. It is frequently difficult to be sure about the precise position of some lights in the distance. Your estimates of your own speed will also be affected—it is not uncommon for your car to seem to be going faster at night.

Any long journey, particularly late at night, is likely to make you

fatigued. Eat only light meals beforehand, stop at regular intervals on the journey (at least every three hours) to take a refreshment break or some brisk exercise. Do not take any drugs or alcohol, and remember that your body's alertness falls to its lowest peak in the early hours of the morning. Keep the car well ventilated, and if you feel you are becoming drowsy, pull off the road (not onto the hard shoulder of a motorway), and either have some exercise or a short sleep.

Although it may appear to be easier to spot other vehicles at night, it is an unfortunate fact that a large proportion of the vehicles on the road have lighting defects. You should therefore be constantly on the alert for vehicles, including cycles, with no lights, or only one light, or very dim and dirty lights. You can easily make a dangerous mistake if you act on first impressions under these circumstances. You could also find unlit vehicles parked on dark, country roads. Flashing your lights on the approach to a crossroads is a useful warning signal to other drivers that you are there. It is no more than that, however.

Make sure there are no bright lights in your car to distract you when driving at night. In rain, the problems of dazzle will be worse because of the multiple reflections of all the other lights, and, in addition, stopping distances will be increased. Extra caution is called for in this case.

Consideration for other drivers can be exercised at night by thoughtful use of your indicators. If you are in a queue of traffic waiting to turn, unless you are the first or last in the queue, other drivers

will be grateful if you do not allow your indicator to continue to flash unnecessarily. Keeping your foot on the footbrake, in addition to being bad practice, will also have the effect of dazzling following drivers with your brake lights.

You should also be particularly watchful at night for pedestrians, children, animals and vehicles pulling away from the kerb.

Breakdown

In the event of a breakdown at night, get the car off the road if possible. The hazard warning lights should be switched on if the vehicle is likely to obstruct other traffic, and an emergency triangle should be set up 50 yards behind the car (150 yards on the hard shoulder of a motorway). It is always wise to carry a torch in the car for any unexpected incident at night.

Parking

You should not park on the road at all if there is somewhere else convenient to leave the car. Do not leave your vehicle on the right hand side of the road at night (except in a one-way street). Switch off your headlights when you stop to avoid the risk of dazzling other motorists.

Cars, motor cycles and other vehicles under 30 cwt unladen weight can park at night without lights provided that:
a the road is subject to a speed limit of 30 mph or less
b no part of the vehicle is within 15 yards of a road junction
c the vehicle is parked close to the kerb and parallel to it, and, except in a one-way street, with its nearside to the kerb.

Driver's view using dipped beam

Driver's view using main beam

Rain All weather driving

Wet weather driving demands gentle use of all the main controls —steering, clutch, brake and accelerator—and a larger-than-normal allowance for errors and emergencies. The presence of rain means reduced visibility, a deterioration in the car's stopping ability and increased risks of skidding and aquaplaning.

Rain is most dangerous when it falls after a long dry spell on to roads that have become polished and smooth. The water blends with oil and rubber deposits on the road surface to form a mixture on which the risks of skidding are greatly increased.

Remember that the soles of your shoes will be wet when it rains and that they will slip on the control pedals. Scuff them on the carpets or matting to give you a better and safer grip on the pedals.

Basic rules

There are four basic rules which apply to driving in the rain:
1 Reduce speed so that you can manoeuvre safely through bends, roundabouts, busy road junctions and in mixed traffic.

2 Switch on dipped headlights, even in daylight, so that you can see and be seen.
3 Use windscreen wipers and washer, and also if necessary, demisters and screen heaters to maintain the best possible forward and rearward vision.
4 Do not change speed or direction suddenly, or a slide may be induced.

Visibility

Visibility in rain is all-important. The wipers will often clear light rain from the windscreen with a few sweeps, but then if they continue on an almost dry screen they can leave smears of drying dirt. Use the windscreen washers liberally and operate the wipers in short, frequent bursts.

Heavy rain, on the other hand, can overload the wiper blades, allowing an almost continuous sheet of water to flow over the screen. Reduce speed even more than you would otherwise have done. If the reduction in visibility is severe, pull into a side-turning or lay-by until the storm passes. This usually takes no more than a few minutes.

Rain can also cause windows to mist up inside the car. The windscreen is easily cleared by the demister, by fresh air or by the use of an impregnated cloth. Above all, when visibility is reduced, switch on dipped headlights.

Adhesion

No one has yet perfected a tyre whose grip in the wet is as good as it is in the dry. Nevertheless, some good modern tyres have wet grip as good as the dry grip of some tyres made in the 1960s.

The grip of a tyre on a wet surface depends on two factors:

Tread: the grooves in the tread dispel most of the surface water. The greater the tread, the more water can be displaced, and yet as the car travels faster, larger amounts of water must be pumped through the grooves.

Sipes: These allow the tread to act as a squeegee, mopping up the quantities of water left by the tyre's main grooves.

The area of contact of a tyre on the road is very small, about the size of a large footprint. The space between the neighbouring groove flanks on a crossply tyre changes significantly as it rolls through its contact patch. The faster the speed, with these tyres, the more restricted the drainage passage becomes.

This change in tread pattern is negligible with radial ply tyres because all the deflection takes place in the side walls. This is why radial tyres tend to give a better wet grip than crossply ones. It is, nevertheless, not uncommon to have a difference in emergency braking stopping distances in the wet of up to 20% between radial tyres of similar tread patterns but made from different types of rubber. Thus, allowance should be made for the

Stopping distances — Emergency stop in a straight line from 60 mph

Tyres	Stopping distance in feet	Type of road
Good tread pattern	190 feet	Dry smooth concrete
Good tread pattern	310 feet	Just wet concrete or polished asphalt
Tread depth 1 mm	460 feet	Just wet concrete or polished asphalt
Tyre grooves filled with oil/rubber sludge	760 feet	Just wet concrete or polished asphalt
Tread depth 2 mm	360 feet	1 mm water on road surface
Near bald	1,360 feet	1 mm water on road surface
Crossply tyre tread depth 4 mm	490 feet	2 mm water on road surface
Radial ply tyre Tread depth 4 mm	420 feet	2 mm water on road surface
Crossply tyre tread depth 4 mm	990 feet	4 mm water on road surface
Radial ply tyre tread depth 4 mm	570 feet	4 mm water on road surface

(Thinking distance 60 feet)

fact that the braking performance of the car in front and that of the car behind may differ markedly from yours.

Trucks and coaches, particularly older ones, have braking characteristics which are inferior to those of cars. When they are lightly loaded they tend to swing out of line, so they should always be given a wide berth.

The tyre's grip depends on the weight on the tyre as well as on the adhesion between the rubber and the road surface. Abrupt changes of direction or speed have the effect of transferring weight from one tyre to another and this can upset the handling and braking balance of the car in the wet. It could reach the point where the driver loses control.

The road surface is another important consideration for the driver in the wet. The uneven cracks in coarser surfaces tend to fill with concrete dust, rubber and oily deposits, particularly during a dry, hot summer. A downpour of rain can turn this into a thick sludge which clings to and fills the tread grooves.

The tyres perform in a most peculiar fashion under these conditions. The road adhesion is even lower than on a water-covered surface, since the tyres cannot bite through the film on to a hard, continuous surface.

The only practical way to deal with this sludge is to wash it out with a strong jet of water over the tyres.

Reduce speed

There are several reasons for driving more slowly in rain:

1 The grip of the tyres on the road surface is reduced.

2 Directional stability is impaired, and a sudden slide is not uncommon when braking or accelerating rapidly.

3 Compared with a dry road it takes longer both in time and distance to pull up on a wet surface, especially when you are travelling fast.

4 Rain can impair visibility, particularly through side and rear windows and the dirt-speckled areas of the windscreen not swept by the wipers.

5 Rain tends to muffle the sounds of other traffic, which are frequently the first warning to the driver that there are other road users not far away.

6 Pedestrians, in trying to escape from the rain, tend to dash across the road without taking due note of other traffic. In addition, they frequently overestimate the ability of motorists to brake safely and avoid them.

Periods of heavy rain can induce conditions for which many motorists may be unprepared. As far as possible, of course, one should try to avoid these situations, but there could be circumstances when it is valuable to know what to do should the unexpected take place.

Unfortunately the phenomenon of aquaplaning is not as rare as it should be. Much depends on the condition of the tyres as to whether or not it will occur. The importance of good tyres is nowhere more evident than in this situation.

Aquaplaning

How does aquaplaning occur? As the car is driven at speed into surface water, it builds up a cushion of water ahead of the rolling tyre. If the tread grooves cannot allow sufficient water to be passed through them, the tyre will lose road contact and float off on a wedge of water. The action is like water skiing, depending on forward speed.

Aquaplaning speeds

40mph
Smooth tyre, crossply or radial

45 mph
1mm tread depth crossply or radial

55–60 mph
7–8 mm tread depth, new crossply

65–75 mph
7–8 mm tread depth, older pattern radial

85–90 mph
Radial with drainage channels

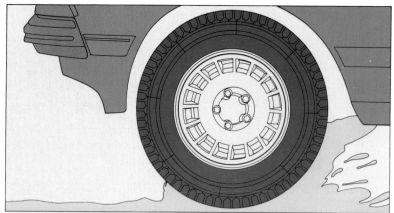

Once you are aquaplaning, the application of brakes or steering becomes ineffective, for there is no solid surface for the tyres to grip against. Ease off the throttle and brakes until the speed drops sufficiently for the tyres to make ground contact again.

The speed at which aquaplaning may occur depends on the depth of water on the road, and the tread depth of the tyre. The minimum tread allowed by law in Britain is 1mm. Tyres with only 2mm of tread may become unsafe at normal cruising speeds, often due to the deteriorating state of heavily-trafficked trunk roads. Tyres with 3mm of tread are much less prone to aquaplaning, although on some roads the depth of surface water might be greater than 5mm in tracks left by heavy trucks. These conditions may be found in the slow lanes of dual carriageways and motorways.

Conditions of aquaplaning will be reached at different speeds for different types of tyres. In a situation where there was $\frac{1}{8}$in (3mm) depth of water on the surface of the road, the chart shows the speeds where aquaplaning occurred.

Contrary to popular belief, lowering the tyre pressure, far from helping, merely brings on aquaplaning at a lower speed.

Flooded roads

Driving into flood water at speed is almost like hitting a wall. You may lose control, then come to a violent stop, risking injury to passengers. However, provided the speed is not too high it is perfectly feasible to ford fairly deep water without loss of control.

If the water is no deeper than the bottom of the cooling fan blades—on average 10–12 inches or roughly to the centre of the wheel hub cap—it is possible to drive through it. Engage a sufficiently low gear, 1st or 2nd (L or I in an automatic), so that the engine can propel the vehicle through the water without risk of stalling.

Use about half-throttle and keep it constant, neither easing it off nor depressing it suddenly as you feel the resistance of the water. Keep the speed slow or moderate to reduce the water splash swamping the electrics and/or the air intake. If it feels as though the engine is about to stall, slip the clutch to keep it going.

Should the engine stall some water may be sucked back through the exhaust system into the engine cylinders. This could result in permanent and costly damage to the piston, connecting rod or crankshaft, and it may not necessarily manifest itself until 100 miles or so later.

Changing gear almost invariably means a change in engine speed and manifold depression, with a similar risk of sucking back water through the exhaust pipe.

Good observation, particularly at night, should give warning of flooded roads. Places where the road is undulating, or where there is a dip under a railway bridge, should warn you that rain tends to collect there quickly. If the contours of the fences, trees, hedges and buildings at the side of the road appear to be unnaturally low, beware of flooding, and slow down at once.

Immediately after passing through deep water test the brakes. They may be saturated, and only driving very slowly and braking lightly at the same time will generate enough heat to dry them out. Be sure they are pulling evenly on all wheels before building up speed again.

River floods

Should you be confronted with a fast-flowing stream which has burst its banks, do not panic, but try to estimate the depth of water, direction and the speed of its flow. Consider your car to be a shallow draught boat, and position it so that, allowing for the deflection caused by the current on the wheels of the car, you can cut across the stream to reach the opposite bank.

Should the water reach the height of the sills and the driving wheels thrash uselessly in the water you will be getting close to floating. However much it may run counter to your instincts, open a door, preferably on the down-stream side. This will reduce the unwanted buoyancy and allow the tyres to grip solid ground again. Do not let the engine revs drop, and above all, do not switch off.

Escape from a sinking car

If you have been swept out into really deep water, it will be necessary to abandon the car. You may find it very difficult to open the doors against the rush of water. The inside of a saloon car will hold sufficient of an air bubble for you to breathe while you deliberately prepare to abandon the sinking vehicle. The car will not drop like a stone, it will sink relatively slowly, heavy end first. In these few seconds you should:

* Free yourself and your passengers from all restraints such as seat belts and child safety harnesses. Use as little energy as possible in order to conserve the air in your lungs.

* Keep the heads of all occupants above the level of the water as it rises inside the car.

* Release all door safety catches.
* Wind down the windows to allow water pressure to equalise inside the car and out.

* Push the doors wide open and step out.
* Form a human chain and swim or float to the surface.

This method should also be used for escape from soft-topped cars, rather than making an escape hole in the canopy. The stays and brackets are so close together they could easily impede the upward exit.

Wind All weather driving

Although the problems of driving in wind may not appear to be great, studies of accident figures have indicated that on some sections of road which are prone to windy conditions, a large proportion of the accidents which took place there occurred on days when wind conditions were worse than average, many of these accidents happening on the exposed sections of the road. A wind blows on most days of the year, even though strong winds are experienced relatively infrequently, and the experience of driving in strong cross-winds is sufficiently unnerving to justify every driver taking the subject seriously.

Observation

It will not always be immediately obvious that a wind is blowing, particularly if you have been travelling for some time and the wind has sprung up during the course of your journey.

The movement of the trees is not a consistently reliable guide to the force of the wind. Some trees do not deviate very much even in high winds, while others appear to be permanently bent in the direction of the prevailing wind. Unusual movement of roadside trees, however, will warn of the possibility of strong winds.

Other warnings of the presence of high winds come from observation of flags or bunting on petrol station forecourts, the effects of wind on the telephone wires, and the behaviour of other vehicles. If you see the cars ahead of you suddenly veer to one side, it is quite likely that there will be gusts of wind at that point.

Observation of the terrain ahead

Strong winds across the Severn

Trees blown by a high wind

Further evidence of wind

can also warn of the likelihood of strong cross-winds. If you are emerging from a section of road protected by trees or woodland on to an area of barren heathland, you could expect to be subjected to sudden cross-winds. Stretches of open motorway can also be crossed by strong winds.

Country roads

The main hazards of high winds when driving in country areas are not so much the deviations to which the car may be subjected, but rather more the risk of finding branches, twigs and even whole trees blown down in the road. Drive more cautiously than usual on minor country roads because of these possible hazards.

Towns

Gusts of wind in built-up areas will be very haphazard, appearing to come from almost any direction. Alleyways and narrow streets between tall buildings can funnel the wind into strong gusts across the road. These gusts will tend to blow rubbish into the air, and can blow pedestrians and cyclists off course.

Wind speed

The speed of the wind is generally given in terms of a force number. This relates to the Beaufort scale of wind force.

Beaufort scale wind force number	Wind speed mph	Description
0	less than 1	calm
1	1–3	light air
2	4–7	light breeze
3	8–12	gentle breeze
4	13–18	moderate breeze
5	19–24	fresh breeze
6	25–31	strong breeze
7	32–38	moderate gale
8	39–46	fresh gale
9	47–54	strong gale
10	55–63	whole gale
11	64–75	storm
12	75 +	hurricane

Motorways

The problems of driving in high cross-winds appear to be worst on motorways. The path of the road cutting across large areas of open country makes them more susceptible than other roads to cross-winds. Deflection of the wind by the parapets of the bridges can produce gusts appearing to come from all directions and requiring quick responses from drivers. The response should not be too violent, however, or the car could be provoked into a skid. You should, generally, reduce your speed in high winds.

Passing high-sided vehicles in strong winds is an unnerving experience. As you approach a high-sided vehicle you are steering a course which compensates for the strength of the side-wind. When you get alongside it, however, and are shielded by the other vehicle, this force disappears, and you appear to be sucked towards it. In fact, this is because you were not steering a completely straight course, but were compensating for the side-wind. As you approach the front of the other vehicle the force of the side-wind will be felt again. This force is usually experienced at a point slightly behind the front of the other vehicle.

The most important thing to do when driving in such windy conditions is to avoid over-correcting the steering. Your tyres are very well able to handle quite strong sideways forces and you retain control better by working with them rather than against them. The main danger to avoid is allowing the path of your car to be blown sideways such that it gets in the way of other traffic.

Roof racks

The use of a roof rack will always affect a car's handling, particularly in windy weather. In addition it will also increase fuel consumption even when the rack is empty. All luggage placed on a roof rack should be well fastened as low as possible to optimise air flow over the car. Make sure the roof rack is securely attached to the car.

Caravan towing

Towing a caravan can be particularly difficult in high winds. If your speed is too high and your caravan is not well-loaded a cross-wind can induce the phenomenon of 'snaking'. The appropriate course of action to take is described on pages 186–187.

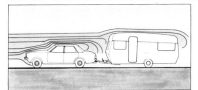

Experiments have been carried out with 'spoilers' fitted to the roof of the towing car to see whether this will improve the airflow over the caravan and therefore reduce its drag, improve its stability and reduce overall fuel consumption.

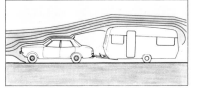

It has been found during tests with models in a water tunnel that a shaped spoiler, fitted at an angle of 45° as far back on the roof as possible (or 30° if placed farther forward) will direct the airflow over the caravan.

Lights in fog All weather driving

The most important reason for using lights in fog is not in order to see better, but so that you may be seen by others. For this to be effective, all lights need to be kept clean, in good working order, and accurately aimed.

Headlights

The use of dipped headlights when visibility is restricted is mandatory in Britain and many other countries. This is especially important in fog, as they allow your car to be seen by other road users before its shape is evident.

Sidelights should never be used on their own under these conditions. An area of fog reduces the amount of light which can penetrate it, and effectively blocks out such a low-powered light source, so rendering the car invisible.

The main, full beam of the head-

Sidelights alone barely show up in fog

Dipped headlights are always necessary when driving in fog

100

lights should also not be used in fog. The angle and spread of the beam is such that the fog particles will reflect a large proportion of the light back into the driver's eyes, severely dazzling him. Modern headlights with their sharply cut-off dipped beam provide as effective a performance in fog as many fog lights did eight to ten year ago.

The quality of the light emitted by the headlight depends more on the cleanliness of the lens and the brightness of the reflector mirror than on the wattage of the bulb. Whenever the weather is bad, as in fog, all lenses should be cleaned at regular intervals to remove caked-on dirt.

It is especially important in fog to avoid dazzling other motorists. Modern headlights are of great optical precision, and must be carefully aimed for this reason.

Fog particles

The water vapour in the mist clings to minute particles of dust or dirt in the air to form fog particles. These then attract more moisture and, in turn, get bigger. These fog particles:

*float or drift with the slightest change in local air pressure or temperature

*absorb sound

*act as a series of half-mirrors

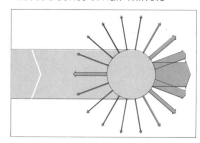

When a beam of light (pale blue here) hits a fog particle it is scattered in all directions. The thickness of the dark blue lines shows what proportion is scattered in that direction.

The last effect means that each particle reflects light hitting it from, for example, a headlamp beam. But it also allows some of the light to pass through it to the next particle, where the same thing happens. Some of the reflected light returns and hits the eye of the driver, and some of it is scattered in other directions. In addition, the light beam cannot penetrate far through the fog layer. The denser the fog the more the scatter and the less the penetration of the light beam. This is the reason why dipped headlights are more effective in fog than lights on main beam.

Fog lights

Visibility in fog can be greatly enhanced by the use of foglights. A pair of lights should be fitted, so that they indicate the width of the vehicle. If only one light is fitted, it must be used in conjunction with the headlights. This is to avoid the risk of possible confusion with a motorcycle.

Foglights should be mounted low on the front of the vehicle, in a zone which does not attract splash and road dirt. When they are not in use, protection against stones can be provided by a plastic cover.

The beam should be flat and wide with a sharp cut-off to prevent back scatter of the light. If a pair of lights is fitted, the nearside one should be angled on the kerb, about 15 feet in front of the car. The other one should be angled about two or three degrees to the right, so that it will pick up cat's eyes and lane markings.

Fog lights need to be cleaned regularly, when driving in fog. The spray from the vehicles in front, aerodynamic forces sucking up dirt, and the heat generated by the bulb all combine to form a thin coating over the lens which progressively reduces the amount of light passing through it. In some conditions, a 50% reduction in light intensity can take place within 30 minutes.

Rear fog lights

New cars now have high intensity rear fog lights fitted as standard. This regulation also applies to new caravans and trailers.

Not all other cars have these very useful lights fitted, and it is worth

Tail lights

Rear fog lights

Rear fog lights with brake lights

Siting of rear fog light

considering their purchase as an accessory. In some cases, these lights have been wired into the brake light circuit, so that they come on simultaneously with the brake lights. This is dangerous.

The greatest danger in fog is being rammed from behind by a vehicle which was following too close. The intensity of a good rear fog light is such that it can be seen from about the same distance as that where opposing fog lights or dipped headlights would become apparent as a pair of small white specks. It is also about the same distance as that at which brake lights would become visible, and is about twice that at which a normal rear light or a clean reflector would be seen.

The intensity of the rear fog light should be about the same as that of a brake light, so that they will be seen together when the brakes are applied. If it is any brighter, the brake lights might not be seen in time. The lights should be fitted low enough not to dazzle following

drivers. Their positioning is specified by law.

It is important that these lights should be switched off when it is not foggy and that they should be wired to a warning light inside the car clearly visible to the driver.

Law

Single fog or spot lights may only be used in conjunction with dipped headlights.

A pair of lights must be mounted equidistant from the centre line of the vehicle, and must be of the same colour, white or amber. The positions are defined as follows:

Vertically: At least 19·6 inches (500mm) from the ground. If the distance is less than this, they may only be used in conditions of fog or falling snow. The maximum height from the ground is 47·2 inches (1200mm). The lights must be permanently dipped, or capable of being dipped. They should not dazzle an observer 7·7 metres away with an eye level of 1·1 metres.

Horizontally: Cars registered before 31 December 1970: 13.8 inches (350mm) separation between the lights. Cars registered on or after

1 January 1971: 15.75 inches (400mm) maximum distance between the outer edge of the light and the edge of the vehicle.

Coloured lights

One of the less-commonly realised effects of fog is that it can change the colours which lights appear. Those at the red, amber and yellow part of the spectrum can pass through fog, although with some changes. Those at the blue and green end do not, however, and sometimes cannot be seen at all. So, in a dense fog, a red light may appear to be amber; an amber light might seem white; a white light almost green but a green light may not be seen at all.

Clean windows

In fog, as in all other adverse weather conditions, both the inside and outside of all windows should be kept clean and free of moisture. Use the wipers intermittently.

On the inside, you may usually rely on the car's ventilation system, but under really muggy conditions this may be too slow-acting or not powerful enough. It may well be possible to disperse the interior fogging of the windscreen by directing hot air on to it to evaporate the moisture. At times, however, it may be preferable to accelerate its condensation by directing cool air on to it and turning it into tiny water rivulets. Then warm air can be turned on to keep the windscreen unobscured.

Use a slightly damp chamois leather cloth to clean the windows, or a leather kid glove will do. Never use your hand, a handkerchief a tissue or a woollen or cotton glove.

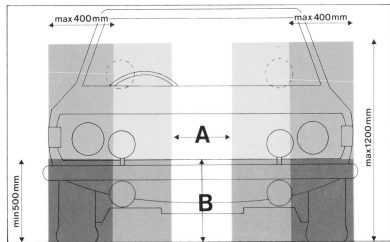
*Fog light positioning, Note **A** Cars registered before 31 December, 1970 may fix their lights not less than 350mm apart rather than 400 mm from the outside edge of the vehicle. Note **B** Lights sited less than 500 mm from the ground may only be used in fog or falling snow*

Fog provokes greater fear among motorists than most other adverse weather conditions, and with good reason. Not only does it strain all the driver's senses, but it also produces illusions to mislead him. Anyone who can avoid driving in fog is well advised to do so.

Why does fog form?

In Britain there is always some moisture in the air, and relative humidity rarely drops below 60%. A drop in temperature will cause the moisture in the air to form into finely-dispersed vapour droplets.

Generally, when the ground temperature drops fairly fast in relation to the air temperature, mists form and do not rise more than a few inches above the ground. Where the land has been warmed and there is little or no air movement, however, the mists may rise and hover over or drift across roads.

Air pollution from industrial plants, power stations or domestic heating appliances can turn this mist into a blanket of swirling fog. The fog blanket then acts as a heat shield, this prevents the cooling of the earth during the night from turning the fog into drizzle, and it also stops the sun's rays from warming up the ground sufficiently for the moisture to become re-absorbed in the air.

This situation can only be changed by strong winds or a substantial rise in the ground temperature. The moisture is then taken up in the air to form clouds.

Signs of fog

Fog tends to occur in early spring, autumn and winter when the heat of the sun is not sufficiently strong to vaporise the fog and lift it. But the situation can vary greatly along almost any route, so it is important to recognise the signs of fog formation.

Meadows, rivers, lakes, gravel pits and some woodlands can all give rise to fog. The moisture from freshly-tilled fields, however, can aggravate the situation still further. A substantial rise or fall in temperature and wind will disperse it. Early morning mists are soon soaked up by the summer sun, but less so in autumn and winter. If there is not sufficient change in heat during the day the fog can hang about for several days.

Fog driving rules

There are a number of basic considerations which should always be followed when driving in fog.

Lights: Immediately visibility becomes poor, switch on headlights, not sidelights. In fog, also switch on rear foglights, and front foglights (see pages 100–101), if fitted. Use dipped headlights, or you may be dazzled by the backscatter of the fog particles. Keep all lamp glasses cleaned regularly during a journey in fog.

Speed: Bring the speed right down. The correct speed for the circumstances will often be lower than intuition might indicate, and should always be the speed at which you can stop within your range of vision. This may be no more than 5 mph in some cases. Never drive faster than the safe speed, simply in order to keep in sight of another vehicle's lights.

Turning: Turning right is a particularly dangerous manoeuvre in fog. If it cannot be avoided, turn very carefully, signalling in good time. Keep a sharp watch out for

Dipped headlights and a slow speed are essential in fog

other traffic, and open the window to listen as well. Flash headlights or sound horn to be more certain your presence is realised.

Windows: It is important to be able to see as well as possible. Use the windscreen wipers, washers, demister, rear screen heater and rear screen wiper, if fitted. Open a window to prevent other windows misting up, and also for ventilation. The presence of fog will tend to make the car windows mist up on the inside. An open window will also help you hear other traffic.

Stopping: Take great care when stopping in fog, and always get off the road or carriageway. If you cannot avoid creating an obstruction, switch on hazard warning lights when stationary, and put out a warning triangle at least 100 yards behind the car (150 yards on a motorway or dual carriageway). However, do not hesitate to stop and park safely if the density of the fog is great. It will also be necessary to stop regularly in order to clean the windows and the lights, and this should also be done in a safe and careful manner.

Extreme care is required when turning or stopping

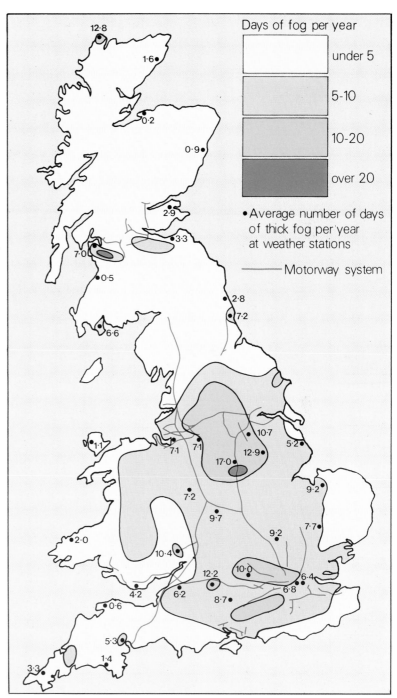

Days of fog per year

under 5

5-10

10-20

over 20

● Average number of days of thick fog per year at weather stations

—— Motorway system

103

Fog driving All weather driving

Understanding how to drive safely in foggy conditions requires an appreciation of the psychological effects on the driver as well as due attention to safe driving. Knowing and recognising the illusions which fog can produce helps to combat their insidious effects, and these factors should be taken into account by every driver when travelling in fog.

Disorientation

Quite apart from the fact that fog makes it more difficult to see, there are other effects which are less obvious. These effects can all rob a driver of his sense of orientation.

Fog muffles sound; the denser the fog the more it absorbs sound. It is not until noise disappears that we realise how much we depend on it to warn us of the presence of other vehicles. It may thus be advisable to use the horn to warn any other vehicles which may

be unaware of your presence, particularly for example when making a right turn.

The other effects which fog has can add to the sense of disorientation. In the uncertain half-light produced by fog, trusted landmarks can become difficult or impossible to recognise.

In any case, it is always more fatiguing driving in fog. More concentration is called for, and the pulse rate, heart beat and sweat rate (an indication of stress) increase considerably. Many motorists drive faster and overtake more in order to get ahead of the queue, in the false hope that driving conditions will ease there. Usually, as weather conditions get worse, most drivers moderate their driving style, but this does not seem to occur in fog. This failure to reduce speed sufficiently undoubtedly contributes to the severity of accidents in fog.

Speed fallacies

Press reports of multiple collisions in fog tend to accuse the motorists of behaving irresponsibly, incompetently and dangerously. But why do motorists drive too fast in fog? Research has uncovered some possible explanations.

First, there is the theory of 'speed hypnosis'. When the fog blots out familiar landmarks and reference points a driver can lose all sensation of speed, and this is more pronounced on a featureless motorway than on a country lane with hedges on either side.

The subconscious fear of being run into from behind may cause the driver to speed up on the dangerous assumption that the situation is safe ahead. The result is that the speed becomes too fast for the prevailing conditions.

In thick fog, drivers have been shown to be unable to estimate their own speed correctly, or the distance between them and the

vehicle in front. For example, a driver believing he had reduced his speed from 70 mph to 20 mph was actually travelling at 48 mph.

To complicate this even further it has been found that fog produces the optical illusion of making objects appear to be farther away than they really are. Also, objects seen in peripheral vision appear smaller than they really are.

These different facts show how easy it is to misjudge not only one's own speed, but also the distance of other objects. The muffling effect of fog on engine noise distorts the information normally available from that quarter about the car's speed. It now becomes more than usually important to regularly refer to the car's speedometer (it is best for the passenger to tell the driver what the car's speed is). Add to this the optical illusion about the distances involved, and it can be seen how easy it is to drive too fast in fog. It can also be seen how to avoid doing so.

Not too close

Many drivers believe, erroneously, that the safest policy in fog is to keep within sight of the tail lights of the vehicle in front, and never to lose visual contact. This is often dangerous because it can result in the vehicles being too close together. When the front vehicle puts his brakes on, others may not be able to react quickly enough to avoid hitting the vehicle in front.

For example, suppose a line of ten vehicles were travelling at 50 mph in fog. The first driver sees a blank wall of white fog and applies his brakes. The driver behind him applies his brakes $\frac{1}{2}-\frac{3}{4}$ second later. This is repeated down the chain. The driver of the tenth vehicle will not apply his brakes until perhaps $7\frac{1}{2}$ seconds after the first driver. In that time he

will have travelled 550 ft farther than the first driver. Collisions are inevitable unless each vehicle in the chain was at least 55ft behind the one in front. Even if that were the case, however, not every driver may be alert enough to react within $\frac{3}{4}$ second, and some vehicles may have worse braking characteristics than others.

An additional hazard of following another vehicle in fog is that one does not get an accurate picture of the fog's density. The fog thins out immediately behind each vehicle, and it may suggest that visibility is sufficient to overtake this vehicle. When you pull alongside however, you may find you cannot see far enough ahead to complete the manoeuvre safely. This can lead to dangerous errors of judgement resulting in serious multiple accidents.

Fog appears deceptively thin in the wake of a large vehicle

Always conform to speed restrictions, especially in foggy conditions

Fog at night

It is a mistake to drive on full beam during night time fog, not because it may dazzle oncoming traffic but because it may dazzle you. Dipped beam headlights should always be used.

In an urban environment with street lighting, the driver may be caught in a very difficult situation. The quality of the street lighting is important under some fog conditions—the amber light of the sodium vapour lamp is better than the blue-white light from the mercury vapour strip light. Depending on the quality of the street lighting, and the vertical thickness of the fog blanket, the motorist may find himself in a situation where there is a finely dispersed mantle of illumination everywhere, but no shadows. This makes it extremely difficult to pick out objects ahead or to the side.

Generally, the motorist relies on his headlights to pick out other objects, not only by illuminating them, but also from the shadows they cast. He can also observe the lights and reflectors of other traffic. In an urban situation when

it is foggy, these points of reference are missing, and orientation becomes much more difficult.

Freezing fog

This is the worst kind of fog. It usually starts as fog when the ambient air temperature is already quite low, about 2°C–4°C. As the earth cools, or in a cooling wind, the fog particles turn into frost, and are deposited on any surface as a thin covering of ice. A car driven through such fog soon tends to look like a box encrusted with icing sugar.

When the trunks and branches of trees begin to look white and glistening in the weak light, be prepared for that ill-defined mist ahead to turn into freezing fog.

In these conditions the windows tend to distort the already limited view. The windscreen washers may cease to work and the wipers often do not give a clear sweep either. Also, it is difficult to be picked out against a background of fog. The illuminating power of the headlights drops dramatically, and the roads tend to be covered in thin layers of black ice.

Preparation for winter driving All weather driving

Every motorist is likely to have to use his car during the winter months, so preparation for adverse weather conditions should be regarded as a matter of routine, rather than anything exceptional.

The first priority is to ensure that the car is in first class condition, and is well serviced. The driver should also prepare himself for driving in adverse weather conditions, by learning what he can, from books or courses, and practising the necessary driving techniques, off the road if possible. Much of the inconvenience brought about by severe weather can be minimised by careful forethought and by keeping a few simple items in the car.

Car preparation

A car that is well maintained and regularly serviced should have no problems with winter driving. Certain aspects of the car need special attention, however.

Air intake Some air cleaner inlets have summer and winter positions, and, if so, they should be adjusted for the winter.

Anti-freeze Although anti-freeze will last for two to three years, check before winter that the concentration is adequate for low temperatures. If the time has come to replace it, flush out the system thoroughly beforehand. Check all the hoses for possible leaks. Finally, do not forget to use a solution of anti-freeze and water when topping up the radiator during the winter.

Battery Cold weather reduces the performance of a battery. Clean the terminals and cover them with Vaseline, keep the electrolyte level properly topped up and re-charge it whenever necessary. When starting the car from cold, minimise the strain on the battery by applying the starter motor in bursts of no more than 5 seconds, followed by an interval of about 30 seconds. Turn off lights, heater blower, wipers and radio when trying to start the car, as these all take power from the battery.

Brakes Always keep the brakes in good order; any which work unevenly are especially dangerous on wet or icy roads.

Choke cable Extra use will probably be made of the choke during the winter, so make sure it works freely and that when pushed home, the choke mechanism is fully released.

Exhaust system Any leaks from the exhaust system could result in poisonous carbon monoxide fumes seeping into the car. The system should be checked at least every six months.

Fan belt The battery's problems in winter will not be helped if the fan belt is not correctly tensioned. Check its general condition and tension at the start of the winter, and always carry a spare.

Heater The heater will be subjected to extra use during the winter. See that the vents are not blocked with paper, dirt or rubbish, and also check that the hoses are not blocked or leaking.

Ignition system Damp in the winter months can affect the distributor cap, the low- and high-tension leads, the plug connection caps and the top of the ignition coil. These parts should be checked and thoroughly cleaned, before being given a protective spray of ignition sealing lacquer.

Lights The normal checking of lights should be more thorough than usual, and their aim should also be checked. Dirty road conditions will mean that they all need cleaning more often than usual. Keep enough cloths in the car for this purpose. Carrying a set of spare bulbs is especially important in winter.

Oil If a summer grade oil has been used, it should be replaced with winter-grade. A multi-grade oil will work just as well in winter as in summer.

Rear screen heater This useful item should be well cared for by cleaning it regularly with a damp cloth and a few drops of windscreen wash additive. If one is not fitted as standard, it is an accessory worth consideration.

Shock absorbers Worn or broken shock absorbers will seriously affect the car's handling and the tyres' grip, and will be particularly dangerous under slippery conditions. If the car bounces more than once when a corner is pressed down, the hydraulic damper is due for replacement.

Throttle linkages The smooth driving pattern essential for safe control and economical motoring cannot be maintained if the throttle is stiff. The linkages should be cleaned and lubricated, and any kinks in the accelerator cable straightened out.

Tyres Normal-use radial ply tyres will need about 3mm thread depth in order to cope satisfactorily with winter conditions. Apart from that, their general condition and pressures should be checked regularly.

Underbody Good protection of the underneath of a car will help protect it from the corrosion inevitable in a damp climate. Factory-applied PVC coating is the most effective currently available protection. The salt and grit used by Local Authorities in keeping roads free of ice and snow is a major factor causing bodywork and structural corrosion but dirt and dust particles are also important contributors.

Washers Windscreen washers get a great deal of use in the winter, and driving can be made difficult and dangerous if they fail. Clean the washer reservoir, the pipes and the jets, then fill with water containing a suitable additive which will help remove windscreen grease as well as prevent the water freezing. Check regularly that the reservoir is full. Do not use anti-freeze in the washer liquid.

Windows Clean windows are essential for safe driving, and they will need cleaning more often than usual in winter. It is also as well to check that there are no leaks which could let in water or exhaust fumes.

Wipers The blades should be cleaned and inspected for cracks. They may need to be replaced if they are more than 12 months old, or if they produce streaks across the windscreen.

Extra equipment

A survey of a wide range of accessories which help to make winter motoring safer and more enjoyable is given on pages 176–177.

There are many simple and inexpensive ways the motorist may reduce the inconvenience caused by winter conditions, which should be considered before winter sets in.

Anorak A useful precaution against getting wet or cold during an unexpected stop is to carry an anorak in the car.

Cloths A clean wash leather for the interiors of the windows and other cloths for the outsides and the lights will all be found necessary in winter.

Damp-start Starting difficulties can sometimes be overcome by spraying damp-start lacquer on to parts of the ignition system before starting the car.

De-icer Ice on the windows can be easily and quickly removed by the use of aerosol de-icer and a plastic scraper.

Driving shoes The heavier footwear appropriate for walking in snow or rain is not always ideal for driving. A pair of lightweight driving shoes should be kept in the car. It is also useful to keep a spare pair of waterproof boots in the car in case of emergency.

Jump-leads An extremely useful item to keep in the car is a set of jump-leads. Connect the positive terminal of your battery to the positive terminal of the other car's battery, and do the same with the negative terminals. Run the engine of one car and then turn the starter motor of the other. Take great care connecting and disconnecting these leads.

Lights Fitting extra lights to the front and rear of your car can make winter driving, especially in fog, easier and safer, although take care not to overload the battery. See pages 176–177 and 100–101. Keep spare bulbs in the car for all the lights.

Sacking Problems of getting stuck in the snow or on ice can often be overcome by driving over some sacking placed under the wheels.

Scraper A plastic scraper is an almost essential item for clearing the windows of ice and frost.

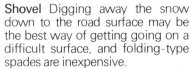

Shovel Digging away the snow down to the road surface may be the best way of getting going on a difficult surface, and folding-type spades are inexpensive.

Snow chains Under some circumstances of deep snow, a set of snow chains or snow-grips can be an asset.

Torch It is always useful to keep a torch (in working order) in the car, not merely during the winter.

Tow-rope It may be possible to help stranded motorists if a good, strong tow-rope is carried. It is unwise to use it for tow-starting another car, however.

Tyres A set of winter tyres may be helpful, even necessary, under extreme conditions. See pages 176–177.

Prepare yourself

Although some winter conditions require considerable care, adequate preparation can prevent them from becoming an ordeal. The preparation of the car, and planning for winter motoring, will remove many travel uncertainties.

The more a driver can study how to deal with wintry conditions, the better equipped he should be to deal with them. If frost is likely and the car is parked outside, leave the car in gear, chock the wheels and release the handbrake before it freezes in the on position.

It is wise to start to think about your journey further in advance than usual. Avoid routes which include steep hills and uncleared roads in snowy conditions. Minor roads with relatively little traffic, however, may not be too difficult to negotiate after snow, as it will not have been compacted into ruts. In foggy and swirling snow conditions, try to avoid right turns.

107

Snow and ice All weather driving

Brief spells of snow and ice are not uncommon in Britain, nor are isolated areas where deep snow and drifting occur. Local Authorities generally keep the motorways and principal roads free of snow, spreading grit and salt to turn the snow into slush, or using snow ploughs to deal with deep drifts.

Starting off

1 Be sure to remove the snow and ice from all windows and mirrors. Clearing a small patch on front, rear and some side windows is not enough. The complete window surface needs to be clear, and wing mirrors should have the ice scraped off them.

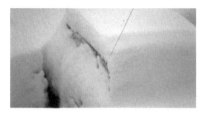

2 If the car has been parked out-of-doors, direct hot air from the heater against the windscreen before heating up the car interior. Heat the rear window as well if possible.
3 When attempting to start the engine apply the starter for up to 5 seconds with a long pause in between, rather than using a series of short, sharp bursts. Then, pull away as soon as possible to help the engine, transmission and the

car itself warm up quicker and avoid wasting fuel.
4 Do not drive in boots which have accumulated deposits of snow or ice. They are often quite wide, they will slip on the pedals and you will lose any sense of feeling. It is better to change into a dry pair of soft shoes for driving.
5 Select the highest gear possible when moving off, usually second. Let the clutch out gently to avoid wheel spin. If wheel spin occurs, ease off immediately. The tyre tread can only bite when the wheels revolve slowly, and in cold conditions, the rotating wheels may turn the snow into ice. The front wheels must be straight to offer the least resistance.

6 Be sure to use headlights if visibility is in any way reduced.

Driving on ice

One of the most frightening experiences while driving is to find suddenly and unexpectedly that you are driving on ice. It should not be sudden or unexpected, however, because good observation can warn you of your approach to an icy stretch of road.

The first thing to remember on a cold day is that although your car may feel warm inside, the temperature outside could be at freezing point or below. Watch for any indication that ice could be about, looking at puddles by the side of the road, and reading the

road ahead for areas which are more prone than others to the formation of ice patches.

The patches of road under overhanging trees are unlikely to feel the warmth of the sun, and ice is likely to persist on the road there until well into the day. Where there is danger of falling rocks there can also be the possibility of ice on the road in winter, because rocks are often dislodged by water.

Your ears will also tell you when you are driving on ice. Unlike the swishing sound made by the tyres as they roll through water, on ice there will be much less noise and no swishing sound. In addition the steering will feel very light. To maintain control and stop the car skidding use all the controls very gently indeed. Make no sharp or sudden movements. Allow a great deal of extra space for braking by looking well ahead and anticipating the actions of other road users. If the car slides when you brake do not panic, but release the brakes immediately, even if it takes courage to do so. Then re-apply them quickly but extremely gently.

Steering and braking

It is important to know the nature of the snow-covered road surface you are driving on. Slushy snow has a high moisture content and a texture rather like a viscous fluid. It offers reasonable resistance to movement but little sideways control. As it is squashed down on to the road surface, tyres with insufficient width and depth of grooves will tend to fill. Road grip will be poor and intermittent, resulting in some loss of traction. This calls for gentle throttle, brake and steering application to prevent the car sliding out of control The granular type of snow neither compacts nor adheres to other

layers, and should be treated in the same way as sea sand. It is easy to sink into it when driving a car shod with ordinary tyres. Wide tyres spread the load, making sinking less likely.

Soft snow is relatively harmless—tyres can bite into it well, and it is not always necessary to drive slowly. A hard-packed snow surface demands much greater restraint, but most dangerous of all is a snow-covered road with ice underneath. Three inches of powdery snow on top of an icy road surface may prove more difficult than six inches of crunchy snow.

The important guide for both steering and braking in snow is to do both very gently, but never to do both at the same time. Either steer or brake. Braking distances may well be 3 times those experienced on dry roads, but on icy roads these braking distances can be increased by as much as 10 times.

All steering should be careful and slow. In order to get going, it is usually best to have the wheels as straight as possible. In a difficult situation, when it is necessary to steer and brake, avoid locking the wheels. First brake gently, then release the brakes; turn the steering wheel gently and then apply the brakes again when the vehicle is moving in the right direction.

When braking, apply feather-light pressure, and remember that the driver behind may not have such good brakes or tyres as yours. His vehicle may also be heavier and more difficult to control. Using a gentle pumping action minimises the risk of locking up the brakes and the flashing of your brake lights provides a more effective warning of your actions.

Do not be misled into believing that it is better to slow down by changing to a lower gear. The action of letting in the clutch can cause the vehicle to skid, as the engine braking is transmitted to the driving wheels which may be having a difficult enough time.

Traction

Modern car tyres are generally suitable for all-year-round motoring. Their ability to deal with powdery snow and ice is, however, limited.

A snowfall in Britain is frequently followed by gritting and salting

to keep most motorways and principal roads free of snow. The grit and salt turns the snow into slush and water by lowering the freezing point. The heat generated when tyres run over it assists the melting process. Any delay in starting gritting operations makes the job much more difficult. The surface layer turns into ice when the temperature drops and snow gets compacted by the traffic into ruts. Further de-icing salt and heat generated by the passing traffic is then required to melt it.

When the road temperature falls to around −5°C, the heat generated by the passing tyres fails to turn the snow into slush. Under these conditions, the half-melted snow fills the tyre grooves, and lowers their grip on the road. Increasing the pressures by around 20% sometimes helps in the case of wide grooved radial tyres, but lowering them locks in the melted snow.

Special winter tread tyres are better at coping with roads covered with a layer of dry snow. A fairly open tread pattern allows the snow to be flung out in spurts. For very severe conditions a chunky pattern may be preferable. Heavily ribbed tyres are unsuitable for fast motoring on dry roads because they heat up quickly at speed.

109

Snow All weather driving

For many people driving in snow is relatively rare and best avoided if possible. During a severe winter, however, most drivers are affected in one way or another and for some motorists snow is a common aspect of winter driving. Nevertheless, the skills of handling a car on snow can be acquired by everyone prepared to practise and these skills will always stand them in good stead.

Climbing and descending hills

An important attitude to winter motoring is to have confidence and consistency of driving style, particularly when tackling snow-covered hills. A steady speed should be maintained since to stop might cause trouble not only for yourself but for those behind. Avoid having to change gear half-way up the hill, so engage a low gear earlier than you would normally do. Removing the foot from the accelerator can have the effect of applying a brake.

If you do get stuck, going up a hill or on the flat, it is important not to persist in spinning the wheels. This can have the effect of turning the snow to ice and will make it more difficult to get going again.

*Make a track in the snow by moving the car forwards and backwards. Otherwise, shovel the snow away from all four wheels.

*Straighten up the front wheels.

*Put sand or gravel in front of the driving wheels. Alternatively put twigs or sacks there.

*Get your passengers to help by pushing. They should not stand in the path of the twigs or sacks, as these may be thrown out with quite a force. At times they may need to steady the vehicle sideways because when it is stuck in a rut or in deep snow it may follow a path tending to slew it sideways.

*Engage second gear and use just enough throttle to get out of the rut. Once on the move do not stop

to retrieve the sacks or to pick up your passengers until you are on firmer ground.

If none of these measures gets you going again, the only course left is to roll back, with care and as much warning as possible, to a more level part where the run-up to the hill can be resumed. Remember, however, that steering precision may be lost under these circumstances. Accelerate gently in second gear and

avoid slowing down or stopping until you are on easier terrain.

In spite of the problems which beset drivers climbing hills, it is actually much more dangerous descending steep hills in snowy weather. In these conditions, your speed should be so slow that you are completely in control of the vehicle and can stop at any time. In general, you should select a gear lower than that in which you would ascend the hill. Be more cautious in applying the brakes than you would be on the level to avoid the risk of skidding.

Should you find that the slope becomes even steeper, it is best to

stop. Then select a lower gear and proceed once more. When descending a steep hill it is courteous to give way to vehicles coming up it, but never apply the brakes hard or suddenly.

In heavy traffic on undulating roads it is advisable to plan the approach to hills so that you will not get stuck half-way up. This may mean waiting at the bottom of a hill until it is possible to make the ascent without interruption.

Snow drifts

If your car is stranded in deep snow or in a blizzard, it is always best to stay with it. The most important things to do are to keep warm and to keep awake. A hot drink, chocolate and sweets all help. In order to keep warm use everything that is to hand. Wrap yourself in blankets, carpets, sacks; even newspaper stuffed into your clothing will help to retain body heat. Be careful to avoid carbon monoxide poisoning when running the engine to heat the car interior. Only run the engine and the heater if the exhaust pipe can be kept clear of snow. Occasionally, open a window slightly (on the side which is free from drifting snow) to let fresh air into the car. Violent exercise or allowing yourself to drop off to sleep are both to be avoided. Conserve your energy and keep a channel of fresh air supply open if your vehicle is likely to be trapped and engulfed by increasing drifts.

If several other drivers are trapped in the same predicament, it is advisable for groups of people to sit together in one car, rather than in isolation.

Snow chains are quick and straightforward to fit

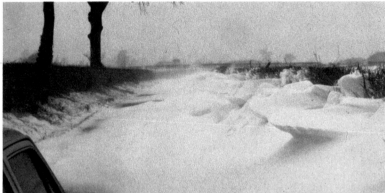

Snow traction clamps are intended for use in emergencies

Studs fitted to tyre

Close up of studs

Studded tyres

Special tyres fitted with hardened steel studs or spikes can be effective when driving on ice, but are of little practical use on deep, soft snow. Many countries limit their use to certain periods of the year, or ban them altogether,

because of the damage they can do to the road surface.

If the studs come into contact with the road surface, they wear grooves which quickly fill with water when the snow melts, or during summer showers. These can cause the serious hazard of aquaplaning.

Snow chains

Roads in hilly or mountainous areas are frequently left uncleared by snow ploughs, particularly if the snow fall is widespread. Snow chains or special snow traction clamps can be useful in these circumstances. Not all cars are suitable for the fitment of chains. Before fitting them ensure there is enough clearance in the wheel arch to allow unrestricted up and down movement and full steering

lock when chains are fitted. Practise fitting them at home before use. The action of snow chains is to transform the tyre into a primitive type of track-layer, with each link biting into the surface. Forward traction is good, but the sideways force which they can develop is very limited. This makes for poor steering and, occasionally, a sideways lurch. Vehicles fitted with snow chains should be driven at moderate speeds only, particularly on dry roads.

Test yourself All weather driving

Are you confident you can drive safely in all weathers? Do you know the points to watch out for in different weather conditions? The preceding section of this book has surveyed the driving hazards associated with all different types of weather conditions. The quiz on this spread gives you a chance to test your own knowledge.

1 When approaching a long tunnel, after driving in bright sunlight, how can you ensure the best vision in the tunnel?

2 What type of sunglasses are most suitable for driving straight into low sun on a winter afternoon?

3 If you are dazzled when driving at night, will it help your vision to wear dark glasses?

4 Is it necessary to dip your headlights earlier on a left hand bend or on a right hand bend?

5 If there is light rain after a dry period, why should you be especially careful?

6 Under what circumstances does aquaplaning occur?

7 When driving through deep flood water should you use a high or a low gear?

8 What should you beware of when driving in high winds on exposed motorways?

9 Does the use of a roof rack affect petrol consumption?

10 Why should you not follow the rear lights of another vehicle when it is foggy?

11 Do yellow lights penetrate fog better than white ones?

12 Why should high intensity fog rear warning lights not be wired up so that they come on at the same time as the brake lights come on?

13 What should you be especially careful of when driving in thick fog on a motorway?

14 Which gear should you select when you are driving up snow-covered hills?

15 Should your car become stranded in blizzard conditions, is it better to stay with the car or to walk to safety?

16 How can you tell you are driving on black ice and not merely on a wet road?

Answers

1 You will probably have been wearing sunglasses while driving in bright sunlight. If they are of the photochromic type they will not lighten instantly when entering the tunnel.

For a second or more they will remain dark and you will be unable to see. Ordinary sunglasses will also remain dark, of course. Your eyes, unaided, will adapt much more quickly to the darkness of the tunnel, so, if you were wearing sunglasses you should remove them before entering the tunnel.

2 Photochromic sunglasses are unlikely to be suitable for this task. Their darkening depends on the intensity of the light which, in this case, may not be quite bright enough. This darkening is also affected by the temperature and if it is on the cold side in the interior of your car that also may reduce the darkening effect. It is preferable, in these circumstances, to wear normal sunglasses.

3 Dark glasses should not be worn when driving at night. In some countries it is illegal to wear them. The amount of light available to the driver at night is very limited, and to reduce this light by wearing dark glasses is most dangerous.

4 On a left hand bend you should dip early. An oncoming car will cross the beam of your lights before you cross his. On a right hand bend you will not risk dazzling the oncoming driver until slightly later. Meeting another driver on a straight stretch of road, however, you should always try to be the first one to dip his lights.

5 The rain water mixes with the oil and rubber deposits on the road to form an extremely slippery surface film which can also fill the treads of your tyres. Be extra cautious in such circumstances and allow plenty of room for braking.

6 When the depth of water on the road is greater than the tread on the tyre there is a risk of aquaplaning. As the car's speed rises, a wedge of water is formed just in front of the tyre and the tyre lifts so that it loses contact with the road surface. It begins to slide along the surface of the water and stops rotating. Control of the car can then be lost unless the speed is reduced so that the wheels stop aquaplaning. The speed at which aquaplaning occurs depends on several factors, including the depth of the water on the road, but a critical contribution is made by the tyre. The more tread there is on the tyre the less the chance of aquaplaning at any given speed.

7 The important points to ensure when driving through deep flood water are that the car keeps going and that no flood water enters the exhaust pipe or the engine. It is best to drive slowly in first gear, minimising the bow wave and keeping the revs up (slipping the clutch if necessary).

8 There are several possible hazards to consider when driving in a high wind on a motorway. Exposed stretches of the road will be liable to cross winds, and side gusts will also be felt when passing under bridges. Buffeting will be experienced when passing or being passed by high sided vehicles, and it is important not to be panicked into making excessive steering corrections when this happens.

9 Yes, dramatically so. Even an empty roof rack can increase fuel consumption by up to 5%. The loading of a roof rack is important too. Try to keep the load as low as possible and arrange it so that airflow over the top of the car will be smooth. Do this by placing the smaller items at the front.

10 There are several reasons why it can be dangerous in fog to follow another driver's rear lights. Your eyes can become hypnotised by the lights, stopping you from looking in other directions in order to orient yourself. You will also be given a false impression of speed and this may result in your driving too fast. The fog in the wake of another vehicle is thinned by the passage of that vehicle, so you could also be led to believe that the fog is thinner than it actually is. In addition to all this, the driver in front may be going too fast for safety. It is much better to rely on your own perceptions of the conditions and drive at a speed which will ensure you can stop within the distance you can see to be clear.

11 They do not, in fact—the penetration of fog by yellow lights is less good than by white lights. Yellow lights produce less "glare" however and this may give an impression of good fog penetration.

12 Because their value is that, when switched on, they enable the car to be seen from a greater distance when it is travelling in fog. This is not achieved if they do not come on until the brakes are applied. The bulbs have a similar intensity to brake light bulbs, so it is unlikely that they will show up a braking car from a greater distance. There is also a fire risk from the wiring overheating. The most important reason for not wiring up these lights with the brake lights, however, is that it is against the law.

13 The most essential consideration when you are driving in fog is not to drive too fast for the conditions. Your subjective assessment of speed is extremely unreliable in fog due to the illusions it creates. Other vehicles travelling too fast can lead you to believe the fog is thinner than it really is. Look at your speedometer from time to time (or get your passengers to do so) and check that you are not allowing your speed to increase.

14 You should use the highest gear suitable for the gradient. Too high a gear will probably result in the need for a gear change on the hill which could result in your getting stuck. Too low a gear could produce wheelspin because of the greater degree of power available at the wheels.

15 In general, if you are some way from safety and the weather is bad, it is better to stay in the car. You will be able to keep warm better and rescue services will probably find it easier to locate a car than someone walking through the snow. When waiting in the car, keep moving and do not allow yourself to go to sleep.

16 When driving on a wet road you will hear a swishing sound from the tyres. This sound will not be present when you are driving on black ice. You should be expecting black ice, in any case, by observing the temperature, the nature of the road and the roadside ahead.

4 Emergencies

Emergencies

Everyone hopes they will not need to deal with a difficult emergency situation on the road. It is sound common sense, however, to be prepared for an emergency to arise at any time and to know how to cope with it if it does.

Basic to the ability to cope with an emergency is confident car control and the avoidance of panic. Everyone who follows the rules of better driving should be able to anticipate possible emergencies in plenty of time; looking sufficiently far ahead, keeping up good observation of traffic and road conditions ahead and driving at a safe speed should prevent a tense situation from developing into a dangerous emergency.

In spite of every reasonable care exercised by yourself, another vehicle, less competently handled, may transform the situation into an emergency. At that point all a driver's skill will be called upon in order to avoid an accident or to try and minimise its results.

Not many drivers really understand how to control a skid correctly. This is partly because so little instruction is available and partly because there is seldom a chance to practise skid control before the emergency arises. Spreads in this section explain how to handle the car in a skid using a skidpan.

The statistics of the road accidents which take place during any one year are complex and need interpretation. Many factors contribute towards the causes of these accidents, but there are few in which a driver is not partly at fault. If you were involved in a road accident, or came upon one, would you know what to do? Advice is given here as well as some basic First Aid tips.

Emergency situations
pages 118–119

In spite of every care on your part for safe driving, a situation may arise in which you need to take emergency avoiding action. This section explains the techniques for avoiding or minimising a variety of unpleasant situations.

Mechanical failures
pages 120–121

A properly maintained car should not cause an emergency through failure of one of its mechanical parts. It is wise, however, to know what you would do if, for example, the brakes failed or the windscreen shattered.

What would you do?
pages 122–123

Your chance to test how you might behave in an emergency situation is provided on this spread. You are faced with a difficult incident and asked to decide how you would cope with it.

Preparing for emergencies
pages 124–125

There are several ways you can prepare to cope successfully with emergency situations. Your driving should always be of the highest possible standard while your car should be in first-class condition. Practical advice is given about learning all you can about how your own car handles and behaves in different situations.

Skidding
pages 126–127

The loss of car control indicated by a skid should never arise if the car is being driven carefully. Knowing how skids can arise, however, and how to control the different kinds of skid can prevent a difficult situation becoming worse.

Skidpans
pages 128–129

Facilities for practising the control of skids are provided by skidpans. This spread explains what they are, how they work and the ways in which they can help every driver.

Skidding quiz
pages 130–131

Do you know how to control the different kinds of skid? Do you know why they arise in the first place? Should you always steer into a skid? You may think you know how you would respond to a skid but it is worth checking your knowledge more thoroughly. The quiz on these pages will help you you do just that.

Causes of accidents
pages 132–133

There may be several factors involved in the causes of an accident. Many of these factors involve human error but there can be other causes as well. This spread looks at the contributions made by these other factors.

Accident statistics
pages 134–135

Detailed statistics about all road accidents are published on a regular basis, but it is not always easy to make good sense of them. This review highlights the main features which every motorist should know and bear in mind when driving.

What to do at an accident
pages 136–137

Most people will probably come across a road accident situation at some time, but it is unlikely they will feel confident that they know exactly what to do. This spread describes the steps to take and in which order, and it also explains the role of the emergency services.

First Aid
pages 138–139

A basic knowledge of First Aid could be extremely valuable in certain accident situations, although a book can be no substitute for practical tuition obtained through a First Aid course. The essential items in a First Aid kit are described here as well as the principles behind some simple procedures.

Casualty rate during an average week ☐

	0700	0800	0900	1000	1100	1200	1300	1400	1500	1600	1700	1800	1900	2000
Monday														
Tuesday														
W'nesday														
Thursday														
Friday														
Saturday														
Sunday														

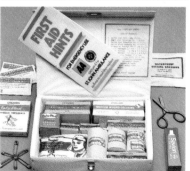

Emergency situations Emergencies

An unexpected situation demanding immediate action can happen to any driver at any time. A great deal can be done to prevent a situation catching a driver unawares, and it is also possible to learn how to handle such a situation safely.

Avoiding emergencies

There are some basic rules which should govern everyone's driving. If these are followed properly, few situations should develop unexpectedly.

Keep alert Driving is a task which demands full concentration. If you are being distracted, perhaps by children or pets in the car, you should stop and try to minimise the distraction. You should not drive if you feel tired, ill or unable to concentrate properly. Always expect the unexpected.

Drive within your capabilities Recognise that many factors such as your age will affect your reactions and also your eyesight, so adjust your driving accordingly. Gear your driving to the changing weather conditions.

Anticipate developments Good and thorough observation of everything that is going on all around will enable you to anticipate a situation before it develops. Feet, noticed under a parked vehicle, should warn you of the hitherto unseen presence of a pedestrian. One of the children fighting on the pavement may run in the road in front of you. A ball rolling into the road will probably be followed by a child. Any suspicion that another road user is acting dangerously or is in trouble should prompt you to slow down and give him plenty of room. Keep asking yourself what you would do if someone around you did something unexpected.

Know your car A well-maintained car should behave predictably in response to your handling, and you should be thoroughly familiar with what it will do under different conditions. The car will, of course, behave differently when it is fully laden with passengers and luggage, compared with its performance when you are driving on your own. You should also know how it will behave in response to sudden action on your part. Lack of knowledge or experience of your car's capabilities can severely hamper your reactions in an emergency.

Avoid head-on collisions A head-on collision, particularly with another moving vehicle, and even at slow speeds, will usually cause a great deal of injury and damage. If a collision is inevitable it is always preferable to try and make it a sideways scrape, or to drive obliquely on to a soft verge or through a hedge. Do not risk turning your car over, however. In every emergency situation you have a choice. Always try to minimise the danger to car passengers and other road users, before protecting the car.

Overtaking car committed to dangerous manoeuvre

Blue car brakes firmly in a straight line

When speed is low, verge is closely inspected

Blue car then steers into verge to avoid collision

Coping with an emergency

An emergency can happen at any time, so always be prepared. Careful observation and considerate driving should prevent you being taken by surprise. In spite of these precautions, you may nevertheless be presented with a situation demanding emergency action. Every situation is different, of course, but there are several points to remember in every case.

Blue car travelling at speed

There is no time to brake and stop before reaching red car

Blue car brakes in a straight line for as long as possible

Steering control must be retained to avoid red car

Do not brake too hard The instinctive reaction to an emergency is to brake hard. In some cases, however, it may be better to accelerate out of trouble. If braking is called for, apply the brakes firmly and in a straight line. Do not swerve while braking, and do not allow the wheels to lock up. If they do so, release the brakes at once, then re-apply them more sensitively. This allows you to be able to steer out of trouble to some extent.

Brake progressively rather than harshly and give the vehicle behind as much time as possible to react to your brake lights so that he will not run into the back of you. When the road surface is not dry or even, braking should always be carried out more carefully to ensure adhesion of all the tyres. If this adhesion is lost the car will get out of control, and you will no longer be able to minimise the effects of the emergency.

Always brake in a straight line, and not when you are swerving. If the wheels lock release the brakes momentarily, then apply them again. This avoids loss of control

Warn other road users Generally, other road users will be unaware that an emergency is developing, so sound your horn to warn them.

Never give up Keep control of your car all the time. This will usually turn an emergency into a problem you have managed to solve.

Mechanical failures Emergencies

Not all emergencies are produced by the behaviour of other road users. Some of them are caused by a failure of one or more of the mechanical components on a car, although this is less likely to happen if the car is properly maintained.

Should a failure occur unexpectedly, the most important consideration is to retain control of the car. Let other road users know that something is wrong by sounding the horn and switching on the lights, then check the mirrors, indicate and move to the side of the road.

Brake failure

Most modern cars have dual braking circuits so complete brake failure is unlikely. If one circuit fails, perhaps due to a break in the hydraulic pressure line, the other will usually be sufficient, although less effective.

As the speed drops gently ease the car to the side of the road and stop. Should there be insufficient time to stop using handbrake and gears, it may be necessary to scrape the side of your vehicle against walls or banks.

The brakes may become ineffective if they get wet after you have driven through a ford or a flood. Dry them by applying the brakes gently for a short distance whilst the car is moving at moderate speed. A leaking oil seal can also drastically reduce braking efficiency.

If the brakes get too hot they can also lose their effectiveness. This could happen, for example, when descending a long hill in top gear. The brake fluid may partially vaporise and the pedal would sink to the floor with little effect on the brakes. Pumping the pedal rapidly up and down frequently restores braking power.

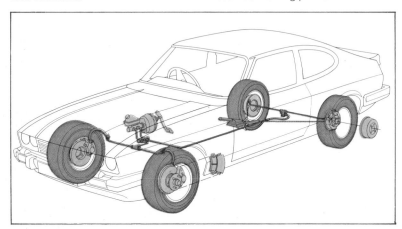

In the event of complete brake failure slow down using the handbrake and changing down quickly through the gears. Attempts to change gear too quickly or over-harsh use of the handbrake can make the car unstable, however.

Should the brake pads get so hot that they 'fade', there will be no feeling of sponginess when the brake pedal is applied. A short stop usually allows them to recover, but they should be checked at the soonest opportunity.

Suspension failures

Although suspension failures are relatively rare, calm, deliberate control will prevent an accident if failure should occur. Coil springs are least prone to failure, Hydrolastic and Hydrogas units usually give some indication before they fail completely, but should a leaf spring break, it may puncture a tyre or it could sever a hydraulic pressure line.

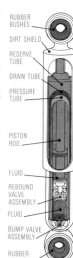

RUBBER BUSHES
DIRT SHIELD
RESERVE TUBE
DRAIN TUBE
PRESSURE TUBE
PISTON ROD
FLUID
REBOUND VALVE ASSEMBLY
FLUID
BUMP VALVE ASSEMBLY
RUBBER BUSHES

In all these eventualities let the car slow down naturally, steering and braking gently to bring the car to rest at the side of the road. Should the fuel lines or petrol tank have been damaged, avoid a possible fire by switching off the ignition and disconnecting the battery if possible. Keep well clear of the car and inform the police.

Steering failure

It is very rare indeed for steering to fail without some warning, such as an increase in steering wheel movement, or steering "wander" when attempting to keep a straight line. As soon as any of these symptoms are detected, the system should be checked by a fully qualified mechanic.

A sudden jolt to badly worn steering joints could cause them to part, resulting in steering loss. On no account try to crash stop but brake gently and progressively.

Burst tyre

If a front tyre bursts, there will be a strong pull to one side. This must be controlled by deliberate and jerk-free counter-steering to retain a straight course. A rear tyre burst may provoke a tail slide, which, again, requires restrained, smooth steering correction. In either case, do not change gear, but take your feet off the accelerator and clutch pedals, then brake gently and bring the car to a standstill. Use a hard shoulder if possible, but do not attempt to stop the car on a soft verge. A firm base will be required when jacking up the car to change the wheel.

The essentials of tyre maintenance are to keep the correct tyre pressures, to ensure that the treads are adequate and that there are no cuts or bulges in the side walls.

Loose wheel

Warnings of a wheel becoming loose are "clanking" noises and unusual handling. If these symptoms occur, slow down gently and stop. If the cause is loose wheel nuts, tighten them, then drive gently to the nearest garage where a competent mechanic can check the wheel, its nuts and bolts, wheel bearings and allied parts.

If the wheel comes off suddenly and without any warning, the car will drop at the corner affected. It will pull strongly to one side and this must be countered by firm steering and gentle, progressive braking to bring the car to a halt and prevent it slewing.

Engine failure

A frequent cause of an engine faltering is lack of fuel, usually the result of an empty tank rather than a carburettor fault. If, when the engine splutters, a quick change into a lower gear does not jerk the engine into life again, change into neutral and use the momentum of the car to move to the side of the road in order to stop. Under damp conditions a neglected ignition system can produce the same effects as lack of fuel.

Engine seizure is another matter and is often due to overheating because of a broken fan belt or lack of coolant. Increasingly poor engine response will be felt when the car slows progressively at the same throttle opening on level ground. In these circumstances pull to the side of the road as soon as it is safe to do so.

If the engine seizes up completely the driving wheels will lock up. De-clutch immediately and move the gear lever into neutral so that the car can move under its own momentum. Check the mirrors, signal and move to the side of the road, without cutting in front of another vehicle.

Bonnet flies up

This is only a problem with bonnets which open from the front of the car. There is no need to panic if this should occur. Steer on the same course, brake progressively, signal and move carefully to stop at the side of the road. Some forward vision may be obtained by winding down the driver's side window.

Windscreen shatters

Laminated windscreens present little problem as they remain transparent even after an impact by a stone causing nothing more than a star-shaped scar. Toughened glass screens usually incorporate a zone in front of the driver which gives fair visibility even when the rest of the screen cannot be seen through with clarity.

Toughened windscreen

When the windscreen shatters do not punch a hole through it immediately. Check your mirrors, signal, move gently to the side of the road and stop when it is safe to do so. Remove as much of the broken glass as possible by pushing it out onto a sheet or newspaper on the bonnet. Do not push the glass into the car interior or allow it to block any heater vents.

Impact on laminated windscreen

A temporary windscreen will allow you to proceed safely, but if you do not have one you can still drive, although with great care and at a low speed. In that eventuality make sure that all the glass fragments have been removed from the windscreen surround.

Accelerator sticks down

A first reaction to this problem is to try to get a toe under the pedal and lift it. In many cases, however, the cause is a broken throttle return spring and the pedal stays down.

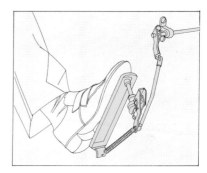

The appropriate action is to check mirrors, move the gear lever into neutral, then signal left. Switch off the ignition, but do not withdraw the ignition key as this can lock the steering, then coast to the side of the road, and stop.

Maintenance saves emergencies

A check of the tyres, brakes and steering at the start of every journey, plus regular maintenance and the immediate replacement of any suspect components would prevent most of the emergencies described here from taking place.

Emergency problem Emergencies

How would you react if you were faced with an emergency situation. Having read about the subject you would know enough to deal with the situation in theory. Would your reflexes be quick enough to assess and review every option to you and still leave you enough time to adopt the right course?

Imagine you are confronted with the situation described on this page. It is based on an incident which actually happened, although the details have been changed. In the real incident a collision was avoided. What would you have done in this situation?

You are driving a family car towards a cross-channel port en route for a summer holiday abroad. The sun is shining, the road is dry and smooth. About 15 miles before the port you enter a built-up area. The speed restriction is 40mph, the road has two wide lanes bordered by normal width pavement and kerbing, with fences beyond.

Driving at a safe 35mph you approach a left hand bend. Buildings on your left restrict forward vision to around 50 yards. You have taken up a position to the left of the centre line in order to obtain the best view through the bend. On entering the bend you find an oncoming car driving directly towards you on your side of the road.

You sound your horn to alert the other driver. Generally, you will have been driving with sufficient care and anticipation to avoid an accident, but in this case the other driver makes no attempt to steer his car back to his own side of the road. In the first split-second you notice that it carries a French registration plate.

Approaching the bend at 35 mph visibility is restricted to 50 yards. At first all seems clear

Suddenly an oncoming car is seen approaching on the wrong side of the road

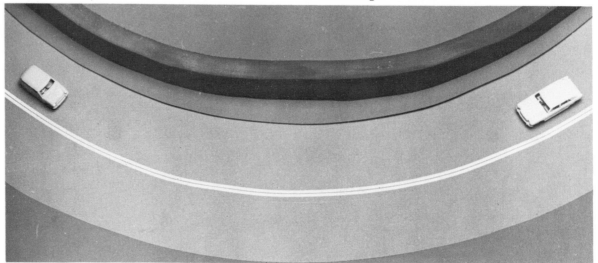

When the cars first see each other 1½ seconds are left for avoiding action

What would you do?

a Freeze up completely

b Brake hard
c Swerve to the right
d Swerve to the left

e Brake firmly and swerve out of the way at the last moment when you see where the other driver moves.

a It will be too late to avoid a head-on collision if you do not react instantly. Suppose both cars are travelling at 35mph, the closing speed is 70mph or about 34 yards a second. When the two cars are 50 yards apart, there are about 1½ seconds in which to take positive avoiding action.

b Panic braking will lock up the front wheels and the car will slide straight on with no steering control at all, or the rear end may break away and the car will slew. It would be impossible to swerve out of the way at any point.

c A sudden swerve to the right can easily result in loss of control. If the back wheels start to slide there will be a collision.

d A sudden swerve to the left could also result in a loss of control. In this case it would also have resulted in a head-on collision. The oncoming car was, indeed, French. He had just come off a cross-channel ferry and had not yet oriented himself to driving on the left hand side of the road.

The fact that the driver made no attempt to return to the correct side of the road even after your horn warning confirms that this is so and also that he believes he is perfectly in the right. In fact, his reaction to the situation is to behave as he would have done at home, and he swerves to his right, (your left) and into the kerb. If you had swerved left, you would certainly have hit him.

e The correct response is to get your speed right down while keeping firm control of the car.

Knowing you were near a port would, in any case, have forewarned you to expect some cars to be on the wrong side of the road. You will have been driving with the appropriate degree of caution when this incident arose and have been prepared to react quickly if necessary. Firstly, avoid any kind of panic reaction.

Brake firmly in a straight line, but not so hard that you lock the wheels and lose control. At this point the other driver begins his turn towards your left. With your speed now much reduced, and steering under control, you turn your car to the right, towards the centre of the road, thus avoiding contact. A careful study of the situation as it developed, while remaining firmly in control of the car, enabled you to react quickly but without panic.

Initially, brake firmly in a straight line

Steer right when you see what the other car does

Everyone can prepare themselves to cope with emergencies. Each time you go out in a car, whether as the driver or not, you should observe and study the road in order to anticipate what will develop. Accurate anticipation often prevents emergencies. Keep asking yourself what you would do if the situation ahead of you changed suddenly and dramatically.

You should take every opportunity to practise and improve your car control. This should not be done on a public road but on a specialised training area, skid-pan, or on a disused airfield.

Several specialist courses are available in advanced and high speed driving and these are extremely useful as a start towards preparing yourself to deal with emergencies. A most valuable feature of these courses is that they reveal any weaknesses or bad habits in your driving, enabling you to overcome them. After that, continue to practise the relevant techniques.

Anticipation and control

Most emergency situations can be prevented by good observation and intelligent anticipation. Careful reading of the road scene and gentle car handling should ensure that you enter each situation at the right speed and in perfect control.

Reading the road well ahead enables you to spot hold-ups such as lorries turning in good time, so you can avoid braking harshly

When following a large vehicle, particularly on a narrow road, keep a safe distance behind and when possible look along its nearside

Observing the road beyond the lorry would have given you advance warning of the parked car and helped avoid sudden manoeuvres

Sharp observation is needed when driving in busy streets to spot the pedestrians stepping into the road, as well as other hazards

Seeing the broken-down lorry in plenty of time helps you make an early lane change, minimising disruption to traffic flow

The parked van actually conceals some road works, as the observant driver will have noted from the warning sign ahead

Braking

The general rules about braking, whether in an emergency situation or not are :
1. Brake in plenty of time.
2. Brake firmly only when travelling in a straight line.
3. Vary the brake pressure according to the condition of the road surface

When preparing to handle a possible future emergency situation, an important aspect of car control to practise is braking from speed. You should know just how hard you can brake in your car without locking the wheels and losing steering control.

Practise, off the public roads, driving at a series of different speeds, then slowing the car down in a straight line by adjusting the braking pressures. When you have mastered control at one speed try a slightly higher one.

Once you can control the braking of your car from speed, start gently swerving to one side while braking and keeping steering control at all times. This will increase your confidence in your own driving ability and will help you to react positively to emergencies.

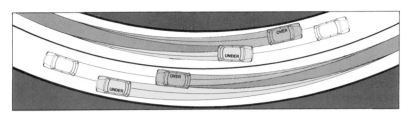

Under-steer

A small degree of understeering characteristics are designed into most modern cars. This gives them stability in a straight line at speed, under crosswind conditions and also when cornering.

The front of the car tends to run wider than the curve of the bend and this must be countered by greater movement of the steering in the direction of the bend.

Over-steer

The behaviour of an over-steering car on a bend is the opposite of one with understeer. The car tends to turn in towards the bend, because the centrifugal force

moves the rear of the car outwards. This requires a steering correction in order to maintain control. An oversteering car will not have the inherent stability of an understeering one in gusty crosswinds, and will need constant steering correction. Correction will also be required on roads with pronounced changes in road cambers.

As the speed at which a bend is taken is increased, so the steering characteristics of a car will change. One which normally has a degree of understeer will, at high speed on a corner, develop neutral steer and then change to over-steer. This transition should, ideally, be progressive and predictable. If it takes place too rapidly it can be unexpected and dangerous.

Car care

However proficient the driver in coping with an emergency, it is essential that the car behaves and responds reliably and as expected. This is only achieved if it is maintained in good condition.

Great stress will be thrown on the brakes, tyres, steering and hydraulic dampers in dealing with an emergency, and these should always be kept in first class condition. The driving exercises above will indicate whether any of them is deficient.

Brakes If these are not working at full efficiency, it will take you longer to stop. Have the brakes and brake fluid levels checked regularly and do not wait to replace friction linings until they are worn down.

Tyres The steering response can be critically affected by the wrong, or incorrectly inflated, tyres. Tyre pressures should be checked regularly, and tyres inspected for signs of over- or under-inflation.

Hydraulic dampers Weak dampers can cause the car to pitch badly with an increased tendency to roll. This can seriously affect braking and steering, particularly in an emergency situation.

Windscreen A clean windscreen free from smears will aid observation and visibility, particularly if an emergency should arise. Good windscreen wipers and an effective screen wash are also important.

Headlights Properly adjusted headlights will maximise your own vision when driving at night, and also minimise dazzle to others.

Seat belts Make sure your seat belts work properly, and, if you have children, install approved safety restraints to the back seat. Never allow a child to travel in the front seat.

Parcel shelf Keep the rear parcel shelf free from loose objects which could fly forward during a collision, into the necks of the driver or passengers. Even light objects can be dangerous if propelled with enough force.

Roll-over bar If driving an open car have a roll-over bar fitted. If a car without one turns over, the occupants have no protection.

Skidding Emergencies

No good driver should ever find his car skidding unintentionally. A skid is usually the result of poor observation, too high a speed, harsh use of the controls or a badly-maintained car. Knowing how to control a skid is essential, however, since even a good driver may skid sometime.

Four wheel skid

When harsh braking locks all four wheels and the car skids, the only way to regain control is to release the brakes and then re-apply them more gently. This allows the tyres to roll again and re-establish their grip on the road. If the steering is not straight ahead, it is important to straighten up before trying to get back on course.

Skid control is not taught to learner drivers, and for many people the first skid will be a completely unexpected experience. The most important consideration is not to panic. Look in the direction you want to go, not where you appear to be going. The next thing to remember is not to over-correct a skid. It is better to let the car sort itself out than to induce a secondary skid by over-correction. Most modern cars respond very quickly to even a slight steering correction. Radial ply tyres react in a fraction of the time that cross-plies used to do, at a fraction of the steering input formerly required.

Tyre grip

A skid is caused when a tyre loses its grip on the road surface and starts sliding instead of rolling. As soon as this happens, control of the car is lost. The area of contact between tyre and road is very small, no bigger than a size 9 shoe. It is critical that this small area remains effective.

The tread of the tyre is an important factor in retaining grip, particularly if the road is not dry. Water on the road surface is dispelled by the channels and slots of the tread pattern so that the tyre can grip on the road surface proper.

Suspension and steering

The design of the car's suspension and steering are inter-related and have important effects upon its handling.

Worn dampers cause unsteady cornering, a bumpy ride when on the move and unpleasant dipping movement when braking. The tyres may not be kept in sufficiently close contact with the road surface and skidding is much more likely to occur. Badly misaligned steering geometry can also increase the risks of skidding.

Road surfaces

A good appreciation of the nature of the road surface and its camber is an important aspect of skid prevention. In fine weather, dust or gravel on the surface can dramatically reduce tyre adhesion, as can mud on country roads. Light rain on roads which have been dry for some time causes a potentially dangerous situation. The rain water can mix with the oily and rubber deposits which are lying on the road surface to form a very slippery surface, and a mixture which could block up the tyre tread.

Rain on the road surface will obviously reduce tyre adhesion. Autumn and winter bring their own skid hazards to road surfaces. Fallen leaves in the autumn produce a very slippery surface.

Road observation

Accurate reading of the road ahead and to the side will prevent most skids, particularly in adverse weather. Judging the severity of an approaching bend is not always easy, but the line of the roadside hedge in the distance can provide an indication. Do not always trust the line of telegraph posts, however, as these can sometimes cut straight across a field, while the road bends in a different direction.

Smooth handling

Skids can be induced or made worse by harsh or sudden braking, harsh acceleration, jerky steering and excessive speed. If the car handling were carried out more smoothly and with greater delicacy, the risks of skidding would be halved. Too heavy a grip on the steering wheel is sometimes a cause of harsh car handling.

Wheelspin

The definition of a skid, in which the grip of the tyre on the road surface is lost, could include wheelspin, with which most drivers are familiar. It is usually caused by harsh use of the accelerator, and can only be cured by easing off. Continuing to press the accelerator will not increase the chances of getting a grip on the road.

Front wheel skid

The car tends to travel straight on in this type of skid despite the direction in which the driver is trying to steer. It is usually brought on by harsh acceleration into a corner, when the front wheels lose their grip. It may seem as though the steering has failed, but do not attempt to apply more steering lock. The first thing to do is to take your foot off the accelerator. Then straighten up the front wheels, so that they can start rotating again. Once grip has been restored steer gently in the direction you wish to take.

This steering correction must be applied very briefly and very gently. Over-correction could result in a rear wheel skid which will be very difficult to control. On no account apply the brakes.

Front wheel drive cars

When a front wheel drive car gets into a front wheel skid, do not take your foot off the accelerator suddenly, as this would have the effect of braking. Reduce the acceleration, but keep a light pressure. Continue to steer into the corner until the car regains its course, then gently start to increase the acceleration.

Rear wheel skid

When driving too fast round a corner or bend, the rear of the car may break away and cause a rear wheel skid. The commonly-stated advice is 'steer into the skid', but this is not always easy to interpret.

Modern radial ply tyres and recent types of suspension system are extremely quick to respond to a skid. They can react a great deal more quickly than most drivers will be able to. Steel-braced tyres generate a self-straightening effect very much more quickly than older generation tyres, particularly cross plies. For the same steering correction, steel-braced tyres will develop up to three times the sideways guidance force that cross ply tyres used to do. This sideways guidance force restores straight line running.

Because of these developments in tyre technology, it is now frequently the best course of action to take your foot off the accelerator (do not touch the brake or clutch pedals). Apply only very slight steering correction for a short time, very quickly but not jerkily. Do not attempt to steer into the skid for any length of time since this could provoke a dangerous aggravation of the skid. As soon as possible return to a neutral steering position.

A major danger with this type of skid is over-reaction, resulting in excessive correction of the initial skid. A secondary skid is set up, often worse than the first one, and this again could provoke excessive steering response. The result can easily be a 'sawing' motion of the steering wheel, rapidly leading to loss of control.

It is not necessary to grip the steering wheel more tightly than usual during skid control. A light but firm handhold is preferable, and allows the car's course, once it starts to skid to be corrected quickly and accurately without nearly so much risk of over-correction.

One cause of a front wheel skid

Demonstration of how a rear wheel skid would be induced and controlled on a skid-pan

Skid-pans Emergencies

Practice at recognising a skid and learning to control it can only be gained on a skid-pan. This is a specially prepared area, set away from public roads, where members of the public may learn about skids. Unfortunately there are not many skid-pans in existence, partly because they are expensive to run and seldom attract sufficient support. Their value, however, cannot be over-estimated.

Skid-pan construction

The surface of a skid-pan is usually designed to give minimum

The skid-pan is coated with special compounds to facilitate skidding

tyre grip, especially when the surface is wet, as it normally will be. In some cases, in addition to watering, the surface will have been specially treated to deliberately induce slipperiness.

It is often the case that you do not use your own car, but one which is supplied. This may be fitted with 'slick' tyres which have no tread at all, so skids will happen at low speed. Occasionally, after completing a course of instruction, you may be encouraged to take your own car on to the skid-pan to discover how it handles.

Instruction

Different arrangements are made at every skid-pan. In some cases the sessions last several hours and include lectures and demonstrations. In others, the sessions are one hour or less. The use of the skid-pan may be linked to a course on better driving run by the Local Authority. The qualified instructors may come from the Police, the Institute of Advanced Motorists or be Approved Driving Instructors. Details of current opening times, charges, how the courses are organised, the use of your own car, etc., are best obtained from your local Road Safety Officer.

Recognising a skid

One of the advantages of a skid-pan is that it teaches you what the onset of a skid feels like. This is particularly valuable if you have not experienced it before. Failing to recognise that a skid is developing, and thus reacting to it too slowly or too abruptly are common causes of loss of control in a skid. It is important to recognise it quickly and to respond smoothly and in good time.

In some ways a skid-pan gives an artificial idea of what a skid is

like. The treated surface means that a skid is induced at a relatively low speed. In addition, however, you will be expecting a skid to occur on a skid-pan. Some skid-pans have one area treated differently from the rest to make things less predictable. This will teach you how to cope with differing degrees of adhesion.

Familiarity with the sensation of skidding, achieved through practice on a skid-pan, is the first step to avoiding the panic over-reaction which so often occurs. The results of over-correction of a skid will become apparent at an early stage and you can then learn to appreciate how effective the strategy is of making only the minimum necessary steering corrections, taking the feet off all the pedals and letting the tyres correct the skid.

Another important benefit of skid-pan experience is that you learn to recognise the point at which control has been regained. Just as you will feel when tyre to road grip becomes marginal, that is when a skid is about to happen, so you will be able to tell that you have regained control. Skid-pan practice will accustom you to the feeling of skids of different types.

Practising cornering on a skid-pan. By avoiding a front wheel skid control is retained through the bend

Skid practice

A skid-pan provides an opportunity to keep practising a particular type of skid until it is familiar and understood. In most real life situations, however, events will happen much more quickly for loss of tyre grip will occur at higher speeds.

A **front wheel skid** can be pro-voked by turning the steering wheel and braking hard. The front wheels will lock and steering control will be lost. By releasing the brakes, some steering control will be restored and you can practise trying to keep to a proper steering line.

A **rear wheel skid** can be provoked simply by going a little too fast round the skid-pan circuit. It can also be induced at a moderate speed by turning the steering wheel, pulling the handbrake on briefly and then releasing it. This will lock the rear wheels while retaining front wheel grip, and the rear of the car will slew. Take your foot off the accelerator, do not touch the brake or clutch pedals, apply any necessary steer-ing correction, then return the steering to a neutral position until control of the car is regained.

A more advanced driver can use the skid-pan to make the basic manoeuvre from which to engineer more problems, allowing the driver to improve his skill further. It is possibie, for example, to learn the knack of sliding the car from lock to lock under complete control, while maintaining speed by keep-ing the foot on the throttle.

A rear wheel skid is provoked on the curve. Skid-pan practice will enable it to be controlled

Quiz Emergencies

It may be easy to feel that the essentials of skid control are understood after reading about them in a book. Experience on the road is very different, and can be assisted by practice gained on a skid-pan. One way to check whether you would do the right thing if you were involved in a skid is to try the quiz on this page. Although the answers are given here, try to work out your own answer before reading them.

1 What are the factors that could cause a skid?

2 Which pedal must you not press when you have got into a skid?

3 Which pedal would you press in a car with a manual gear box if you get into a skid?

4 In the event of a rear wheel skid on a left hand bend with the car sliding to your right, in which direction would you turn the steering wheel?

5 What effect do weak shock absorbers have on road adhesion?

6 Under what road conditions are you most likely to skid?

7 What should you do if, when braking for a bend, your front wheels lock up?

8 In a similar situation what should you do if the front wheels start to skid outwards towards the crown of the road?

9 What is a secondary skid and how is it caused?

10 Is a front-wheel-drive car more prone to front wheel skidding than either a front engine rear-wheel-drive car or a rear engine car?

11 What should you do if a front-wheel-drive car gets into a front wheel skid?

12 How would you deliberately induce a skid on a skid-pan?

13 What is the most important aspect of skid-pan practice?

14 What is done to some skid-pans to give varying degrees of adhesion?

15 Which tyres, radials or cross-plies, have better cornering power?

16 Why do bald or badly-worn tyres lose adhesion on wet roads?

17 Apart from bald tyres, what other tyre conditions contribute to skids?

18 What tyres should you fit to your car to minimise the chance of any form of skid?

19 What is the essence of skid prevention for a driver?

20 In the event of getting into a skid what is the first requirement of the driver?

Answers

1 Poor driving involving perhaps driving too fast, insufficiently good observation of the road ahead or harsh use of controls.

2 The brake pedal. Applying the brakes in a skid will tend to lock up the wheels, making it even more difficult to regain control. Control is only regained when the tyres are in rolling contact with the road surface. The best strategy when in a skid is not to press any of the pedals at all.

3 It has sometimes been suggested that depressing the clutch may help, but as stated in the answer to question 2, it is better not to press any of the pedals. You may get into another skid when you let in the clutch.

4 Any movement of the steering wheel must be carried out as soon as the slide is detected, and then with great care. In this case, steer slightly to the right, enough to 'catch' the slide, then return the steering to a neutral position. Do not steer too far to the right, or keep the steering in that position for more than a very short time or the car will start to slide to the left.

5 Weak shock absorbers allow the wheels to bounce excessively on the road surface. This means that road contact is only poorly maintained, resulting in reduced tyre-to-road adhesion. They will also cause imbalance in the car's handling.

6 Under almost any road condition if you are inattentive. In general terms, anything on the road surface which is loose such as gravel, anything which will provide a film between the tyre and the road, such as rain or ice, increases the risk of skidding. Particularly hazardous is light rain after a long dry spell. This spreads a film of water over a surface covered with an oily, rubber deposit and the road becomes extremely slippery.

7 Release the brakes for a fraction of a second to regain steering control, then re-apply them more sensitively.

8 Release the accelerator and straighten up the steering so that, for a very short time you are steering in the direction of the skid. Once steering control has been regained continue your course round the corner. Do not brake under any circumstances.

9 A secondary skid is caused by over-correcting the first skid, either by applying too harsh a steering correction or continuing it for too long. The result is to make the car go from one skid to another on the other side, the second usually more difficult to control than the first.

10 The idea that all front-wheel-drive cars have superior road-holding to other cars is not borne out in practice.

11 You should ease off the accelerator smoothly, but not completely. A small amount of power should still be applied to the front wheels. Otherwise, removal of the power can have a braking effect which could result in the rear of the car breaking away.

12 There are several ways of doing this. Driving too fast into a curve will provoke a skid, so will steering into a curve and braking hard or steering left or right and pulling very hard on the handbrake.

13 To get used to the feeling of the car's loss of adhesion. Once you can recognise the onset of a skid you will be able to react quickly and smoothly enough to control it before it goes too far. Practice in dealing with the different types of skid is also most important.

14 Certain sections of the skid-pan may be treated with a liquid having a low co-efficient of friction or may have a permanent special surface treatment which simulates a greasy patch offering less adhesion than other parts.

15 Radial ply tyres have better cornering performance as a built-in feature.

16 The tread of a tyre dispels the water lying on the road so that the tyre can grip on the surface below. When the tread is very thin or absent, the tyre cannot make such good contact with the road surface even at low speeds. At high speeds the tyre may 'float' off the surface and aquaplane.

17 Underinflated tyres distort excessively when cornering and this reduces their grip on the road surface. Unevenly worn tyres offer reduced tyre to road grip. Unequal pressure distribution side to side can also promote the onset of a skid.

18 In most cases you should fit the tyres recommended by your car's manufacturer, but you should seek the advice of a tyre specialist before changing to anything very different.

19 To read the road well ahead, to be at the right speed and in the right gear for every situation, especially when cornering. You should always bear in mind the road surface conditions at the time, whether the road is dry, or covered in rain, mud or ice.

20 The first requirement is not to panic. If you can think quickly and clearly and recognise the type of skid involved you are well on the way to taking the correct action. Remembering that modern car and tyre design is such that a great deal of the correction will be carried out automatically by the car itself without active participation of the driver, you should try to make any steering correction precisely and smoothly. This is better than reacting suddenly and losing all control.

Causes of accidents Emergencies

Accidents are rarely accidental. They may be unforeseen or unexpected events but they rarely happen by chance. They are caused by specific factors or combinations of factors, not by fate. It is often possible to determine their causes, and therefore many accidents could be prevented.

There are three general groups of factors which contribute to accidents: the road user, the environment and the vehicle. Of these categories, road user factors are the most important; $\frac{2}{3}$ of all injury accidents are due to driver error. Environmental conditions, which include the road layout as well as the weather, contribute to just over a quarter of accidents. The vehicle, its loading and condition of maintenance play a leading role in just under 10% of all road accidents.

The role of the road-user is discussed at length in other parts of this book. The other two factors are analysed in detail here.

Although it may not be readily apparent the main road turns right at this junction

Many road accidents involve pedestrians, especially children

The road environment

In about one quarter of the adverse environmental conditions which contribute to accidents, the driver's vision is restricted. This restriction may be caused by buildings, the line of the road, or as the result of parked cars, trees, road signs, lamp standards or bollards.

Pedestrian accidents make up a major part of the urban road toll. The most effective and most expensive solution is complete segregation of pedestrians and vehicles, but this can usually only be achieved in a new town.

Road signs and markings

The design of road signs and markings is laid down by the Government so that the motorist is presented with a consistent set of signs and markings at any given situation. These should provide clear information about potential hazards, but they sometimes fail to do so. Poor siting or inadequate signs and markings contribute to around 15% of the environmental factors in the causes of road accidents.

The sign itself may be misleading. For example, a direction sign at a junction may suggest, by the relative thickness of the lines, that the minor road approach to the junction is, in fact, the major road.

The direction sign may be complicated. To read and understand an unfamiliar sign at a complex multi-road junction may require the motorist's complete attention for several seconds. During this time he may overlook hazards such as pedestrians and parked cars, thus increasing the likelihood of an accident occurring.

Reduced visibility

The human eye can, generally, adapt successfully to most levels of light during the day. Where bright, direct sunlight is present, however, glare can occur. Sun, dazzle and glare comprise about 4% of the environmental factors in the causes of accidents. This factor seems to be more prevalent in accidents involving turning manoeuvres, and those in which the right of way is violated.

Visibility is also greatly reduced when driving at night. Indeed, about 1 in 3 of all accidents occur during the hours of darkness. The severity of these accidents tends to be greater than for daytime accidents: the proportion of fatalities is almost twice as high at night. This increased severity is not due solely to the lighting conditions. The incidence of drinking drivers and pedestrians on the road is also higher at night.

Inadequate street lighting is associated with about 3% of the environmental factors in the causes of accidents, but is thought to be a much more important factor in pedestrian accidents alone.

In the summer, especially, road signs can become obscured by overhanging leaves and branches

A detailed signpost with a number of destinations can take several seconds to read properly

In some conditions of bright sun light visibility is greatly reduced

Weather conditions

The roads in Britain are damp or rain-soaked for about 20% to 40% of the times of principal traffic flow, although there are geographical and seasonal variations. Even so, over half the road accidents occur in conditions when the roads are dry and the weather is relatively good.

Wintry road conditions reduce the density of traffic; most accidents in winter are the results of losing control and skidding

Water on the road surface greatly lengthens stopping distances and increases the risk of skidding

Rain: About 17% of all injury accidents occur in rain and double that number take place on wet road surfaces where it is not raining.

Rain causes increases in the numbers of accidents in daylight and to a greater extent in darkness. The numbers of accidents are always increased both in summer and winter when visibility generally is impaired. In daylight, wet road surfaces without rain, however, cause greater increases in accidents during the summer, when water accumulating on a highly polished road surface increases the chances of a vehicle skidding and causing an accident.

Snow and ice: Approximately 3% of injury accidents in Britain occur on snow-covered or icy roads. About half the vehicles in such accidents are involved in a skid prior to the impact, usually because of harsh use of the controls. Snow usually reduces traffic flow by about 15% overall, but even so the number of accidents on snowy days increases by about 25% compared with dry weather. The main reason for this increase is the icy road surface rather than the falling snow.

Fog: Traffic flows in foggy weather are generally reduced by up to 20%. Around 1% of all injury accidents occur under these conditions. On both urban and rural roads accidents in fog, although they take place more frequently, in fact cause no more serious injuries than accidents occurring in clear weather. Only 3% of all motorway casualties occur in fog, although some of these accidents involve multiple collisions and the injuries may be more severe.

Vehicle defects

Vehicle defects and design do not form a major part of the causes of accidents and sudden component failure is rare. More commonly, the standard of a particular component, although apparently adequate for normal driving, is not good enough to cope in an emergency situation. Overall, mechanical failure is a contributory factor in about 1% of accidents.

Steering defects: Free play in the steering system is likely to affect seriously the steering performance of the vehicle, and contributes to the causation of less than 1% of all accidents.

Tyre defects: Despite the excellent performance of the modern products, tyre factors are involved in the causation of about 3% of all accidents. The three commonest causes are deflation before impact, inadequate tread or tyre combination and incorrect inflation (usually under-inflation). Tyre blowouts due to catastrophic failure of the structure of the tyre are thought to be rare. Punctures are more common and are usually caused by nails or screws lying on the road.

Tyre deformation due to kerbing

Inadequate brakes: Even though it has been estimated that about half the cars on the road have inefficient braking systems, inadequate brakes are causal factors in only about 3% of accidents. Typical causes of poor braking are worn linings, chafed or swollen hoses, leaky pipes and cylinders.

Vision restrictions: A driver's vision may be restricted by condensation on the windows, thick windscreen pillars, stickers, and luggage or large passengers obscuring rearward vision. Vision restrictions are involved in the causation of less than 1% of accidents.

Lighting defects: These usually prevent a vehicle being seen easily by other motorists, rather than posing a problem for the driver. They contribute to the causation of less than 1% of accidents.

Other factors: Doors, bonnets and boot lids may open when the car is in motion, but normally the vehicle can be stopped safely.

Accident statistics Emergencies

Road accidents are the major cause of accidental death in Britain today. Air, rail and industrial accidents result in relatively few fatalities, and only accidents in the home (involving mainly the very young and the elderly) are anywhere near as important as road accidents. Among young people, however, road accidents do the greatest damage, being responsible for one death in every three from all causes in the 5–24 age group.

The number of casualties reported is approximately 300,000 every year, but this does not include all of them. In many cases, the victim of an accident is taken directly to hospital by the motorist involved, or is treated only by a general practitioner, and the accident is not reported to the police. It is believed the true casualty figure is nearer 400,000–500,000. Accidents which involve only damage to other vehicles or to property are rarely reported to the police, but it is believed there are about 6 damage-only accidents to every injury accident.

Traffic accidents cost a great deal of money, as well as causing suffering and inconvenience. The costs of emergency services and medical treatment, vehicle and property damage, the courts, the administrative costs of accident insurance and loss of economic output was estimated to be well over £946,000,000. The true cost of the pain, grief and suffering involved, however, is impossible to calculate with any accuracy.

In spite of these terrible figures, it is encouraging that the serious and fatal casualty rate per 100,000 people has been falling since the mid 1960s partly due to road safety legislation and campaigns and partly due to education of the most vulnerable pedestrian group, the 5–9 year olds, in roadside behaviour. A great deal of research is also being carried out in many countries in the world identifying the causes of accidents and injuries, and suggesting appropriate solutions. Without doubt this work has saved lives.

Road casualties in Britain

Deaths	6,614
Serious injuries (limb-fracture or in-patient hospital treatment)	81,681
Slight injuries	259,766
Total	348,061

Top Ten Accident Causes (not in order of importance)

Lack of attention

Turning right without due care

Excessive speed in the circumstances

Failure to comply with traffic sign or signal

Emerging from junction without due care

Pedestrians walking or running into the road

Overtaking error

Pedestrians crossing the road, not concealed by other vehicles

Pedestrians crossing the road, masked by a stationary vehicle

Driving under the influence of drink or drugs

When do accidents occur?

Accidents are most frequent during the weekday morning and evening rush hours, the times of peak traffic flow. Saturday shopping and the Sunday afternoon outing also result in many casualties. Late night driving, particularly on Fridays and at weekends, can be very hazardous because of the suspected presence of alcohol in many motorists and pedestrians.

Seasonally, summer and autumn have the highest number of casualties, winter and spring the lowest. These variations are due to seasonal differences in traffic flow as well as weather conditions. Casualty figures and traffic flow are highest in the summer.

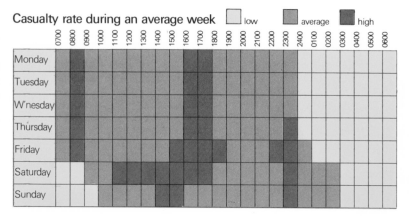

Casualty rate during an average week — low, average, high

Where do accidents take place?

Most accidents occur in urban areas because of the greater density of traffic there and the larger number of hazards such as junctions, parked cars and pedestrians. Motorways have the lowest number of casualties and the lowest casualty rate (number of casualties per 100 million vehicle-miles). Because of the higher speeds, however, motorway accidents and rural accidents (accidents on roads, including trunk roads, going through rural areas) tend to result in more serious injuries. If involved in an injury accident on a motorway or a rural area, the chance of its being a fatal accident is more than twice as high as for an injury accident in an urban area.

Injury accidents on the road

	Motorway accidents (including A (M) roads)	Urban accidents (excluding motorways)	Rural accidents (excluding motorways)	Total
Fatal	175	3,553	2,363	6,091
Serious	1,089	47,159	19,747	67,995
Slight	2,641	155,096	33,965	191,702
All severities	3,905	205,808	56,075	265,788

Who has accidents?

Car occupants and pedestrians together comprised about 72% of all road fatalities and 64% of all casualties (1977 figures). Accidents to moped and scooter users and motorcyclists accounted for about 18% of fatalities. (This is the fastest growing category partly because of increases in two-wheeler traffic over recent years). Bus and coach passengers and the occupants of goods vehicles make up the remainder.

Deaths for different road users

Pedestrian	35%
Pedal cyclist	4%
Motor cyclist	18%
Car occupant	37%
Goods vehicle occupant	4%
Bus or coach occupant	1%
Other vehicle occupant	1%

Pedestrians

Almost all pedestrian casualties result from accidents in built up areas—84% of the deaths and almost 96% of the serious and slight injuries in 1977. The most vulnerable groups are the young and the old. Many motorists make little or no allowance for the pedestrian and some pedestrians, having never been drivers, are unaware of the problems faced by the motorist.

Children More than 2 out of every 5 pedestrian casualties are children and the 5–9 age group has the highest casualty rate per 100,000 population. Few children below the age of 9 can fully understand the traffic environment and they cannot accurately predict the movements or speeds of traffic. A 6 year old child is only two-thirds the height of an adult and

thus it is difficult for him to obtain an unobstructed view of the road. Many accidents to children occur in inner city areas where children play on the pavements or in the road. When playing children become absorbed in their games and they are hardly aware of passing traffic.

Adults Between the ages of 20 and 59, the pedestrian casualty rate drops significantly. Most people are able to drive or ride, so less time is spent as a pedestrian. In addition, physical and mental fitness reach a peak during this time, increasing the ability to cope with traffic situations. A major factor in accidents to adult pedestrians is the presence of alcohol. Surveys have shown that amongst men aged 15–39, 90% of fatalities occur between 7 pm and 3 am. Nearly three quarters of these men had been drinking and most of them had consumed quite large amounts of alcohol.

Women tend to be less likely to be involved in pedestrian accidents, and a much lower proportion of those involved have been drinking.

The elderly The pedestrian casualty rate increases steadily after the age of 60. With increasing age, females comprise a larger percentage of the population, and thus the proportion of female casualties rises—60% of casualties over 70 years old are women.

Most accidents to elderly pedestrians occur during the day, and fewer of them involve alcohol. Impaired vision and hearing make the assessment of a traffic situation more difficult, and loss of agility increases the time they spend when crossing a road.

Pedal cyclists There are more than 23,000 casualties among pedal cyclists every year, and although the figures have more than halved since the late 1950s, increased cycle usage since 1974 has reversed this downward trend. Even so, the number of child cyclists injured has remained about the same, 1 in 3 of all casualties being between the ages of 10 and 14. Three out of every four accidents occur in built-up areas in daylight when the child cyclist is going to and from school.

Motorcyclists Between 1970 and 1976 the popularity of mopeds and motorcycles soared, and moped casualties more than tripled while motorcycle casualties increased by over 60%. Today, casualties to riders of powered two-wheeled vehicles comprise nearly 1 in 5 of all casualties and about 1 in 6 of all deaths which happen on the roads.

Goods vehicles By virtue of their size, goods vehicles (over 1½ tons unladen weight) have a higher involvement rate in fatal accidents than cars. In such accidents, it is generally the occupant of the other, usually smaller, vehicle who is killed rather than the HGV driver. Their involvement rate in other injury accidents is less than for cars and other vehicles partly because about ⅔ of goods vehicle traffic is found in rural areas.

Most articulated vehicles are now fitted with anti-jack-knifing devices and account for only about 2% of all HGV injury accidents. On motorways, rear-end shunts are common types of accident, but the use of reflective markings on the rear of the goods vehicle and the provision of under-run bars have helped to reduce the consequences of such accidents.

Buses and coaches In terms of the death rate per 100 million passenger miles, buses and coaches are the safest form of transport, some seven times safer than travelling by car. A substantial proportion of the accidents, however, occur to people, often the elderly, when they are boarding or alighting from the vehicle.

What to do at an accident Emergencies

Accidents of one kind or another are far from uncommon and very few motorists will escape ever being involved in one. The accident may involve no more than a minor collision where the damage is limited to bodywork blemishes or it may be a major accident where several people are injured or even killed. Today's motorist must be prepared to cope with any of these situations.

Damage-only accidents

Several different situations may occur. The table below summarises what to do in the more common cases. In every instance where other people or vehicles are involved, your insurance company should be informed, whether or not you make a claim. This need not jeopardise your 'no claim' bonus. Failing to do so quickly can cause serious complications.

Injury accidents

If any person is injured in an accident, the drivers involved must produce their insurance certificates to anyone who has reasonable grounds for asking. If this cannot be done, they must report to the police within 24 hours, and produce the certificate at a police station with 5 days of the accident.

It is especially important to keep an accurate record of the accident, prepared on the spot if possible, and recording the names, addresses and statements of any witnesses. However one may feel, however, no admission of liability should be made. It is advisable to say as little as possible, particularly whilst still suffering from shock.

Serious accident

If you were the first to arrive at the scene of an accident where there were injuries, would you know what to do?

Accidents, sadly, are an everyday part of road travel. Even though you may be careful and lucky enough not to be involved directly yourself, sooner or later you are likely to be confronted with an accident. Before anything, overcome panic. Those involved in the accident will probably be panicky already. Three steps should be taken immediately.

1 Warn approaching traffic
Traffic approaching from both directions must be warned of the situation, to prevent the accident becoming more extensive and complex than it already is at present. This warning should be well away from the accident scene, allowing for the speed of the approaching traffic, the road layout and the prevailing weather and road surface conditions. Uninjured people on the scene can often be usefully deployed to do this job.

Emergency services regularly hold training exercises to help them deal with motorway accidents

The first step is to rapidly protect the accident scene

By the time the ambulances arrive the police are already starting to free trapped drivers

Ambulance crews assess the situation and apply First Aid where it is necessary

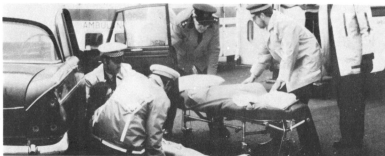

Victims needing hospital treatment are moved quickly into ambulances, which will be constantly arriving at and leaving the scene

Some police vehicles have a telescopic stalk on the roof which can be raised to illuminate an accident scene with powerful lights

2 Assess conditions

The next step is to assess how many people and how many vehicles are involved.

Is anybody trapped in the wreckage?

Is there any danger of fire from a leaking petrol tank? In any case impose a ban on smoking at the accident and, if time and equipment permits, disconnect the vehicles' batteries.

Locate First Aid kits, if any.

Find out if anybody present has received First Aid training. There may be an ex-nurse present.

3 Summon help

If there is a house near by, send the calmest person you can find to locate a telephone and make the 999 emergency calls. If there is no telephone in the immediate vicinity, deploy a vehicle to the nearest telephone. It is often wise to duplicate such arrangements in case one telephone is not working or involves delays.

You should ask for the police first, keeping the message as straight-forward as possible. They need to know the exact location of the incident, the types of vehicle involved, and an estimate of the number of injured people. They will call the other services.

Motorway accident

In the event of a serious motorway accident, there is little the ordinary motorist can do beyond driving to the next emergency telephone to summon help. He will usually be advised not to stop unless this is absolutely necessary.

The job of the emergency services is made infinitely harder by the presence of onlookers or would-be helpers. The more the traffic can be kept moving, the quicker the victims can receive any necessary hospital treatment.

The first priority of the police in a motorway accident situation is to protect the scene by coning off the area. This prevents other traffic driving into the situation and causing more trouble.

Normally, they would not attend to the victims of the accident until the scene was satisfactorily protected. Even then, however, they would be unlikely to administer First Aid, because the ambulance will almost certainly have arrived by that time, and the ambulance crews will be well-trained in the appropriate medical techniques.

The police will usually also alert the motorway control centre who will switch on the warning signals and any of the message signs in the locality. The importance of obeying these signs is obvious.

Damage	Whose Fault?	Should you stop?	Should you tell the police?	Further Action
Your own car; no other damage.	Yours	Yes	No	Insurance claim depending on cost of damage
Your own car and another vehicle: minor damage to either.	Either yours or the other driver's	Yes	No, provided names and addresses were exchanged at the scene. Yes, within 24 hours if names and addresses were not exchanged.	Insurance claim, depending on the agreement reached with the other party. Do not admit liability.
Your own car and another vehicle; serious damage to either	Either yours or the other driver's	Yes	Yes	Insurance claim, if agreement reached with the other party. Do not admit liability.
Property near the road.	Yours	Yes	No Yes, if damage is serious or involves a traffic sign.	You must give your name and address to anyone who has grounds for wanting them.
Animal injured or killed.	Yours	Yes, if a dog, horse, sheep, pig, ass, mule or cattle, involved. No, if any other animal involved.	No Yes, if damage or injury is serious.	You must give your name and address to anyone who has reasonable grounds for wanting them.

Hazchem Labels

Should an accident involve a road tanker, the police and fire brigade will deal with its contents according to the information provided by the Hazchem Label attached to it.

Box 1: the number denotes the type of fire appliance and how it should be used; the letters following indicate the type of chemical and its effect.
Box 2: International Hazard Sign.
Box 3: the United Nations chemical number or its name.

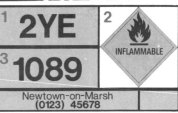

Inflammable Gases	Inflammable Solids	Spontaneously Combustible Substances	Substances which are Dangerous When Wet	Oxidising Substances	Organic Peroxides

Harmful — Keep Away From Food	Toxic Gases	Poisonous Substances	Radioactive Substances	Corrosive Substances	Compressed Gases

137

First aid Emergencies

It is an unfortunate fact that, sooner or later, you are likely to come across an accident in which people are injured. Everyone hopes that, in such a situation, they may be of some help.

While it is possible to anticipate what one would do at the scene of an accident, in reality it will be much less easy. For most people without any First Aid training, the best advice is: do nothing beyond telephoning the police who will summon the necessary emergency services. The sight of injured people is far from pleasant, and it is better to leave well alone than to risk injuring the victims even further by well-meaning but untrained assistance.
See also pages 136 and 137.

Basic training

The most positive single step which every motorist can take needs to be made well before he meets an accident situation. An elementary grounding in First Aid can be acquired at very low cost, and a short evening course may last no more than three hours.

These are laid on in most localities by St. John Ambulance, and information about them can usually be obtained via the local library. At such a course, proper training will be given about the procedures described here, so that they are carried out safely and without further risk to the victim. Road accidents rarely involve a single injury, however.

First Aid kits

Every car should carry a good First Aid kit. The contents of such a kit are shown here.

The instructions on the kit should be read when it is first obtained, and then kept with the kit for reference. The container should be kept closed and clean, and stored in the glovebox rather than the boot, which may be inaccessible in the event of an accident. Items used up should be replaced as soon as possible. In certain European countries it is obligatory to carry a First Aid kit.

At an accident, particularly where several people are injured, all First Aid kits should be located.

Shock

Many accident victims, whether injured or not, are liable to be in a state of shock. Reassure them and keep them in absolute rest, lying down with the head turned to one side. Clothing about the neck, chest and waist should be loosened, and the patient wrapped in a blanket, rug or coat. Anyone likely to receive hospital treatment should not be given any food, alcohol or other fluid. Heat should not be applied in any form, and limbs should not be rubbed.

Lie unconscious victims like this

Breathing

The single most important thing to do is to ensure that all casualties are breathing. The air passages should be cleared, restrictive clothing round the neck should be loosened, and false teeth and any other obstructions should be removed from the mouth.

If the tongue is blocking the airway, lay the patient on his back on a firm surface. Press the top of his head backwards, while supporting the nape of the neck. If breathing does not start, lift the tongue out of the throat by pressing forward the angles of the jaw, or by pressing the chin forward. Alternatively, hold on to the tongue with a handkerchief, pulling it forward.

When the patient gasps and starts to breathe, place him on his side with his legs drawn up, until he is fully conscious.

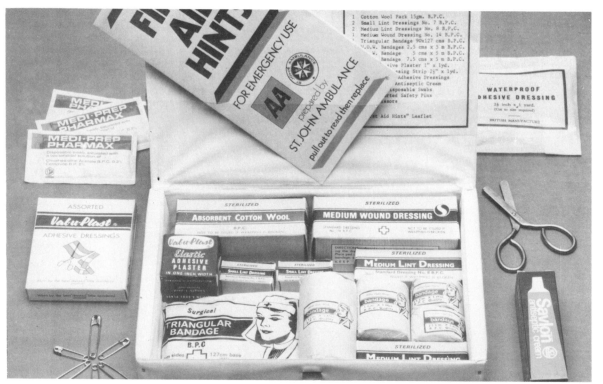

Before giving mouth-to-mouth resuscitation, clear victim's mouth and air passages

Raise the shoulders slightly so that the head can be tilted back with the jaw jutting out

Close the nostrils with one hand keeping the jaw well up and opening the mouth with the other

Seal your lips round the victim's mouth, take a deep breath and blow steadily into the lungs

Mouth-to-mouth resuscitation

If the casualty is not breathing as a result of clearing the airway, attempts at mouth-to-mouth resuscitation should be tried quickly. Keeping the casualty's head extended, give the first four inflations as rapidly as possible.

Open your mouth, take in a deep breath, then, pinching the casualty's nostrils with your fingers, seal your lips round his mouth and blow into his lungs until they are filled. Remove your mouth and watch his chest empty. Repeat this process at the normal rate of breathing, until the casualty starts to breathe; then place him on his side with his legs drawn up.

Re-starting the heart

If no pulse can be felt, and the injured person is beginning to look blue/grey, steps should be taken to restart the heart.

As a first step, put the casualty on his back, making sure his airways are clear. Strike his chest smartly, to the left of the lower part of the breastbone, with the edge of the hand. If there is no response at first, continue striking rhythmically once per second for 10 seconds, while feeling for the pulse.

If the heart still does not start, heart compression should be started, combined with artificial respiration. First make 15 compressions. These compressions should alternate with two inflations of the lungs.

For this procedure, take up a position at the side of the casualty. Place the heel of your hand on the lower half of the breastbone (holding the palm and fingers off the chest). Cover the heel of your hand with the heel of the other hand, and, with straight arms, rock forward and press down on the lower part of the breastbone. Repeat the process as necessary.

In an unconscious adult it can be pressed 1–1½ inches towards the spine. In adults repeat the pressure once per second, but in children the pressure of one hand will be sufficient and the rate is 60–100 times per minute.

Bleeding

Minor wounds should be exposed and the bleeding controlled by applying an adhesive dressing. The skin round the wound can be cleaned with antiseptic lotion.

If there is considerable, but not severe bleeding, expose the wound, removing or cutting as little clothing as possible. Raise the bleeding part, except in the case of a fractured limb, without disturbing any blood clot that has formed. Remove any foreign bodies which are visible and loose. Then immobilise the injured part and apply treatment for shock.

Where the bleeding is severe, the casualty should be lying down, and pressure applied to the bleeding part with a suitable clean pad. This should be bandaged firmly in place with a folded triangular bandage. If the bleeding is not controlled, more pads should be applied and the pressure increased by hand or bandage.

Broken bones

No casualty should ever be moved if any fracture or dislocation is suspected. The only exception to this is if they are in serious danger from fire or something falling on them. The injured limb should be supported at once so that no movement is possible. If an arm is thought to be fractured, move it gently and bandage it to the body in the most comfortable position.

Medical information tags

Knowing how to help an unconscious victim may be made easier if he is wearing some disc or bracelet containing medical information about himself. Sufferers from diabetes, epilepsy and various allergies sometimes wear these to avoid the risk of wrong treatment should they become unconscious. Anyone attempting to render First Aid at an accident scene should check for these tags on unconscious victims.

Of the two types commonly used, one is the Medic-Alert disc, worn either on a bracelet or a necklace, which states the illness or allergy, together with a phone number and a reference number for further information. The other type of tag is the SOS Talisman, a capsule fashioned as decorative jewellery, which contains a strip of paper containing all relevant medical details.

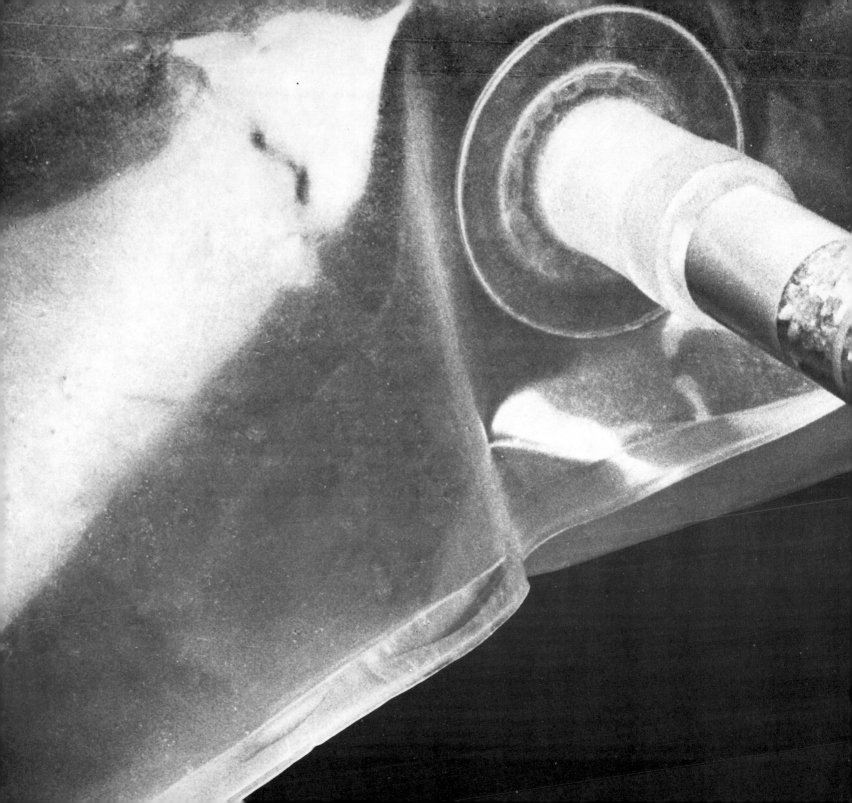

5 Fit to drive

Fit to drive

Every motorist's standard of driving is affected not only by his or her skill and experience, but also by many other factors such as his health, whether he has been drinking or is taking medicines of various kinds, and the stresses and anxieties under which he is living.

A good driver needs to understand what governs his driving performance. Even in perfect health, accidents can still be caused by drowsiness, lack of attention or panic reactions. Many driving tasks become almost automatic after years of experience, yet they can be affected by many subtle influences of which the driver may be unaware.

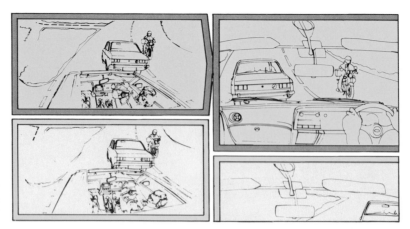

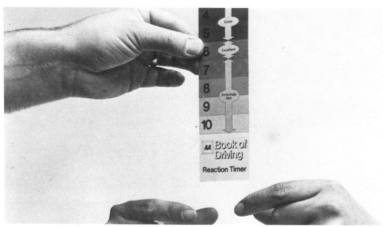

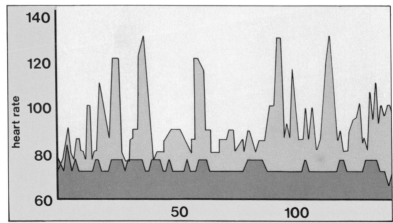

Driving decisions
pages 144–145

Although it may appear to be a simple task to cope with most situations, the brain carries out several quite complex processes in order to produce the appropriate response. There is plenty of scope for mistakes to be made and they can happen all too easily. An imaginary situation is analysed in detail in order to show just which processes are involved and the mistakes that can be made at every stage.

Reaction times
pages 146–147

Everyone may pride themselves on the speed of their reactions but, in fact, this reaction time can vary from one occasion to the next depending on its complexity and a host of other factors. Tiredness or drinking alcohol can also slow down reaction times, when even a very slight increase can make a big difference while driving at speed. The factors affecting reaction times are explained and a simple game is outlined enabling anyone to compare their own reaction times.

Fatigue
pages 148–149

The drowsiness brought on by fatigue is one of driving's more insidious hazards. It may not be recognised in its early stages and it may also not be taken sufficiently seriously. Indeed, a number of accidents, some of them fatal, have been brought about by fatigue. There are several ways to minimise this danger, and there are warning signs to be recognised and heeded. Regular breaks for refreshment and exercise provide the best means of avoiding fatigue.

Drink and driving
pages 150–151

The dangerous results of drinking and driving are well known in general, but seldom in detail. How many drinks can be taken before the blood alcohol level rises above the legal limit? How soon after drinking should you drive? What is the effect of mixing drinks? What is the alcoholic content of different types of drinks and how do they compare? All these and many other questions are explored in detail in this section.

Illness and drugs
pages 152–153

Many everyday minor complaints can have a bad effect on driving, particularly if certain medicines are taken for them. Many drugs in common use, such as tranquillisers, can affect driving performance. Women drivers may find that their driving is affected by the menstrual cycle and by pregnancy. Advice on the effects of all these aspects of health and illness is given on these pages as well as the side-effects on driving of many common drugs.

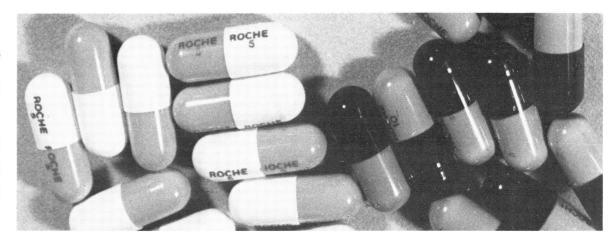

Keep fit exercises
pages 154–155

Every journey can be tiring for both driver and passengers and regular breaks are essential for alertness. Blood circulation can be improved with a specially devised set of exercises which are simple and enjoyable to carry out. These can be practised at any rest break. Even traffic jams can be put to good use by doing a programme of exercises, starting from the feet and working up to the neck and shoulders. These are all carried out from the driving seat and are an antidote to rising blood pressure.

Driving decisions Fit to drive

Situation

Looking

Seeing

It has been estimated that drivers make about 10 to 20 decisions every mile, yet are rarely conscious of the fact. Driving should not be a matter of over-deliberate concentration all the time, however. This can provoke over-reaction. Driving decisions can be of an infinite variety, depending on the situation involved, but they all involve the same sequence of mental processes. Most accidents are due to driver error, so every attempt to understand why mistakes are made could help to reduce the number of accidents.

Every time a driver is faced with a changing situation or a hazard, four basic processes take place:
1 looking at the hazard
2 recognising the hazard
3 deciding how to cope with it
4 responding, using the appropriate controls.
A mistake in any of these four processes increases the chances of an accident. It does not necessarily mean that a collision will occur, because that depends on how the other traffic behaves, but nevertheless there is an increased risk of an accident.

Looking

Many different objects require or attract the driver's attention. Some, such as parked or moving vehicles, pedestrians and mandatory signs require action to be taken. Others, such as direction signposts, provide information, particularly for strangers. Many other objects are not directly relevant to the driving task, although drivers may, nonetheless, look at them.

The driver must not only look at the hazard, he must look at it in time to respond properly. In many accidents, by the time the driver has looked at the hazard, it is too late for any avoiding action to be taken. Under normal traffic conditions it takes only about $\frac{1}{2}$ second to 1 second extra anticipation time to be able to avoid 80% of collision accidents. This means looking farther ahead than many drivers tend to do.

Failure to look at the hazard is the commonest error committed by road users, and about one-third of all errors leading to accidents are of this kind.

The driver was usually looking elsewhere at the critical moment. Most people will look at things which are:
a important to them
b bright, colourful, or associated with a loud noise
c novel
d moving

All potential hazards should be important to a driver, but many of them, such as parked cars or pedestrians, are not novel and may be too easily taken for granted. Any distraction, however momentary, such as lighting a cigarette, turning to talk to a passenger, waving to a friend, looking at a

direction sign, or countless other examples, can lead to a collision if there is not enough space between the vehicles.

Seeing

We do not always see what we think we see. The brain must interpret what the eye sees, and if the image is indistinct or ambiguous, the brain may have difficulty in recognising it.

First impressions have a strong effect, particularly in traffic. A driver may continue to believe in his first impression of a situation until he is presented with

eciding

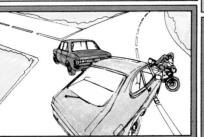

Responding

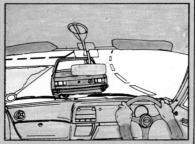

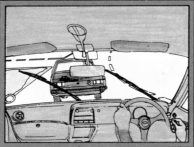

*Driver's errors: **looking**: does not see turning car; **seeing**: misunderstands intention of car, or does not see motorcycle; **deciding**: panic reaction or late braking; **responding**: operates the wrong control.*

overwhelming evidence to the contrary. This error is known as 'misperception,' and it accounts for about 1 in 5 of all errors leading to accidents.

Many errors are misperceptions of the road environment. The general lie of the land, or inadequate signposting, may cause a driver to mistake the severity of a bend or the priority at a junction.

Misperceptions of the speeds or the separation distances between vehicles are common, particularly in conditions of poor visibility and when speeds are high. At night, or in rain, fog, slush or snow, dirty

rear lights producing a dim light may make a following driver believe that a vehicle in front is at a greater distance than it really is. In fog, vehicles tend to look smaller and further away than they are. The intensity of rear lights plays an important part in the judgement of distance.

A vehicle's position on the road is often used to predict its future movements. One close to the crown of the road may be assumed to be turning right, even if its indicators suggest otherwise. Illuminated brake lights are generally assumed to mean that the vehicle is stopping, rather than slowing to turn.

A common cause of motorcycle accidents is their not being seen by drivers turning on to a major road. Most car drivers expect to see cars on the road, and when they look to see if a main road is clear, they are looking for relatively large vehicles, not for small motorcycles often ridden close to the kerb. Many motorcyclists now use their headlights and wear bright clothing to make themselves more conspicuous.

Accurate predictions of traffic movements about to take place are an important part of every driver's skill, but when rash assumptions are made without any confirming evidence, a potential accident situation is created.

Deciding

After the driver has seen a hazard and has recognised it correctly, he must decide on the appropriate course of action. Many mistakes can occur at this stage, but there are two general types.

One is the panic reaction. For example, when a hazard appears suddenly, the motorist, rather than reacting rationally, simply tries to stop as quickly as possible. He applies the brakes hard and often swerves as well, resulting in a loss of control of the vehicle. About 10% of errors are of this type.

A larger proportion of errors, about 25%, come about because of excessive speed with regard to the conditions. On approaching a hazard the driver does not reduce his speed sufficiently to negotiate it safely. Many mistakes of this kind are made on the approach to a bend or near the crest of a hill. The motorist may enter the bend too fast and then run out of road,

for there are limits to the sideways forces which tyres can exert to keep a vehicle on its chosen path.

Alternatively, the bend itself can cause a sight restriction, such that the motorist is unable to stop within his available sight distance. In most cases the radius of the bend, or the degree of sight restriction, is obvious a long way prior to the hazard, but usually, the reason why the driver was going too fast was an over-estimate of the road-holding capability of his vehicle, particularly on a damp or slippery surface.

There are many other errors made at the decision stage. They include delay in coming to a decision, incorrect overtaking, following too close, wrong evasive action, and changes of mind part-way through a manoeuvre.

Responding

The common error at this stage is to choose the wrong manoeuvre or, sometimes, select the wrong control. A mistake such as pressing the accelerator when intending to press the brake is generally made only by novice drivers.

Confusion over the minor controls can result from the present lack of standardization. The positioning of dip switch, wiper, indicator and horn controls can vary from one car to another, and under stress conditions in a strange car, drivers may revert to old habits and operate the wrong control. In certain situations, such errors may be potentially dangerous for it takes 1 to 2 seconds to cancel the wrong action and substitute the correct one. About 1% of errors leading to accidents involve errors of response.

Reaction times Fit to drive

It is simple to explain what reaction time means, but it can be affected in so many different ways that it is easily misunderstood. It is the time taken for:

a the brain to receive information from the senses (eyes, ears and the sense of movement, as, for example, in detecting the onset of a skid);

b a decision on the course of action required (this may be a reflex action);

c transmission of the message to the appropriate muscles;

d response by those muscles.

The critical factor determining the reaction time is **b** the decision making process.

Reaction time varies greatly with age, experience, alertness and physical fitness. The same driver's reaction times may vary as follows:
0·6 seconds at the beginning of the day
0·8 seconds after a meal
1 second when tired
1·5 seconds after a few drinks or when taking drugs
2 seconds when drowsy or in poor health.

The standard reaction time is usually given as $\frac{2}{3}$ of a second. This translates into the thinking distance listed in the Highway Code, 30 feet at 30 mph, 40 feet at 40 mph and so on. This reaction time is not the same, however, for every driver, or for all circumstances.

Simple decisions

Where there is only one course of action possible, the decision is simple. After continuous practice, it may not be perceived as a decision at all. A driver at the peak of his mental and physical alertness can react in 0·3 seconds, if he is tensed to do so.

Choice situations

In most situations, there is a choice of reactions. The most likely response and the one the driver is prepared for will be the quickest. An unlikely response and one the driver is unprepared for will take longer. The reaction time will depend on the personal characteristics of the driver and the driving conditions, and reaction time can vary from about 0·5 seconds to over 2 seconds. Alternatively, the choice may be to do nothing.

Complex decisions

In complex circumstances the brain must fit together a number of different features of the situation before making a decision. Reaction times here are even longer than for situations where there is a straight choice of reactions.

Reactions in traffic

In heavy traffic the driver must be alert to many different eventualities. Normally, the stimulation of driving in traffic sharpens up one's reactions. Faced with a multitude of choices, however, the driver will respond more slowly than in a less complex situation.

No driver should depend on sharp reactions to keep him out of trouble. Sudden, emergency actions may catch other people by surprise, causing trouble for other nearby road users.

Excessive speed and very close following place a high premium on a driver's quick reactions. Events can happen so quickly that the brain and muscles simply do not have time to respond. The driver's attention becomes overconcentrated on too few events, and when something unexpected happens, such as a child dashing out from behind a parked car, the driver may be unprepared for this eventuality and react too late.

Following a line of vehicles for a long time can become monotonous which tends to slow reaction times. Drivers, attempting to keep their place in the queue, often follow too close behind the vehicle in front. It is easy for drivers to become so unalert that they fail to see the brake lights when the car in front slows down. This may result in a collision when rapid braking is required.

The good driver will anticipate traffic events and road conditions ahead so that he responds smoothly without panic. Good training and experience will produce fast reactions because the driver knows what to expect under different circumstances. This helps him to distribute his attention properly, to make the correct response when necessary. He will also be aware of what effect his actions will have on the safety margins of those around him, and thereby prevent others colliding with his vehicle.

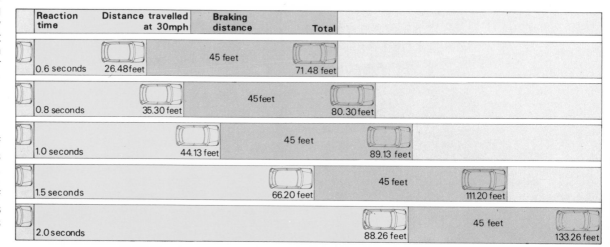

Reaction time	Distance travelled at 30mph	Braking distance	Total	
0.6 seconds	26.48 feet	45 feet	71.48 feet	
0.8 seconds	35.30 feet	45 feet	80.30 feet	
1.0 seconds	44.13 feet	45 feet	89.13 feet	
1.5 seconds	66.20 feet	45 feet	111.20 feet	
2.0 seconds	88.26 feet	45 feet	133.26 feet	

Overtaking

Some of the most difficult driving decisions are required when overtaking. Critical judgements must be made about the speed of the vehicle to be overtaken, the road conditions ahead, the distance and speed of any approaching vehicles and the acceleration capability of the vehicle being driven. The speed of other vehicles is judged by the rate of change of their perceived size.

As the situation becomes more complex and the decisions become more difficult, so the reaction time increases, possibly up to 2 seconds, for any situation with multiple options extends the mental sorting-out process. It would be lengthened still further by distraction, lack of driving experience, tiredness, alcohol, or the awkward siting of controls. As the delay is extended, so the chances of successfully carrying out the manoeuvre are reduced.

Age

Young drivers will usually have fast reactions, but lack of experience sometimes results in an unwise decision. If they make a mistake about a developing situation, they tend to persist in that error beyond the point where an older, more experienced driver would have introduced corrective action. In complex situations they may attempt first one course of action, then another. A delay of 2 to 3 seconds may elapse before the appropriate step is taken.

Reaction time is slowed down with advancing age. Experience can compensate to some extent, but both the under 25s and over 65s are at greater risk.

Eyes and ears

Good eyesight (particularly the ability to resolve fine detail a long way ahead, and good peripheral vision), and sound hearing, are essential for the brain to be able to perceive the road scene correctly and in good time.

Alcohol

The driver's reaction time can be affected in several ways by drugs and alcohol:

a it can blur his perception of moving objects and make stationary objects appear to be moving, lengthening his reaction time because the brain receives inadequate or inaccurate information

b it can produce badly co-ordinated responses, so that the physical actions take longer to perform correctly

c it can produce less caution, so the reaction may be the wrong one

d it can make the driver slow to respond to the unexpected

e large quantities of alcohol will cause tiredness, which slows down the reactions of both the brain and the muscles.

Fatigue

The responses of the brain and the muscles are both slowed down by fatigue. A less-commonly appreciated effect of fatigue is to make the driver give less attention to important events than they deserve.

A common danger for tired drivers is not seeing a bend, driving off the road at corners, or running into stationary objects.

Test your own reaction time

A very simple test of visual reaction time is to make a ruler marked as shown. Ask a friend to hold it up, and, without warning, to let go of it. You must then catch it, and the point at which you catch it can be used to indicate your reaction time. The higher up you catch it the slower you are.

1
2
Slow—you could have slow reactions when driving
3
4
Good
5
Excellent
6
7
8
Amazingly fast
9
10

Daily changes

The body's level of activity varies through the day in a regular fashion. For most people its activity and speed of reaction are highest during the late afternoon or early evening. Its activity lowest around 2am to 4am, when the person is normally asleep, so driving should be avoided in the early hours of the morning, particularly on a long-distance journey.

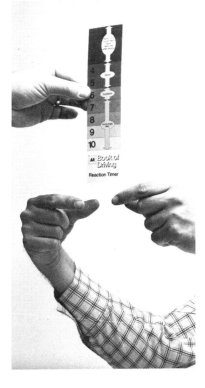

A better test of the problems of choice which exist in driving situations is to use two rulers, marked in the same way. The friend holds up both rulers, but only releases one of them, and, again, you must catch it.

Fatigue Fit to drive

Most drivers will admit they have experienced feelings of drowsiness, yawning and general aches and pains while driving. These are all symptoms of fatigue.

At the same time, it is possible for a driver to be seriously affected by fatigue, yet be totally unaware of the fact. He may not feel tired and may only have started his journey half an hour ago. Yet this short time is amply long enough, in certain circumstances, for his driving performance to have been badly impaired by fatigue.

There are many factors which can bring about fatigue. Drugs or alcohol will make these effects worse than they might have been.

How to recognise fatigue

Sometimes the symptoms of fatigue will be obvious. These will include a feeling of drowsiness and perhaps a feeling of fullness after a meal.

The onset of fatigue may be less well-marked, however. Many drivers, particularly commuters who regularly travel the same route, may suddenly find themselves at a particular spot on this route, without knowing how they got there. This is a warning of fatigue. They must stop for a breather and to stretch their legs before continuing the journey.

Another experience may well be familiar to those who use motorways a great deal. The driver will suddenly come to, and find himself bearing down on an obstruction ahead. He has to take rapid avoiding action, and this is a warning that he is seriously fatigued and must stop for a rest.

A high proportion of accidents

| Early morning low point | | | | | Mid-day peak | Afternoon low point | Evening peak |

6 7 8 9 10 11 noon 1 2 3 4 5 6 7 8 9 10 11

involving only a single car, particularly on long, straight stretches, is attributed to the driver nodding off at the wheel.

The effects of fatigue on driving performance are very subtle and can be quite startling. As time passes and fatigue gets hold, the driver pays less attention to hazards just outside his field of view.

Mental fatigue

It is not always sustained physical effort which brings on fatigue. Stress, worry, irritation and mental tiredness can also be important factors in provoking mental fatigue.

His responses become more automatic and less adjusted to the different situations he meets.

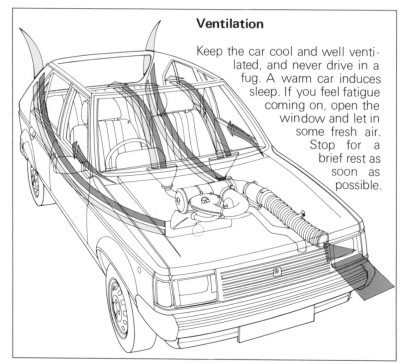

Ventilation

Keep the car cool and well ventilated, and never drive in a fug. A warm car induces sleep. If you feel fatigue coming on, open the window and let in some fresh air. Stop for a brief rest as soon as possible.

A violent argument before you set out on a journey, or, worse still, en route, will leave you mentally and physically limp and your driving performance will often deteriorate.

Even the weather can affect you— the atmospheric disturbance associated with heavy storms can make you irritable, susceptible to headaches and accident prone.

When below-par in your general health you are half-way to fatigue, even before you start driving. Any drugs you are taking, or the use of alcohol in these circumstances will hasten the onset of fatigue.

The mental stimulation involved in driving also plays an important part in provoking fatigue. Most people perform best at a middle level of stimulation. Low stimulation slows down all reactions, whereas a high degree of stimulation cannot be sustained for prolonged periods behind the wheel.

A monotonous period of driving may provide too little stimulation and could make the driver bored and drowsy. This is most likely to happen on an empty motorway, and particularly in fog, or at night when driving along the never-ending swathe cut by your own headlight beam.

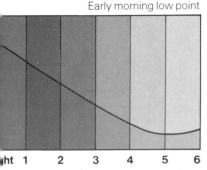

Early morning low point

ht 1 2 3 4 5 6

Deliberately vary your speed, from time to time. Glance in your mirrors occasionally and listen to the radio set to a volume which does not obliterate the noise of other traffic.

Discomfort

Alertness begins with comfort and an uncomfortable seat leads to fatigue. Although the design of car seats is improving, it is, nevertheless, wise to spend a few minutes getting it exactly right to suit your individual requirements. Most drivers agree that in normal driving, your knees should be slightly bent, and the elbows also flexed with the hands resting naturally on the steering wheel. The correct driving position will provide a commanding, all-round view and leave you relaxed, yet alert. The head should be held straight to give the eyes an un-obstructed, level gaze forward, and minimise strain to your back and neck muscles.

Both the thighs and the back need proper, firm support or physical fatigue will follow, bringing about discomfort or cramp. Adjusting the seat back, rake and runner position may help. Occasionally a back rest may do the trick, particularly on a well-worn car seat.

Long journeys

Use the Rule of Three:

Never drive for more than three hours without a break. Frequent short stops are better than one long stop. This interval between stops should be less if you are an inexperienced driver.

Do not aim to cover more than about 300 miles in one day, unless you are sharing the driving with another driver.

Beware of the third day away from home on a very long journey. At this time you will be at your lowest ebb, unwound from the tensions at home, but not yet refreshed. You may be irritable, and any arguments, particularly in the car, increase the risks of an accident. It is better to plan the third day as a rest-day.

Eat wisely

Too little food can be as risky as too much. Certainly, heavy meals before and during a journey should be avoided, as the digestive process leads to drowsiness.

Starting the day without a cooked breakfast, however, can be dangerous because of drowsiness resulting from the lowering of blood-sugar when the stomach is empty. This can happen whether you actually feel hungry or not.

Picnics en route provide a better way of eating. Even after a light meal, however, there is a little-recognised threat of tiredness. Some twenty minutes after the meal, a comfortable feeling of drowsy somnolence will be experienced. This could be dangerous when driving, so take a little physical exercise. Even a gentle walk will be sufficient before setting off again. Exercise tends to accelerate the circulation of the blood and speed up the digestive process.

Noise

Noise is always tiring. Rattles, body-drum and wind noise will quickly set your nerves on edge and induce irritation and fatigue. It is worth spending some time searching out the rattles, checking doors, window seals and panels for proper fit. Move any objects which rattle about or resonate, and alter your speed to get out of a resonance band.

Eye strain

If your eyes have to strain, peering through a dirty windscreen (or dirty spectacles), that strain will soon be transmitted to your neck, body and limbs. Another cause of eye strain is insufficient illumination provided by the headlights. Equally, if you grip the steering wheel too hard, premature fatigue will be the result.

What to do

Understanding the causes of fatigue should help you to minimise the times when it will occur. Ensure adequate rest before starting a journey (avoid starting a long holiday journey after finishing work on Friday). Avoid driving in the early hours of the morning, when general body alertness is low.

Sit as comfortably and be as relaxed in the car as possible. Avoid heavy meals and stop every two or three hours.

If you feel tired, prepare to stop the car. Until you can do so safely, open the window, turn the radio on, talk to the passengers (or even yourself) in order to keep awake.

When your passengers notice the driver becoming strangely quiet, or see him driving erratically, they should realise he is tiring, and alert him.

Similarly, if you see another car behaving erratically, perhaps due to the tiredness of the driver, do not startle him with a sudden horn-blast or flashing of lights.

When you can stop, pull off the road into a lay-by. Do not stop by the edge of the road, or on the motorway hard shoulder. Go for a short walk to exercise the muscles and stimulate blood circulation.

If that does not help, have a sleep. Even a few minutes' sleep can have a reviving effect.

Driver's heart rate

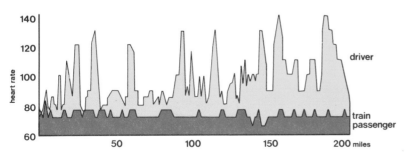

heart rate

140
120
100
80
60

50   100   150   200 miles

driver

train passenger

Alcohol is probably the biggest single cause of road accidents. One in 10 of all accidents involve someone who has been drinking, and this figure rises to over 1 in 3 amongst fatal accidents.

In spite of the danger, drinking alcohol is a social habit which is not easily broken. When the breathalyser was first introduced in 1967, road casualties and deaths due to drunken drivers were reduced. Since then, per capita consumption of alcohol has gone up, so has the amount of traffic, and drunk driving accidents have increased again.

The action of alcohol

Most people cannot accurately judge the effects of alcohol on themselves. They usually under-estimate its effect, particularly on their driving performance. Confidence is increased, but actual driving ability is decreased and instinctive caution is also suppressed.

When alcohol is consumed it enters the bloodstream and it acts as a depressant, impairing vision, co-ordination and muscular activity, and tends to concentrate in the brain and the nervous system. Its effect is quick, although it can take a long time to wear off.

After a single drink, the level of alcohol in the blood (blood alcohol concentration or BAC) rises to a peak 30 minutes to 1 hour later, then gradually falls. When several drinks are consumed over a period of time, the peak alcohol level may not be reached until after drinking has stopped. Following a night of heavy drinking, a person could still have a high concentration of alcohol in the blood by the next morning.

The figures in bold type denote the concentration of alcohol in the blood (in mg of alcohol per 100 millilitres of blood) after drinking the measure quoted.

The blood alcohol concentration can be measured, and is usually expressed as a number of milli-grammes for a given quantity of blood. The present legal limit is 80mg alcohol per 100ml of blood.

Accident risk

The likelihood of having an accident is directly linked to the amount of alcohol absorbed. At 30mg/100ml, the chances of an accident start to increase. By 80mg/100ml, they are four times greater; by 100mg/100ml they have become five times greater, and at 150mg/100ml the risk has risen to twenty-five times greater. That point could be equivalent to five pints of beer or ten small measures of whisky.

How many glasses?

The only completely safe rule about drinking is not to drink when you are driving.

How soon should you drive?

To work out how soon you should drive after drinking calculate your consumption using the chart on the left, then read off the time you should wait from this table below. This table is worked out for an average 8–10 stone person. If you are below this weight, add approximately one hour to the times given. Those above this average weight should subtract about one hour from the times given.

| | driving affected by the alcohol | | | | | | | |
| | blood alcohol level above legal limit | | | | | | | |
Consumption (mg alcohol/ 100 ml blood)	After 1 Hour	After 2 Hours	After 3 Hours	After 4 Hours	After 5 Hours	After 6 Hours	After 7 Hours	After 8 Hours
15	0	0	0	0	0	0	0	0
30	15	0	0	0	0	0	0	0
45	45	30	15	0	0	0	0	0
60	60	45	30	15	0	0	0	0
75	75	75	60	45	30	15	0	0
90	90	90	75	60	45	30	15	0
105	105	105	90	75	60	45	30	15
120	120	120	105	90	75	60	45	30
135	135	135	135	120	105	90	75	60
150	150	150	150	135	120	105	90	75
165	165	165	165	165	150	135	120	105
180	180	180	180	180	165	150	135	120
195	195	195	195	195	180	165	150	135
210	210	210	210	210	210	195	180	165

It is impossible to give an accurate indication of the effects on every individual of drinking a certain amount of alcohol. Its influence on behaviour depends on the personality of the individual concerned. Some become morose and sleepy, while others turn boisterous and talkative.

Body weight makes a big difference. A large man can drink more alcohol than a very light-weight person. A small wife who has had less to drink than her bigger husband may possibly have a higher blood alcohol concentration than he has.

Food eaten before or during drinking can slow down the rate of absorption of alcohol into the blood. Fatty foods are best because fat lines the stomach, but milk is also good. The speed of drinking also makes a difference. The body eliminates alcohol at the rate of about 16 grams per hour. One pint of beer may contain 20 grams of alcohol, so it should not be drunk in less than about $1\frac{1}{4}$ hours. The blood alcohol concentration will then reach 30mg/100ml.

No alcoholic drink is safer than any other, they simply contain different concentrations. Mixing drinks will not make you any more drunk, but it may make you ill. As a general rule, half a pint of beer contains about the same amount of alcohol as a small measure of whisky or a glass of table wine.

Effects on driving

Different individuals will be affected in different ways by similar amounts of alcohol. People who drink only rarely will suffer the effects after only a few drinks. Heavy drinkers may show no outward signs until the alcohol in their blood has reached much higher levels.

The effects on driving are more subtle. At levels as low as 30mg/ 100ml, the likelihood of having an accident starts to increase. By 50mg/100ml, one's judgement is impaired, although one may not realise it.

One of the effects of alcohol is to

increase confidence. Another is to restrict the driver's attention to a limited part of the road scene, concentrating particularly on what seems likely to happen. If everything works out well and the driver negotiates it successfully, the feeling of confidence is reinforced, making him believe he is handling the car better. This phenomenon makes it difficult for many people to believe that drink affects their driving.

The outward effects of drink are usually obvious.

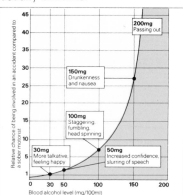

If an unexpected development takes place on the road, however, the driver will be less prepared for it, and also less capable of reacting correctly. This increases the chance of an accident.

Alcohol slows down one's reaction time, and also affects vision. It affects the clarity of vision, it slows down the eye's adaptation to the dark after the pupil has been exposed to glare (from oncoming headlights, for example), and it reduces the ability to distinguish colours. Double vision can sometimes be caused, and, with it, a reduction of the ability to judge distances. It also reduces peripheral vision, particularly when driving over 45 mph.

The law

The 1967 Road Safety Act specified a maximum permitted blood alcohol concentration of 80mg/ 100ml. Any driver suspected of driving with more than this amount of alcohol in his blood may be

stopped by the police and asked to take a breath test. Motorists may not be stopped at random—the police must have some ground for suspicion.

The breath test

An indication of the blood alcohol concentration can be obtained by measuring the amount of alcohol in the breath. The breathalyser bag is operated by blowing through a tube of crystals to fully inflate a bag. Alcohol in the breath turns the crystals green, and if those beyond a marked line change colour, the blood alcohol concentration is probably above the legal limit. The usual sequence of events is shown in the chart.

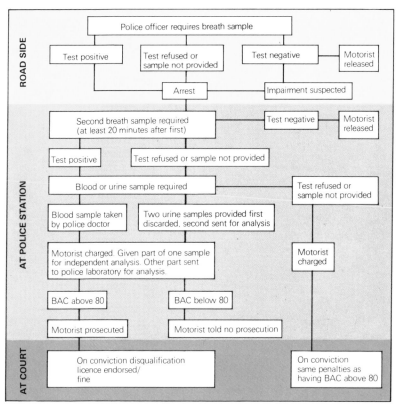

Illness and drugs Fit to drive

Any illness, however minor, will have a bad effect on driving ability. In some cases, even with a very minor ailment, such as a cold, the effect may be unexpectedly great, particularly if any medicine is being taken.

The driver's emotional state can also have an effect on his driving. A serious row before starting out can affect concentration, and bring on fatigue.

Driving licence requirements

Certain illnesses and disabilities preclude the issuing of a driving licence. These include the inability to read a number plate at 75 feet (if glasses are worn for this test they must subsequently be worn for driving), uncontrolled epilepsy (under certain conditions), liability to sudden attacks of disabling giddiness or fainting, any mental disorder requiring treatment as an inpatient, severe subnormality or mental deficiency. In addition, all drivers applying for a licence are required to declare if they are suffering from any other disease or disability likely to cause them to be a danger to the public.

Ailments and allergies: Coughs, colds, flu, hay-fever, asthma, other allergies, travel sickness, any painful conditions.

All will have some effect on driving performance, a lowering of concentration, an increase in reaction time, and possibly effects on vision. No one should drive with a high temperature or similar symptoms. Even a sneeze is a common, but little recognised driving danger. If it lasts for 5 seconds, a car at 70mph will have travelled 106 yards while the driver was almost blind and hardly in control. To stop a sneeze press a finger hard against the upper lip, or slap a thigh hard.

Car sickness is sometimes a problem for children, but the risks can be minimised by careful planning, avoiding rich food, keeping the children occupied, driving smoothly, and taking a break frequently (every hour). Ensuring correct tyre pressures, and soundness of shock absorbers and suspension will help prevent car sickness.

Emotional disturbance: Feeling 'one degree under', emotional problems, anxiety, tension, insomnia, depression.

It is not commonly realised that the subtle but common emotional upsets such as grief, anger, personal and business problems can seriously affect one's driving performance.

A wide variety of drugs is prescribed for anxiety and depression. The use of tranquillisers is widespread and increasing. These can have a marked effect on driving performance, by depressing the brain's activity, inducing drowsiness, fatigue and even mental confusion. Like all drugs, they should never be taken with even the smallest quantity of alcohol, if intending to drive. In certain conditions they may induce aggressive behaviour. Anti-depressants are being increasingly prescribed for mild cases of depression, but can make people take greater risks.

Women's problems: Pre-menstrual tension, period pains, effects of pregnancy.

The combination of irritability, depression and lethargy frequently found with pre-menstrual tension can have an affect on a woman's driving performance and could cause accidents. Everyone should appreciate that this is a time when reactions will be slower than normal and concentration will decrease. Tranquillisers may relieve the tension but should not be taken if driving.

Pregnant women should be able to drive perfectly satisfactorily provided they can adjust the seating position and seat belts to reach the controls comfortably and safely. In the later stages of pregnancy long spells of driving should be avoided.

Aches and pains: Toothache, stomach ache, migraine.

Severe pain, such as toothache, is usually thought to be insufficiently serious to stop one from driving. Yet, this pain together with the emotional struggle to 'keep going', can result in faulty judgement, loss of concentration and poor performance, all of them dangerous on the road. Many pain-killers, such as aspirin or distalgesic may affect driving performance.

Migraine is an even more serious problem. In addition to the pain, visual disturbances and nausea may be produced. Any sufferer from migraine should stop driving when he or she feels an attack coming on.

Drugs to avoid if driving: Amphetamines found in some nasal decongestants, inhalers, cold cures, tonics, appetite curbs, slimming pills; Anti-histamines found in some cold cures, asthma remedies, catarrh treatments, hay-fever remedies, travel sickness remedies, sea sickness pills; Opiates found in cough and stomach medicines.

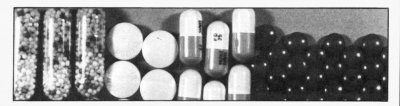

Drugs to avoid if driving: Sleeping pills some common brand names are Nembutal, Seconal, Sodium Amytal, Tuinal; Tranquillisers such as Equanil, Librium, Nobrium, Serenid D, Stelazine, Valium; Anti-depressants such as Marplan, Nardil, Noveril, Parnate.

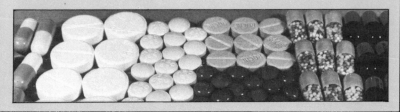

Drugs to avoid if driving: Anti-histamines used in some preparations for the control of morning sickness during pregnancy; Tranquillisers such as Debendox, Librium, Nobrium, Tofranil.

Drugs to avoid if driving: Belladonna used in stomach medicines and indigestion mixtures and tablets, can seriously blur a driver's vision; Anti-histamines used in stomach medicines and travel sickness preparations; Painkillers such as distalgesic, aspirins and Aludrox.

Epilepsy

The sufferer from epilepsy may take out a driving licence provided he has been free from daylight attacks for at least three years, and that he would not be a source of danger to the public. Many epileptics take anti-convulsant drugs, and they should consult their doctor about possible side effects which may impair driving. Certainly, no alcohol should be taken with these drugs.

Nervous disorders

Nobody with a history of disabling giddiness or fainting should drive. Many nervous disorders develop progressively and patients should not decide for themselves, but should consult their doctor, in order to establish whether or not to drive. Those whose condition remains static for long periods may be allowed to drive.

Diabetes

Mild cases of diabetes, controlled by diet, should present no problems for the driver. All diabetics, whether the disease is controlled by diet or by drugs, should keep in their vehicles an adequate supply of sugar lumps, glucose tablets or semi-sweet biscuits, to avoid the dangers of a hypoglycaemic attack.

Heart disease

Anyone who has suffered a coronary thrombosis should not drive for at least two months after they have recovered. Angina sufferers, however, whose attacks are provoked by the exertions and frustrations of everyday motoring, should stop driving completely.

Hypertension should not affect driving ability apart from the side-effects of visual disturbances. Anti-hypertensive drugs, however, can impair driving, and a doctor's advice should be sought.

Orthopaedic problems

Stiff or painful joints, temporary or permanent, such as a stiff neck, can be hazardous while driving if they restrict the driver's normal movements. Backache can be highly distracting, but if its cause is by a bad seating position, a cushion or backrest may alleviate the situation.

Driving after medical treatment

A patient should never drive immediately after treatment which involves an anaesthetic, even in a minor case. A common effect on coming round is automatism, in which the patient appears normal, but is completely unaware of his surroundings.

For certain eye examinations, the doctor uses eyedrops to enlarge the pupil. These give blurred vision and the patient should not drive for several hours afterwards.

Drugs—Ask your doctor

So many different preparations are available, either over the counter or on prescription, that the only safe guide to their use while driving is your own doctor.

Alcohol and drugs

Alcohol should never be mixed with other drugs if driving. Tranquillisers and barbiturates are particularly seriously affected. Every patient should ask his doctor about the likely effects of mixing their drug with alcohol.

Keep fit exercises Fit to drive

Alertness while driving is all-important. The major problem affecting a driver's alertness is the onset of fatigue (see page 148). This danger can be minimised by avoiding heavy meals (although breakfast should never be missed), keeping as comfortable and relaxed as possible in the car, and taking regular rest-breaks.

Morning exercise

The regular morning inspection of the car, wiping the lights and windows all the way round, will get the circulation flowing and wake you up. Spectacle wearers should not forget to clean their lenses. Clear vision is important, not only for good observation, but it also minimises eye-strain and reduces the risks of fatigue.

Rest breaks

Especially on motorways, 'wheel-weariness' is apt to set in quite insidiously, and often quite unsuspected. Almost mesmerised by the seemingly unending ribbon of road unrolling in front of them, your eyes still see the traffic pattern, but your brain no longer consciously analyses the information presented.

Never drive for more than about three hours without a break. Pull safely off the road, into a motorway service area, or a lay-by. Do not stop on the hard shoulder, or by the edge of the road. Once safely stopped, counteract the tiredness of the eyes by deliberately focusing on stationary objects such as trees or houses. After getting out of the car remember to lock it.

Stretch your limbs and back while doing some breathing exercises:

Raise yourself on tip-toe

Stretch your arms above your head

Take a deep breath in

Hold it briefly then relax

Sink back on your heels

Let your knees sag and arms dangle loosely from the shoulders, while forcibly breathing out.

Repeat about a dozen times, and always breathe through your nose, mouth closed.

Take a short, brisk walk (off the road), or jog round the car. If need be, run on the spot for a couple of minutes.

Have a snack. A cup of tea or coffee and a small bar of chocolate are excellent revivers. In less than ten minutes you will feel much fresher, and able to resume your journey without risking the results of fatigue.

Traffic jam exercises

Instead of fretting at the delay caused by a traffic jam, welcome it as an opportunity to freshen-up and relax. Turn on the radio to help pass the time, but choose light music rather than a controversial debate.

A systematic series of exercises can be carried out while sitting in the driving seat. This is far better than drumming the steering wheel with increasing irritation. The principle is to set the blood flowing through the entire system by alternately contracting and relaxing groups of muscles. These then act as a pump to the blood vessels embedded in them.

The programme starts from the feet and works up:

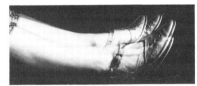

Curl and straighten your toes in your shoes, ten times for each foot. Firmly wriggle your ankles, first up and down, then from side to side. Then rotate them, first clockwise, then anti-clockwise.

With feet on the floor, make as though to bend the knees, then extend them, but without causing any visible movement.

Lift your thighs from the seat, then press them down again.

Grip the steering wheel firmly with both hands, at the ten-to-two position. Without actually moving them, try to bend and then straighten your elbows.

While still gripping the steering wheel in the same position, hold the body in the seat, try to pull it towards the wheel, then push away, but without causing any actual body movement.

Let go of the steering wheel. Clench and unclench your fists, and end up by circling your wrists in mid-air.

Clasp your hands in front of your chest. Try to pull them apart, and then push them together again. Keep doing this, alternately, several times without letting go completely.

Throw back your head and yawn.

Then roll it around your neck in both directions in turn.

Shrug your shoulders, and rotate them forwards and backwards.

When you move on you will be feeling better and more relaxed, while around you others are fuming impatiently and increasing their blood pressures.

6 Living with the car

Living with the car

Good driving depends, to a considerable extent, on having a sympathy for and an understanding of your car. This need not extend to a skilled mechanical ability, but every driver should realise the importance of handling the car gently and without straining its mechanical parts. If it is carefully and sensitively driven, and is well maintained, the first steps will have been taken towards controlling the high costs of running a car.

In today's driving conditions, safety is an increasingly important factor and the design of modern cars incorporates a great many safety features never dreamed of years ago. The most important single item is, of course, the seat belt, which even now is worn less than it should be. A wide range of accessories is also available to help every motorist make his car as safe as possible in all weathers. A contribution towards more relaxed, and therefore safer, driving is made by trying to increase the comfort and convenience of the driver, and a variety of useful accessories can do this.

Seen in the most unimaginative light, a car may be thought of as no more than another form of transport. For many people, however, it is much more than that. It gives greater freedom, and allows them a richer use of leisure time. In most cases, the driving skills required to make the most of one's car have already been discussed in this book. In two specific instances, however, specialised driving skills are required.

The popularity of caravans means that many people must learn how to tow them. This is a skill which needs to be acquired, and it involves modifications to one's normal driving habits. The fact that there is no obligatory caravan towing test does not mean that everyone can tow a caravan without some form of preliminary instruction. The rudiments of the necessary techniques are explained in the relevant section in this part of the book.

A great many people derive considerable pleasure from the wide variety of motor sports. For those whose interest in driving leads them to wish to participate in one or other of these sports, a brief section in this part of the book explains what will be involved.

Economy driving
pages 166–167

The way you drive has a considerable effect upon the running costs of your car. Awareness of economy driving techniques will not only cut fuel costs, but will also save wear and tear on the car.

The safe car
pages 168–169

Modern cars contain a great many safety features, and more are being researched for inclusion in future cars. This section looks at the latest ideas in car safety.

Seat belts
pages 170–171

The widespread use of seat belts can make an invaluable contribution to reducing the number of people killed and injured on the roads. This section explains how to wear a seat belt and why they should be worn.

Safety accessories
pages 172–173

Every motorist can improve his own and his passengers' safety by investing in certain accessories. These can range from restraint systems for children to breakdown warnings and fire extinguishers.

Driving comfort
pages 174–175

A comfortable, relaxed driver is a safer driver. A great deal can be done to increase a driver's comfort, and this section surveys a range of useful accessories.

Winter driving accessories
pages 176–177

The special problems brought about by winter conditions can be overcome to a considerable extent by having the right equipment.

In-car entertainment
pages 178–179

In-car entertainment can be beneficial to the driver on certain types of journey, and it also has great advantages as a source of traffic information.

Security accessories
pages 180–181

As cars become more expensive, and while car thefts increase, the value of good security becomes more and more apparent. A wide variety of different systems is available, and this section provides a general review.

Caravanning
pages 182–187

A series of three double page spreads covers a great many aspects of owning and towing a caravan, from how to select the best model, to hitching up, simple manoeuvring and basic towing techniques.

Motor sport
pages 188–189

Many different forms of motor sport are available, quite apart from rallying and motor racing. The first of this series of three spreads describes these other forms of motor sport.

Rallying
pages 190–191

The most popular motor sport is rallying, and general information is given here about how to take up the sport. Some idea is also provided of the ways in which rally driving is different from normal road driving.

Motor racing
pages 192–193

The excitement of motor racing is captured here by a dramatic account of what it is like to drive round a Grand Prix circuit. Information is also provided for those who wish to take up motor racing.

Basic car care Living with the car

A car that is well looked after will be cheaper to run, safer and more pleasant to drive. The owner's handbook will usually indicate which items need attention at the regular service intervals, and this work can be carried out by a reputable garage or by the owner himself if he is properly equipped with tools and the relevant knowledge. Details of this kind of work are not given here.

In addition to the main servicing tasks, there is a series of simple checks on the car's condition which every driver should make at regular intervals, daily, weekly or monthly. Carrying out these checks in a routine manner will provide early warning of developing faults, which, if repaired in time, will save money and keep the car safer. They will also reassure the conscientious driver that his car is functioning properly. A car which gets heavy use should have the weekly and monthly checks done at more frequent intervals.

Every day

A detailed routine which should be followed every day before driving away in the car is set out on pages 16 and 17. A summary of it is given below:

Brakes: Carry out a quick brake test every time the car is taken out, even if it has stopped for only a short while. This should be done soon after you start motoring, after checking carefully that the road is clear, front and rear.

Lights: Clean the lenses of the lights and indicators all round the car, and check that they are all in working order.

Mirrors: Wipe interior and exterior mirrors clean and check that they have not been knocked out of alignment.

Petrol level: Always check the petrol level as soon as the ignition is switched on. A great many breakdowns are caused by nothing more complex than running out of petrol.

Seat belts: Make sure they are adjusted properly and not twisted before putting them on.

Tyres: Walk all round the car and carry out a visual check that the tyres are properly inflated and not damaged.

Windows: Clean all windows inside and out.

Windscreen: Ensure the windscreen is clean inside and out. Check that the windscreen washer reservoir is full and that the wipers and windscreen washers work properly. All cars must have these items in good working order, by law.

Every week

Battery: The electrolyte level should be about $\frac{1}{4}$ inch above the battery plates. If any of the cells have a lower level than this, they should be topped up with distilled or de-ionised water.

Brake fluid reservoir: Check that the fluid level is up to the recommended mark, and, if necessary, top up with clean fluid as recommended by the manufacturer. If it needs topping up every week, check for possible leaks.

Car cleaning: Thoroughly wash the whole of the outside of the car, rinse and dry. A quick tidy-up of the books, maps and rubbish inside the car will make it more pleasant to drive. A suggested routine is given on the facing page.

Clutch fluid reservoir: Check the level in the reservoir and, if necessary, top up with the recommended fluid.

Radiator: Inspect the coolant level when the engine is cold and, if necessary, top up with anti-freeze/water mixture or water. If the car has a semi-sealed system inspect the level in the reservoir and top it up if necessary.

Oil level: With the car on level ground, remove the dipstick and, after cleaning it, note the oil level. If it is below the maximum line, top up with the recommended type of engine oil.

Tyres: Check that all tyre pressures are correct, using your own pressure gauge. Also check the pressure in the spare wheel. Then go over the tyres removing flints and stones from the tread and looking for cracks or bulges.

Every month

As well as the usual weekly checks, some additional ones should be carried out at monthly intervals, or more frequently if the car gets heavy use.

Battery: Clean the battery terminals and smear them with petroleum jelly (not with grease). Also clean the earth strap, make sure it is unbroken and has a good, firm contact with the metal body of the car, and check the case for leaks. If you have any reason to suspect that the battery is not fully charged, supplement it with a trickle charge.

Dampers: Test whether the dampers are becoming worn by pressing down heavily on each wing in turn. The car should bounce up once and then return to the normal rest position.

Hoses: Bend or squeeze the radiator and heater hoses to check for signs of cracking or perishing. Also check the hose clips for adequate tightness.

Leaks: Any indications of leaks seen on the ground or garage floor should be pinpointed by parking the car on newspaper overnight.

Lubrication: Door locks, boot and bonnet catches should be well lubricated.

Rattles: Try and locate then cure all rattles noticed during the past few weeks.

Rust: Any rust found during the weekly car cleaning session should not be allowed to go untreated for a long period of time.

Tyres: Check the tread depth on each tyre, including the spare.

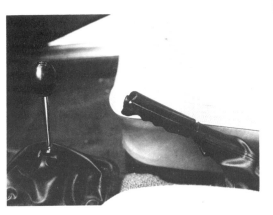

Car cleaning Outside

1 Roof:

2 Bonnet:

3 Boot lid: Wash or sponge with plenty of clean, tepid water, possibly containing a little car shampoo. Most car polishes afford only slight protection.

4 Rear: Wash paintwork with plenty of tepid water. Clean the light lenses with warm water and dry with a leather. Remove stubborn marks with window-cleaner.

5 Front: Wash paintwork with plenty of tepid water and clean light lenses as above. Clean out the dirt from the radiator grille and around the lamps with a flexible brush. Dry them thoroughly. Occasionally clean both sides of the chromed bumpers and coat them with chrome cleaner. Steel and plastic-coated bumpers need only be washed and dried.

6 Nearside:

7 Offside: Wash paintwork with tepid water. Remove any tar spots with a cloth soaked in white spirit, then rinse.

8 Windows: Wash all the windows with clean water (never use washing up liquid or window polish) and a clean chamois leather. Clean the windscreen wiper blades with a clean sponge (not the one used for the bodywork) using undiluted windscreen washer liquid. Dry the wipers thoroughly. Brush out dirt from the window guides.

9 Wheels: Remove caked on dirt from the wheel arches with a piece of soft wood, then wash off loosened dirt.

Inside

Ashtrays: Should be emptied and cleaned regularly.

Boot: Should be cleaned and vacuumed whenever the car interior is cleaned.

Carpets: All mats, carpets and underlay should be vacuumed and stains removed. From time to time they should be removed, beaten and cleaned with carpet cleaner. Any tears in carpets or mats should be repaired. When the carpets are out check the floor for rust.

Dashboard: Clean all dials and switches, ensuring they are secure.

Door trim: Wash, rinse and dry interior paintwork and trim panels with minimum water and a leather. Ensure window winders, armrests, etc. are secure.

Gaiters for handbrake and gear lever: Check for wear or perishing, and replace if necessary.

Interior light: The lens should be cleaned and the switches in the door jambs checked. If the switch is sticky, free by applying a few drops of light oil.

Interior mirror: The mirror glass should be cleaned regularly and any looseness in the fixing should be tightened.

Pedals: Wash and dry the pedal rubbers, replacing them if they are split or worn. At the same time check and lubricate the pedal linkages.

Roof lining: Apply a suitable fabric cleaner very gently onto the roof lining. Cloth linings should be brushed lightly or vacuumed, then wiped with cleaning fluid and a soft rag.

Rubbish: All rubbish, books, maps, etc. which have been allowed to clutter up the car's interior should be tidied up.

Seats: Use a special cleaner for upholstery, never detergents. Dry thoroughly and carry out any necessary repairs. Wipe leather with a damp cloth and dry with a soft cloth. Slide the front seats from one end of the runners to the other and check that the runners are securely fixed to the floor.

Seat belts: Check that all mountings are secure and free from rust; also that the belts run freely and are not badly worn or frayed. If so, they should be replaced.

Steering wheel: Wipe the steering wheel with a damp cloth. Check that the column support brackets are not loose. Ensure that an adjustable steering wheel is securely clamped in the desired position.

Costs of car ownership Living with the car

A proper analysis of all the costs involved in owning and running a car needs to be done carefully, and in detail. A number of factors, in addition to the costs of fuel and servicing need to be taken into account in order to establish the true costs.

There are four main aspects to car running costs:

Standing charges

These costs are incurred by every motorist no matter what sort of car he drives, nor how far he travels per year.
These are:
Road fund tax £50·00
AA subscription £15·00
Parking costs £104·00 (an average of £2 per week)
Total £169·00

Standing charges will obviously increase from one year to the next. The only variation is likely to be in the parking costs, which depend on an individual's movements.

Money lost

The mere fact of paying for and keeping a car means that capital has been tied up in an asset which will depreciate. A full assessment of the cost of owning a car takes these factors into account.

If the money spent on buying a car had been invested instead, interest would have accrued from that investment. At an interest rate of 8% £2,000 would have yielded £160·00, £5,000 would have yielded £400, and so on. This can be seen as one of the penalties of buying a car.

Every car depreciates year by year. The depreciation in the first year

after the purchase of a new car is generally greater than in subsequent years, but the effects of inflation on the behaviour of the secondhand car market make it impossible to give a standard figure for an average rate of depreciation.

The AA Schedule of Estimated Standing and Running Costs uses the figure of 12½% as a basis for calculation, but this will not apply to an individual case. Everyone must work out the depreciation for their particular car by studying the secondhand car market.

For those whose annual mileage is low, it may well be worth investigating the alternatives of hiring or leasing a car. The breakdown of figures given here should provide sufficient information for this comparison to be fully evaluated.

Insurance

The costs of car insurance are an important part of the running cost of a car. The sum involved will depend on a great many different factors relating to both the car, the driver, and any no-claim bonus. A general indication based on some average figures obtained for a sample of popular cars is as follows:

up to 1,500cc	£150·00
1,501cc–2,000cc	£200·00
2,001cc–3,000cc	£250·00
3,001cc–4,500cc	£375·00

These figures are based on average rates for Class 1 policies and make no allowance for no-claim discount.

Running costs

The items which make up this category comprise petrol, servicing,

oil, repairs, replacements and tyres. They vary according to the type of car involved, and the annual mileage. An indication of the likely sums involved can be assessed from the chart on this page, which has been calculated for new cars. It is, of course, only a very general guide, as the cost of each item can vary widely from one year to another.

An intricate schedule of running costs is calculated every year by the AA, and used for detailed calculations by many organisations. The information in this book is intended, not so much for detailed calculations of costs, but more as a guide to the general sums involved, against which every motorist can work out his own expenses.

The contributions made by the different aspects of general running costs are, on average, as follows.

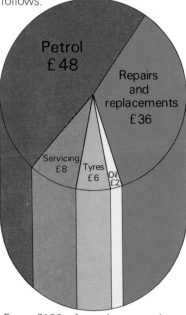

Every £100 of running costs is divided approximately as above.

Monitor your costs

Using the information on this page, it is possible for every motorist to estimate an approximate annual cost for owning and running a car. Against this, a detailed record of expenses should be kept, using the following headings:
Petrol
Repairs and replacements
Servicing
Tyres
Oil
Insurance
Depreciation
Interest on capital
Road fund tax
Parking charges
AA subscription

This will allow accurate monitoring of overall costs, as well as providing information about any increases of any of the items.

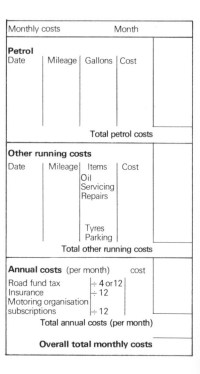

Analysis of running costs

Attention to the individual items which make up your total running costs can reveal possible ways of saving money. In some areas, however, economies can be counter-productive and even dangerous.

Petrol

The price of petrol is far from stable and appears likely to continue so. Every motorist's figure for this item will vary according to the size of the engine, its condition, the way the car is driven and the grade of petrol used. You should use the grade of petrol recommended by your car's manufacturer. It is a false economy to use too low a grade of petrol and it is wasteful to use a higher grade. It is wise to keep a regular check on petrol consumption in order to spot signs of an increase. This will allow you to correct it before much money is wasted.

Repairs and replacements

The costs of repairs and replacements vary a great deal from one model to another and depend, among other things, on its country of origin. This factor is being taken into account increasingly by purchasers of new cars. Economies in this area are generally counter-productive, usually resulting in greater expense at a later date.

Servicing

The costs of servicing are often seen as an area for potential economy, but this should never be allowed to affect the safety of the vehicle. Their level varies from one garage to another and savings must be related to the standard of workmanship involved. Every car must be serviced at regular intervals and servicing costs naturally depend upon the type of car involved. They also become greatest when the car's mileage exceeds 40–60,000 miles.

Tyres

The annual cost of tyres depends on the mileage covered, but it is also influenced by your driving pattern and the type of tyre used. Gentle and careful motoring can extend tyre life quite considerably. Radial-ply tyres, although more expensive than cross-ply ones, can last for up to double the mileage covered. They are either steel or fabric-braced and because they have a lower rolling resistance, they can thus save petrol in the long run.

Oil

Consumption of oil can vary widely, even between similar examples of the same model. Buying cheap oil is a false economy, as is delaying an oil change. Oil must be added to the engine as necessary in order to maintain and prolong its life.

Alternatives to car ownership

There are some situations where it is worth considering hiring a car rather than buying it. There are, in general, three major alternatives when hiring. Short-term hire charges are based either on mileage covered or on the period of hire. Contract hire enables a car to be hired for a continual period of up to three years and it is also possible to lease a car for a monthly rental charge.

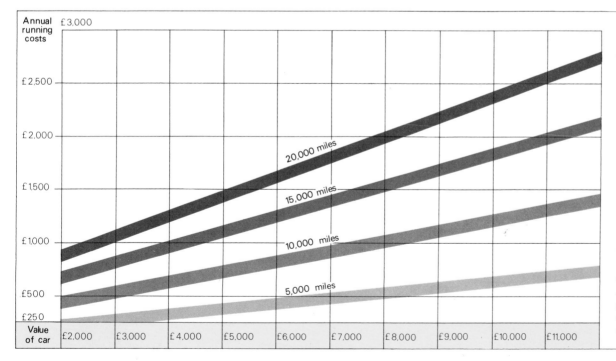

The precise figure for the annual running costs of any car can only be worked out in accordance with the prices pertaining at the time and after taking into account specific factors relating to the car in question. A very general indication of the total annual running costs can be estimated from this chart, however, which relates them to the value of the car. The running cost figure includes all the items described here as contributing to that figure, and the types of car covered by the chart obviously excludes specialised cars of relatively high value. The figures are all averages and are not specific to the nearest pound, but in general this chart will give an indication of what order of expenditure can be expected during the year.

Some of the costs of motoring can be reduced by careful attention to the car itself. Although the overall petrol consumption depends on one's mileage and driving style it is affected by the car's mechanical state, and the regularity and efficiency of the servicing it receives.

It is frequently difficult to decide how savings could be made unless you know how much you are spending on each aspect of running your car. Apart from retaining all receipts, it is helpful to keep a notebook in the glovebox and note down all expenses as they occur. Increasing costs can then be spotted.

Carburettor

The most crucial factor affecting a car's petrol consumption is the state of its carburation. New cars have seals on the carburettor, which prevent any adjustment by the individual owner. A carburettor specialist will have an exhaust gas analyser so that he can set the mixture accurately.

A visual check on the richness of the petrol and air mixture is provided by inspecting the inside of the exhaust tailpipe. If all is well the colour will be ash-grey. If it is sooty-black the mixture is too rich; if white, the mixture is too weak and potentially damaging to the engine's valves.

Automatic chokes

Increased fuel consumption can result from an automatic choke becoming sticky in action, and remaining closed or semi-closed longer than it should. If the mixture is thought to be over-rich, an expert should check the automatic choke control.

Tickover speed

This should be only as high as necessary to give smooth idling. More than this wastes fuel when driving in traffic.

Sparking plugs

An inspection of the sparking plugs will also indicate the state of tune of the carburettor. Sooty plugs are the result of a rich mixture, white of a weak one. A correct mixture is shown by a light brown deposit on the plugs. Plugs covered with a film of black oil indicate possible ignition malfunction or engine wear.

Worn spark plugs are wasteful and, if in doubt, should be replaced. The life of a plug is generally between 8,000 and 10,000 miles, depending on the usage to which the car is put. Regular cleaning and gapping may extend this life up to 15,000 miles, but a 10,000 mile replacement makes economic sense. Electronic ignition can extend plug life to two or three times that.

Ignition timing

Fuel consumption is directly influenced by an engine's timing. The gap between the contact breaker points should be neither too wide nor too small. The automatic advance systems should also be operating correctly. For most people, the checking and, if necessary, rectifying of ignition timing is best left to a qualified mechanic using proper equipment.

Servicing

Regular and efficient servicing, not only of the ignition and carburation, will keep running costs as low as possible.

Doing all your own maintenance may not be cheaper in the long run. If some part of the manufacturer's servicing schedule is missed, or carried out incorrectly, a costly repair could be necessary at a future date.

Many of the simpler servicing tasks are within the capabilities of a relatively inexperienced mechanic.

Checking coolant level, screen washer level, hydraulic fluid reservoir levels and battery electrolyte level; **Lubricating** locks and hinges.

Modern cars have fewer and fewer servicing points which require attention, so many owners should be able to carry out some aspects of car servicing. Garage labour costs can be reduced by carrying out those aspects of routine servicing of which you are capable, and detailing in writing precisely what the garage is to do.

Petrol grades

The belief that engines perform better the higher the grade of petrol used is mistaken. The grade recommended in the manufacturer's handbook should always be used.

Rolling resistance

Binding brakes, incorrectly adjusted wheelbearings, and misaligned steering all increase rolling resistance, and therefore increase fuel consumption.

Tyres

Under-inflated tyres waste petrol because they increase rolling resistance. The type of tyres fitted may also have an effect on fuel consumption. Radial tyres, particularly steel belted ones, develop less friction than crossplies and therefore consume less power. This can lead to a small reduction in fuel consumption. The fact that radials last longer than crossplies also represents a saving.

Spare parts

It is wise to shop around before buying spare parts. Competition in this market is considerable and prices vary widely.

A set of basic spares in the boot can save inconvenience and money. Essential items are a spare fan belt, top radiator hose, and a set of spare bulbs.

Sparking plugs that are worn as badly as this waste fuel and should be replaced now

White, powdery deposits on the plugs show that the carburation is set far too weak

The appearance of black, sooty deposits on the plug shows that the carburation is over-rich

Normal plugs in good condition ought to be checked and cleaned every 3,000 miles

Bodywork

The value of a car can best be retained by taking care of the bodywork, as many buyers are strongly influenced by a clean, rust-free body. If the paintwork becomes chipped, touching-in with paint as soon as possible will ward off corrosion.

Getting the best price

Prices for second-hand cars vary during the year. A periodic study of the market price of cars similar to your own will reveal the best time of year to sell. Timing the sale correctly can make a difference to the overall cost of owning a car.

Economy gadgets

Although there are large numbers of these devices available, the improvement they make is usually found to be only marginal.

Fuel leaks

Any leak of fuel, oil, coolant, etc can be expensive and even dangerous. The location of many leaks may be pinpointed by placing newspaper underneath the car when it is garaged overnight. Sources of leaks are shown here.

Leaks of oil, water, or hydraulic fluid may originate from the top of the engine but will find their way downwards, the exhaust system excepted. As an example, the rocker box (or valve cover) gasket can leak oil which will seep down and you might think that an oily sump is due to the sump gasket failing. The way to check is to clean the engine and then examine it carefully after a run. You should then be able to see where the leak originates.

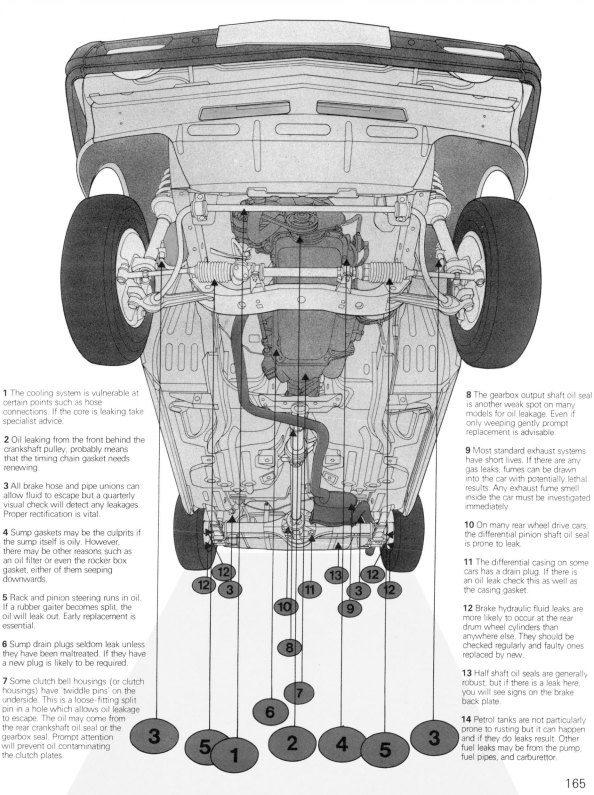

1 The cooling system is vulnerable at certain points such as hose connections. If the core is leaking take specialist advice.

2 Oil leaking from the front behind the crankshaft pulley, probably means that the timing chain gasket needs renewing.

3 All brake hose and pipe unions can allow fluid to escape but a quarterly visual check will detect any leakages. Proper rectification is vital.

4 Sump gaskets may be the culprits if the sump itself is oily. However, there may be other reasons such as an oil filter or even the rocker box gasket, either of them seeping downwards.

5 Rack and pinion steering runs in oil. If a rubber gaiter becomes split, the oil will leak out. Early replacement is essential.

6 Sump drain plugs seldom leak unless they have been maltreated. If they have a new plug is likely to be required.

7 Some clutch bell housings (or clutch housings) have 'twiddle pins' on the underside. This is a loose-fitting split pin in a hole which allows oil leakage to escape. The oil may come from the rear crankshaft oil seal or the gearbox seal. Prompt attention will prevent oil contaminating the clutch plates.

8 The gearbox output shaft oil seal is another weak spot on many models for oil leakage. Even if only weeping gently prompt replacement is advisable.

9 Most standard exhaust systems have short lives. If there are any gas leaks, fumes can be drawn into the car with potentially lethal results. Any exhaust fume smell inside the car must be investigated immediately.

10 On many rear wheel drive cars, the differential pinion shaft oil seal is prone to leak.

11 The differential casing on some cars has a drain plug. If there is an oil leak check this as well as the casing gasket.

12 Brake hydraulic fluid leaks are more likely to occur at the rear drum wheel cylinders than anywhere else. They should be checked regularly and faulty ones replaced by new.

13 Half shaft oil seals are generally robust, but if there is a leak here, you will see signs on the brake back plate.

14 Petrol tanks are not particularly prone to rusting but it can happen and if they do leaks result. Other fuel leaks may be from the pump, fuel pipes, and carburettor.

Economy driving Living with the car

It has been found that substantial gains in fuel economy can be made by adopting a new attitude to driving. These will be in addition to savings made by improving the maintenance and tuning of the car.

Maximum fuel economy is obtained, in general, by driving smoothly in top gear with the accelerator pedal pressed as lightly as possible. When the engine labours, change down.

Journey planning

Road and traffic conditions can make substantial changes to fuel consumption, and a short time spent with a map planning the best route will result in substantial fuel savings.

The shortest route is usually the most economical. Avoid large towns and the times of peak traffic density. City rush-hour traffic can double a car's fuel consumption compared with conditions on main roads.

Travel on motorways is not necessarily more economical, because of the higher speeds involved. There will, however, be steadier speeds and fewer gear-changes than on a comparable cross-country journey, and these factors promote improved fuel economy.

While preparing for a journey, take out any unnecessary objects which may be cluttering up the car interior, possibly left over from winter. Any reduction in weight will help to save fuel.

Starting

Once the choke has been used to start the engine, it should be returned as soon as possible.

Driving on the choke is a great waste of fuel, and most cars, properly adjusted, should be able to dispense with it in a mile or less.

Petrol is wasted by running the engine before moving off, so do not start the engine until you are ready to drive off. Revving the engine when it has just started is also a waste of petrol. It will warm up most economically on the move.

A car's fuel consumption can be expected to be twice as high as normal during the first 3 miles of a journey, after starting from cold, then only slightly better during the next 3 miles. If short journeys have to be made they are best planned, either in a consecutive sequence, or at the end of a longer journey, when the engine is warm.

Acceleration

Use the accelerator gently at all times. It has been said that one should imagine there is a raw egg on the accelerator pedal, in order to achieve better fuel economy. Thin-soled driving shoes provide the sensitivity necessary for delicate accelerator control.

In general, a car will consume as much fuel moving the first 20 yards from a stop, as it does to cover $\frac{1}{3}$ mile at 30mph in top gear.

Gentle acceleration may take a little longer, but it will result in greater economy. Looking and planning

ahead while driving will avoid the need for sudden, wasteful sprints of acceleration. Pumping the accelerator when stationary, or before turning the engine off, wastes fuel.

Slowing down

The most economical way to slow down is simply to take your foot off the accelerator pedal. Good observation of the road ahead should enable most situations to be treated quite safely in this way.

Harsh braking increases the wear on both brakes and tyres. Braking should be started gently, then continued with firmness.

Braking through the gears wastes petrol. It is more economical, to brake gradually and then change gear from top to 2nd gear for smooth acceleration from a slow speed. In all cases, however, the gear appropriate to the situation should be selected.

Every time the brakes are used, the energy built up by the car is wasted, then extra fuel is needed to build it up again. Looking well ahead and anticipating traffic conditions will help you to keep moving smoothly.

On the approach to traffic lights, for example, if they are red, it is wise to slow down gradually; they may have turned green by the time you reach them, allowing you to continue in top gear.

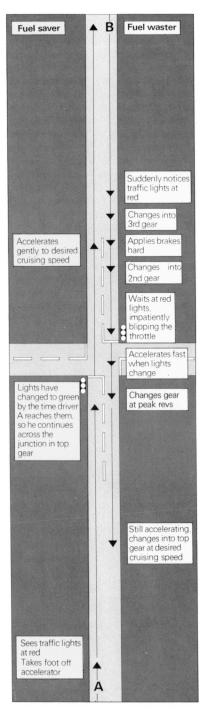

Fuel saver ▲ B Fuel waster

Accelerates gently to desired cruising speed

Suddenly notices traffic lights at red

Changes into 3rd gear

Applies brakes hard

Changes into 2nd gear

Waits at red lights, impatiently blipping the throttle

Accelerates fast when lights change

Lights have changed to green by the time driver A reaches them, so he continues across the junction in top gear

Changes gear at peak revs

Still accelerating, changes into top gear at desired cruising speed

Sees traffic lights at red. Takes foot off accelerator

A

The approach to a set of traffic lights at red where:

Driver **A** saves fuel by looking well ahead and using the controls gently.

The approach to a set of traffic lights at red where:

Driver **B** wastes fuel by driving impatiently and with poor anticipation.

Stopping

If you are stationary, in heavy traffic, for a long time and it is unlikely you will be able to move off for a while, switch off the engine to save petrol.

When applying the handbrake, press the release to avoid wear on the ratchet.

Changing gear

The best fuel economy is achieved by changing smoothly through the gears to reach top gear as quickly as possible with a moderate throttle opening. Gear changes should be made at the right road speed so that the engine does not labour or surge.

A gear change made when the road speed reaches about half the maximum recommended speed for that gear will generally produce smooth, economical driving. Avoid peak revs in each gear.

Overdrive is fitted to some cars, and gives greater fuel economy when cruising at high speeds. Changing too soon into overdrive, however, can waste fuel. Many cars have a five speed gearbox, the fifth gear acting as an overdrive.

Speed

Driving at high speeds is obviously uneconomical. For most cars the best fuel consumption is obtained at around 30mph. The engine's best performance, however, is usually developed at around 50mph.

Driving at a steady 40 to 50mph is preferable to keeping at 30mph. Other road users will probably cut in front of you, forcing you to keep braking, then accelerating.

Great fuel economies can usually be made by reducing the cruising speed. A car in the 1,100 to 1,600cc range will probably give an extra 10 miles per gallon by a speed reduction from 70mph to 50mph.

Hills

It is illegal to try to save petrol by coasting down a hill with the car out of gear or the engine switched off. In addition, the fuel saving is negligible.

Driving uphill, the best economy is achieved by maintaining a steady speed in top gear, rather than changing to a lower gear. As soon as the engine labours, change to a lower gear and use sufficient acceleration to finish the climb.

Where possible, speed should be built up on the approach to the hill so that it can be climbed in top gear involving the minimum acceleration. Avoid driving unnecessarily fast over the crest of the hill, however, or you may be forced to brake sharply to avoid some unseen hazard on the other side.

Corners

Reading the road well ahead and good anticipation will allow corners to be taken smoothly without the need for fierce acceleration or braking. The precaution of keeping a safe distance from other traffic will save you having to brake every time the driver ahead does so. You should not drive so fast round bends that you are forced to brake by an unexpected hazard on the far side.

Keeping the amount of steering to a minimum during a bend or corner will maintain the car's hard-won speed, and also reduce the amount of wasteful resistance through tyre scrub.

Parking

Reverse into a parking space or a garage, when the engine is hot. When starting the car from cold, a clear run out saves some of the time which must be spent in running the car with the choke out, with the resultant fuel savings.

Roof racks

A heavily loaded roof rack restricts the smooth flow of air over the car body, and can increase a car's fuel consumption by as much as 25%. Indeed, driving with an empty roof rack will also waste petrol.

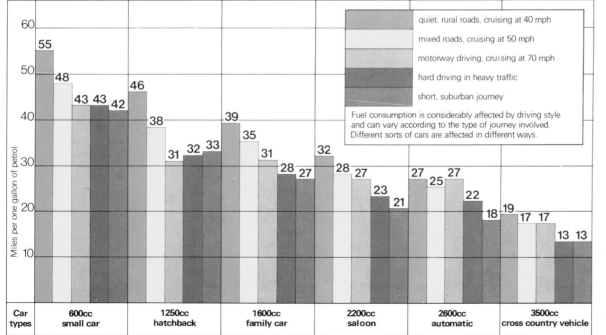

Legend:
- quiet, rural roads, cruising at 40 mph
- mixed roads, cruising at 50 mph
- motorway driving, cruising at 70 mph
- hard driving in heavy traffic
- short, suburban journey

Fuel consumption is considerably affected by driving style and can vary according to the type of journey involved. Different sorts of cars are affected in different ways.

Miles per one gallon of petrol

Car types	600cc small car	1250cc hatchback	1600cc family car	2200cc saloon	2600cc automatic	3500cc cross country vehicle
quiet, rural roads 40mph	55	46	39	32	27	19
mixed roads 50mph	48	38	35	28	25	17
motorway 70mph	43	31	31	27	27	17
hard driving	43	32	28	23	22	13
short suburban	42	33	27	21	18	13

The safe car Living with the car

Every year throughout the world, approximately 300,000 people die because they have come into sudden, violent contact with some part of the motor car.

During the last 10 years, increasing attention has been paid to the design of cars which limit the injuries inflicted on the occupants. Most modern cars give good protection for their occupants against front and rear impacts, and greatly improved protection against side impacts will be introduced over the next 10 years.

Pedestrian protection

As the protection of car occupants improves, so a larger proportion of casualties in accidents will be pedestrians, and riders of two-wheeled vehicles. Research is under way to redesign the car exterior to minimise injuries to this group of road users.

The height and resilience of the bumper is being studied, so that injuries to children as well as adults are minimised. The shape of the car combined with the car's speed affect the severity with which the pedestrian's head hits the car.

Steering assembly

The steering column and steering wheel can be a major source of injury to drivers in an accident.

The steering wheel might break, and the rigid steering column then act as a spear, transmitting the force of a striking object directly to the driver's chest.

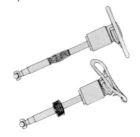

Steering wheels are now designed to deform and distribute the blow over a contact area wide enough to avoid concentrated loads on only part of the chest.

A method of limiting the penetration of the steering column into the passenger compartment is one where the column has a number of flexible joints, which will readily break away in a collision. Alternatively, one element will slide down and over another when the front of the car is struck a severe blow.

In another very effective design the steering wheel boss is connected to the column through a fine mesh or concertina-type tube. When the driver's chest strikes the steering wheel rim, these collapse into a much shorter length tube.

Windscreen

The most common type of windscreen is made of toughened glass. This is cheap to produce, but in a crash it fractures into lots of small, round-edged pieces. These can cause serious injury, especially to the eyes, and the occupant is not retained by the glass, but travels through it. Forward vision is lost except for a pre-stressed, zone-toughened area in front of the driver.

Laminated glass, the other type commonly used for windscreens, is made from a layer of transparent plastic, sandwiched between two thin layers of glass. On impact it will not shatter across the screen but only produce a localised dent, resulting in no real loss of vision.

The car occupants are generally restrained by the windscreen and suffer less-serious lacerations than with toughened glass.

Whichever type of glass is fitted, if the windscreen gets dirty or smeared it becomes a safety hazard. Thin films of fine dust, dirt, traffic haze and tobacco tar on the windscreen all add to the problem of glare.

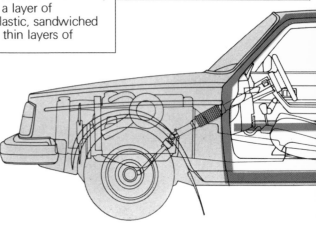

Mirrors

The interior rear-view mirror leaves substantial blind spots, depending on the size of the rear window. A mirror mounted on the driver's door is mandatory on new cars under UK and European regulations.

There is little point in fitting wing mirrors in addition to door mirrors. Wing mirrors can restrict forward vision, and endanger others. If used, they should be so positioned that the driver views them through that part of the windscreen which is swept by the wipers.

Slightly convex mirrors allow the driver to take in a wider field of vision; but convex exterior mirrors, combined with a flat internal mirror, can make judging size and distances difficult. The convex mirror makes objects appear smaller.

Head restraints

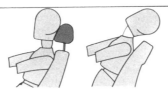

An effective restraint should be stronger than a mere head rest, and set high enough to be effective. In a head-on collision, a properly padded head restraint prevents the rear seat passengers from striking their heads on the front seat passengers or the seat frame.

In the much rarer cases of rear-end shunts, the passengers' necks are pressed backwards over the seat backs. This sudden neck stretching can cause a 'whiplash' injury to the neck vertebrae and the spinal cord. If the head is twisted back through more than about 90° it can be fatal. This injury can be prevented by a well-designed head restraint.

Door locks

During a crash, the risk of injury to those thrown out of the car is five times as high as for those remaining inside. Many countries now demand that new cars must be fitted with anti-burst door locks. These restrain the doors from flying open, even in severe crashes, yet can be opened with ease by rescuers, in spite of the fact that the car may be severely mangled.

Another valuable safety feature for rear doors is the fitting of child-proof door locks. These isolate the interior door handle so that the door can only be opened from the outside.

Blind spots

All-round 360° vision, even with the aid of external mirrors, cannot be achieved on modern cars. Attempts to reduce roof and door pillars and rear quarter panels to the minimum width possible, however, conflict with the requirements of overall rigidity, strength and occupant protection, to which these pillars contribute. International and national regulations lay down minimum requirements of driver vision and vehicle structural strength.

Fire prevention

Fire causes less than 2% of occupant fatalities, and the greatest danger is that of fuel spillage. An electric spark or a hot spot can set off the vapour. In many modern cars, the fuel tank is located inside the crush-resistant zone.

Should the interior trim of the car catch fire, there is a danger of asphyxiation due to the gases given off. Flame-retarding materials are now being included in car interiors.

The car structure

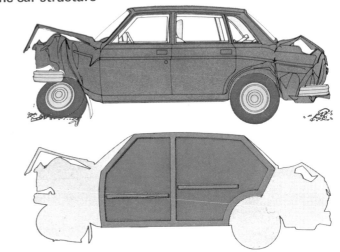

Cars are not made rigid all over, but are designed to have a strong passenger compartment with crushable front, side and rear zones. In an impact, the energy taken up in deforming these crushable zones reduces the forces transmitted to the passenger compartment, and hence the occupants. The human frame can withstand steady pressures much better than a sudden sharp blow.

In a collision between a small car and a bigger one, or a commercial vehicle, the occupants of the small car come off worst. Much research is being done to optimise the structures of cars of different sizes to give the best compatability for impacts of different kinds.

Seat belts Living with the car

The wearing of seat belts by front seat occupants is compulsory in most European countries. It has led to a considerable reduction in both the number and severity of accident injuries, and also the saving of many lives.

What a seat belt does

When a moving vehicle suddenly stops, everything inside it, including the driver and passengers, will continue to travel forwards, unless they are restrained. The car occupants will be lifted more completely out of their seats, and will hit the windscreen or parts of the car interior.

The seat belt is designed to limit the movement of the car occupants as quickly as possible. The webbing stretches in a controlled way to help absorb some of the body's kinetic energy, and the loads generated are distributed over those parts of the body which can best absorb them with the minimum injury.

Wearing a seat belt

Some injuries are caused to drivers and passengers who wear seat belts, but have not adjusted them properly. Any excessive slackness allows the body to move some distance before the belt grips and thus can lead to bruises, abrasions and injuries of the soft organs of the abdomen, and allow contacts with the car interior which may produce injuries.

The lap section of the belt should always be comfortably tight and low across the top of the thighs, on or below the hard, bony area in the front part of the pelvis. Any load will be transmitted into this bony structure, which is quite capable of withstanding considerable shock loads. There should be no twists in the belt and the loads should not be transmitted directly to the abdomen, which cannot withstand them without injury.

The diagonal belt should also be comfortably tight with just enough room for one hand to be slid beneath it. The belt should run over the centre of the collar bone, not across the neck or upper arm.

The buckle should not be over the abdomen, but at the side of the hip, close to the pelvis.

The seat belt must be adjusted tightly because, in the few milliseconds of a crash, the body could easily move forward and hit something in the confined space inside a car.

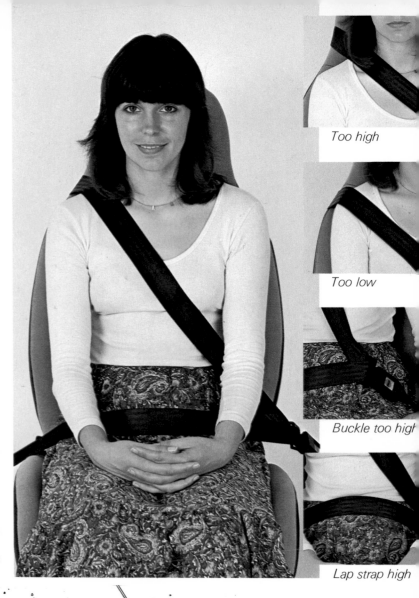

Too high

Too low

Buckle too high

Lap strap high

170

Care of seat belts

A seat belt will not last for ever. It needs to be kept clean using warm soapy water, not petrol or white spirit. The anchorage points need to be checked regularly to make sure they are still secure and free from rust.

After a crash, the webbing will have been stretched. New seat belts should be fitted by a specialist and the anchorage points should be checked.

Inertia reel belts

Any inconvenience in wearing a seat belt is minimised by an inertia reel belt. These belts give a considerable degree of free movement, but they lock the wearer in a safe position when the vehicle stops suddenly.

The important factor in the performance of an inertia reel belt is its sensitivity. An oversensitive belt, which locks on too easily, can be a nuisance to the wearer. On the other hand, a system which locks only under severe emergency braking (upwards of 0.6g), allows too much webbing to be paid out before locking so that the wearer could hit some part of the car interior.

There are three types of inertia reel belts. Some are activated by the forces on the vehicle as it decelerates, some by the forwards or sideways movement of the wearer, and some combine the features of both types.

European regulations on the sensitivity of inertia reel belts allow easy disengagement while the car is stationary on a steep slope. They require a reel to lock at 0.45g.

Seat belt development

The effectiveness of seat belts could be further increased by eliminating the slack in the belt, and controlling the forces applied to the wearer with a load limiting device. At the moment of impact, the belt slackness is tightened up, usually by the firing of a renewable explosive cartridge. As the occupant moves into the belt, it yields by a small, but controlled amount by allowing a progressive tearing of a series of folded-over stretch joints. The shock load applied to the wearer is thus minimised. Should the cartridge fail, the restraint system works as an ordinary lap and shoulder seat belt.

Passive restraint systems

In an effort to overcome the reluctance of many people to wear seat belts voluntarily, several manufacturers are experimenting with various systems which work automatically, without the direct participation of the car occupants.

Airbags: these work by being explosively inflated when a sensor is triggered. After inflation, the occupant is cushioned by riding down on the bag which deflates under his load. Unfortunately, airbags are expensive to install and their reliability in service is still uncertain. The complex triggering system needs to be checked regularly for effectiveness, and this is expensive. The fact that airbags are not very effective in side-impacts, mean that a lap seat belt should always be worn.

Automatic belts: linking the belt to the car door as well as to the other internal anchorage points produces a system which automatically places a seat belt on the car occupant when the door closes.

Injuries without seat belts

Most serious collisions involve impact to the front of the car. Impacts from other directions are also important, but it is difficult to provide the same degree of occupant protection for side impacts.

The best protection is to minimise the side penetration and prevent the doors from bursting open as a result of the collision.

The passenger in the front seat runs the highest risk of injury if no seat belt is worn, the driver is next and rear seat passengers run the lowest risk. All these risks would be reduced if seat belts were worn, and belts are now available for passengers in the rear seats as well as those in the front. The head and chest are most often damaged when car occupants who were not wearing seat belts are injured. Head and chest injuries are the most frequent cause of death in vehicle collisions.

It is sometimes suggested that being thrown clear of the car during an accident is preferable to remaining strapped in the seat. In fact, death or serious injury is at least twice as likely if the occupant is thrown out. Being trapped in the car if it catches fire is also most unlikely. Very few accidents involve fire, and all belt buckles are quick-release.

Seat belts should be worn on all journeys and at all speeds. The risk of accidents is actually greatest in built-up areas. Many injuries occur at relatively slow speeds.

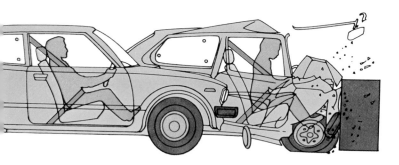

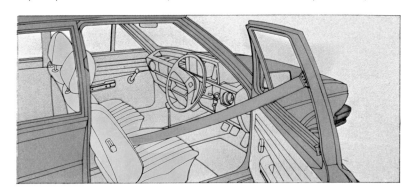

Safety accessories Living with the car

Although thoughts of danger and accidents while driving are unpleasant, the prudent motorist can, nevertheless, acquire several accessories which will significantly increase his own and also his passengers' safety.

Seat belts

Front seat belts have been fitted to all cars since 1 January 1965, so almost every car on the road today should have them. Most cars have belts fitted with spring loaded inertia reels. These allow the wearer freedom of movement, but will lock during any sudden deceleration.

Spare parts for belts are not available, except through approved reconditioning centres, because seat belt manufacture is subject to very stringent BSI quality controls, to ensure proper functioning in an emergency.

Any belt which was worn during a severe accident should be immediately replaced. The stitching may have been strained, and the webbing over-stretched. A single belt can be replaced by an authorised fitting centre. Any new seat belt must bear the BSI 'Kite Mark' label indelibly.

APPROVED TO BRITISH STANDARD
BS. 3254

Rear seat belts

Mounting points for rear seat belts are frequently incorporated in current cars. Their advantage is that they protect the rear-seat passengers from being flung into the front seat or its passenger, during a frontal impact; they also protect the driver and front seat passenger.

It is possible to buy rear seat belts, and one very ingenious type of belt adjusts so that it caters for both adults and older children.

Child safety

In 1977, 9,741 children in Britain were killed or injured as passengers in cars. It is likely that only 10% of children aged 1 to 5 used any safety seat or restraint system.

The safest way for children to travel is properly restrained in one of the systems which has BSI approval, in the rear of the car.

A variety of systems is available. A small baby, up to sitting age (20lbs.), should be strapped into its carrycot, which in turn should be secured in the back seat by a webbing harness.

Children between 9 months (20lbs.) and approximately 4½ years (40lbs.) should sit in a child safety seat. Several different makes are available, although surveys have found big differences between their safety performance. A useful guide to the effectiveness of these safety seats is the BSI 'Kite Mark' label.

It is extremely important that the fitting instructions of these seats should be strictly followed. Parents who have fitted these seats themselves are advised to have them checked by a garage. An insecurely anchored seat would undoubtedly wrench free on impact, and the child could be injured.

Children aged between about 4 years (40lbs.) and 12 years (80lbs.), should wear a full child safety harness. These are suitable for all children too small to wear an adult belt and they have

Carrycot restraint

Child safety seat

Adjustable rear seat belt can cater for both adults and children

Safety play seat

Child safety harness

shoulder and lap straps. Wearing these belts not only restrains the child safely but also encourages the habit of wearing a seat belt.

Breakdown warnings

Many new cars have, as part of their standard equipment, a hazard flasher system for emergency warning. A conversion kit is available for those cars not so

Emergency warning triangle in use

equipped, allowing all four indicator bulbs to be operated together.

Many countries require motorists, by law, to carry an advance warning triangle, although this is not the case in Britain. A robust red, reflective triangle on a strong base should stay up even in very windy conditions.

It can be stored easily in the boot, and, when needed, should be erected at least 50 yards (150 yards on the hard shoulder on motorways) away from the car on the lane it is partially blocking. Different European countries have their own regulations. See page 78.

First aid kit

Many European countries require motorists to carry a first aid kit in the car. This is not the law in Britain, but it is a very sensible idea to carry one. The instructions should be studied when the kit is bought, then kept with it. The kit should be stored inside the car, preferably in the glove-box, rather than in the boot. See page 138.

Fight fire

Nearly 20,000 cars a year go up in flames. Nearly one-third of these cases are due to faulty wiring, and almost as many to underbonnet petrol fires. Other causes are crashes or collisions, welding work, careless smoking and vandalism. It is a sensible idea to carry a fire extinguisher in the car, but it is important to ensure that it is effective. An aerosol extinguisher should be at least 1½lbs content.

Many aerosol extinguishers are filled with BCF liquid gas. This is bromo-chloro-difluromethane, and is most effective. It is slightly toxic,

so if it is used in a confined space the area should be well-ventilated after the fire is out. It can be used also on electrical equipment. It evaporates completely, leaving no deposit, so there is no mess to clear up afterwards. BCF is generally better at putting out petrol fires than dry powder, an alternative extinguisher filling.

Every extinguisher should show its nett weight, so that the contents can be checked to ensure there is enough extinguisher material left.

The extinguisher should be mounted where it is accessible, such as in the driver's foot-well, or close to hand on the transmission panel. These positions are preferable to keeping it in the boot or under the bonnet.

Make sure you know how the extinguisher works before being

confronted with a fire. The contents of the extinguisher should be directed at the base of the fire, rather than generally over the flames. Starve the area of oxygen — open the bonnet just enough to be able to direct the spray at the base of the fire.

See better

The driver must be able to see properly all round the car. The windows must always be kept

clear. The inside of the front windscreen and side windows can usually be de-misted using the car's heater system. Wiping the glass with a damp cloth and a few drops of windscreen wash additive will usually clear off dirt and nicotine particles.

The rear windscreen can be cleared by using the rear window heater. If this is not fitted as standard, a range of different types are available as accessories, but they must be fitted with care.

The external surfaces of the front and rear screens should always be kept as clean as possible. The windscreen wiper blades should be regularly renewed, and the windscreen washer reservoir kept full. Anti-smear preparations can be added to the wash in order to improve its performance. Kits are also available for fitting washer and wiper equipment to the rear windscreen of some cars. Great care should be taken, however, to ensure that they are properly installed and electrically insulated.

Mirrors

Full all-round vision can only be obtained with the help of external and internal mirrors. A mirror fitted to the driver's door has become standard equipment on new cars. It has the advantage that it can be adjusted from the driver's seat, and it does not interfere with forward vision in the same way as wing-mounted mirrors.

In some circumstances, such as when towing a boat or a caravan, wing mirrors may be preferable. These should be of the boomerang type, springing back on impact. Where the trailer is wide, special mirrors are available.

Typical door mirror

Door mirror meeting EEC standard

Electrically adjustable door mirror

The internal mirror should be as good as possible. If the standard mirror fitted to the car does not give a sufficiently wide rear view, it should be replaced with one that does. Some mirrors can be found which give a very wide panoramic rear view.

A very useful type of rear view mirror is the dipping variety, which can be dipped at night to reduce the glare from the headlights.

Driving comfort Living with the car

A comfortable driver will be safer at the wheel than one who is uncomfortable, particularly on long journeys. The driver who does not have to strain forward to reach the controls, whose seat is comfortable, who is neither too hot nor too cold, will be better able to maintain the high level of concentration that even the most ordinary journey requires.

Clothes

Wear clothes which do not restrict movement and which do not make you too hot or too cold. Lightweight, flexible, flat-soled shoes are best, preferably without over-wide welts. An anorak may usefully be kept in the car in case of emergency.

Driving gloves are not worn so often now that car manufacturers cover steering wheel rims with leather or synthetic material. If necessary a steering wheel glove can be fitted, taking care to ensure that the lacing is tightly done up.

Seat position

The range of seating adjustment provided on most cars is limited, because the seat has to suit drivers of every shape and size. The full potential of the existing seat should be explored.

A common mistake in adjusting the seat is to slide it too far back, in an effort to drive with the arms straight. This position is far from comfortable on a long run, and is not appropriate to a production car whose steering requires delicate steering movements by the driver. Conversely, the seat should not be so near the steering wheel that an adequate range of steering movements cannot be carried out.

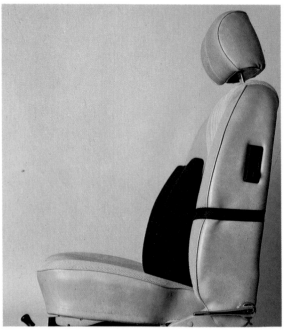 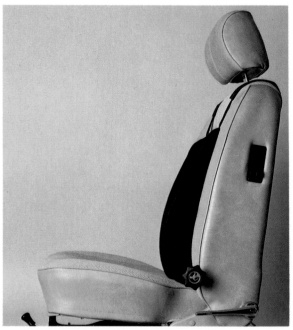

Backrests may help improve the sitting posture

Seat covers

The simplest change you can make to the seating is to fit seat covers. In recent years, however, the incorporation of cloth or brushed nylon fabric in car upholstery has made this less necessary. Vinyl covered seats can be made cooler in summer and warmer in winter by fitting covers of cord or cloth. It is also possible to buy seat covers which have built-in support padding — these improve a seat with an ordinary profile to give more side support.

Specialised seats

Motorists for whom standard seats do not provide comfort and support can choose from a range of specialised seats, which take into account considerations of orthopaedic and comfort importance.

Back problems afflict a large proportion of the British population, and these are increasing. One reason is the increasing amount of time spent sitting down, particularly for some people, who spend long periods at the wheel of a car.

The correct position for the spine when sitting, is in an S-shape, with its base tucked into the corner between the seat cushion and rear squab. Some backrest support accessories aim to produce this effect, but few achieve it.

Some specialized seats have been produced with the competition driver in mind, but these will not necessarily suit the general motorist. Other ideas have been produced for the ideal car seat. These seats include a wide range of possible adjustments as well as good ventilation and heating.

They are certainly expensive, but they may be worth consideration by the driver who values comfort and freedom from backache. These seats are bulky and restrict the space available for rear-seat passengers.

Frequently, the best option is to invest in the seat fitted to the top of the range of your own car. This should present the least fitting problems.

Head restraints

A good head restraint is designed to protect the front seat passenger from either a whiplash injury, in the event of a rear shunt, or impact from the rear passengers during a frontal collision. It should be integral with the seat top, or very securely plugged into the top of the seat's frame. It is also helpful

Specialised seats have a sophisticated range of features including full adjustment of the back and squab height

if it is possible to see through the head restraint, for safe reversing.

Head rests which fix onto the seat back often provide comfortable repose on a long journey, but have no value as head restraints in an accident.

A good head restraint should be fixed sufficiently firmly that, in a rear-shunt, the head and neck will not go back more than 45° relative to the torso. In addition, the head restraint should be adjusted correctly. The top of it should be at eye level.

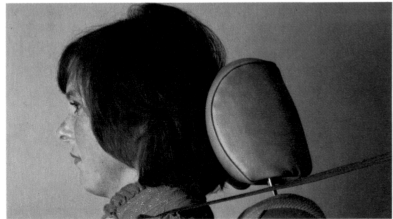

Sound insulation

Driving comfort is, undoubtedly, aided by a reduction in the interior noise level. Good results are sometimes obtained by using a sound-deadening kit but in several cases where these systems have been the subject of any acoustic testing the end result has been a negligible improvement.

The effects of badly worn suspension will be felt in the car's handling and ride. Worn shock absorbers are likely to affect, not only the car's comfort, but also its safety. The only remedy is replacement of the affected parts. Special hydraulic damper kits are available, but it is important to make sure they are the correct ones for your make and model. Attempts to improve on factory-approved shock absorbers rarely succeed.

Other accessories

A great many accessories are available for the enthusiastic motorist. Gear levers can be extended, and gear lever knobs can be found for every taste. Toggle switch knobs can also be extended, and central consoles can be fitted to bring these switches nearer the driver.

The standard steering wheel can be exchanged for a more sporting one, although some wooden rimmed ones can be dangerous. A wheel with a small diameter, however, will make steering excessively heavy at slow speeds.

Fresh air without draughts can be provided by fitting a plastic shield around the driver's window. An air freshener can clear stale air inside the car, particularly stale tobacco fumes.

Winter driving accessories Living with the car

It is usually possible to avert most of winter's difficulties by planning and thinking ahead. Neglect of one's car can often lead to problems, and a few simple precautions will usually remove the worry of being unable to complete a journey. A wide range of accessories is available to help ease the problems of winter driving and these are surveyed here.

Getting started

One of the more basic aspects of winter protection for a car is the addition of anti-freeze to the cooling system. A mixture of 25% of anti-freeze in the water will give sufficient protection for usual conditions of frost, but in extremely cold circumstances the ratio should be increased to a $33\frac{1}{3}$% solution.

Topping up should be done using water and anti-freeze mixed in the same proportions. It is best to leave anti-freeze in for about 2-3 years, and then flush the system and completely replace it with a fresh charge.

Window cleaning

It is always important to be able to see clearly out of the car, never more so than in winter.

An ice scraper is essential for removing frost from the windows, although frosting up can be minimised by covering the windows with newspaper before leaving the car in the evening. The scraper should always be cleaned after use to remove any grit that may have been collected.

An aerosol can of de-icing fluid will remove the need for laborious scraping, although if it is kept inside the car, frozen door locks may make it difficult to reach. A lock mechanism may be unfrozen by heating the key with a match or cigarette lighter.

Windscreen wiper blades wear out after about a year, if they are used frequently. Many replacement blades are available. The tension from the wiper arm spring reduces after a time, so the arms need to be

periodically changed. Wash-wipe kits are available to clear the rear window, and so are rear screen heaters, if one is not fitted as standard on the car.

The screen wash reservoir should always be kept topped up. Special additives will minimise smear and prevent the washers freezing.

A manual screen washer can be converted easily to one which is electrically-operated by means of a simple kit.

Tyres

The most important consideration when preparing for driving in winter is that all tyres should be in good condition, with adequate tread. This should, of course, be the case all through the year.

Winter-treaded tyres are a useful accessory for those who drive in rural areas, where snow, slush or mud can be expected for part of the year. Some of these can be used all year round, but they tend to be noisy on dry roads and wear out more quickly than standard profile tyres. It may be preferable to change to summer tyres once the severe weather has passed. Studded tyres are the ultimate for severe conditions, although their use is illegal in certain countries. They do, however, cause severe damage to the road surface if they come into contact with it.

Detachable chains and clamp-on snow driving aids are not widely used in Britain, but are compulsory for certain sections of mountain roads in Europe. Practise fitting them before driving in snow.

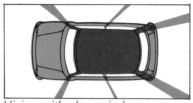

Vision with clear windows

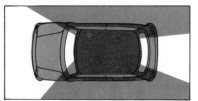

Restricted vision when only small areas are cleaned front and rear

Winter tyre tread may be pre-moulded for stud holes

Studs fixed in tyre

When studs are used only 1·5mm should protrude above the surface

Snow chains in use

The spring steel grip is quickly fitted for emergency use

Lights

Extreme weather conditions can seriously limit visibility. Before contemplating buying additional lights, however, you should check that your standard equipment is working properly. All the bulbs or sealed beam units should be functioning correctly, the reflective surfaces must be in good condition, and you should see that none of the lenses is cracked and letting in water.

Quartz-halogen bulb conversion units make a great improvement to ordinary headlights. These bulbs produce more light for the same wattage than conventional bulbs.

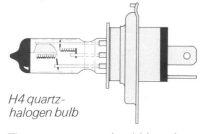

H4 quartz-halogen bulb

The greatest care should be taken when handling quartz-halogen bulbs. The touch of a finger on the quartz part of the bulb can seriously reduce its life, and, if accidentally handled, it should be cleaned with a rag soaked in methylated spirit before being fitted.

Fog gives rise to the most worrying visibility difficulties. Special fog lights, whose beam is very wide

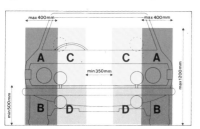

but cut off at the top to reduce back-scatter, are widely available. The light may be white or amber, according to choice.

A very sensible auxiliary light is the rear fog light. A pair of these should be fitted, and all new cars are required to have at least one. They should not be wired in such a way that they come on with the brake stop lights. More details about the fitting of fog lights are given on page 100.

Auxiliary driving lights are now more commonly used than spot lights. They give a wide spread as well as penetration up the road, in preference to the narrow, pencil beam of the spotlight.

Reversing lights are another very useful accessory. No more than two should be fitted, and they can only be used when reversing. The use of a fog or spotlight for this purpose is prohibited. The bulbs in these lights should be no more than 24 watts in strength.

Control of reversing lights is usually automatic from the gearbox. Where this is not the case, there must be a warning light on the dashboard or on the switch.

A wise precaution is to carry at least one spare bulb for each of the main lights. This will save a great deal of inconvenience in the event of bulb failure.

Cars registered after 31.12.70
Fit lights in area A. If in B use only in fog or falling snow.
Cars registered before 31.12.70
Fit lights in areas A or C. If in B or D use only in fog or falling snow.

The range of the dipped head-lights' beam

Switching to main beam improves vision at night

Auxiliary driving lights provide greatly improved vision

In-car entertainment Living with the car

The benefits of listening to the radio or a cassette while driving have been argued over for some time. Listening to music can help a driver's concentration, particularly if the driving conditions are monotonous, as happens on motorway driving or in traffic jams.

In addition, of course, a radio can provide traffic information. This field is rapidly developing, both in Britain and in Europe.

Radio

The development of car radio systems has come a long way since the days of the AM radio,

receiving long and medium waves only, and requiring manual tuning.

Increasingly, sets are being provided which receive FM(VHF), and this is the most usual type in Europe. FM radio has many advantages, particularly in sound quality, but there are areas of poor reception in Britain.

Tuning may be carried out manually, or by using push buttons which are geared to pre-determined wavelengths.

Electronic microprocessors are bringing further refinements to the tuning of car radios. One model

now contains a memory for up to 16 stations which can be located and fastened onto at the touch of a button.

Cassette players

Most in-car tape players use the standard cigarette-packet-shaped cassette. These are more convenient in size than the bulkier cartridge. With cartridges, however, it is possible to obtain a continuous loop, providing non-stop sound.

Refinements available in cassette players are automatic ejection of a completed cassette, and auto-

reverse, which avoids the need for the driver to reverse the cassette, enabling him to keep his attention on the road.

It is becoming increasingly common for tape players to be combined with radios, although, naturally, at a relatively high price.

An additional use for a blank cassette is to include on it journey details, prepared at home in advance of the journey. This can greatly help the driver on his own, or the navigator with many different maps to consult, for example, on a long distance journey, perhaps to Europe.

Tuning is carried out manually on this type of radio

Push-buttons are used on this radio to select pre-determined stations

A great many stations can be selected using this radio's electronic memory

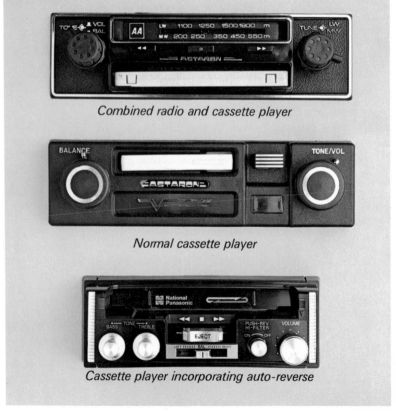

Combined radio and cassette player

Normal cassette player

Cassette player incorporating auto-reverse

Speakers

Good sound quality on the move is obtained by using two speakers, even for a mono system. For a stereo system, four speakers are even better. The quality of the speakers should match the quality of the radio or cassette player. It is always wasteful to buy inferior speakers for an otherwise sophisticated system.

The best position for a single speaker is in the place provided by the manufacturer. This is usually located above the dashboard or in the rear parcel shelf.

For stereo systems, the speakers should be separated, so it is usual for them to be located in the doors. In two-door cars they may be positioned in the rear side panels.

Aerial

The quality of the aerial is most important. An inefficient or badly-fitted aerial will have noticeably inferior reception to weak signals. Reception quality depends more on the aerial and its correct positioning than on the radio itself.

The optimum position for the aerial varies from one car to another, and is usually as far from the engine as possible.

Several car manufacturers recommend specific fitting points for their cars, and this advice should be followed.

The aerial can be retracted for protection against vandals or the damage sometimes caused in an automatic car wash.

Traffic information

Motorists usually receive traffic information via the interruption of a normal radio programme. It is often primarily of local importance, and this activity has therefore fallen within the brief of local radio stations.

The BBC are starting trials of a CARFAX traffic information system, for implementation in the early 1980s. A special receiver would be needed, either added on to an existing set or built into a new radio. When a vehicle enters the area of any of the chain of transmitters, normal AM radio reception would be interrupted for the traffic information broadcast.

Another system, pioneered in Germany, is Automatic Road Information (ARI). This system is already in widespread use in Europe, and is not an automatic system. When a driver enters a particular area, information signs tell him which FM (VHF) frequency he should tune to, in order to receive the traffic information.

An extension of the ARI idea is for traffic information to be stored on tape, and made available for motorists to hear in Motorway Service areas.

Specially-built radios can be tuned to ARI traffic information broadcasts

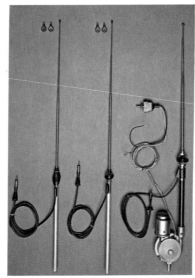

Mono speaker, shelf mounted

Shelf mounted speakers

Flush fitting speakers

Three element hi fi speakers

From left to right:
Wing or body mounted retractable aerial
Roof mounted retractable aerial
Electrically retractable aerial

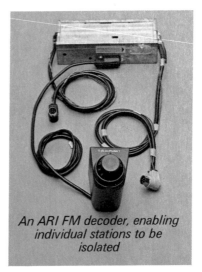

An ARI FM decoder, enabling individual stations to be isolated

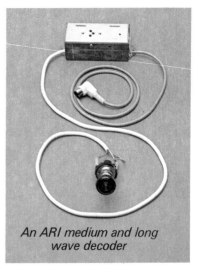

An ARI medium and long wave decoder

'Auto-crime' is a rapidly growing activity, and now accounts for more than a quarter of all crime. Approximately 500,000 cars are stolen a year, and three-quarters of these thefts are by amateurs for joy-riding or theft of property in the car.

Initial precautions

Many motorists are careless when leaving their cars. Doors are not locked, windows are not closed and the keys may even be left in the ignition. These mistakes make the task of the amateur thief very easy.

Door locks and even steering locks are usually not of very good quality, and one of the simplest and most popular anti-theft devices fixes onto the steering wheel to prevent it from being turned. These are easily seen and usually act only as deterrents.

Extra locks

Several different locks of varying sophistication can be added to a car which will make it much more difficult to steal.

Theft of petrol is extremely irritating, and a locking petrol cap is a relatively inexpensive precaution. These should be properly designed to be safe, and should be appropriate for your car.

Wheels are sometimes stolen, and this can be prevented by fitting locking wheel nuts. A sophisticated development is that of magnetically locking wheel nuts, which do not require keys.

Handbrake and gear lever locks are not often found. One system, which must be fitted by a garage, locks on the brakes, and this has been found

to be effective.

Some bonnets have external catches only, and, for these, a bonnet locking kit with an internal release is a wise addition.

Auxiliary lamps are easily stolen, and a few devices to counteract this can be obtained.

Devices to cut off the fuel supply are relatively easy to fit. A tap can be inserted into the fuel line, which is concealed and locked, although easily reached by the owner. A more complex alternative is to fit an electrically-operated valve into the petrol pipeline. This can also cut the ignition or sound the horn.

Alarms

Several different sorts of alarms are available. These usually open-circuit the ignition system to prevent the thief driving away with the car, and they may possibly also sound the car horn.

The traditional design is activated by a pendulum, and the alarm is set off by a slight movement of the car. One major disadvantage is that, unless the sensitivity of the pendulum is adjusted carefully, the alarm can also be set off by a high wind or a passing vehicle.

The use of the car horn as the alarm has its disadvantages. Passers-by tend to ignore them; they are often not built for continuous sounding; the thief can also pull off the wires. It is usually preferable to fit a separate alarm siren.

Other alarm systems work in different ways. Some respond to high frequency vibrations only, some use ultrasonic signals to detect

intruders, some detect a change in the electrical load on the battery.

Identify your car

Kits are available which allow the car's registration number to be etched on to the windows. This may be a setback to the car thief who steals a car for re-sale.

These systems will not prevent the theft of your car, but they will make it easier to identify if the car is recovered and you are able to reclaim it.

The professional thief

About 5% of car thefts are carried out by professionals. They will not be deterred by any security system, no matter how good. They may be slowed up, but if they are determined, they will tow the car away.

Petrol caps With the rapidly rising price of fuel, properly vented, locking petrol caps become increasingly useful.

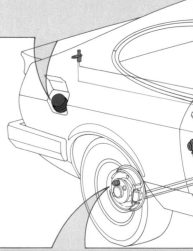

Magnetic wheel nuts The theft of car wheels is relatively simply prevented by the fitting of locking wheel nuts, using one nut per wheel. The magnetic nuts are unlocked by simply touching the nut with the special magnetic key.

Brake lock The lock which can be inserted into the braking system is extremely difficult for the thief to overcome. Its action is to lock the brakes of the vehicle when they are first applied. They cannot then be released until the lock is switched off. Because it is designed to be inserted into the braking system, this device

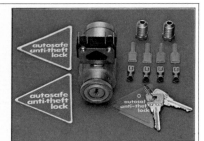

should not be fitted by anyone other than a fully-qualified garage.

Alarm systems It is usually not too difficult to fit an alarm system to the car yourself. An increasing number of kits is becoming available with which it is possible to do this. Many of these devices are extremely sensitive and can be set off by passing vehicles, and even, in some cases, by the movement of the car's clock. Those which incorporate a pendulum must be mounted vertically with the pendulum lined up to swing across the width of the car, not along its length.

The development of alarm systems has been extended to

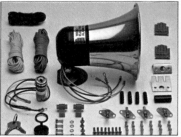

cover the contents of the car as well as the car itself. These work by being connected to sensitive switches on the bonnet and boot as well as to all the doors; any forced entry activates the alarm, and also immobilises the ignition, preventing the engine from being started. The alarm sometimes uses the car horn, although it is better to use a special alarm siren. This is because the horn may not

withstand the load placed on it by the continuous sounding of the alarm, and a siren will also have a more distinctive and louder sound.

When fitting an alarm system ensure that any wires are well hidden from view, preferably by running them through the bodywork channels which will save them from being cut through. Some alarms are activated by an external switch, and this should be placed in an inconspicuous place.

Bonnet lock An exterior bonnet catch can be replaced with a bonnet lock.

Krook lock One of the most popular devices, to deter the casual thief and the increasing number of joy riders, is a lock which links the steering wheel and one of the pedals. It is easy to fix and to unlock, but it will not

deter the serious thief. The lock can be opened quite easily, the metal can be sawn through, or the steering wheel bent to release it.

Steering wheel lock An obvious steering wheel lock may deter the casual joy-rider.

Caravanning Living with the car

The freedom of movement brought about by the car is greatly increased by linking it to a caravan. Care needs to be exercised, however, in the matching of car to caravan, and skill must be acquired in towing techniques in order to make the most of this enjoyable activity.

The right caravan

The most important criterion when selecting a caravan is its weight, as this determines how easy it is to tow, as well as how safe it will be. After this, consider its size, trying to balance the accommodation you need with a vehicle that is not too cumbersome when towed.

Weight

Most car manufacturers recommend that the maximum gross weight of the caravan (i.e. the weight it should not exceed when fully laden and travelling on the road) should be about three-quarters of the kerb weight of the car. The lighter the caravan, the better will be the performance.

The kerb weight of the car is the weight of the car without any luggage, driver or passengers, but otherwise ready to drive. The figure is usually given in the owner's handbook.

All caravans must be marked with the delivered weight of the van (i.e. the weight without personal belongings and equipment) and the maximum gross weight. The difference between these figures gives the loading capacity.

It is important to ensure that the loading capacity is enough for your needs. Most families require between 280 and 450lb (127–204kg) for their food, water, crockery, cooking utensils, other equipment and holiday gear.

The items shown here, for a family of four, weigh 336lb (152 kg).

Examples of suitable combinations are:

Car's kerb weight	Caravan's delivered weight	Loading capacity	Caravan's maximum gross weight
1,792lb (813kg)	1,008lb (457kg)	336lb (152kg)	1,344lb (610kg)
2,688lb (1,219kg)	1,568lb (711kg)	448lb (203kg)	2,016lb (914kg)

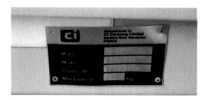

Evidence of weight

The manufacturer will provide details of the delivered weight and maximum gross weight of a new caravan. The maximum gross weight must be marked on the nearside of the caravan if there is not already a weight plate attached.

The same information may be more difficult to find for a secondhand caravan, but it should be obtained. Sometimes the manufacturer can help, given the model name and year of manufacture.

Nose weight

Car manufacturers sometimes state the maximum weight which can be

Nose wheel balance

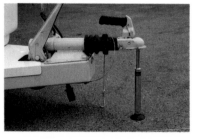

imposed by a caravan on the rear of the car. This is usually between 70 and 120lb (32–55kg), and it should not be exceeded without modifying the car's rear suspension. The correct nose weight is important for stability when towing, and should be around 6% to 10% of the caravan's maximum gross weight. It is possible to measure the nose weight using a nose wheel balance.

Caravan size

Although a large caravan may provide the best accommodation, it will present problems when towing, parking and storing. Caravan body length varies from 9 to 17 feet and more, but the most convenient size is between 12–15 feet.

Width is also important. All caravans are more than 6 feet wide, yet some country lanes can be as little as 7 feet wide. A wide caravan is difficult to negotiate through narrow gateways and in busy traffic. A typical caravan width is 6ft 6in.

The height of a caravan is usually around 8 feet. This means that it cannot be taken into multi-storey car parks, or some open-air car parks with a low arched entrance. Sharply cambered roads will require care to avoid the caravan hitting trees.

Caravanning law A-Z

Brakes The brakes should work automatically whenever the car footbrake is applied. The linkage and the brakes must be in good condition. This applies to all trailers made after 1 January, 1968.

Handbrake The caravan must have a mechanically-operated handbrake that will hold the van on a 1 in 6·25 (16%) gradient. The handbrake must be applied whenever the caravan is detached from the tow car. This applies to all trailers made after 1 January, 1968.

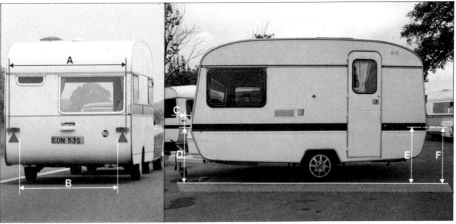

Positioning caravan lights

A *not less than 600mm*
B *not less than 21 inches*
C *not more than 12 inches from outside edge of trailer*
D *not more than 1700mm*
E *not more than 42 inches nor less than 15 inches*
F *Alternatively not more than 1500mm nor less than 350mm*

Indicators Caravans must have two amber flashing indicators at the rear, operating in unison with those on the towing car. The frequency should be between 60 and 120 flashes per minute. They must be fitted symmetrically, at least 15 inches (381mm) from the ground and linked to a device giving warning of failure.

Licence Drivers towing caravans must have a full driving licence. Holders of a provisional licence cannot tow. There is no special driving test for towing a caravan.

Lights Two white side lights must be fitted, symmetrically, to the front of the caravan, not more than 12 inches from the outer edge of the body and not more than 1700 mm from the ground. Two red tail lights must be fitted, symmetrically, to the rear of the body, not more than 42 inches nor less than 15 inches from the ground. An alternative arrangement is that they should be not more than 1500 mm nor less than 350 mm from the ground. Two red brake lights must also be fitted, symmetrically, to the rear of the body, within the same parameters as the red tail

lights. Caravans made prior to 1 January, 1971, must have at least one red brake light. All lights must work in unison with those on the towing car, and be kept in good working order.

All new caravans must have at least one rear red fog light, or a symmetrical pair. They should be fitted between 9·8 inches (250mm) and 39·4 inches (1,000mm) from the ground and not less than 3·94 inches (100mm) from any part of the stop light lens. They should be connected to a warning light inside the car.

Mirrors It is not a legal requirement to fit external mirrors when towing a caravan, but it is a requirement that the driver should be able to see clearly to the rear of the caravan from the driving seat of the towing car. This is usually achieved best by using external mirrors, although there are periscope devices which provide a view through the caravan windows.

Motorways A car towing a caravan must not use the right hand lane of a three-lane motorway.

Number plate The number plate

must bear the same number as that of the towing vehicle. It must also be illuminated at night. The towball fitted to the car should not obscure any part of that car's number plate. If necessary, the number plate must be re-sited to avoid its being obscured.

Parking Parking overnight in a lay-by or on any land within 15 yards of the verge of the road could constitute obstruction.

Passengers No passengers may be carried in the caravan when it is being towed.

Reflectors Two triangular red reflectors must be fitted, symmetrically, to the rear of the caravan. They should be not more than 42 inches nor less than 15 inches from the ground, or, as an alternative, not more than 1500 mm nor less than 350 mm from the ground, and at least 21 inches (533mm) apart. The triangles must be equilateral, with sides between 6 and 7½ inches (150–190mm). If the caravan is over 16ft 5 inches (5m) long (excluding drawbar) it must also carry two amber reflectors on each side.

Road tax No additional road tax is payable on a caravan.

Size The maximum size for any caravan towed by car in Britain is: length 23ft (7m); width 7ft 6 inches (2·3m).

Speed limits A general speed limit of 50mph is imposed for a car towing a caravan, provided it fulfils a given weight ratio. This condition is that maximum gross weight of the caravan must not exceed the kerb weight of the towing car. A caravan meeting this requirement must have its maximum gross weight marked on its nearside, and the car's kerb weight must also be marked in a conspicuous position on its nearside. In addition, an approved 50 sign, 4 inches (100mm) in diameter, must be displayed vertically at the rear of the van. If the maximum gross weight of the caravan equals or exceeds the kerb weight of the towing car, the speed limit is 40mph.

Tyres The minimum legal tread depth on caravan tyres is 1mm. Radial and cross-ply tyres may not be mixed on a caravan.

183

Caravanning Living with the car

Safe and trouble-free caravanning depends on thorough preparation of both the towing car and the caravan. The regular maintenance and servicing of the car will need to be supplemented before it is used to tow a caravan. A new or second-hand caravan will also need to be checked over before it is taken out on the road.

Preparing the car

The parts of the car which will come under extra strain when towing are the clutch, the cooling system, the brakes and the suspension. These items need to be in good working order, carefully maintained and regularly checked.

Maintenance of the clutch should be thoroughly carried out when servicing the car, but it may also need more frequent adjustment.

The cooling system should, generally, perform satisfactorily when towing. If contemplating a journey to high altitudes, or one with long, steep slopes, it is wise to have an oil cooler fitted. When towing with an automatic it is always advisable to fit a transmission oil cooler.

The car's suspension system may, perhaps, be inadequate for towing a caravan, even if it is properly balanced. A long rear overhang or soft rear suspension can lead to a reduction of ground clearance beneath the brake gear at the front of the caravan, and this could be dangerous.

A variety of assisters or special rubber cone springs are available to stiffen the suspension systems of most types of cars. Some cars have load levelling built in, however. The hydraulic dampers may be inadequate, and they may be

replaced with more specialised types. Some of these can be adjusted to cope either with the normal use of the car on its own, or when towing a caravan.

The new caravan

A brand new caravan should come ready to use. Even so it is wise to check that:
Tyre pressures are correct
Wheel nuts are properly tightened
Correct number plate is fitted
Braking system is adjusted correctly
All the equipment is in good working order
Any extras are fitted properly

Caravan maintenance

Regular maintenance will ensure

the safety of the caravan and also prolong its life. Essential points are:
Check all the lights
Grease all nipples on the brake over-run mechanism
Top up the auxiliary battery, if fitted
Check the wheel nuts for tightness
Adjust the brakes regularly and oil the linkages
Check and control rust development on the chassis
Examine tyres for embedded stones, cracks and loss of pressure
Grease the coupling mechanism. Also check and maintain the inside and outside of the body

Winter storage

The best place to store a caravan over the winter is close to your

house, but this may not always be possible. The steps to take when laying the caravan up for the winter are:
Take most of the weight off the tyres by jacking up the caravan under the axles
Ensure good air circulation round the van
Leave the brakes off
Grease the corner steadies and running gear
Securely cover the socket and hitch with a water-proof material
Remove all valuables
Open all cupboards and drawers

Towing bracket

The considerable loads imposed by the caravan when it is towed require a strong towing bracket to be fixed securely to the towing car. A temporary or improvised fastening is dangerous. Make sure your car is structurally sound and that the towing bracket is of a type approved by the vehicle manufacturer for your model.

The load should be spread over the car's sub-frame and the towball should be sited centrally and as near as possible to the rear axle. Fitting of the towing bracket should be carried out by a specialist.

Towball

The international standard size of the towball is 50mm. Some older couplings use a 2 inch ball, and the two systems should not be mixed.

The height of the towball on the car should be between $13\frac{3}{4}$ inches (350mm) and $16\frac{1}{2}$ inches (420mm), and it should always be higher than the coupling head of the caravan when the caravan is level. This takes into account that the rear of the towing car may be depressed with luggage and passengers.

When not in use, the towball should be greased and covered with a cap.

Electrical connections

The standard connection used for towing a caravan is a 7-pin plug and socket. Its fitting is best left to a specialist. With the introduction of rear fog lights on caravans, a second plug will be needed for such things as interior caravan lighting, refrigerator, or similar electrical equipment.

Wiring inside the plug and socket

In addition to the socket, it will be necessary to add a warning light to the car dashboard, in order to detect a fault in the working of the caravan indicators. The additional load imposed by the caravan indicators on the car's flasher unit may cause the flashing rate to be too low, so it will need to be replaced or supplemented by a heavy-duty flasher unit or relay control.

The load imposed by the caravan's brake lights may also require a relay to reduce the load on the stop light switch.

Mirrors

Several types of wing mirror are available for use when towing a caravan. Those which are not a permanent fixture may vibrate, so it is better to fix a mirror with an extension arm which can be adjusted or folded up when the car is not used for towing.

It is also possible to fit a periscope to the roof of the car which gives a view through the front and rear windows of the caravan provided they are not obscured by items stored in the caravan.

Coupling car and caravan

1 Check that the caravan handbrake is on.
2 Drop and clamp tight the jockey wheel.
3 Wind up the corner steadies.
4 Turn the handle of the jockey wheel until the coupling is slightly higher than the towball on the car.
5 Manoeuvre the car so that the ball is as close as possible to the coupling.
6 Release the caravan handbrake.
7 Move the caravan by hand until the coupling is directly over the towball.
8 Releasing the safety plunger, wind down the jockey wheel until the head fits snugly over the towball. Then apply the safety plunger again.
9 Plug in the electrical connection.
10 Switch on car's sidelights and check that the side, rear and numberplate lights on the caravan all work.
11 Switch on left and right indicators in turn, and check that the indicators on the caravan also work, and at the right frequency (60–120 flashes per minute).
12 While the indicators are still flashing, apply the car's footbrake,

Fitting coupling over towball

and find out if the brake lights on the car and caravan light up.
13 Try all the lights again, individually.
14 Raise the jockey wheel and lock it in the highest position.
15 Fasten the safety chain.
16 Release the caravan handbrake, and the caravan is ready to move.

Loading and balance

When the car and caravan are coupled, and while they are unladen, check that they are level. If they are out of line consult a towing specialist who may recommend modification to the height of the towball, or the use of spring assisters.

When loading the caravan, the weight should be distributed evenly over the axle and as low down as possible so as to give the nose weight recommended by the manufacturer.

If the nose weight is too heavy, the front of the tow car will rise, putting greater load on the car's rear tyres, possibly overloading them and the rear suspension. Steering will become excessively light, and the hitch may hit the ground, with damage to the road and to itself, particularly when driving over uneven surfaces, or emerging from a slope to a level stretch of road. Headlights will also be aimed too high.

Plug in electrical connection

Too little nose weight can cause the rear of the car to be lifted slightly, promoting pitching and swaying.

In addition to redistributing the load in the caravan to achieve the right balance, it may also be necessary to move some of the luggage in the boot of the car forward, into the footwells between the front and rear axle, for example.

Most domestic trailers, such as boat trailers, camping trailers, and small loose boxes have to conform to the same regulations as those applying to caravans. There are complex regulations, however, for other trailers.

Caravanning Living with the car

Towing a caravan is a skill which can be acquired only by practice or training. It is quite possible to tow a caravan without either, but it could be dangerous and will certainly be unnerving.

Checks before starting

These quick checks should be carried out before starting a journey, and after every stop, no matter how short.

1 Make sure everything is secure inside the caravan and the doors are closed and locked

2 Check that the coupling and the electrical connector are secure, then ensure that the jockey wheel is securely retracted and the caravan handbrake is off

3 See that all the caravan's lights are working

4 Check that you can see in the mirrors along the offside and nearside of the caravan and to the rear of it as well.

Moving off

A smooth start will take practice to achieve, because the caravan's weight will affect clutch control. Once on the move, however, the extra weight will be less noticeable, and, indeed, there is a danger of forgetting the caravan is there until you need to brake.

Acceleration will be less rapid than in a solo car, but it will be more important to maintain a steady speed. Read the road sufficiently far ahead to avoid the need for sudden braking and allow plenty of time and distance for every manoeuvre.

Considerate towing

Allow extra space all round you

when towing a caravan. Remember that because your speed is restricted to 50mph you will be regularly overtaken, and allow room for overtaking vehicles to come back in front of you. If you see you are collecting a queue of cars behind you, pull into a convenient lay-by and let them past.

Overtaking calls for a great deal of care. Signal well in advance, particularly in busy traffic, pull out in good time, leaving plenty of clearance, and do not cut in too early after overtaking. Be especially careful of bicycles and motorcycles.

Turning right across oncoming traffic calls for patience and practice. Allow plenty of time for the manoeuvre and, remembering the length of your outfit, do not cut the corner too fine.

Do not drive too near the edge of the road: keep about one yard away from the kerb so that the nearside caravan wheel is clear of the edge. In some countries the road edges are ill-defined, crumbly and liable to collapse

especially under the weight of a heavy caravan wheel.

When driving on motorways use the nearside lane, unless traffic is such that you would be constantly changing lanes to overtake. In that case, stay in the centre lane for longer periods and avoid the need to keep pulling out and cutting back. Do not, however, allow a queue of traffic to build up for a distance behind you.

Use all the controls, the clutch, brake and accelerator, very gently, and never jerk the steering wheel.

Tackling hills

Steep hills should be avoided until some experience has been acquired. On all uphill gradients, however, keep up as much momentum as possible, changing down a gear at an early stage.

Care is required when driving downhill because the caravan's brakes only go on once the tow car begins to slow down. It is helpful to change into a low gear and assist the car's brakes with

engine braking to counteract the additional momentum of the caravan. If you need to stop on a slope, hold the car and caravan on the car's handbrake, never on the footbrake or by slipping the clutch. For a longer stop place a chock under a wheel. Practise starting on a hill when conditions are quiet.

Should you become stuck on a hill, unable to continue upwards, it is usually possible to move forward again by, firstly, letting out the passengers to lighten the load. This may be sufficient to get going again, perhaps also giving a push to the car.

If it is still impossible to move, slip back slightly with the car's steering on full lock so that the caravan is at an angle to the road. Get passengers to warn other traffic of this hazard. The caravan's angle reduces the immediate load on the car, and it is usually possible to start off again up the hill.

Stopping

Do not stop on the road if it can be avoided, and certainly never on the crest of a hill or on a bend. If it is impossible to get off the road, switch on the hazard warning lights, and place the emergency warning triangle 50 yards (45m) down the road in the direction of the oncoming traffic.

Snaking

One result of incorrect loading of the caravan, and placing too much weight towards the rear is that a violent, side-to-side swinging motion is set up, known as snaking.

This can also be provoked by cross-winds, particularly on a motorway, going too fast on the level, and, when going downhill, by a caravan which is too heavy for the car.

Initially the snaking may be merely a periodic weaving motion but it must be checked early on. It can easily build up until the car and caravan are swaying out of unison, becoming difficult to handle.

Control of snaking must be very gentle. Do not steer against the snaking or brake sharply, but lose speed slowly and brake gently until control is restored. If you are travelling at a slow speed when snaking occurs, accelerate gently and briefly to straighten out the two vehicles.

Pitching

Incorrect loading of the caravan or weak suspension on the tow car can cause the up-and-down movement of the front of the caravan, known as pitching. It is an unpleasant sensation which can only be cured by correcting the loading. Pitching is often felt in conjunction with snaking and stems from similar causes.

When a pitching sensation is experienced slow down gently.

Reversing

Should it be necessary to reverse the caravan into a tight corner it is better to unhitch the caravan and manhandle it into the space. This is preferable to scratching your own or someone else's paintwork.

Reversing is a skill which is only acquired with practice. It should be carried out extremely slowly, preferably with the aid of someone to guide you.

The first step is to disconnect the over-run brakes with the reversing catch, unless the caravan has automatic reversing. First practise reversing in a straight line. Having done this you should practise reversing round a corner. Choose a right hand corner for preference, so that you can see the caravan through the driver's window. The car must first move very slowly, at right angles to the way the rear of the caravan should go. This will nudge the front of the caravan out and move the rear in the intended direction. Take care not to hit the front of the caravan with the car.

Halfway through the manoeuvre, when the caravan is turning at the correct angle, slow right down, gradually turning the steering wheel to the opposite lock. Continue slowly, making the car follow the caravan round the corner. Finally, straighten up. If the caravan has a reversing stop, this will be released, automatically, when the van moves forward.

There are many aspects of motor sport to cater for those who wish to drive competitively. The public highway is no place for this attitude, but there are many ways in which a driver can realise these competitive ambitions under supervision.

Rallying and motor racing are the most well-known forms of motor sport, and these are described in more detail on pages 190 to 193.

Drag racing

A speed event like sprints and hill climbs, drag racing usually takes place on one of the main runways of a disused airfield. Two cars, each with only the driver, are released in pairs down a straight line of 440 yards. The first of each pair to cross the finish line qualifies for the next run, and eventually just two cars fight out the final.

Hill climbs

These are speed events on tarmac where the challenge is to beat the clock. The course is often laid out in the driveway of an ancestral home. An RAC Competition Licence and a crash helmet are required.

The driver only may be in the car, and each run involves a standing start with the engine running. Cars tackle the course singly.

After an obligatory practice run, two timed runs are usually allowed, the fastest to count for the awards.

Autocross

Autocross events are held on grass, or an unsealed surface, usually on farm land. Amateur and road cars are catered for with some of the classes.

At the smaller meetings, competitors will be started singly at intervals. They are timed over one standing lap, followed by a further flying lap. Results may be determined either by the best time, or on the aggregate of two timed runs. At the larger events, cars can be started in pairs, fours or more.

Sprints

A sprint course is usually laid out on a disused airfield, frequently utilising a stretch of perimeter track. Occasionally it may be held at a proper motor racing circuit.

It is a speed event where competitors challenge the clock. As with hill climbs, an RAC Competition Licence and a crash helmet are needed. A similar procedure is followed in a sprint to that described above for a hill climb.

Rallycross

The sport of rallycross was evolved primarily for television. It involves a combination of loose and sealed surfaces, usually parts of a motor racing circuit. It is faster than autocross, and attracts a more professional approach.

Multiple starts are usual and the result is determined either on the cumulative time achieved over several runs, or by preliminary eliminators concluding with a motor racing type final.

Autotests

Sometimes called driving tests, these are an inexpensive form of sport for standard cars. The event usually takes place on a car park or old parade ground.

A series of tests is laid out for competitors to tackle one at a time. Each test is indicated by posts, marker cones and lines. In addition, the competitor is given written instructions and a diagram showing the directions to take around the various pylons. He will, therefore, need to remember such details, or he will be penalised.

The test is timed, and competitors are penalised, usually as follows:

not attempting a test:	30 points
not performing a test correctly:	30 points
striking a marker:	10 points
crossing one of the lines:	10 points
failing to cross, or stop at or astride a line if required by a test:	10 points

The winner of an autotest meeting is the competitor who completes all the tests with the minimum number of penalties, and in the shortest total time.

Trials

The most popular type of trial today is the production car trial, for which a completely standard car will suffice. A club membership card and an RAC Competition Licence are required.

Competing cars run in different classes and the trial takes place at one venue consisting of a set of sections laid out in a field on the side of a hill.

There may be as many as fifty sections, each having its start line clearly marked, usually on level ground. The edges of each defined section are indicated by a series of marker posts or flags, which determine the twelve sub-sections.

Each competitor drives as high up the hill as he can, without wheel-spinning to a halt. The higher he goes, the fewer points he collects; the category winner is the driver who amasses the least score.

Karting

Although it requires a special vehicle, karting has all the excitement of circuit racing at a fraction of the cost of a formula car.

Karts of up to 100cc may be obtained at relatively low cost, especially second-hand. These can now be raced by youngsters over the age of 11. At the sport's more sophisticated extreme, however, karts attain speeds of 130mph or more on the big circuits.

Karting is a growing branch of motor sport with an increasing number of recognised clubs.

Rallying and motor racing are described on pages 190 to 193

Rallying Living with the car

There must be few motorists who have not, at one time or another, fancied their chances as a racing driver, yet the most popular motor sport in terms of the number of people who actually compete is rallying.

However, as with any motor sport, the rally driver's equipment is expensive. In addition to the basic cost of the car, the cost of specialised preparation can often exceed the price of the car.

Simply taking part in a rally is not cheap. The entry fee, insurance, maps, petrol, spares, and such items as the crew's refreshments, can all amount to a sizeable bill.

The basic rules

For those sections of events held on public roads the normal speed limits must be observed, and the organisers are required by the RAC to adhere to a schedule which will not exceed the permitted maximum average speed of 30 mph.

Control points are set up to provide proof either that competitors are following the prescribed route (passage controls) or that they are keeping within the time limits set (time controls). Competitors are also given a time schedule, showing penalties awarded per minute late at time controls. There will also be a maximum lateness allowed at the final control for competitors to be classified as finishers.

Unlike the road sections which are timed to the nearest minute, the special stages are recorded to the nearest second.

The cost

A used rally car capable of lasting a season of finishes in Club events could cost as little as £1500, but a factory replica fast and strong enough to win an International rally outright could be £15,000 or more. A night's Club rallying costs about £30. An International rally, lasting several days and nights and requiring your own service crew,

could cost several hundred pounds. An indication of the annual cost for those who are lucky enough to get through a season unscathed, could easily add up to £5000 for Home Internationals—and that is without venturing abroad.

The next step

To go rallying you must first join a Motor Club which is registered with the RAC's Motor Sport Division, the governing body in Britain. They can put you in touch with the Secretary of a suitable Club.

Nearly every competitor starts off by tackling a few road events. These rallies call for a much less modified car, there being no special stages. About the only requirements are that the auxiliary lights conform to the law, and that the exhaust passes the organiser's noise check.

For the smallest events, which are only open to members of a particular Club, you only need the Club's current membership card. Where

members of other Clubs are invited to take part (a Restricted Event), you need a Competition Licence from the RAC.

Rally school

The great majority of serious rally drivers concentrate on special stage events where the real battle is on private property, mainly Forestry Commission tracks where there are no speed limits. Getting practice for this type of driving is far from easy. Unlike motor racing the rally school is a rarity, and about the only one is the Ford Rally School.

Rather than having a permanent home, the School sets up a variety of venues. The instructors are all professional rally drivers. Pupils use the School's Ford Escort Mexicos and the cost is only the equivalent of a pair of tyres for their day's tuition.

On the course, instructor Andy Dawson advises pupils to approach corners so that they can drive straight out of each bend from the apex and enter the straight ahead as fast as possible. "Remember, a couple of miles an hour faster out of a bend means a couple of miles an hour faster down the straight.

"If you do find yourself in an unavoidable accident situation, think quickly about how you are going off and how to get your car back on the road. If you go off in a straight line it is quite likely you can reverse out the way you went in. But if you go off sideways the chances are you will find a rut, ditch, or bump which will roll the car over.

"Anybody can drive a rally car quickly, it is how long you stay on the road which matters".

The specialised techniques required for rallying are very different from those for everyday driving. Particular expertise is required for car control during fast cornering on loose or icy road surfaces.

Rally car equipment

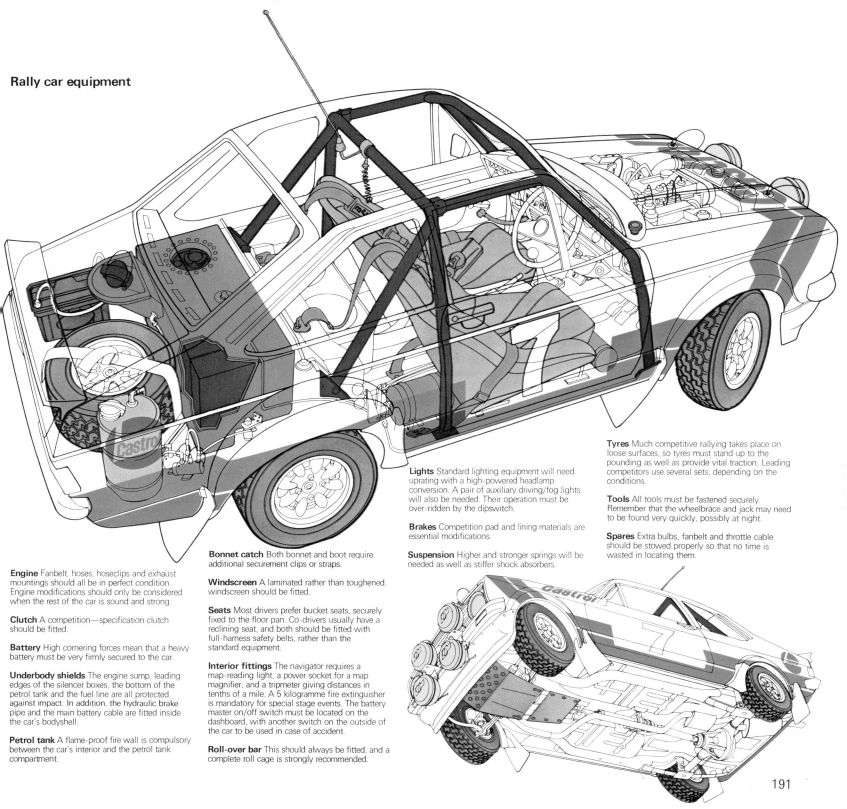

Engine Fanbelt, hoses, hoseclips and exhaust mountings should all be in perfect condition. Engine modifications should only be considered when the rest of the car is sound and strong.

Clutch A competition—specification clutch should be fitted.

Battery High cornering forces mean that a heavy battery must be very firmly secured to the car.

Underbody shields The engine sump, leading edges of the silencer boxes, the bottom of the petrol tank and the fuel line are all protected against impact. In addition, the hydraulic brake pipe and the main battery cable are fitted inside the car's bodyshell.

Petrol tank A flame-proof fire wall is compulsory between the car's interior and the petrol tank compartment.

Bonnet catch Both bonnet and boot require additional securement clips or straps.

Windscreen A laminated rather than toughened, windscreen should be fitted.

Seats Most drivers prefer bucket seats, securely fixed to the floor pan. Co-drivers usually have a reclining seat, and both should be fitted with full-harness safety belts, rather than the standard equipment.

Interior fittings The navigator requires a map-reading light, a power socket for a map magnifier, and a tripmeter giving distances in tenths of a mile. A 5 kilogramme fire extinguisher is mandatory for special stage events. The battery master on/off switch must be located on the dashboard, with another switch on the outside of the car to be used in case of accident.

Roll-over bar This should always be fitted, and a complete roll cage is strongly recommended.

Lights Standard lighting equipment will need uprating with a high-powered headlamp conversion. A pair of auxiliary driving/fog lights will also be needed. Their operation must be over-ridden by the dipswitch.

Brakes Competition pad and lining materials are essential modifications.

Suspension Higher and stronger springs will be needed as well as stiffer shock absorbers.

Tyres Much competitive rallying takes place on loose surfaces, so tyres must stand up to the pounding as well as provide vital traction. Leading competitors use several sets, depending on the conditions.

Tools All tools must be fastened securely. Remember that the wheelbrace and jack may need to be found very quickly, possibly at night.

Spares Extra bulbs, fanbelt and throttle cable should be stowed properly so that no time is wasted in locating them.

Motor racing Living with the car

The flavour and attraction of motor racing can be brought vividly to life by understanding what a racing driver does and plans as he drives round a circuit. Here, a racing driver explains how he tackles the Silverstone circuit. The course runs clockwise.

11 Pits 'In about three seconds I am passing the pits at 155mph or so. I have just enough time to glance at my pit signals on my way to Copse again. A flying lap at Silverstone takes around one minute nineteen seconds!'

10 Woodcote Corner 'The run under the bridge and down to Woodcote is the second fastest part of the circuit, and I reach nearly 170mph here'.

'The chicane to slow cars down as they go through Woodcote and past the grand stand calls for very hard braking. I go straight from sixth to third, entering the right-hand part at about 95mph, leaving at over 125mph'.

8 Club Corner 'The straight after Stowe always seems very, very short. I am in fifth and have to snatch sixth for a second or two before Club'.

'The corners are almost identical but there is more adverse camber on this one, and a nasty bump on the apex which can throw the car off line. A good exit speed would be 130mph'.

Woodcote Corner 10 ▼

1 Start ▲   11 Pits ▲   Copse Corner 2 ▼

1 Start At the start of the race, the cars are moving forward on the grid, all raring to go.

9 Abbey Curve 'Safely out of Club I accelerate all the way through Abbey Curve, not braking and doing about 165mph'. Corner 4 ▶ Becketts

9 ▶

Abbey Curve

Chapel Curve 5 ▶

8 Club ◀ Corner

7 Stowe Corner 'Here I brake hard and go from sixth to fifth and, as long as nobody is right on your tail, it pays to go in very wide as the apex is fairly late. The cars go through at 125mph'.

6 ◀ Hangar Straight

Stowe Corner 7 ▼

2 Copse Corner 'I am in fifth before Copse where I brake and go down to fourth. The corner can be taken at about 110mph but it has an adverse camber and a late apex, which can be rather tricky as you cannot see the apex until you are committed to the line'.

3 Maggotts Curve 'It is very important to get the power on early leaving Copse, there being a longish uphill straight leading to and through Maggotts Curve. I will be accelerating in fifth, taking top and reaching 155mph before having to brake for Becketts'.

4 Becketts Corner 'This is the tightest corner on the circuit and I have to brake very hard—but not until I am within the "100 Yard" area. When I reach the right speed to take the corner, I go straight from sixth to fourth'.

5 Chapel Curve 'Exit speed from Becketts is critical as it determines your eventual speed down Hangar Straight. If I do a good Becketts, Chapel will be taken in fifth at about 140mph without lifting off'.

6 Hangar Straight 'Almost at the start of the straight I am in sixth, and my engine will be pulling its maximum of 12,000rpm just before the "100 Yard" board'.

'Even though the fastest cars will be doing more than 175mph on the straight, the ten seconds or so it allows is very useful for having a look at your instruments'.

3 Maggotts Curve ◀

Learning to race

The techniques used by a racing driver in tackling a circuit are important for those interested in taking up the sport. They also have relevance, however, for the ordinary motorist interested in safer road driving.

For those interested in learning to be a racing driver there are basically two ways to start. It is possible simply to take part in races and to pick up the skills as you go along.

Competition cars are now sophisticated and expensive, however, so mistakes can be costly. Nevertheless, the essential requirements are:

1 a full driving licence;

2 membership of one of the racing-orientated clubs (such as the British Automobile Racing Club);

3 a Competition Licence from the RAC, and their Medical Certificate;

4 a car which complies with the RAC basic vehicle regulations for racing.

It is a wise investment, however, to consider attending one of the racing schools. Many leading drivers, including World Champions like Emerson Fittipaldi and James Hunt, went to racing schools.

Racing schools

Two organisations which have been running racing driving schools for several years are the Jim Russell Racing Drivers' School at Silverstone (Northamptonshire), Mallory Park (Leicestershire) and Snetterton (Norfolk), and Brands Hatch Racing (Kent). The schools plan their training as follows:

Jim Russell International Racing Drivers' School

Trial lesson: Each pupil drives the school's single-seater racing cars in two sessions on a marked out course for braking and gear changing. If his standard is suitable he is invited to enrol in the school.

Stage one: The lessons give detailed instructions on the correct braking and gear changing points, as well as the correct line to take, using the major corners of the circuit. Each pupil's performance is then analysed in the classroom.

Stage two: Twelve further lessons of eight or twelve laps each include three lapping sessions at a progressively increasing engine rev limit. During these sessions, instructors situated on the corners check each pupil's braking, gear changing and line. Lap times are recorded. Skid training is also available during this stage.

Drivers' racing club: After completion of the full course, pupils may join the school's own club. This is registered under the RAC and runs its own race meetings. The school provides the cars and the helmets and visors.

Brands Hatch Racing

Using your own car: A one day session of 17 laps, either solo, or with an instructor travelling with you for three of the laps. An instructor could drive your car and advise you for five of your laps at an extra charge.

The safe condition of your car is your own responsibility, and a crash helmet must also be worn (these can be hired from the school).

Using school cars: It is possible to use one of the school's racing Ford Escorts for an exploratory drive, driven either by the instructor or by yourself.

A more serious introduction to motor racing is provided by the initial trial. After a blackboard briefing, an instructor accompanies you for three laps of the track, noting those aspects of your driving technique which need correction and improvement. This is not an assessment of your potential as a racing driver. If your driving is basically sound, you may then take one of the single-seater Formula Fords for five untimed laps. The instructor is interested only in whether you can drive safely, sensibly and according to instructions. He is not interested in speed.

Drivers' club: Once a pupil has completed the initial trial, and obtained clearance from his instructor, he may take part in one of the races organised by the drivers' club, exclusively for pupils. Meetings take place every weekend.

Most people, however, require several instruction sessions before taking part in their first race. The full training course involves five steps. In order to move through these steps, candidates must better lap times set by the instructor on the day.

Learning to drive

The process of learning to drive should be seen as a means of acquiring the skills of driving competently, rather than merely a way to pass the official driving test. The driving test itself should be seen as no more than a milestone along a continuing path of learning. Driving lessons are just a beginning albeit a very important one. Even when you are a certified driver you can improve your driving.

Section contents

The material in this section will form a comprehensive adjunct to a formal course of instruction as given by anyone else acting as an instructor, whether they are providing a full course of driving lessons, or simply accompanying the learner driver on a practice session. All the information should be related to what has been taught.

Instruction
pages 198–199

Good instruction is important in order to establish sound driving habits and pass the driving test.

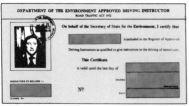

Driving position
pages 200–201

A good and comfortable driving position is one of the first things to establish.

Car cockpit
pages 202–203

The learner should become familiar with the functions of all the controls in the car cockpit.

Gears and handbrake
pages 204–205

The way these controls work must be understood before the car is set in motion.

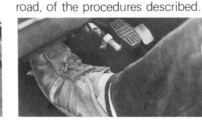

Starting off
pages 206–207

A regular routine should be followed every time you prepare to start off in the car.

Steering and stopping
pages 208–209

The most basic and essential control movements when learning to drive are fully explained here.

Practice 1
pages 210–211

Suggestions are given for a variety of practice manoeuvres, off the road, of the procedures described.

Turning
pages 212–213

Cornering techniques, and what to do when turning left and right are the basis of this section.

Hills
pages 214–215

Anxieties about the problems of driving on hills should quickly be dispelled with this material.

Reversing
pages 216–217

The use of reverse gear is explained for reversing round corners, and for turning.

Use of speed
pages 218–219

Several considerations are used to determine the appropriate speed for different circumstances.

The Highway Code
pages 220–221

The central importance of this publication is brought out through examples and some test questions.

Proper teaching

Proper teaching will give you a sound foundation upon which to build, but if the tuition is inexpert you are likely to pick up faults without realising you are doing so, and will have great difficulty in eradicating them later. The test is designed to find out if you are competent to drive under normal road conditions without supervision. Good teaching will also help establish good, safe driving habits which will influence you up to the driving test and beyond it for the rest of your motoring career.

Other road users
pages 222–223

Consideration must always be shown to other road users, from the earliest days on the road.

Signalling
pages 224–225

The learner must soon become familiar with the different signals in use on the road.

Practice 2
pages 226–227

These pages review ways of practising basic aspects of driving which have now been learned.

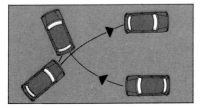

Observation
pages 228–229

Every learner driver should study and develop good observation to ensure safer driving.

Corners, junctions, roundabouts
pages 230–231

The more complex road environments can now be tackled.

Overtaking
pages 232–233

Overtaking skill can be acquired if a few basic considerations are borne in mind.

Practice 3
pages 234–235

The final practice suggestions revise and consolidate all that has gone before.

Test yourself
pages 236–237

A wide-ranging quiz enables every learner to check any gaps in his driving knowledge.

The driving test
pages 238–239

A review of what the driving test involves and what happens before, during, and after the test.

The test

During the 25 minutes or so which the test lasts, the examiner will be looking for general ability, car control, and safety, not special expertise. The Department of Transport chooses its personnel very carefully, giving strict training at the Driving Establishment at Cardington, and the examiners have a proper understanding of the job and the problems the test poses for many of the candidates.

When you receive your Provisional Driving Licence, you will also receive a booklet entitled 'The Driving Test and How to Pass', which is a good indication of the Department's attitude to the test and its desire you should pass first time. This booklet, known to the profession as 'DL 68', contains a great deal of very sensible guidance.

Practice

One way in which relatives and friends may be of help is to accompany you if you wish to practise provided, of course, they hold full licences. You will find this more useful after you have had several lessons and are becoming more accustomed to the controls and the car's handling, rather than early on.

It is important, however, that anyone accompanying you when you practise should not try to teach, because this may very well conflict with any professional instruction you have received. You should first get used to being behind the wheel, with your feet on the pedals. If you do this on private ground there is no need to have a qualified supervisor with you. But do not start the engine or try to drive at this stage.

Instruction Learning to drive

The selection of your driving instructor is of great importance. There may be a temptation to rely on a friend or relative, but there are drawbacks in this arrangement. Because the amateur has had no instruction it is likely there will be no set programme to follow. This tends to result in haphazard explanations which may confuse the beginner.

The professional instructor has the advantage of being a comparative stranger and is less likely to become involved in an argument with a pupil. He will, therefore, be better able to preserve a calm manner when giving instruction which will help the pupil.

Choosing a school

The best way to select a school is through the personal recommendation of someone you know and who has used their services. Failing this, look for one which is a member of a responsible organisation such as the Motor Schools Association.

When trying to find a driving school the first place to look is in your local classified telephone directory. It is better to arrange with the school to start your lessons from their premises rather than have them pick you up, since then you can be sure of getting the full time for your money. Always read the small print on the contract.

Driving schools

Driving schools vary in size and scope. Two-car schools are quite common, but one-car schools are probably in the majority, while some have several branches. Each branch should be regarded as a separate school since it is the local supervision which is of prime importance to its success.

Some schools augment practical driving lessons with indoor instruction in a classroom. Some members of the public regard this as a waste of time, but whilst it is true you can only learn to drive in a car, it is also true that you can learn to understand a great deal about driving in the classroom, provided the lessons are objective and properly linked with the practical driving programme.

A good driving school will teach you more than merely how to pass the driving test. As well as providing you with knowledge about driving on the road and the skills of controlling and handling a car, it should also teach you good and safe attitudes to driving which will influence you always.

All schools must employ ADIs. (Approved Driving Instructors), but they may also have a trainee or two on the staff. However, no school is permitted, by law, to have more than one trainee for each ADI employed, and every trainee must be properly supervised.

Ask to see the Department of Transport certificate of the instructor who is going to teach you. If he proves to be a trainee and you prefer a qualified teacher, say so and refuse lessons unless the school meets your wishes.

Do not be guided by what appear to be high prices, nor tempted by low ones; look for the qualifications first. First impressions are important. A tidy office, prompt and efficient reception, and a clean, well tended car all point to a well run school.

Many schools have sales ploys to try to attract business. Some will offer a free half hour trial lesson, others a full hour at half price, and there are still others with different persuasions to get you to take up a course of lessons. These business methods are perfectly

---

Reading Material

A wide range of material is published to help the learner driver but there is a basic reading list which every learner should possess.

Your driving test and how to pass (Department of Transport) This is code-numbered DL68 and is issued free with your Provisional Driving Licence. It explains how to prepare and apply for the test, the knowledge and ability you will be expected to acquire and information about what happens after the test.

The Highway Code (HMSO) Every applicant for the driving test will be tested on his knowledge of the Highway Code so it is wise to buy a copy and study it, even before starting driving lessons.

Driving (HMSO) All the driving techniques needed by the learner driver, and, indeed, by any driver are explained and illustrated in this book. It cannot replace practical instruction, but it is a useful reference book for revising or explaining what you have been taught.

A comprehensive review of all the books available on the subject of driving is given on pages 250–251.

legitimate and need not reflect adversely on the school's efficiency but, as with all special offers, look closely at 'the small print', and make sure you are not letting yourself in for something for which you did not bargain.

The cost

Fees vary a little from school to school but not by a great deal, so the total cost of bringing your driving standards up to or, preferably, above test level will simply depend upon the number of lessons you need to have. Regular practice, with a friend or relative to comply with the law's requirement that a learner driver must have a qualified passenger, could help reduce the number of lessons you will need. But the friend or relative should not try to alter a technique you have been taught or the practice sessions could become a hindrance rather than a help.

It is said that most people will need $1\frac{1}{4}$ as many lessons as their years of age, but this is a very rough guide indeed. It is true that as you grow older your reactions become slower so you have to learn to act earlier through more mature judgment, and this is likely to extend the number of lessons you will need. However, so much depends on the individual and his aptitudes that it is very difficult to predict how long it will take to learn to drive. Your instructor will soon be able to advise you.

Younger pupils who are impatient to get on may sometimes fail to fully absorb what the instructor is trying to teach them. This may mean that more lessons are needed. Everything the instructor says during the lessons is intended to help you improve your driving, so pay full attention to what he or she is saying and try to commit it to memory.

What you will learn

The object of the lessons you receive is to teach you to drive safely and competently in all normal traffic conditions. It will be explained where all the controls are, what they do, and how and when they should be used. This does, in fact, mean you will be taught how to pass the driving test, but it is better to think of the lessons as instructions in how to become a good driver.

In addition to understanding the controls and how to use them, you will be taught correct handling, steering, accelerating, braking, and gear changing so they will be right for the road and traffic conditions confronting you. As the lessons progress you will be instructed in some of the more involved manoeuvres such as hill starts, reversing round corners, and the correct approach to junctions and roundabouts.

Qualifications

A professional driving instructor will either be an ADI or a trainee. The trainee must first obtain a licence from the Department of Transport before giving professional tuition, and must be properly supervised by an ADI.

To become an ADI the applicant must pass a written test and then, at a later date, take a practical test to demonstrate driving ability, followed by another test of instructional knowledge. Both tests last three hours each.

At present there is no legal requirement for formal training before applying to become an ADI and some professional instructors consider that any expert driver who knows the Highway Code could qualify, provided the instructional part of the test was carried out properly. Many schools, however, insist that their instructors are adequately trained before they are allowed to teach.

The combination of a good and conscientious instructor with an apt and attentive pupil is the key to the making of a good driver.

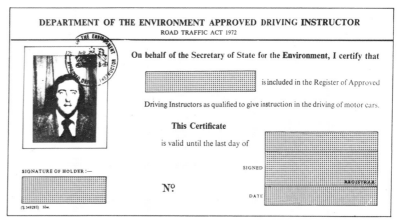

Main aspects of learning to drive

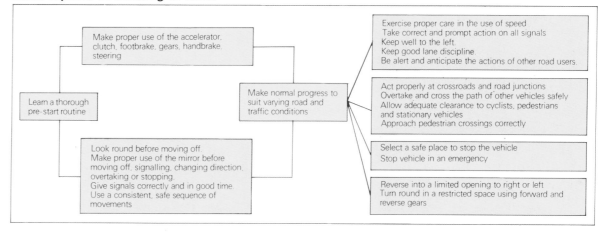

Before anything else, the driving position must be as comfortable as it can be made. If you are not at ease in the seat you will develop muscular tensions which hinder your use of the various controls—accelerator, clutch, brakes, gear lever, and your driving comfort.

It may seem very elementary to say you should begin by getting into the driver's seat correctly, yet some people appear to have difficulties in getting themselves behind the steering wheel easily.

Before opening the door, check in front and behind for the space available for moving away. Look up and down the road for any other hazards which may be present such as a broken milk bottle in the gutter which could lacerate a tyre. Wait until the road is quite clear before opening the door, and when doing so take a firm hold to keep it secure, especially if the day is very windy.

Getting in

For the driver, the best way to get into the driving compartment is to put the left foot into the well, swing into a sitting position, and then bring your right foot alongside the left foot. Next, manoeuvre your body back so you are leaning against the back rest with as much support from the base of the spine to your shoulders as the seat allows.

Once settled comfortably in the seat, reach for the steering wheel with your hands at the 'ten-to-two' position or, if it is more comfortable, at 'quarter-to-three', with your arms slightly bent at the elbows. If this means that you have to lean forwards a little, it will be necessary to alter the seat adjustment.

Take care when opening the door

Swing body into the seat

Place left leg in first

Close the door

Before making any adjustment to the fore-and-aft position of the seat, you should make sure your leg position is also comfortable. With your left foot resting lightly on the left pedal (clutch), and your right foot resting on the right pedal (accelerator), when the seat is correctly adjusted your legs should be slightly bent at the knees, so that when you need to depress either pedal you can do so simply by pressing down. This can

normally be done without having to shift your position in the seat.

If you find that, although your leg position is correct, you still cannot reach the steering wheel and, just as important, the gear lever without having to lean forwards, then you should adjust the rake of the seat back. Not all cars have this facility, and if the one which you are driving does not, you will have to make the best compromise

you can between your leg and arm positions.

When you are driving along with your hands at 'ten-to-two' or 'quarter-to-three', never rest your elbow on the window ledge, and even if there is an arm rest on the door do not use it when on the move. Remember that both hands should be on the wheel except when changing gear or operating some other control.

Fasten the seat belt

Check for tightness

Blind spots

It may seem that since the interior mirror gives a wide view of the road behind, and is backed up by the wing or door mirror, you should have all round visibility. Unfortunately, there is almost always a blind spot over your right shoulder, so before you move off, turn your head to make sure the road is clear and nothing is concealed in the blind spot.

The steering wheel should be held firmly but not hard. If you hang on to it you cannot have proper steering control since an over-strong grip will restrict smooth movement of the wheel. Your grip is also affected by leg position, for if you have to straighten your legs to operate the pedals, you will find you automatically grip the wheel too hard to pull yourself forwards so as to be able to depress the pedals.

Adjust the interior mirror every time you get in

Seat belt

Having achieved the best driving position you can, put on your seat belt. If the car is fitted with static belts you will probably find the adjustment too loose or too tight. You should pull up—or slacken off—the running buckle so that your body cannot move forward more than about two inches before being arrested by the webbing. In this position, the essential controls—gear lever, handbrake, indicator switch, and windscreen wiper switch must all be reachable. If they are not, you will have to make another compromise with the seating position.

This may seem to be a tiresome and lengthy procedure, but in practice it does not take long and is essential if you are to be able to drive efficiently and safely.

Once you have arranged your driving position suitably, you should then check your rear view mirrors. The interior mirror on level ground should line up with the whole frame of the rear window, to give as wide a vector of vision behind as possible. This you can adjust yourself although it may entail releasing your static seat belt in order to reach it. Having made the adjustment, put your belt on again and re-check the rear view.

Wing mirror adjustments require the assistance of someone angling the mirror to suit your view. Door mirrors, which are standard on most cars, can easily be adjusted by the driver.

Seeing

At all times your all round vision should be clear of unnecessary obstructions. Never dangle miniature football boots, dollies, or similar toys from the interior rear view mirror, and keep the rear window clear of impedimenta on the parcel shelf. A light coloured object such as a newspaper, while not directly obstructing your view, can reflect in the glass partially obscuring your vision.

If you suffer from sun glare and need to use dark glasses, make sure they are optically suitable. Some types exaggerate the toughened zones in windscreen glass and with the sunshine at certain angles your forward vision may become obscured.

Look round before moving off

Car cockpit Learning to drive

Every time you get in the car you should check that the doors are firmly closed, your seat belt is fastened, the seat is adjusted correctly and so are the mirrors. When you have settled yourself as comfortably as possible behind the steering wheel, you should familiarise yourself with the essential controls and instruments. From right to left the foot pedals will always be accelerator, brake, and clutch, and on most cars the gear lever will be between the two front seats. A few cars have the gear change on the steering column, and with some cars it protrudes from the dashboard.

The pedals

The three foot pedals will always be found in the same positions.

The **accelerator**, on the right, controls the engine revs. The harder you press it, the more power is produced.

The **brake**, in the middle, slows the car down and stops it.

The **clutch**, on the left, is used when you wish to change gear. Pressing it down disengages the engine drive from the gearbox. Releasing it re-engages the drive.

Switches

Direction indicators are controlled by a stalk on the steering column which may be on either side. More often than not the stalk serves other purposes such as a horn push, but there are many cars which have more than one stalk, each having a separate function, so it is very important than you should remember which does what.

Although the horn 'switch' may be on a steering column stalk, many cars have it either in the centre of the steering wheel or on one or more of the spokes. When the

buttons are on the spokes it is possible to touch them inadvertently when negotiating a corner, so you should try to avoid this.

You may find that some lessons take place in wet weather and you must, therefore, locate the windscreen wiper switch. In some cases this may be on the dashboard, in others controlled by a stalk on the steering column. Windscreen washers can be manual or electric. The manual type may be operated by a button in the dashboard, but the electric type will vary as to their location. Some will be on the wiper stalk, others may be a separate switch situated on the dashboard.

Some of your lessons may take place after dark, so you will need to locate the lighting switch. Its position varies widely from model to model. It may be a knob on the dashboard, a toggle switch, or it may be a stalk on the steering column. Almost invariably the headlamp dip switch will be a stalk on the column, and it may incorporate other functions such as the indicators.

Heater controls also vary widely in design and are sometimes difficult to understand. You will find it safest to leave any adjustment to your instructor.

Seat belt fastened correctly

Choke control pushed in

Choke control pulled out

Windscreen wipers and wash controlled by a steering column stalk.

Lights, indicators and horn control

Dials

When it comes to dials, the only one which the learner needs to watch is the speedometer. As your driving expertise progresses, you will also, from time to time, check the temperature gauge and the fuel level, but you should be able to take it for granted when driving a school car that there will be plenty of petrol in the tank.

Instrumentation varies but many models have supplementary instruments, such as an ammeter to tell you if the generator is charging properly, an oil pressure gauge so that you can tell if the pressure is high enough, and a tachometer—sometimes incorrectly termed a rev counter—which tells you how fast the engine is turning over. None of these need distract your attention during the early stages of instruction.

Instrument dials

Heater and minor controls

Warning lights

Some models have a large number of warning lights telling you such things as that the choke is in use, the handbrake is on, the sidelights are on, seat belts are not being worn. The important ones from the learner's point of view are the ignition warning light, oil pressure, and direction indicator warning lights. When you switch on the engine two lights should appear: the ignition warning light, which is almost always red, and the oil pressure light which may be green but is amber in some cases. The indicator warning, usually green, may be a single light for both sides or one for each.

If you are driving after dark with headlights, a blue light will warn that they are on main beam.

On the road

Before you start driving your instructor will point out all the important controls to you, explain their functions and how they are operated. If, while you are driving along you need to use a switch—such as the windscreen wipers—but cannot locate the switch without having to peer for it, stop the car at a safe place before looking for it. Taking your eyes off the road while driving except for a split-second glance at the speedometer or regular checks of the rear view mirrors, can be very hazardous indeed.

For a beginner it is best not to drive with a cold engine since it is much easier to stall the engine or to over-choke it. Moreover, with the choke out the engine revs are automatically increased which may make driving very much more difficult for the learner.

Operating the ignition switch

Releasing the handbrake

Ignition switch

The ignition switch will have several different positions but the two which the learner must know about are the one for switching on the ignition, and the other which operates the starter motor. When you turn the key to the first position, the ignition and oil pressure warnings should light. Pause in this position for a brief instant, and then turn on to the starter position against the spring-loading. Immediately the engine fires, release the key so it returns to the ignition-on position.

If the car you are driving has a steering column lock, you will probably find you have to exert slight pressure on the steering wheel before turning the key. Never try to force it or it may break. When the engine starts, the ignition light should dim and go out, as should the oil pressure light.

Should the engine not start after a three to four second burst from the starter motor, release the key and wait for a moment before trying again. Because the current required to turn the engine is heavy, the pause will allow the battery to recover from its effort.

Choke

Pulling out the choke control helps a cold engine to start by enriching the petrol to air mixture.

Handbrake

The handbrake has two functions —to secure the car when it is stopped or parked, and to hold it on an incline when starting off. When applying the handbrake keep the ratchet-release button pressed to minimise wear on the ratchet.

Gears and handbrake Learning to drive

The clutch forms the link between the engine drive and the gearbox. Pressing the clutch pedal disconnects the engine from the gearbox, and releasing it connects them again. When the engine has been started and the gear lever is in neutral, some of the gears will be turning, others will be stationary. In order to bring the stationary gears into mesh with the moving ones, the moving ones have to be stopped, temporarily, by operating the clutch.

In the gearbox there are secondary clutches known as synchromesh which help equalise the speeds of gears when on the move, so making it easier to change from one gear to another. In most cases the gear change lever will be floor mounted conveniently near your left hand. In a few models the gear change will be mounted on the steering column, or the dashboard.

Changing gear

Having taken all your pre-start precautions and made sure the road is clear in front and behind, depress the clutch as far as it will go, and engage first gear by pushing the lever not fiercely but firmly to the first gear position. Now allow the clutch pedal to come up slowly until you hear the engine note slow slightly—this is called the 'biting point'. At this point keep both feet still and start to release the handbrake. As you continue to let the clutch up, depress the accelerator slightly so as to increase the engine revs.

When the car is doing about 10 mph, you will be able to change to second gear. Do not take your foot off the accelerator completely, but allow it to rise to its maximum height while keeping your foot just in contact with the pedal. Depress the clutch, move the gear lever gently back, not snatchily, and pause fractionally in neutral, then pull back again into second gear position.

With second gear engaged, let up the clutch slightly less slowly than when starting from rest, and as you do so depress the accelerator a little to take up the drive

smoothly. Your left foot on the clutch and the right on the accelerator should work in unison so that as the clutch reaches the biting point and beyond, the engine revs increase slightly. The change from second to third and third to fourth is done in the same way.

Changing down from fourth to third or third to second calls for a slightly different technique. Depress the clutch, with the accelerator released, move the gear lever into neutral, pause fractionally, and move the lever into the lower gear. This action should be firm but not snatchy.

Gear positions

Although the popularity of five-speed gearboxes is growing slowly, the vast majority of manually operated boxes will have four forward gears, mostly arranged in an H formation, with first gear being at the top left, second bottom left, third top right, and fourth bottom right. The location of reverse varies but most manufacturers supply a diagram, usually on top of the gear lever knob showing where the gears are.

The gear ratios are arranged so that the lower the gear the greater the 'leverage'. When you start from rest, considerable 'leverage' is required to overcome the car's inertia so you need to select first gear. As the car speeds up second gear can be engaged, then third, and finally fourth. When the engine is at its maximum permitted revs—5,500 to 6,000 for most ordinary cars—you would be doing about 30 mph in first gear. For the same engine revs in top, the road speed could be 80 or 90 mph.

First gear

Second gear

Third gear

Fourth gear

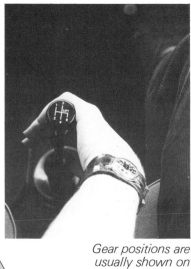

Gear positions are usually shown on the top of the gear lever knob

The chart shows which gears may need to be used up and down hills and on the level

Automatic gearboxes

The design of automatic gearboxes varies, but in most cases the selector lever will be in a console between the front seats. The position of the type of drive selected will be clearly marked—'D' stands for Drive and with this position selected the box will automatically go from the lowest gear to the highest as speed increases. There will also be one, or two, positions for 'L.' In L_1 the lowest of the forward gears will be held and the box will not change up; in L_2 second gear will be held. These positions are for hill descents and similar situations.

In addition to the forward drive positions, there will be 'R' for Reverse, 'N' for Neutral, and 'P' for Park. To engage reverse you will have to press a release device which is there to prevent reverse being selected by mistake. In most cases you can only start the engine in neutral or park.

The Automotive Products automatic gearbox is a little different in that it has four forward gears and the selector lever can be used in 'D', or to change up or down in a similar manner to a manual gearbox. This type of gearbox is to be found in Minis and 1100/1300 BL cars. A third type of automatic box is the DAF Variomatic, in which the ratio is infinitely variable between the highest and lowest.

It is as well to remember that if you pass your driving test in a car with automatic transmission, you will only become licensed to drive automatics. If you want to convert to a manual transmission car you will have to take another test.

Handbrake

You will usually find the handbrake mounted on the floor between the front seats, but some models have it just below the dashboard. Dashboard mounted handbrakes may resemble a spade handle or that of an umbrella.

To release a floor mounted lever, it must first be pulled upwards and then a button pressed to disengage the catch mechanism. The dashboard type have to be pulled towards you and then twisted to release them.

With either type, always try to avoid 'ratcheting', that is to say pulling the brake on with a series of clicks as the pawl passes over the ratchet. This will eventually wear both pawl and ratchet to the point that the brake will not stay on.

The main purpose of the handbrake is to ensure the car is held stationary when it is parked, or to hold the car on an incline when doing a hill start. Whenever the car is brought to a halt (except for stops of only a second or two) the handbrake should be applied. It can be dangerous to wait at traffic lights with the handbrake off, with the car in gear, one foot on the clutch and one on the footbrake. If your foot were to slip on the clutch pedal the car could well lurch forward, possibly colliding with other traffic.

The handbrake is also a back-up braking system in case of footbrake failure. If it has to be used in an emergency, it should be applied with care. Pulling it on hard can induce a rear wheel slide and swing the car broadside on or even spin it completely.

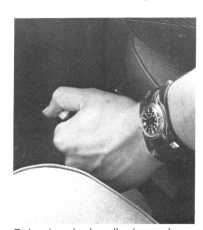
Releasing the handbrake ratchet

Umbrella-type handbrake

Starting off Learning to drive

Now that the layout of the driving position is familiar, the time has come for the first drive. This is not simply a matter of setting off; there are a number of things to check beforehand.

Walk round the car

The first thing to do when starting a drive (and this should be done every time you set out), is to walk round the car. Make sure that no tyre is flat; that there is no ominous pool of water or oil underneath; and there is no broken glass in the gutter which could puncture a tyre.

While walking round the car, see how much room there is between your car and any other vehicles parked in front or behind. This will help you when it comes to moving away.

Carry out the pre-start routine before moving off

Inspect the road in front

Inspect the road at the rear

Look before opening the door

Walk towards the rear

Check the tyres

Getting in

Getting in

It should be unnecessary to slam a door hard to shut it, but having closed it make sure the latch has engaged properly and the door is securely shut. Even in a driving school car it is wise to check the passenger's door, too. It will help to get you into this good habit and is part of correct pre-start drill.

Make yourself as comfortable as possible in the driving seat as described on pages 200 and 201, then put on and adjust your seat belt. Pages 170 and 171 explain how to do this properly. The mirror is the next consideration. Ensure it gives you the widest possible view to the rear and move it if necessary. You are now ready to start the engine.

Starting the engine

Check that the handbrake is on and the gear lever is in neutral by moving it from side to side, then turn the ignition key until the ignition and oil pressure warning lights come on. Pause for a second, then turn the key against its spring loading until the starter motor turns the engine over. The engine should fire immediately and when it does release the key so it will automatically return to the ignition-on position. If it does not fire at the first use of the starter, release the key, and then try again.

Check gear lever is in neutral

Choke control

If you have had to use the choke to start the engine from cold, it should be returned to its 'off' position as soon as possible. Also, once the engine has started, you should be able to push the choke control about half way in without stalling. Some cars have automatic chokes and to operate this type you only need to press the accelerator pedal slowly to the floor once, and then allow it to return to its top position before energising the starter motor to start the engine. The automatic choke should then return to the normal position.

Moving away

Check in the rear view mirror that there is a clear road behind. Look ahead to see if your way is clear, and then you can engage first gear.

Depress the clutch to the floor and move the gear lever firmly into gear. Check the mirror again and look over your right shoulder to take in the blind spot. After you have looked all round and checked that it is clear, switch on your right indicators to signal your intention to pull out from the kerb. Increase the engine revs a little and as you slowly let the clutch pedal come up, release the handbrake and move away from the kerb.

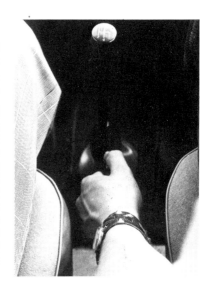

Look behind before moving away

Keeping the car on a straight and steady course is one of the first problems the learner has to overcome. Many learners tend to overreact, steering too strongly against the camber of the road, and then having to correct again.

This process of constant steering correction sometimes means that the car will proceed up the road like a snake. Although this may happen to many learners at first, the skill will soon be learnt of looking where you are going and applying the right amount of gentle pressure on the steering wheel to prevent the car drifting off course.

Before driving the car, however, it is imperative to know how to stop it. Under normal conditions, braking should be gentle but progressive. Every driving test includes an 'emergency' stop, and it is important to learn how to carry this out safely.

Driving position

Maintaining a steady steering line is closely associated with your driving position, especially with the way in which you hold the steering wheel. It should be gripped lightly but firmly with the hands at ten-to-two or at quarter-to-three. The arms should be slightly bent at the elbows so they are in a relaxed state.

Turning the wheel

When negotiating a bend, corner, or making any other steering manoeuvre, you should try never to allow either hand to pass the twelve o'clock position. You will no doubt have seen many drivers 'climbing up the wheel', going hand over hand on one side. This is bad driving.

The correct way to use the steering wheel is based on what is called the 'pull and push' method. When taking a 90 degree left-hand corner, the left hand pulls the steering wheel round, the hand moving from the ten o'clock position to a seven o'clock position. The right hand then moves from two o'clock to five o'clock so it can push the wheel upwards. At the same time the left hand moves back to the ten o'clock position ready for the next move.

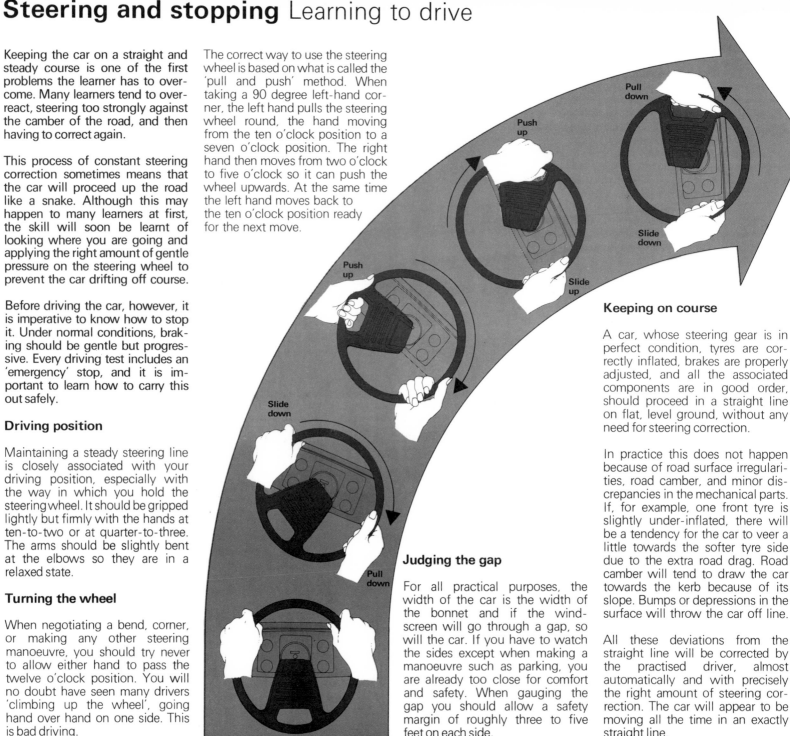

Judging the gap

For all practical purposes, the width of the car is the width of the bonnet and if the windscreen will go through a gap, so will the car. If you have to watch the sides except when making a manoeuvre such as parking, you are already too close for comfort and safety. When gauging the gap you should allow a safety margin of roughly three to five feet on each side.

Keeping on course

A car, whose steering gear is in perfect condition, tyres are correctly inflated, brakes are properly adjusted, and all the associated components are in good order, should proceed in a straight line on flat, level ground, without any need for steering correction.

In practice this does not happen because of road surface irregularities, road camber, and minor discrepancies in the mechanical parts. If, for example, one front tyre is slightly under-inflated, there will be a tendency for the car to veer a little towards the softer tyre side due to the extra road drag. Road camber will tend to draw the car towards the kerb because of its slope. Bumps or depressions in the surface will throw the car off line.

All these deviations from the straight line will be corrected by the practised driver, almost automatically and with precisely the right amount of steering correction. The car will appear to be moving all the time in an exactly straight line.

Engine braking

When you are using the accelerator, even lightly, the engine is driving the road wheels, but when you take your foot off the accelerator, the wheels are trying to drive the engine and the engine is resisting being driven. This is known as engine braking.

As you approach the place where you will have to stop, look in your mirrors, then release the accelerator pedal in good time, and the engine will slow the car. When you use the brake to complete the act of slowing down, only light pressure will then be needed.

Many cars are fitted with power assisted brakes nowadays, which means that the braking effort is made more powerful for any given footbrake pedal pressure, by the action of a servo. Beware, therefore, if you change from a servo equipped car to one which is not, because you will find the non-servo car's brakes will need a good deal more pressure on the pedal to obtain braking equal to that of the servo assisted car.

Progressive braking

Correct braking under normal conditions is known as 'progressive' braking. As you approach a stopping point under deceleration from engine drag, you begin braking firmly, decreasing pressure gradually as you near the stopping point. In this way the car is brought to rest gently without lurching or the risk of a skid. Heavy braking, applied in panic at the last moment, can lock up the wheels causing them to slide out of control.

Slide down

Pull down

Slide up

Push up

Pull down

Pull down

Slide down

Handbrake

The main purpose of the handbrake is to hold the car stationary, and it is applied only after the car has been brought to a halt. The handbrake should never be 'ratcheted', (pulled on in a series of clicks). The correct method is to press the release button, pull the lever up firmly, and then release the button so the catch engages.

Emergency stop

In very, very rare circumstances it may be necessary to put on the brakes and this should only be done if there is no other possible avenue of escape. The danger about this type of emergency braking is that it may lock the wheels, might provoke a skid sideways, and could cause someone to hit you from behind.

Even in an emergency, braking should be only as hard as necessary to stop before, for example, hitting another vehicle which has suddenly emerged from a side turning in front of you. Always try to stop firmly without locking the wheels. If this happens, you will lose steering control and the car will start to slide.

The learner driver should, however, find out how the car behaves in emergency braking conditions. The test examiner will also require the candidate to carry out an emergency stop. Ideally, practice should be at very slow speeds. If it is to be done on public roads, you must make certain it is safe.

The usual procedure is for the examiner to warn the candidate in advance that he will require an emergency stop at a given signal, such as a knock on the dashboard. Instructors prepare candidates for this in different ways. The examiner and the instructor always check that it is safe before they give the signal.

As soon as the signal is given, the driver must stop as quickly and safely as possible. Put on the brakes hard, trying to avoid locking the wheels. In the last yard push in the clutch, so that the car does not stall.

Practice 1 Learning to drive

Everything you have learned up to this point should be practised until it is thoroughly familiar. Get to know your car and where all the controls are. Have a fully-qualified driver sit in the passenger seat during every practice session.

Check the instruments

Sit behind the steering wheel, without the engine running, and make a mental check of what all the instruments are and where they are located. Be sure you know exactly what each one tells you and how it does so. For example, if the car is equipped with an ammeter try to visualise which side of the centre mark shows a charge and which a discharge, then look at the dial. One side will have a 'plus' sign for charging and the other a 'minus' sign for discharging.

The car may be equipped with stalk controls on the steering column for indicators, windscreen wipers and lights. Become thoroughly familiar with each stalk.

You may turn the ignition on in order to check the various warning lights but do not start the engine if you are on your own.

Pre-start drill

Go through the pre-start routine as though you were about to drive off, but do not actually do so. Walk around the car and try to remember all the points you should check before you get into the car. See pages 206 and 207. Adjust the driving seat to a comfortable position and check that the rear-view mirrors are aligned correctly.

When the seating position is correct and comfortable, check that the doors are closed properly. Then fasten your seat belt and make sure you are wearing it correctly.

Ensure that the handbrake is on and that the gear lever is in neutral by moving it to and fro in the gate. If you try moving the gear lever into and out of gear do not use force. When the engine is not running some gears may be positioned so that they do not mesh. Trying to force them into mesh could cause damage.

If you are carrying out the pre-start drill with a fully qualified friend or relative in the car, follow every step of the pre-start drill conscientiously. Pay no attention to any remark he may make such as that the passenger's door is properly closed or that the gear lever is in neutral. Double check every item yourself so that, with practice, the pre-start drill becomes second nature.

Pedal pressures

While the car is stationary, off the road, it is a good idea to become accustomed to the feeling of the clutch, brake and accelerator pedals by getting used to the amount of foot pressure each needs. If the car is equipped with servo brakes, however, the servo action will not work unless the engine is running.

When feeling for pedal pressure and similar actions it is a good idea to place your hands on the steering wheel in the correct position. Do not try to move the steering wheel when the car is stationary, however, as this will put a strain on the steering mechanism.

Clutch control

Any practice with the car on the move should, ideally, be carried out off the public roads on private ground where there will be no need to worry about other road users. You should always have a fully-qualified friend or relative with you for these practice exercises and, in the early stages it is best to allow your companion to drive to a quiet area before you take over.

Clutch control is often found to be a difficult skill for the learner to master. Starting off from rest is a good exercise for getting to know how the clutch behaves.

The tickover speed of the engine should be no higher than normal and when starting off in first gear it will be necessary to press the accelerator pedal slightly. With the engine running, depress the clutch fully and let the clutch pedal up slowly and gently.

As the clutch begins to 'bite' the engine revs will slow. Release the

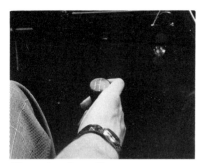

Changing from first gear

From second to third gear

From fourth to third gear

Into second gear

Into second gear

From third to fourth gear

From third to second gear

Engaging reverse gear

handbrake, keeping both feet still. Then slowly let the clutch up completely, at which point the car should move forwards at about walking pace.

Starting in this way is not possible with all cars because of engine design, but the more popular models should present no problem. If you cannot start off from rest by this method either because the car you are driving cannot respond or because your clutch control is not sensitive enough, do not worry. Practise the conventional start as described on pages 204–207 to familiarise yourself with the feeling of the clutch's behaviour.

Steering sense

Because of the self-centring action of modern car steering a car will proceed in a straight line on smooth, level ground, provided the tyre pressures are correct and the suspension, steering mechanism and allied parts are all in good condition. Any corrections should be minimal. The learner driver tends to over-react to any minor deviation so the car veers over the centre line of direction and has to be brought back again.

Steering practice should be aimed at perfecting straight-line steering at this stage. The secret is to have a relaxed arm position and not to grip the steering wheel too tightly. If your shoulders are tensed and your grip too strong jerky steering will result.

Once straight line steering has been mastered, turns will come more naturally. When practising turns

take care that you do not allow the steering wheel to slip through your hands by self-centring action. The correct method is to straighten the steering line by feeding the wheel through the hands, back to the centre position. In this way you will retain control throughout the manoeuvre. This is especially important with front wheel drive cars where the self-centring action is particularly powerful.

Changing gear

While carrying out the steering exercises it is also a good opportunity to practise changing gear. Many learner drivers tend to hurry the gear changes which results in jerky movement. Move the gear lever deliberately, thinking where it should go and pushing or pulling it into position gently and without

force. If you miss the gear, do not snatch at the lever in panic.

When practising gear changing it is important to pay attention to changing down, since this may require you to raise the engine revs slightly when in neutral, in order to match engine speed to road speed.

Braking practice

Although braking often comes naturally, beginners tend to brake too hard and stop rather abruptly. To practise braking choose a spot ahead of you and drive steadily towards it planning to brake smoothly to rest at the spot selected. Repeat this until you have improved the smoothness of your braking. Emergency stops should not be practised yet.

Turning Learning to drive

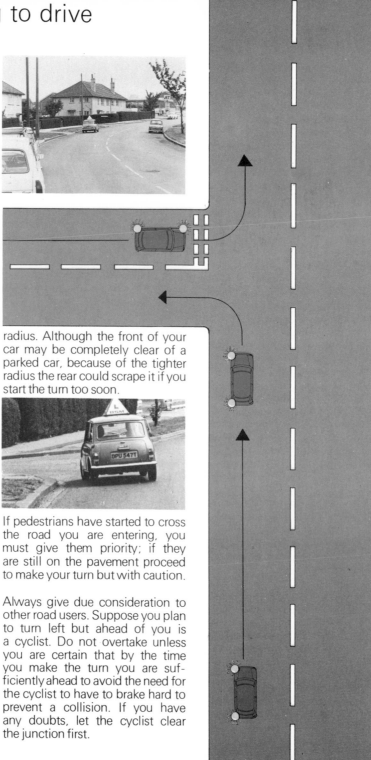

Turning from one road to another always requires care, especially when turning right and when turning into a main road from a side street. In every case the approach to the turn follows the same procedure. Look in the mirrors, make the necessary signal, then carry out the manoeuvre in the correct gear and at the appropriate speed for the circumstances.

Turning left into a side road

A left turn may be 'open' or 'blind'. If you are about to turn left off a main road, buildings may mask the view of all but the mouth of the road, so you will have to proceed with great caution. There could be cars parked on both sides of the side road as well as other traffic approaching the mouth.

Well before you reach the side road into which you wish to turn, check your mirrors—both interior and wing or door mirrors—for traffic from behind. Signal your intention to turn in good time, slow down, and select the appropriate gear for the road speed. This will usually be second gear for a 90 degree turn. Check your mirror again to make sure it is safe behind. It is not unknown for a motorcyclist, foolishly, to come up on your nearside despite your signal and if you continued your manoeuvre there might be a collision.

Your position on the road should be the 'safety line', between three and five feet from the kerb, if there are no parked cars, but giving them a door's width margin if there are. The line you take as you enter the side road should allow you to make such an angle that you keep to your own side of the road, remembering that the rear wheels follow the front on a slightly tighter

radius. Although the front of your car may be completely clear of a parked car, because of the tighter radius the rear could scrape it if you start the turn too soon.

If pedestrians have started to cross the road you are entering, you must give them priority; if they are still on the pavement proceed to make your turn but with caution.

Always give due consideration to other road users. Suppose you plan to turn left but ahead of you is a cyclist. Do not overtake unless you are certain that by the time you make the turn you are sufficiently ahead to avoid the need for the cyclist to have to brake hard to prevent a collision. If you have any doubts, let the cyclist clear the junction first.

Turning left into a main road

Turning left out of a side road into a main road poses slightly different problems. If there are 'Give Way' signs and road markings at the junction you need not stop if the main road is clear. Look right to check for approaching traffic, then left, and finally right again. If both ways are clear, change straight into second gear and drive out keeping as near as possible to your own side of the road. If your steering is too 'coarse', the car will take a wide line bringing you out towards the centre of the road.

You should always plan to stop at the junction if it is necessary to do so. In that case, brake gently and stop carefully. Apply the handbrake and change into neutral. Then, when the road is clear, select first gear and move out.

Turning left at a fork

Fork roads, when you wish to take the left fork, can be treated as if you were continuing along a straight road except that you should signal your intention to take the left fork.

Turning right into a side road

When turning right into a side road you should still use the drill—mirror, signal, manoeuvre. Having checked your rear view mirrors well in advance of the right turning, and if it is safe, signal a right turn and move to the centre of the road, keeping to your side of the centre line. Cars from behind wishing to go straight on can then pass you on the nearside. Having taken up this position you must look ahead for a safe gap in the oncoming traffic to make your right turn smoothly.

It may be that having taken up the correct position for a right turn, you can see the road ahead is clear of oncoming vehicles. If this is the situation, there is no need to stop. Change down from fourth gear to third—or more likely second—and make your turn.

Turning right off a main road into a side road is a hazardous manoeuvre. You have three judgements to make:
1. Does the traffic from behind know what you intend?
2. Do the oncoming vehicles also know your intentions and that you intend to allow them to proceed?
3. Are any vehicles emerging from the side road aware of your intended manoeuvre?

When entering the side road on your right you should endeavour to do so at a right angle. You should make the actual turn in the main road you are leaving, and should have straightened up as the nose of your car enters the side road. Never cut the corner. A car wishing to turn out of the junction may be unable to stop in sufficient time to prevent a collision.

Turning right into a main road

Turning right into a traffic stream on a main road is somewhat different from turning left. Be prepared to stop at the mouth of the junction but select a gear which will enable you to move out without stopping if it is safe to do so. Check the mirrors and signal right, positioning the car left of the centre line.

Having stopped at the main road junction, the gear lever must be put into neutral and the handbrake applied. Look right. If there is any approaching traffic you must wait. Do not assume that if you see an oncoming car signalling a left turn into the side road from which you wish to turn right that it will always do so. The driver may have forgotten to cancel a signal he made farther back down the road.

When the road is clear from the right, look left then right again. If all is clear you can start to make your turn. If not, it may be safe, in some cases, to straddle the lane to your right provided there is not a continuous stream of vehicles coming from your left. After the cars from your left have passed and there is an adequate gap, you will be able to complete your right turn in safety.

Dual carriageways

Treat a left turn into a dual carriageway in the same way as if it were an ordinary left turn. For a right turn you may be able to cross the first carriageway to a gap in the central reservation and wait there for a suitable gap in traffic from your left. If you do this, make sure there is room for your car between the carriageways, and position yourself correctly for completion of the turn. If you are doubtful about the amount of room, wait in the side road until both carriageways are clear.

213

Uphill

The best technique for driving up hills is to remain in top gear until the engine begins to slow a little and then change down into third gear. Should the hill steepen a

Driving techniques on hills are not as complicated as many learners fear. The general aim is to keep the road speed constant as far as traffic and road conditions allow, changing gear when necessary in order to achieve this. Uphill gradients require a different approach to downhill ones from all points of view, whether they be starting, driving or parking.

Downhill

Descending a short hill, even one which is quite steep, can normally be carried out in top gear provided the brakes are efficient (which, of course, they should be).

A decline longer than about 200 yards should be approached with greater caution. Even if the gradient is not very steep, constant use of the brakes will cause them to heat up and poorer braking performance will be produced.

Before embarking on a long down gradient, you should select a low gear so that engine drag will assist the brakes. When it is necessary to change down for a decline, third gear is seldom low enough to give the necessary degree of engine braking assistance. Second gear is usually adequate, but for very severe slopes it may be necessary to proceed slowly in first gear.

It is very dangerous to declutch or coast down a hill, however gentle, in neutral. Should acceleration or drive be necessary at any point, the delay in getting into gear could prove dangerous. The handbrake should also never be used when driving downhill or anywhere else. Its function is to secure the car when parked.

great deal, it may be necessary to change directly from top to second gear. This is not difficult provided you think exactly what you are doing, and make the change sufficiently early.

Some hills steepen progressively. Top gear may carry you about half-way up, then third will take you a bit farther, but second gear will be needed to get over the crest.

If this is the case, do not allow the engine to labour at any point. Make the two downward changes as the engine begins to slow. Do not leave the gear change too late or it may be difficult to make. First gear should not be necessary except on steep hills. If possible, such steep hills should be avoided by the learner.

When tackling a hill for the first time the learner may prefer to assess the severity of the hill and select the appropriate gear before beginning to ascend the gradient. Should a gear change be missed

for any reason, perhaps when trying to snatch a gear change while ascending a hill for the first time, you may, perhaps, need to stop gently. Apply the footbrake, then apply the handbrake (without ratcheting it) and prepare to restart.

In some cases, particularly when the hill is fairly steep, it may not be possible to see the road beyond the crest of the hill.

Do not accelerate or change up too soon at the brow of the hill under these conditions until you have been able to see what lies ahead.

Starting the car on an incline . . .

. . . is not as hard as is feared

Hill starts

Starting a car on an uphill gradient is sometimes presented as a problem, but this is not the case. There are two differences from starting on level ground: the handbrake will have to be used to stop the car rolling backwards, and the engine will need a bit more accelerator to move the car up the slope. An especially careful check in the mirrors for following traffic is important when starting on a hill.

Engage first gear and hold the handbrake on hard but without the rachet engaged. Increase the engine revs to about twice what you would need on level ground but do not race the engine.

The steeper the slope the more revs will be needed. Let up the clutch pedal slowly, and when you feel it beginning to bite start letting off the handbrake. Continue to let the clutch up and, if the engine slows too much, increase accelerator pedal pressure slightly.

If the engine stalls there is no need to worry. Hold the car with the footbrake and pull the handbrake on (without clicking the ratchet) until it is properly engaged. Release the footbrake cautiously so that, if the handbrake is not fully applied, you can stop the car from rolling back. Put the gear lever into neutral, then start the engine and try again.

Starting the car on a decline is quite straightforward. Select first gear and hold the car on the handbrake to prevent it rolling down the hill. Instead of using the accelerator, control the speed of the car with the footbrake as you release the handbrake and move off.

Reversing on a hill requires the same precautions as when reversing on level ground (see pages 216 and 217).

Parking on a hill

When parking on a hill you should leave the car with the handbrake on and in gear. It is always advisable to turn the front wheels at an angle so that the car would be prevented from running away down the hill. The correct positions are:

Uphill: with a kerb—front wheels turned to right; without a kerb—front wheels turned to left.

Downhill: with a kerb—front wheels turned to left; without a kerb—front wheels turned to left.

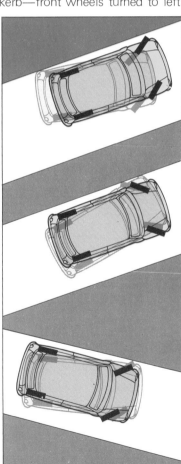

Reversing Learning to drive

There are many occasions, such as when parking or needing to change direction when careful manoeuvring is required, and this will usually involve reversing. One guide to accurate reversing is to carry it out as slowly as possible.

Observation

Before making any reversing manoeuvre you must first make sure it is safe to do so. Your rear view from the driving seat is restricted and, for example, a small child close behind your car may be out of sight, masked by the projection of the boot. Even if you have just come to a halt, a dog or child may suddenly come out of a garden behind you so be alert to the possibility.

Method

When you are quite sure there are no obstructions behind, engage reverse gear. Turn slightly in your seat so you are able to look over your left shoulder down the centre line of the car. Place your right hand at twelve o'clock on the steering wheel. Let the clutch up slightly, and when it begins to bite, increase engine revs a little. Then release the handbrake and check for movement.

Left-hand reverse

Before reversing round a left-hand corner, make sure that the side road you intend to reverse into is clear. Look over your left shoulder to decide how to position your car, then, still looking over your left shoulder, reverse slowly approaching the entry to the side road.

Check over your right shoulder that your line is safe, and look again into the side road to make sure it is still clear. As you reach the corner continue to check that your line is still parallel with the kerb, and then look over your left shoulder once more. While turning you should also look right especially for oncoming traffic. You should come to a halt on your own side of the road, parallel with the kerb.

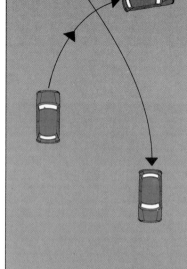

Keep close to the kerb during left-hand reverse

Turning the car round

To turn the car round, first stop on the nearside, as close to the kerb as is safe. Make sure the road is clear in both directions for some distance before starting the manoeuvre, as it takes time. Keep a sharp look out for other traffic whilst making this turn. When safe, steer towards the kerb on the opposite side of the road using full steering lock. When you are between three feet and eighteen inches from the kerb turn the steering wheel to the left. Stop the car using the footbrake, apply handbrake and disengage clutch.

Engage reverse gear, hold the handbrake and look all round to make sure the road is clear. Rev the engine gently and take control with the clutch. When it is safe move back gently across the road looking over your right shoulder to keep the car away from the kerb. Stop the car, engage first gear, hold the handbrake and look left, right and left. When it is safe, take control with the clutch and throttle and move forward, steering to the right then left to straighten up.

Right-hand reverse

To approach a right-hand turning into which you plan to reverse first move to the centre of the road on your own side of the centre line. Check that the side turning is clear of traffic, and when it is safe to do so continue across the road coming to a halt about one or two car's lengths past the mouth of the side road.

Check all round that no traffic is approaching or turning out of the side road. Engage reverse gear, look over your left shoulder then move backwards slowly keeping parallel to the kerb. When the rear offside wheel is just past the side road's kerb, start making the turn. You may need to use both hands on the steering wheel during this manoeuvre. When you have straightened up in the side road, check front and rear, then move forwards across the road to the correct side.

Straight line reverse

Aim to keep the car parallel with the kerb during this manoeuvre. Proceed slowly, watching your line through the rear window but also glancing forwards to check your position on the road.

Never reverse farther than is absolutely necessary and do not be afraid to stop during the manoeuvre if, for example, the car is off line. If necessary, straighten up by going forwards for a couple of yards and then going into reverse once more. Your right hand at the twelve o'clock position on the steering wheel should allow you to counter any small deviations.

Use of speed Learning to drive

Speed, in itself, is not dangerous. It is relative and the correct speed depends on the circumstances. In a car properly maintained and in good condition, 60 mph can be perfectly safe if road and traffic permit, yet passing a school at 30 mph when the children are going home could be too fast. It is important to develop a sense of your own speed as well as learning to assess the speed of others.

The speedometer

Slowing down for the roundabout

The speedometer provides the driver with extremely valuable information. You should not, however, watch it all the time. As your experience increases you will be able to judge your speed without constantly referring to the speedometer. You should try to memorise where the line is for 30 mph so that a split-second glance is all that is needed to see if the needle is above or below it. If you have been driving for a period at a higher speed, say 50 mph, and slow down to what you think is 30 mph, you should periodically check with your speedometer since your actual speed may well be higher than you thought.

Stability

Braking

Accelerating

When you brake the car's weight is thrown forwards on to the front wheels, and when you accelerate the converse is true. The weight is thrown on to the rear wheels. These two factors have an important influence on the car's stability.

You should only ever brake and accelerate in a straight line. Always avoid fierce acceleration since not only does it make the car less well balanced, it also wastes petrol and increases wear on the car, especially on the tyres.

Cornering

The car's stability is very important during cornering. If you go into a bend too fast and have to brake the steering will become heavy and difficult to manage and, at the same time, the rear end will become lighter with reduced rear wheel adhesion. These factors could cause a skid to develop.

As you approach the bend you should reduce speed before you reach it to a level where you can drive round under constant throttle, neither speeding up nor slowing down. This will keep the car nicely balanced. Try to exit from a bend under slight acceleration.

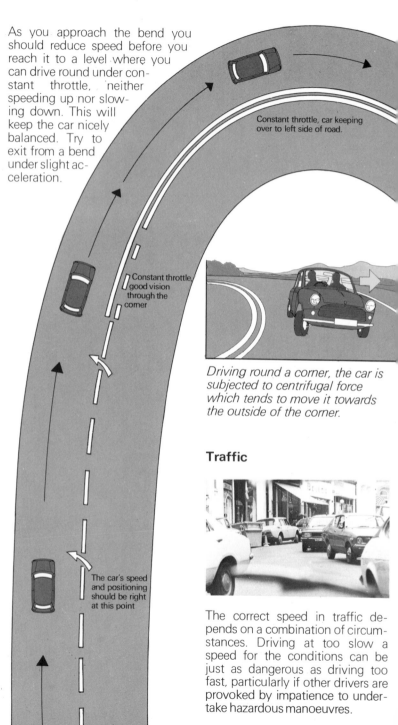

Constant throttle, car keeping over to left side of road.

Constant throttle, good vision through the corner

The car's speed and positioning should be right at this point

Driving round a corner, the car is subjected to centrifugal force which tends to move it towards the outside of the corner.

Traffic

The correct speed in traffic depends on a combination of circumstances. Driving at too slow a speed for the conditions can be just as dangerous as driving too fast, particularly if other drivers are provoked by impatience to undertake hazardous manoeuvres.

Good observation and looking well ahead will help you to avoid harsh braking. Allow the car to decelerate under engine braking if you see traffic slowing in front of you, or you are approaching a hazard. When passing a line of parked cars, for example, watch carefully for any pedestrians or animals between them and for any

sign of one of them pulling out (exhaust smoke or a driver at the wheel will give you a clue), then accelerate firmly without hesitation past them, leaving enough room to your left.

Observe speed limits. At times they may not appear to be realistic, but there may often be good reasons for them which are not apparent at the time. They are worked out after careful consultation and are mandatory. The limit is a maximum speed allowed, however, and there will be occasions when it is only safe to drive

at perhaps half that speed. Do not allow an impatient driver behind to push you into driving faster than you wish. Allow him to pass at the first opportunity by keeping well over to the left.

Overtaking

Overtaking requires very careful observation and planning. You should always check carefully that it is perfectly safe to overtake, and then you should try to accomplish it in the least possible time.

Your position behind the slower moving vehicle is important. You should hold well back to give yourself the best view ahead, then accelerate briskly past the slower moving vehicle. Get past and then return to your own side of the road quickly, without cutting in front of the other vehicle. Too abrupt a manoeuvre can be dangerous.

Visibility

In conditions of poor visibility you must suit your speed to the distance ahead you can see clearly, so you can stop within that distance should the need arise. This is especially important in foggy conditions. After dark your speed will be dictated by the performance of your car's lights, but also remember that other cars at night may appear to be travelling slower than they actually are and proceed with extra caution taking this factor into account.

Speed assessment

Reduce speed when vision ahead is restricted in any way.

Knowing when and how much to accelerate or decelerate comes with experience. There are many situations in which you will need to assess the speed of other vehicles, then make swift decisions and execute prompt actions. It is not always easy to assess the speed of another vehicle, and if you have any doubts, the safest course is to slow down and, if necessary, stop to give the other car priority.

As an example, suppose you are approaching a fork junction and wish to take the right hand fork. You check the mirror, make the correct signal, then position the car just to the left of the crown of the road, as for making a right turn.

A car is approaching from the left hand fork. You must decide whether you can accelerate and safely take the right fork before the other car reaches the junction,

or whether you must decelerate to allow the other car to pass first.

Before deciding you must assess the situation and ask yourself some questions. How fast is the other car going? At constant speed, will you arrive at the junction in time to complete the manoeuvre before he arrives there? If you accelerate and take the right fork, will this give you enough time to cross the path of the other car safely? If you decelerate, can you do so to arrive at the junction after the other car has passed, allowing you to take the right fork without delay?

You will need to consider these four questions in this situation, in order to judge what your speed should be. You will also, of course, need to be constantly watching for any other incident which may affect the safety of the manoeuvre you intend to make.

Highway code Learning to drive

Everyone thinking of learning to drive must satisfy the examiner that he is fully conversant with the contents of the Highway Code. It is a summary of most aspects of correct behaviour on the road and also the legal requirements. If every driver strictly observed everything the Highway Code says there would undoubtedly be a big reduction in the number of road accidents.

Legal status

Disregard of the Highway Code is not, by itself, a legal offence. As the statement on page 5 of the Code says, however, 'This Code, between pages 6 and 45, is issued with the Authority of Parliament (Resolutions passed November 1977)'.

It continues, 'A failure on the part of a person to observe a provision of the Highway Code shall not of itself render that person liable to criminal proceedings of any kind, but any such failure may in any proceedings (whether civil or criminal, and including proceedings for an offence under this Act, the Road Traffic Act 1960 or the Road

Traffic Regulation Act 1967) be relied upon by any party to the proceedings as tending to establish or to negative any liability which is in question in those proceedings. Road Traffic Act 1972 Section 37'.

Both of these statements show clearly that, apart from the wealth of information and useful advice which is contained between its covers, not having a sound knowledge and understanding of the Code could result in a failed test or, when a qualified driver, weigh against you in court proceedings. It could also weigh in your favour if it could be shown that another party had not observed the Code. The purpose of the Highway Code is to lay down criteria for safe driving, to explain different manoeuvres, to advise on the action

to take in special circumstances, to explain the meanings of road signs, and to give a brief resumé of the legal requirements.

Behaviour of road users

The most important section for the learner driver to study are pages 6 to 45 which covers the Code not

only as applied to car drivers, but also to pedestrians, cyclists, motorway driving, and road users in charge of animals. Although your aim may be to simply become a qualified car driver, the advice offered by the Code to other road users will widen your understanding of their problems and improve your own performance.

Signals, signs and road markings

The next section with which you must become familiar are pages 46 to 57. This covers traffic light signals, arm signals by police or other authorised persons such as traffic wardens when controlling traffic, drivers' direction indicator signals (flasher lights) and arm signals, and several pages of traffic signs and road markings.

The law

On page 61 of the Code comes 'The law's demands'. This, under the various Acts and Regulations tells you what you must and must not do. Some of the requirements seem fairly obvious. As an example, you must, 'stop when required to do so by a police officer in uniform'. Also, you must not, 'drive recklessly'. What is not so obvious is that you must, 'use your headlights in poor daytime visibility'.

Do you know the code?

From all this it will be seen that there is much to be learned from the Highway Code. How much have you learned? Try answering the questions which follow—without checking the answers in the Code until you have decided what the correct one should be.

1 According to the Code, what is the shortest stopping distance in feet from 30 mph?

2 At a Pelican pedestrian crossing, what should you do when the amber light is flashing and no pedestrian is on the crossing?

3 When a traffic light signal shows amber alone, what is the next colour which will appear?

4 If the car in front of you has its nearside direction indicator flashing what should this mean?

5 If you see a post-mounted red disc with a horizontal white bar, what does it signify?

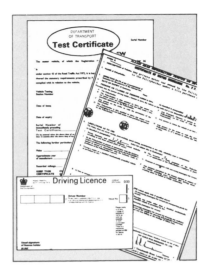

6 If required by the police to produce your driving licence, certificate of insurance and, if your vehicle is subject to compulsory testing, your test certificate, and cannot do so on the spot, how long do you have to produce them at a police station of your choice?

7 When may you not sound your horn?

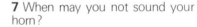

8 When intending to turn left out of a roundabout what, if any, signal should you make as you approach it?

9 When, if at all, may you park on the right hand side of a street at night?

10 If another motorist flashes his headlamps what should this mean?

When you have noted down the answers to these questions, you will probably have to search through the Code to check the answers, which is the object of the exercise. The more often you read through the book, the more familiar you will become with its advice and, therefore, the more likely you will be to drive accordingly. This is the road to passing the test and becoming a safe driver.

Other road users Learning to drive

Everyone has the right to use the roads but must exercise responsibility to others. Even the pedestrian, who is unlikely to cause damage by bodily impact can, by stepping thoughtlessly in front of a moving car, cause the driver to swerve into the path of another vehicle, thus being responsible for an accident.

The Highway Act of 1835 states that you must not, '...by negligence or misbehaviour interrupt the free passage of any road user or vehicle', and this act is still in force. Moreover, there are the more modern phrases such as 'without due care and attention', or 'without reasonable consideration for other persons using the road'.

Pedestrians

Among pedestrians, those most prone to accidents on the roads are under 15 years old or over 60. The driver, therefore, must make allowances for children and old people being less able to judge the speed of vehicles and, quite probably, being absent minded. The child at play concentrates on the game and may behave unpredictably. They also have a restricted view of the road because they are not very tall, and young children are not good at assessing the speed of approaching vehicles. An old person who, perhaps, cannot see very well may be trying to remember what shopping to get. Either may step into the road thoughtlessly.

At crossings which are controlled by lights, the driver needs to remember that when the amber light is flashing at a Pelican crossing, the pedestrian has priority. At a Zebra crossing where there are no lights, any pedestrian with a foot on the crossing must be given priority. If a Zebra crossing is divided by an island, it can be regarded as two separate crossings, and if there is a pedestrian on the other section, you may proceed over the nearside part of the crossing. But do so with care.

When turning at a junction you should give way to pedestrians who have started to cross the road into which you are turning, whether or not the junction is traffic light controlled.

If you see a blind person with a guide dog waiting to cross the road, do not stop to allow the pair to cross—except, of course, at a pedestrian crossing. The dog has been trained to judge when it is safe to cross and stopping may confuse him. Moreover, a car coming from the other direction may not have seen the situation.

School crossings are usually signposted ahead (page 51 in the Highway Code), and if you see one slow down and take particular care. The 'Lollipop' person, in rare cases, may be unable to judge the speed of approaching traffic accurately and, therefore, could walk into the road prematurely.

Cyclists

Some motorists appear to regard cyclists as a nuisance, but they should be given just as much consideration as any other road user. Do not overtake a cyclist too closely, especially at speed, as the displaced air wave can be very disconcerting and cause a wobble. On a hill, a cyclist may zig-zag from side to side, so take extra care.

Remember that when starting from rest, a cyclist tends to zig-zag slightly and make allowances for this if you are alongside at traffic lights when they change to green.

If you overtake a cyclist just before you intend to make a left hand turn, make sure you have plenty of room to make the turn without cutting across his bows. If you have any doubt, hold back.

Motorcyclists

The main problem with motorcyclists is that they are often difficult to see, especially if one is overtaking you. The 'blind spot' over your right shoulder may not entirely mask a car but can hide a motorcycle completely. Although they should not do so, motorcyclists often overtake on the nearside, so if you are about to turn left, in heavy traffic especially, keep a watchful eye on your mirrors for this possibility.

Turning right out of a side road is also hazardous. A car approaching from your right may have signalled that he intends to turn into the road from which you are emerging. The road behind him might appear to be clear but there could be a motorcyclist overtaking him, masked from your sight by the car or other parts of the road scene.

Commercial vehicles

Heavy lorry drivers are expert at handling their vehicles but, because of the length they have special problems. An articulated lorry, for example, has to take a wide line at roundabouts because the rear wheels follow a tighter radius than the front ones, so if you are in the right hand lane give way to avoid the danger of his rear wheels cutting across your line.

The same wide sweep is necessary at any junction so if you see a long lorry about to turn into the road from which you are emerging, hold back to give room for the cab to clear your car.

Van drivers can, certainly, hold you up but they have a job to do and it is not always easy for them to find a good parking place at the point of call, so be patient if your way is temporarily obstructed.

Urban bus drivers have the difficult task of trying to keep on schedule, especially during rush hour periods, so whenever safe and possible, give way to the bus which has signalled it is about to pull out from a bus stop. Do not park, even briefly, at a bus stop. If one comes along it will have to stop out in the road, and it will be a hazard to other road users.

Emergency vehicles

If you hear the warning sound of an emergency vehicle—ambulance, fire engine, or police car—try first to determine whence it is coming, looking for the flashing blue light.

If it is coming from behind, pull over as tightly as possible to your left and stop, with your left indicator flashing. If there are parked cars with no gaps, even take an unwanted left turn to get out of the way. A life may depend on it.

If the vehicle is coming from ahead and there is heavy traffic, it may be necessary for it to come over to your side of the road to get by. Make every effort to allow it to do so, and indicate as clearly as you can to vehicles behind that you intend to do so.

Other motorists

Your responsibility is to treat other motorists with consideration, and although you should be able to expect the same treatment, do not count on it.

Always bear in mind the possibility of the other driver doing something unexpected or foolish. Allow him plenty of room and do not get impatient. With safety the most important factor, exercise courtesy and consideration at all times.

Treat courtesy from other drivers with due caution. If another driver stops and beckons you to move out from a side road, double check before moving out that it is safe and there is not a motorcycle or other vehicle which you may not have seen coming up behind him.

The main method of communication between vehicles on the road is by their electric signals, although arm signals are also used in some circumstances. Because so much depends on these signals it is most important that they should be absolutely clear.

They should also be given in good time so that other road users can react to them, and you should always look in the rear-view mirror before making a signal, in order to make sure you are not creating a hazard.

He intends to move out to the right or turn right.

He is likely to turn left or stop on the left.

There is little doubt that this driver intends to turn left.

Flashing direction indicators

Most drivers use their flashing direction indicators to signal their intentions.

He is slowing down or stopping.

Never take another driver's signals for granted. Wait until you are quite sure his signal is intentional before moving out. He may have forgotten to cancel his left indicator.

At a junction where a policeman or traffic warden is controlling the traffic, your position on the road may suggest, erroneously, that you wish to turn right. The left hand held up palm forwards will indicate that, in fact, you intend to go straight on.

Arm signals

Although they are not used very much nowadays, arm signals can help to reinforce electric signals.

He probably intends to turn right. Do not take it for granted, however, that he will complete the manoeuvre. There may be some other hazard you have not seen.

He intends to move to the left, turn left or stop on the left. If intending to stop on the left the far side of a turning to the left, he should not indicate until he has passed that turning, or confusion may result.

A line of traffic is more likely to let this driver in than if he relied on his flashing indicator alone.

Using the arm signal for 'I intend to slow down or stop' when stopping for pedestrians at a Zebra crossing warns following vehicles that the driver is about to give way to the pedestrians and the pedestrians know what he intends too.

When giving way to pedestrians at a Zebra crossing do not signal to them or wave them across. They should check for themselves that there is no hazard (perhaps one which you cannot see) to prevent them crossing safely.

Signals by authorised persons

Policeman holds up traffic for pedestrians

Police signal to come on

Traffic behind must halt

Traffic ahead to come on

Side road traffic must halt

Traffic wardens have the same authority as the police when controlling traffic, and their signals must be obeyed. Even if they signal for you to go in a direction different from the one you intended, you must still obey their instruction.

The signals of school crossing patrols, like those of the police or traffic wardens, must always be obeyed. School crossings are usually signposted ahead, sometimes incorporating flashing amber lights. When you see one of these signs be prepared to stop, and take especial care if the sign precedes a bend.

Headlamp flashing

Although headlamp flashing is commonly used as a signal it can be very confusing and difficult to interpret. It should only be used to let another road user know you are there, never for any other reason.

Headlights warn 'I am here'

If you are faced with having to interpret a flashing headlight signal make absolutely certain you know what is intended before you take any action. What you might believe signifies 'come on', for example, may not actually mean that at all.

Treat with similar caution any signals given via the tail lights, such as lorry drivers sometimes use. They may be intended to let you know that it is safe to overtake, but it is your responsibility as the overtaking driver to be sure that it is safe to pass.

Horn

Although many people may react adversely to it, you should never hesitate to use the horn to alert another road user to your presence. It should, however, not be used for any other reason.

It is also a wise precaution to sound the horn when driving into an area of greatly restricted visibility, such as round a sharp bend in a country road, or from a narrow side entrance onto a busy main road with many pedestrians.

The horn may not be used when the car is stationary, or between 11.30 pm and 7.00 am when the car is travelling on roads subject to a 30 mph speed limit. It may be used to avoid an accident.

Practice 2 Learning to drive

By this stage you will have already spent some time driving on public roads, and it is now appropriate to keep practising the basic techniques and manoeuvres until you have corrected any faults you may have had. You must, of course, have a fully-qualified and responsible friend or relative in the passenger seat when carrying out these practice exercises.

Try to find some quiet road which offers bends, turns, crossroads and, if possible, hills. For every manoeuvre reassure yourself you are doing it 'by the book'. Even if the roads are quiet, watch your mirrors, give the correct signals, check your speed and keep good observation. It is unwise to prolong a practice session much over one hour and a half. You will be carrying out manoeuvres at far more frequent intervals than you would when driving normally, even in traffic, and this can be tiring.

Starting off

The first part of the exercise involves starting off from rest. Use this as an opportunity to revise the pre-start drill. Once on the move, immediately pay attention to your straight line steering, delicately correcting any tendency for the car to steer off course so that you can maintain a steady line.

Turns

Practise a left turn first. Take all the proper precautions such as checking your mirror, then signalling, adjusting speed then engaging the correct gear, and finally carrying out the manoeuvre. Keep repeating the left turn until you can do it neatly.

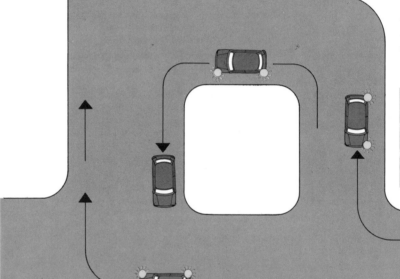

When you feel confident about left turns practise right turns. Keep a careful look out for other traffic and follow the mirror-signal-gear-manoeuvre formula, checking that you position your car correctly. Watch your line carefully so that you do not cut the corner as you complete the turn.

After practising several right turns, repeat a few left turns to ensure you have not forgotten the proper procedure to use.

Reversing

Practise reversing in a straight line, then around a left corner and finally around a right corner. Remember to watch all four corners of the car while reversing, especially when reversing into another road.

You must also look over both shoulders, especially the left one as it gives a view down the centre line of the car.

Turning in the road

Before practising turning in the road make sure you have plenty of time to complete the manoeuvre before any other traffic can appear

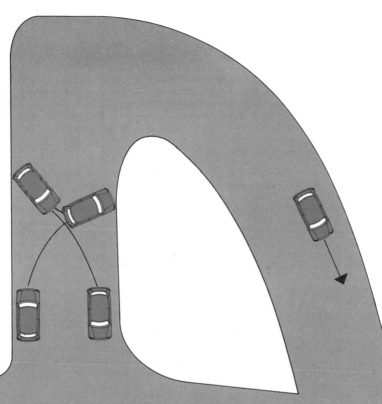

on the scene. You should choose a road that is wide enough to turn the car round completely by using a forwards-reverse-forwards again sequence.

Hill starts

Do not seek out a steep hill to practise hill starts at first. Any slope will suffice if the car will

roll back when not held on the handbrake.

When practising a hill start, do not stop within a few yards. Continue for at least one gear change before stopping and trying again.

Emergency stop

Take great care before practising an emergency stop that the road is completely clear in both directions. Drive up to 20 or 25 mph and get your companion to give you the signal to stop. Before doing so he must check scrupulously that no other traffic is in the vicinity.

A good signal is for your companion to slap a hand on the fascia. There is a tendency for the learner driver is to stamp too hard on the brake pedal, skidding to a halt with locked wheels. The correct technique is to press very firmly on the brake pedal so that the car will pull up in a short distance with the wheels continuing to turn until the very last moment.

You should try not to stall the engine when doing an emergency stop. To prevent this, push the clutch pedal down just as you are coming to a halt. As soon as possible after you have stopped look all round, then move to the side of the road and stop again.

227

Observation Learning to drive

Good observation is the act of looking at a situation, seeing it properly and observing it accurately. You should also be able to perceive how the situation will develop. Your eyes should always be on the move looking ahead, to both sides and in the mirrors.

There is a common tendency not to look far enough ahead along the road. Do not concentrate too much on the vehicle ahead but try to look past it, through it and under it to what lies beyond. Looking well ahead along the road you can prepare your course of action in good time rather than, for example, waiting until you see the other vehicle's brake lights come on.

Road signs

Carefully observing all the road signs will give you a great deal of information about what lies ahead. You will be able to know if the double bends ahead start with a left bend or a right; whether the road narrows ahead from the left, right or both sides, whether to expect children, a hospital and much more. A survey of the signs in general use is given on pages 50 and 51.

Road markings

The white lines marking the centre of the road provide information about the likelihood of a hazard ahead. Where these change from normal centre line markings to the longer dashes of hazard warning lines, proceed with greater caution. The word 'slow' painted on the road is always there for a good reason and should never be ignored.

Road surfaces

Always take note of the condition of the road surface, whether it is dry and firm or likely to be slippery for any reason. After a prolonged period of hot, dry weather a shower can produce extremely slippery conditions.

Autumn leaves on a damp road are a strong indication that the road

will be slippery; on a cold winter morning when the sun has melted the hoar frost in places, keep a good look out for icy patches in the sections where the trees shade the road.

After prolonged and very cold weather, if you notice signs of the road surface crumbling slightly, be prepared to find severely broken up areas and bad potholes also.

Country areas

Country roads may sometimes appear to be deserted, but sharp observation of the road ahead can often give advance warning of some danger. The line of a side road may be observed across a field some way ahead, or a finger-post may indicate where a junction is located. Particular dangers of driving on country roads are the possibilities of finding loose animals, horse riders, children and slow-moving agricultural equipment, sometimes emerging from fields or farmyards.

Towns

The rules of good observation are just the same in towns, but there is usually a good deal more going on which demands the driver's attention. Apart from the road signs, direction signs, traffic lights and pedestrian crossings, there is a great variety of traffic from cyclists and pedestrians to heavy goods vehicles.

In narrow streets where the road bends, reflections in shop windows can often give warning of an approaching vehicle. In slanting sunshine, shadows can also betray the presence of another car. Patches of sunlight across the road can mark a side turning.

During busy times, especially on Saturday mornings, pavements become crowded and people trying to pass one another may step into the road without looking. Advance warning of a bus stop is given when bus passengers are seen to stand up and approach the exit.

In residential areas expect to find children playing near the road. A ball rolling into the road may be followed by a running child. Ice cream vans may also call children across the road.

Navigation through an unfamiliar town is made easier by good observation. Knowing where to look for the direction signposts, and looking well ahead will enable the right course to be chosen in good time. Street name plates will usually be found on a wall or fence at about waist level in residential districts, and above the facia line on the corner of a row of shops.

A street containing a line of parked cars holds a number of hazards. Pedestrians, including children, may be concealed by the cars, so watch for feet visible behind the cars indicating that someone is about to step out into your path. White exhaust fumes from a parked car indicates one which has just been started from cold—it may pull out in front of you. You may see signs of the front wheels starting to turn. Heads seen through the rear window of a parked car should be interpreted as a warning that the driver's door may suddenly open.

The correct positioning of your car on the road is particularly important when tackling corners, junctions and roundabouts. Three main factors are involved. Good positioning will give you the best visibility through the situation; it will also maximise your car's stability; finally it will accurately guide other road users as to the direction you intend to take.

Left hand bend

As you approach a left hand bend, check in your mirror that it is clear behind. Take up the safety line position to the left of the carriageway then slow by braking to the correct speed for the severity of the bend, and if necessary, change down to a lower gear.

If your view through the bend is restricted, by hedges for example, you will need to slow even further. As you enter the bend use constant throttle, neither accelerating nor decelerating, and steer along the safety line course well to the left of the carriageway. Keep this course through the bend. As you straighten up out of the bend, accelerate smoothly, change into top gear and take up a more central position on the road.

Junctions

Turning into and out of side roads and the approach to T-junctions is described on pages 212 and 213 Crossroads pose slightly different problems. When on a main road approaching a crossroads with two minor roads, do not assume that other traffic will automatically give way to you, even though it should.

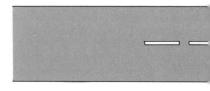

At crossroads controlled by traffic lights you must wait for a gap in the oncoming traffic if you wish to turn right. Should an oncoming driver also wish to turn to his right you should turn offside to offside, passing behind the other vehicle.

If for any reason it is not possible to turn in this way, but you have to turn nearside to nearside, take great care that no other vehicles especially motorcycles are masked by the other vehicle.

Right hand bend

The principle that applies to tackling a right hand bend is that the road position should be such as to give you the safest position all through the bend. You enter the bend on a line two feet from the kerb and stick to this constant line all through the bend. Do not attempt to straighten out the bend by taking a path nearer to the centre line of the road.

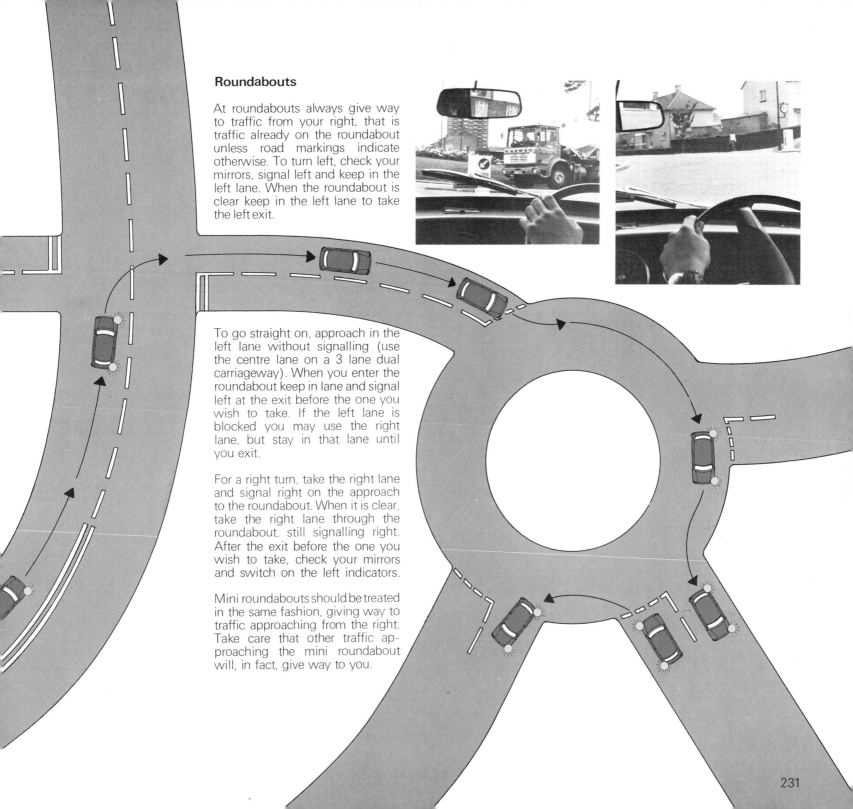

Roundabouts

At roundabouts always give way to traffic from your right, that is traffic already on the roundabout unless road markings indicate otherwise. To turn left, check your mirrors, signal left and keep in the left lane. When the roundabout is clear keep in the left lane to take the left exit.

To go straight on, approach in the left lane without signalling (use the centre lane on a 3 lane dual carriageway). When you enter the roundabout keep in lane and signal left at the exit before the one you wish to take. If the left lane is blocked you may use the right lane, but stay in that lane until you exit.

For a right turn, take the right lane and signal right on the approach to the roundabout. When it is clear, take the right lane through the roundabout, still signalling right. After the exit before the one you wish to take, check your mirrors and switch on the left indicators.

Mini roundabouts should be treated in the same fashion, giving way to traffic approaching from the right. Take care that other traffic approaching the mini roundabout will, in fact, give way to you.

Overtaking is one of the most demanding manoeuvres a motorist makes. With the proper care it need not be dangerous, provided you follow the rules for doing so safely. If you have any doubt at all, however, do not overtake.

Hold back position

Taking up the correct position behind the vehicle in front is a vital 'first step before overtaking. Before taking it up, however, check in your mirrors that it is safe to do so. The 'hold back position' enables you to see as much as possible beyond the vehicle in front. If you get too close your vision is severely restricted and you cannot adopt a smooth overtaking line. No precise figure can be put on this distance. It is whatever distance you need in order to see past adequately.

The correct 'hold back position' will enable you to see oncoming traffic and help you see if there is another vehicle in front of the one you plan to overtake. This situation can be dangerous if you do not discover it until you are committed to the overtaking manoeuvre. From the correct 'hold back position' you will also be able to look beyond the vehicle in front by glancing down the inside of it, over it or under it as the road situation allows.

From time to time other more impatient drivers will overtake you, dropping into your 'hold back' space. This may be irritating but do not decrease the gap on that account. In fact, it will be necessary to drop farther back to allow adequate space between you and the car in front.

Oncoming traffic

The accurate assessment of the speed and behaviour of oncoming traffic is essential for safe overtaking. You should know that you can return safely to your side of the road after completing the overtaking manoeuvre without causing any of the oncoming traffic to slow down or swerve. You should also check that none of the oncoming traffic is likely to start overtaking as it approaches you.

Following traffic

Although the situation ahead will demand a great deal of attention when planning an overtaking manoeuvre, it is important to check your rear view mirrors regularly. Another car may be coming up behind you faster than you had realised. Before signalling to start overtaking, you should always check your mirrors once again.

Let the bus go first

Overtaking speed

While overtaking, you should keep to a minimum the time exposed to danger. Your own knowledge of your car's performance will indicate how quickly the manoeuvre can be accomplished.

As soon as you have satisfied yourself that the road ahead is clear and that no one is coming up fast from behind, check your mirrors, signal, select the right gear to give you smart acceleration, move out to the right and drive firmly past the other vehicles.

Your line should be a gentle curve from the 'hold back position' to the overtaking line, then in as straight a line as possible past the other vehicle's offside, keeping a safe distance away from it.

Plan your overtaking manoeuvre...

Return to the left

When you are well clear of the vehicle you are passing move back to your own side of the road and change into top gear. Although the time exposed to danger when overtaking should be kept to a minimum, do not cut in sharply in front of the slower-moving vehicle. Your line should be a very gentle curve as you return to the nearside.

. . . in plenty of time

No overtaking

There are a number of situations in which overtaking should never be considered.

Road signs and markings warn of some of these situations, and in these cases it is against the law to overtake. Double white lines, for example, must not be crossed when overtaking, nor must those in which the line on your side is solid while the other one is broken. Each side of a Zebra crossing is marked with zig-zag lines and these indicate areas where over-taking is not allowed.

It is dangerous to overtake on a bend or corner, approaching a hump-backed bridge or the brow of a hill. Other vehicles are over-taken on the right, although ex-ceptions to this are sometimes found in one-way streets. Vehicles turning right can be passed on the left, however. On dual carriage-ways and motorways it is even more important to overtake only on the right whatever other motorists might do.

Great caution is required on three-lane roads

Some roads call for extra care when overtaking. Perhaps the most dan-gerous situations are created on three-lane roads when overtaking traffic in both directions can use the centre lane. Take great care before starting to overtake on these roads that no oncoming traffic is overtaking or planning to overtake, and also that no vehicles are coming up fast from behind. When overtaking also try to avoid being the 'meat in the sandwich'—that is overtaking a vehicle while there is another vehicle passing in the opposite direction.

Do not cross double white lines

A deceptive situation arises on straight roads which are slightly hilly. The road can seem to be perfectly clear ahead but, in fact, there could be other vehicles concealed in the dips.

If you are behind a car which pulls out to overtake a slower-moving vehicle never follow it past on the assumption the road is clear ahead. The other driver may have judged his manoeuvre finely and you may be faced by oncoming traffic.

Sometimes another driver may wave you on and indicate that it is clear ahead for you to overtake. Lorry drivers occasionally give this signal with their rear lights. You should regard this signal as nothing more than an indication that the other driver knows you are there, and make your own judgement about when it is safe to overtake.

No overtaking

Do not follow through

Practice 3 Learning to drive

Your driving test will probably not be far away by the time this final practice session is taken. It should be arranged to cover all the aspects of driving that you have learned.

Planning

Detailed planning of the practice session will help you derive the maximum benefit from it. You should select as a companion a fully-qualified friend or relative who will help you go through the practice and who is prepared to test you on different aspects of your driving.

You should no longer seek only quiet roads for practice, but aim to include some traffic driving as well. Plan a route which will last no more than one and a half hours, as anything longer could be tiring. The following features should be included in the route:

Junction of side road into a main road
T-junctions
Crossroads (some with traffic lights)
Roundabouts
Dual carriageway
Quiet roads (to practise reversing and turning the car round)
Hill (to practise moving away on a gradient)

Your companion should give you route instructions (eg 'I want you to take the next road to the left') in plenty of time so that you can make the manoeuvres correctly. Ideally, he should be someone who knows the district well. He should

also test your observation, asking, once or twice, what was the last road sign passed?, and he should help you practise stopping the car properly.

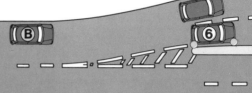

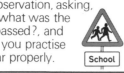

Practice plan

The plan on this page includes all the features which ought to be included as part of one or more practice sessions. Everyone must adapt this to their own circumstances but try to include as many of these features as possible.

1 Pre-start drill. Every time you go out you should practise the pre-start drill so that it becomes a matter of habit.
2 Turn left as the side road enters the main road.
A Your companion asks whether or not a speed limit is in force.
3 Turn right off main road.
4 Turn left at T-junction.

6 If the opportunity arises, practise overtaking on the section of dual carriageway.

7 Turn right at the traffic-light controlled crossroads.
C Your companion asks the meaning of the yellow box marked on the crossroads.

5 Turn right at T-junction.
B Your companion asks what the last road sign was that you passed. You should be expecting the school coming up.

D Your companion asks the meaning of the zig-zag lines marked on the approach to the Zebra crossing.

234

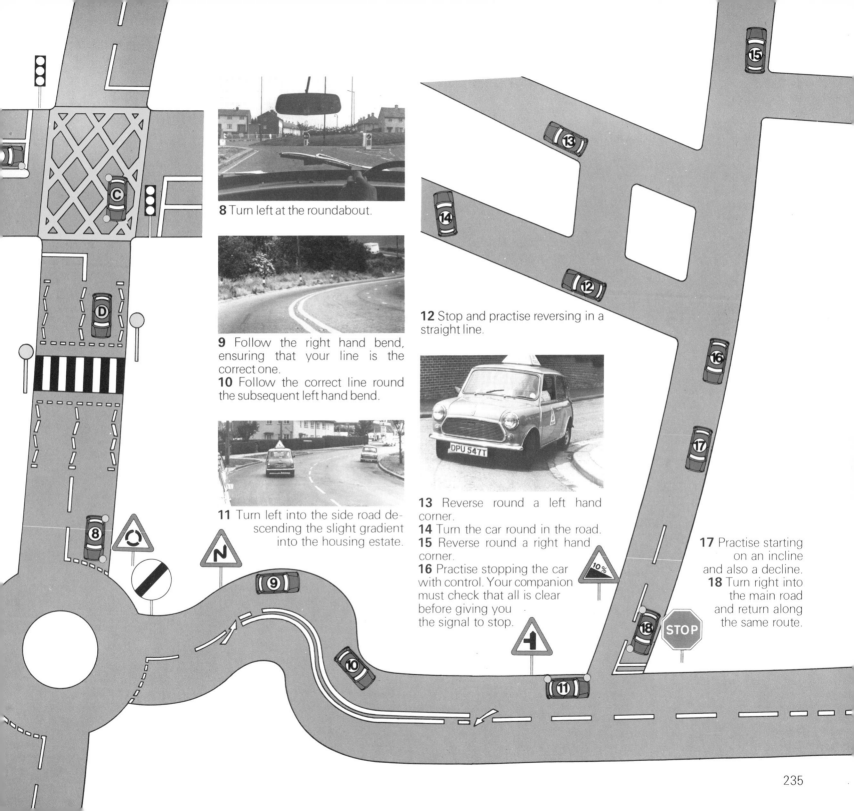

8 Turn left at the roundabout.

9 Follow the right hand bend, ensuring that your line is the correct one.
10 Follow the correct line round the subsequent left hand bend.

11 Turn left into the side road descending the slight gradient into the housing estate.

12 Stop and practise reversing in a straight line.

13 Reverse round a left hand corner.
14 Turn the car round in the road.
15 Reverse round a right hand corner.
16 Practise stopping the car with control. Your companion must check that all is clear before giving you the signal to stop.

17 Practise starting on an incline and also a decline.
18 Turn right into the main road and return along the same route.

Test yourself Learning to drive

The process of preparation for the driving test begins with your first driving lesson. A variety of books will supplement the practical tuition, and your experience can be consolidated with plenty of driving practice. In addition, a knowledge of The Highway Code and other motoring matters is expected for the test. It is inadvisable to try to cram a great deal of revision into the day or evening before the test, so much of this preparation should be carried out further in advance.

The Highway Code

Before you go to the test, you must have got to know The Highway Code properly, and the examiner will ask you a few questions to see if you have a good knowledge of it. Apart from what you must and must not do—such as coming to a complete halt at a 'Stop' sign or straddling double solid white lines—there is a great deal of useful information about driving of great help to the learner driver.

One of the problems with the test is when to apply for it. Because of the considerable delays, there may be a gap of many weeks between your application and the date you are given. Your instructor will have to try to judge how many lessons you are likely to need and, knowing the delay in your area, tell you when to apply.

Relax

When going for your test, try to keep relaxed. Remember, the examiner is not someone chosen for ill nature; his or her object is simply to see if you are a competent driver and know how to behave yourself behind the wheel. If your instructor considers you

have reached the stage where you drive well and can, therefore, pass, he is very likely to be right, and the only thing which might cause you to fail is tension. A tense candidate tends to do things jerkily which is not the sign of a competent driver.

Taking a tranquilliser is certainly not to be recommended and in some circumstances you could be said to be driving under the influence of drugs, which is, of course, an offence.

Do not try to learn the Code parrot fashion; read it carefully and often, so that you get to know what its recommendations are. The driving examiner will want to satisfy himself that you know, as an example, you must not overtake on the nearside of a vehicle except in certain circumstances, but he will not expect a word for word reply.

You should read all sections of the Code, not just those which apply to drivers. It is essential you should know what to expect of other road users so you can take the right action in any given circumstances.

When you have become conversant with its contents, get a friend or relative to ask you random questions from its pages to find out if you have, in fact, digested what you have read. If there is anything which you do not thoroughly understand, ask your driving instructor to explain it to you in detail.

Self-criticism

As the test comes nearer you should have reached the stage where you can be self-critical about your driving techniques, and when you go on a practice run

you should know when you have done something wrong or clumsily. If you find you have certain weaknesses, devote a practice session to trying to eradicate them, and continue to try until you feel you have done so.

Highly skilled drivers sometimes make mistakes, and even an expert can have an off-day, so although your aim should be perfection, do not become too despondent if you find certain things a bit difficult to get right. Practice and self-criticism will smooth out the errors in the end.

A test examiner will not fail you for a couple of minor mistakes. Provided your general driving is safe and competent you will pass, so if at an early stage in the test you miss a gear change, remind yourself not to panic. If you correct the error smoothly, the examiner will be satisfied.

Road signs

You must, of course, know the road signs at a glance and understand exactly what they mean. There are two types of sign, those which must be obeyed, and those which give warnings. In the main, those which are circular give orders, the ones with red circles being prohibitive, and those which are triangular are warning signs. Although learner drivers are not permitted on motorways, you should nevertheless get to know what motorway signs mean.

When you have studied The Highway Code over a period of time, try the questions which follow and see how you get on. You will find the correct answers in The Highway Code on the page numbers given after each question.

If a Zebra crossing has an island in the middle, is it to be regarded as one crossing or two separate ones? (Page 8, para 13).

If a Pelican crossing has a central refuge is it to be regarded as one crossing? (Page 9, para 15).

When may you overtake on the left? (Page 20, para 81).

What is the shortest stopping distance in feet on a good, dry road with a good car from 50 mph? (Page 14, para 47; back cover).

When should you not overtake? (Page 21, para 85).

Are you allowed to stop on a Sunday where the kerb is marked by a single yellow line? (Page 56).

When may you use hazard warning lights? (Page 32, para 117).

What does the amber traffic light mean? (Page 46).

When may you enter a box junction? (Page 23, para 92).

What, according to the Code, does the flashing of headlights signify? (Page 29, para 113).

On a motorway, when may you use the right hand lane of a three-lane carriageway? (Page 38, para 156).

What do these signs mean? (Pages 50 and 51).

What signals should you give when turning right at a roundabout? (Page 28, para 106).

What does this road marking mean? (Page 55).

On a motorway, what does this signal mean? (Page 41, No. 3).

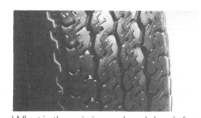

What is the minimum legal depth for tyre tread? (Page 64, CUR Nos. 100 and 99).

What must you do when you stop and leave the car? (Page 65, CUR Nos. 109 and 116).

In what circumstances may you use fog lights instead of headlights? (Page 28/29, para 111).

When may you not use the horn? (Page 30, para 114).

When may you park at night without lights? (Page 33, para 122 and page 66—RVL (Ex) R).

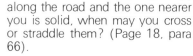

If there are double white lines along the road and the one nearer you is solid, when may you cross or straddle them? (Page 18, para 66).

How far behind your car should you place a warning triangle if you break down on the hard shoulder of a motorway? (Page 33, para 124).

You are approaching a lorry parked on your side of the road. An oncoming car is also approaching. Who should give way? (Page 20, para 84).

The driving test Learning to drive

All the preparation involved in learning to drive culminates in the Department of Transport driving test. Everyone who wishes to drive a motor vehicle on the road must have passed this test, in the form appropriate for that vehicle.

Application for the test

The application form for the driving test is obtained from any post office. There will be a delay, however, between the application and the date set for the test, depending on the waiting list of candidates at the time. Your instructor will advise you when to apply after judging how many lessons you will need, and bearing in mind the delay in your area.

Applying too soon could mean that you will not have reached the required level by the time you take the test. Applying too late may result in your spending more money than necessary on lessons to keep you up to the standard of the test.

Preparation

The right amount of instruction and practice is an obvious prerequisite for passing the driving test, but just as important is the mental preparation. The test is often seen as a psychological ordeal, but suitable preparation and the adoption of a relaxed attitude can help.

The test has been made as standardised as possible in all areas, and the test route will have been selected to provide the fairest possible test of a learner driver's ability. Even the expressions used by the examiner are similar, wherever the test takes place.

The examiner has been carefully chosen and trained to assess your driving skills in a balanced, fair and objective way. He or she will be impersonal and unwilling to be drawn into conversation, but do not infer from this that he is difficult or disagreeable. He will give you precise instructions during the test, such as 'take the second road to the left, please', but otherwise he will probably say very little.

He will certainly understand that you may be nervous, and will want you to pass the test if your driving standard is satisfactory. This is very likely to be the case if your driving instructor considers you are ready for the test. The examiner will observe what you do, but will not be worried by minor mistakes, especially those brought about through nerves. Faults in the first 4 minutes do not count. Serious or dangerous faults will concern him more and will lead to a failure. Provided your general standard of driving is competent, however, you should pass the driving test without too much difficulty. There is no advantage to be gained from attempting a hurried revision of The Highway Code or any other book at the last minute, or the night before. This will cloud your mind rather than help you learn more. Your instructor believes you will pass so there is nothing extra you can do at the last minute to improve your chances.

On the day of the test try to relax as much as possible. Allow plenty of time to get to the test centre and drive there yourself, so you arrive in a relaxed frame of mind. On no account take any tranquillisers. These have a detrimental effect on your driving, and you could be said to be driving under the influence of drugs, which is an offence. Whilst waiting at the test centre try not to think too much about the test to come, but occupy yourself with light reading.

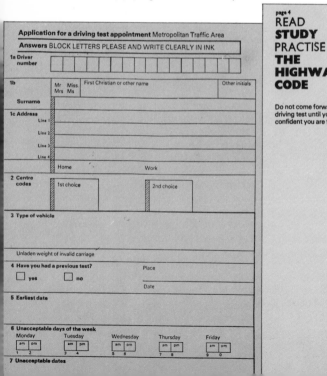

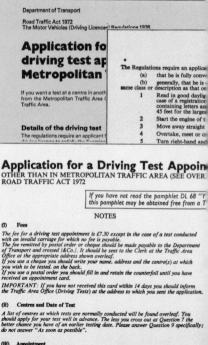

Make sure you have the necessary documents with you. These are:

appointment card
provisional driving licence
insurance certificate (if using a car other than one belonging to a driving school).

The driving test

When the examiner meets you in the test centre waiting room, he will want you to sign the day log and produce your driving licence. He will also ask if you suffer from any disabilities not mentioned on the application form. Then he will ask you to lead him to your car.

As you reach the car he will ask you to read the number plate of a vehicle in the vicinity. If you wear glasses for this test you must always wear them when you drive.

When you and the examiner get into the car go through your pre-start drill as you would in a lesson. The examiner will then ask you to move off when you are ready, and give you brief but precise instructions about the route you are to follow. From now on, all you need do is follow these directions and show the examiner you can drive competently. If you are in any doubt about the directions, ask him to repeat them.

Your test may or may not involve starting on a gradient, depending on the local terrain. It will, however, involve an emergency stop.

The driving test itself lasts for about thirty-five minutes, at the end of which, back at the test centre, the examiner will always ask you a few questions to test your knowledge of The Highway Code and other motoring matters. Then he will tell you that the test has ended.

If you pass

At the end of the test the examiner will tell you immediately whether you have passed or failed. If you have passed it is most unlikely he will make any other remarks about your driving. You will then be given a pass certificate.

If your provisional driving licence still has some time to run you need not apply for a full licence until a few weeks before it runs out. The pass certificate converts the provisional licence to a full one for the groups endorsed on it. It does not entitle you, however, to supervise a learner driver.

At the appropriate time, send the provisional licence, the pass certificate, completed application form and the correct fee to the Driver and Vehicle Licensing Centre. Your full driving licence will be marked with the groups of vehicles you are entitled to drive. The licence also acts as a provisional licence for the groups which are not included in the full licence.

You should note that if you pass your test in a car with automatic transmission, your licence will only authorise you to drive automatics, not cars with a normal gearbox. If you pass the test using a car with a manual gearbox, however, you will also be licensed to drive cars with an automatic gearbox.

If you fail

Although examiners are not officially permitted to discuss their reasons for failing candidates, they help learners who fail by marking on a 'Statement of Failure' the points to which attention should be given before taking the test again. These faults will be those the examiner regards as most serious and this statement should be discussed with your examiner. If you fail the test you must wait one month before you can be tested again.

239

8 Useful information

A number of documents are required by every car owner and some of these must be produced if required by the police. Most of them should be passed to the new owner with any change in ownership of the vehicle.

Test certificate

If a vehicle was first registered in the United Kingdom more than three years ago, it is subject to the annual Department of Transport vehicle test.

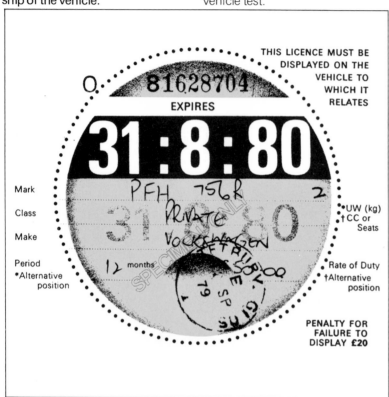

THIS LICENCE MUST BE DISPLAYED ON THE VEHICLE TO WHICH IT RELATES

Q. 81628704

EXPIRES

31 : 8 : 80

Mark

Class

Make

Period
*Alternative position

*UW (kg)
†CC or Seats

Rate of Duty
†Alternative position

12 months

PENALTY FOR FAILURE TO DISPLAY £20

PFH 756R 2
PRIVATE
VOLKSWAGEN

Tax disc

Before a car can be driven or even parked on a public road, the law demands that the owner shows that the appropriate road fund tax has been paid. This is done by displaying the tax disc which must be fixed inside the windscreen on the lower nearside.

It must be clearly visible from outside the car. Failure to display the disc can result in prosecution.

If it is fit for the road, the garage or test station will issue a certificate to this effect. This document is the 'MoT certificate'. Once a vehicle becomes liable for the test, it must be submitted annually to a test station or garage licensed to carry out the test.

The MoT certificate will have to be submitted to the licensing authority (or in certain instances the Post Office) each time the road fund tax is renewed.

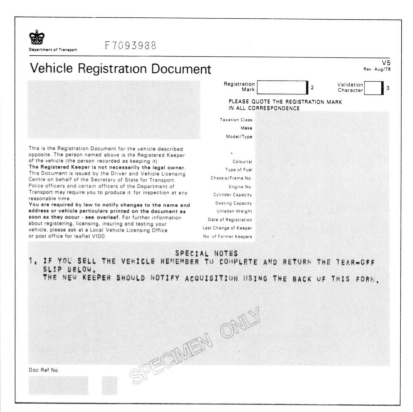

Department of Transport   F7093988

V5
Rev. Aug/78

Vehicle Registration Document

Registration Mark   2   Validation Character   3

PLEASE QUOTE THE REGISTRATION MARK IN ALL CORRESPONDENCE

Taxation Class
Make
Model/Type

Colour(s)
Type of Fuel
Chassis/Frame No.
Engine No.
Cylinder Capacity
Seating Capacity
Unladen Weight
Date of Registration
Last Change of Keeper
No. of Former Keepers

This is the Registration Document for the vehicle described opposite. The person named above is the Registered Keeper of the vehicle (the person recorded as keeping it).
The Registered Keeper is not necessarily the legal owner. This Document is issued by the Driver and Vehicle Licensing Centre on behalf of the Secretary of State for Transport. Police officers and certain officers of the Department of Transport may require you to produce it for inspection at any reasonable time.
You are required by law to notify changes to the name and address or vehicle particulars printed on the document as soon as they occur - see overleaf. For further information about registering, licensing, insuring and testing your vehicle, please ask at a Local Vehicle Licensing Office or post office for leaflet V100.

SPECIAL NOTES
1. IF YOU SELL THE VEHICLE REMEMBER TO COMPLETE AND RETURN THE TEAR-OFF SLIP BELOW.
THE NEW KEEPER SHOULD NOTIFY ACQUISITION USING THE BACK OF THIS FORM.

Doc Ref No.

DEPARTMENT OF TRANSPORT
Test Certificate
Serial Number
GA 534101

The motor vehicle, of which the Registration Mark (s)/Chassis or Serial Number (s)

is
, having been examined
under section 43 of the Road Traffic Act 1972, it is hereby certified that at the date of the examination thereof the statutory requirements prescribed by Regulations made under the said section 43 were complied with in relation to the vehicle.

Vehicle Testing Station Number

Date of Issue

Signature

Inspector appointed by/ for and on behalf of

Date of expiry

Serial Number of immediately preceding Test Certificate

(To be entered when the above date of expiry is more than 12 months after the date of issue)

The following further particulars of the vehicle should be entered:

Make   If a goods vehicle, unladen weight   kg

Approximate year of manufacture   If not a goods vehicle, horse power or cylinder capacity of engine in cubic centimeters

Recorded mileage

KEEP THIS CERTIFICATE SAFELY   CHECK carefully that the particulars quoted above are correct. Certificates showing alterations should not be issued or accepted. They may delay the renewal of your licence.   WARNING A test certificate should not be accepted as evidence of the satisfactory mechanical condition of a used vehicle offered for sale.

(See Notes overleaf)

VT20

Vehicle registration document

Formerly known as the 'log book', this is another item required when the road fund tax is applied for. It carries details of the owner, his or her address and full registration details of the vehicle.

The older log book held details of previous owners also, but this is no longer the case with the current registration document.

The registration document should not be left in the car. If the vehicle is stolen with the registration documents in it, a thief can more easily dispose of it. It should be handed on to the next owner if you sell your car.

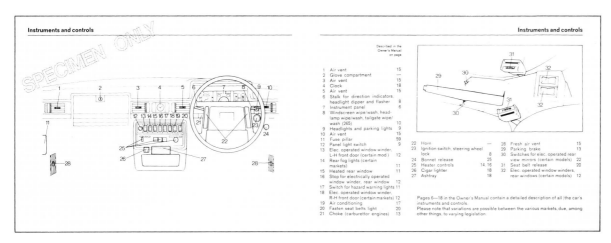

Described in the
Owner's Manual
on page

1 Air vent 15
2 Glove compartment —
3 Air vent 15
4 Clock 15
5 Air vent 15
6 Stalk for direction indicators,
  headlight dipper and flasher 8
7 Instrument panel —
8 Windscreen wipe/wash, headlamp wipe/wash, tailgate wipe/
  wash (265) 10
9 Headlights and parking lights 9
10 Air vent 15
11 Fuse pillar 59
12 Panel light switch 9
13 Elec. operated window winder,
   L-H front door (certain mod.) 12
14 Rear fog lights (certain
   markets) 11
15 Heated rear window 11
16 Stop for electrically operated
   window winder, rear window 12
17 Switch for hazard warning lights 11
18 Elec. operated window winder,
   R-H front door (certain markets) 12
19 Air conditioning 17
20 Fasten seat belts light 20
21 Choke (carburettor engines) 13

22 Horn 23
23 Ignition switch, steering wheel
   lock 8
24 Bonnet release 25
25 Heater controls 14, 16
26 Cigar lighter 18
27 Ashtray 18
28 Fresh air vent 15
29 Parking brake 13
30 Switches for elec. operated rear
   view mirrors (certain models) 22
31 Seat belt release 20
32 Elec. operated window winders,
   rear windows (certain models) 12

Pages 6—18 in the Owner's Manual contain a detailed description of all the car's
instruments and controls.
Please note that variations are possible between the various markets, due, among
other things, to varying legislation.

Handbook

The owner's manual or vehicle handbook is a useful document and should be kept with the car at all times. In the event of a minor breakdown it can provide invaluable information needed for minor repairs.

It also contains information about everyday maintenance of such aspects as tyre pressures, sparking plug types, contact breaker points gap, etc. Keep the book in a polythene bag so that it stays clean and readable. It may often be handled when your hands are dirty.

Service record

A complete service record of all work done on your car should be kept, whether you do the work yourself or have it done by a service station or garage. Not only is it invaluable as a means of keeping a check on running costs and ensuring that your car is kept in tip-top condition, but it is a good selling point to a buyer, who will be able to see that the car has been properly maintained.

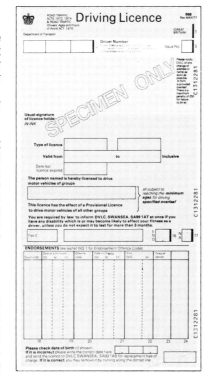

Driving licence

Your driving licence may re required by the police if you are involved in an accident or are apprehended for any reason. You should always carry it with you when you are driving. Make sure it is up to date and that you have signed it. The driving licence is not required when the road fund tax is applied for. It relates to you, not your car.

Membership cards

If you belong to a motoring organisation, do not forget to carry your membership card with you at all times. You will not be able to use their services, unless you can prove membership.

Import licence

If your car was imported from abroad after it had been registered by a previous owner—whether a company or an individual, you may be required to show evidence that it was imported legally and that any duty (if applicable) has been paid.

Selling your car

When you come to sell your car, you will need to complete a small form on the bottom of the vehicle registration document which you send to the Driver and Vehicle Licensing Centre. It is to safeguard you and the buyer that the transaction is in order.

Insurance Useful information

Every motorist is required, by law, to have insurance cover. Motor insurance is a very complicated affair and there are a great many different variations in the cover available. They all have certain basic aspects in common, however, and the following pages identify and compare these. Attempts to reduce the cost of motor insurance are often far from straightforward, as an apparent reduction in premium may be accompanied by an increase in liability in another aspect of the policy which could negate the reduction. Professional advice should always be sought when contemplating a change of policy. One of the most essential requirements, however, is complete openness with your insurance company.

Types of insurance

There are four main types of insurance policy

1 Road Traffic Act
2 Third Party Only
3 Third Party, Fire and Theft
4 Comprehensive

The cover they provide varies, and the premium to be paid varies with it. Which type of cover you need depends principally on you, your car and the use to which you will put it.

The table on this page shows whether or not certain types of loss are covered (usually only up to a stated limit) by the different policies.

Type of loss	Road Traffic Act	Third Party Only	Third Party Fire and Theft	Comprehensive
Your car stolen	No	No	Yes	Yes
Your car damaged by fire	No	No	Yes	Yes
Your garage damaged by fire	No	No	No	Yes
Your car damaged in an accident	No	No	No	Yes
Your car damaged maliciously	No	No	No	Yes
Your property stolen from your car	No	No	No	Yes
Your passengers' property damaged in an accident (your fault)	No	Yes	Yes	Yes
Other people's property damaged by your car in an accident (your fault)	No	Yes	Yes	Yes
Medical treatment costs for injury to you and/or your spouse	No	No	No	Yes
Compensation for injury or death to passengers after an accident (your fault)	No	Yes	Yes	Yes
Medical treatment or compensation for injury or death to other people after an accident (your fault)	Yes	Yes	Yes	Yes
Legal defence costs (by agreement)	Yes	Yes	Yes	Yes

Extent of cover

All insurance policies vary according to the company concerned and most policies will include other items not listed in this table. Examples of aspects of insurance cover which you may wish to examine when comparing the terms of different insurances are as follows:

Is windscreen breakage covered, and also scratches and damage caused to the paintwork by the breakage?

Is the car covered when it is in the hands of a garage for repair or overhaul?

Is there a refund of the premium when the car is laid up?

Does the policy cover trailers when they are being towed by your car?

Is cover provided for travel to countries outside the EEC?

Is the car covered while in transit to a foreign country?

Is the cost covered of towing the damaged car to a garage for repair?

If your new car is stolen or damaged beyond economical repair, will the insurance company replace it with a similar, new car?

Does the cover extend to the car radio?

Is frost damage specifically included?

Every individual will have his or her own personal requirements to consider as well.

Conditions of the policy

There are a number of conditions attached to every insurance policy which must be met to ensure its validity. You should read your policy thoroughly and make sure you understand its limitations.

Lending a car

When lending your car, check that the borrower has a full, current driving licence. You should also check that the car will still be covered by your own insurance. If your policy restricts the use of the car to the owner or to certain named drivers, the policy would need to be changed before the car can be lent to anyone else.

In an emergency you may lend your car to a person not covered by your insurance provided the borrower's insurance will cover them. Damage to the car will not be covered, however.

Borrowing a car

When borrowing a car find out whether you will be covered by the owner's insurance and also check if your own insurance extends to a borrowed car. If it does, it will normally cover claims by third parties only.

Borrowing a car from a garage requires care. Full insurance will usually need to be provided under the borrower's policy, so make sure you have a valid cover note.

Hiring a car

Insurance is usually arranged by the car hire company, although passenger cover and full cover for the car may need to be specifically requested.

Conditions of use

When completing the proposal form you will be required to state the uses to which the car will be put. If the car is driven for a use different from that specified on the policy, it will be invalidated. The standard policies will not cover use of the car for motor sport, rallies, competitions or trials.

Informing the company

The insurance company must always be kept fully up to date with developments or changes affecting your health and driving, or your car and its use. Complete information should have been given on the proposal form, and any changes notified to the company as soon as possible. You should tell the company if you:

Change the particulars on the proposal form

Change your car

Acquire an additional car

Allow it to be used by young or inexperienced drivers

Garage your car in the country but use it mainly in towns

Change your occupation

Suffer a deterioration in health or a physical disability

Are involved in an accident (whether you claim or not)

Are convicted of a motoring offence

Failure to tell the company about changes such as these could invalidate the policy.

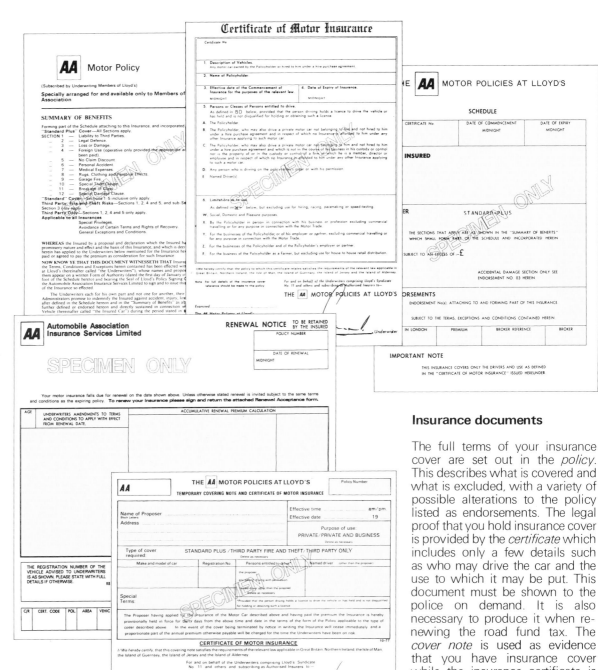

Insurance documents

The full terms of your insurance cover are set out in the *policy*. This describes what is covered and what is excluded, with a variety of possible alterations to the policy listed as endorsements. The legal proof that you hold insurance cover is provided by the *certificate* which includes only a few details such as who may drive the car and the use to which it may be put. This document must be shown to the police on demand. It is also necessary to produce it when renewing the road fund tax. The *cover note* is used as evidence that you have insurance cover while the insurance certificate is being prepared. It is valid for a short period only.

Insurance Useful information

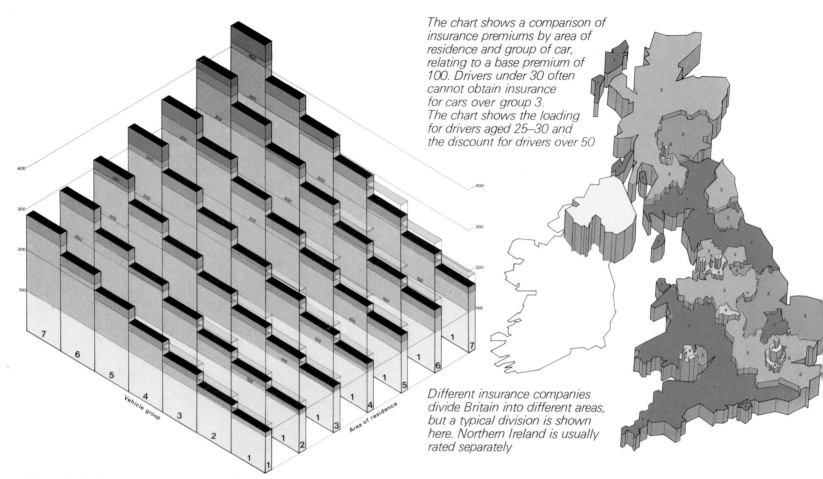

The chart shows a comparison of insurance premiums by area of residence and group of car, relating to a base premium of 100. Drivers under 30 often cannot obtain insurance for cars over group 3. The chart shows the loading for drivers aged 25–30 and the discount for drivers over 50

Different insurance companies divide Britain into different areas, but a typical division is shown here. Northern Ireland is usually rated separately

The calculation of the insurance premium is a complex matter which always arouses great interest. No two companies go about it in exactly the same way, although most follow a generally similar set of rules. It is usually only possible for a company to work out the exact premium after studying the details on the proposal form, so when comparing quotations from different companies, ensure that not only is the degree of cover provided similar, but also that the information given to each company was the same. Generally, a company will take most or all of the following eight points into account when calculating the premium.

Area of residence

Accidents are more common in densely-populated areas and premiums are higher there. Most insurance companies divide Britain into a number of different areas depending on their own experience of claims and accidents. Some may create as many as seven different areas, others only three. As car use in rural areas and long-distance car commuting increases, the difference between these areas grows less.

Type of car

Each model of car falls into one of seven groups for premium rating purposes. Not every company puts the same car into the same group, however. These groups are decided by the car's performance, its repair costs and the company's own claims experience. High performance sports cars tend to be highly-rated and so do many foreign makes because of the frequently high cost and poor availability of spares. The type of car you own and the area of your residence are the two most important factors determining your basic premium.

Age of drivers

The age of the owner and the other people likely to drive the car is taken into account. The age groups seen as being particularly accident prone are:
1 under 20
2 21–25
3 71–80
4 26–30

Driving record

If you have a bad driving record, your premium will be heavily loaded. Convictions for driving under the influence of drink or drugs, or dangerous driving, usually mean a high premium and severely restricted cover.

Car use

Cars used for social, domestic and pleasure purposes attract the lowest premiums. Business use attracts higher premiums, and commercial travelling, even higher premium levels.

Occupation

Certain occupations are considered high-risk by insurance companies. Examples of these are publicans, entertainers and commercial travellers. Other occupations attract better terms, such as accountants, civil servants and teachers.

Country of origin

If you lack driving experience in Britain because you have come from abroad, your premium will be increased.

Car value

High priced cars are likely to carry a loading on the premium.

Voluntary excess

The premium will usually be reduced if you voluntarily agree to pay the first part (up to a stated sum) of any claim for accidental damage to your own car. You can also agree to pay the first part of any claim at all under the policy, and this will qualify you for a larger discount.

No-claim bonus

Most companies operate a scheme of no-claim bonuses, by which your premium is reduced annually to a certain level if you do not make a claim. These are not always the same from one company to another, but the following table gives an example.

Claim-free years	No-claim bonus	£100 premium reduced to
1	20%	£80
2	30%	£70
3	40%	£60
4	50%	£50
5	60%	£40
6	60%	£40

This no-claim bonus can usually be transferred to another company if desired.

If a claim is made after a period of two years without claims, the usual procedure is for the premium to drop back two steps on the discount scale.

Whether or not to claim

Generally, the insurers work on the principle that if they have to pay out on a claim, however small, and whoever is to blame, the policy holder will have his no-claim discount reduced. There are, therefore, certain circumstances where it may be more economical to pay costs privately. The balance between the repair bill and the loss of discount has to be weighed up.

Suppose the motorist pays a basic premium of £150, but is on the maximum discount rate. Given the scale in the table above, his premium will be £60. The repairs will come to, say, £90. The financial comparison is therefore as detailed:

	If he makes a claim	If he pays for repairs himself
Cost of repairs	nil	£90
Premium next year	£105	£60
Premium year after	£90	£60
Premium year after	£75	£60
Total	£270	£270

Not your fault

Claims may be made without prejudice to your no-claim discount if the accident was proved to be not your fault, assuming that the name and address of the third party is known and his insurance is valid.

Your fault

Again, you may choose whether to pay privately or not for your own damage, but if you cause injury or damage to someone else's person or property this cost has to be taken into account too. However, it may still be cheaper to settle privately rather than have your no-claim discount prejudiced.

Knock for knock agreements

These are operated when two companies agree between themselves each to pay for the cost of repairs to the car they insure—as long as both parties are comprehensively insured. It does not matter which party was at fault. As a result of this agreement, a motorist may have his no-claim discount reduced, even if he was not the guilty party but this is certainly not always the case. It is up to the driver to convince his insurer of his innocence and so retain his full no-claim discount.

Making a claim

If your vehicle is involved in an accident, report the matter to your insurers as soon as possible. Never admit liability. If you do your insurers may refuse to deal with your claim. Complete and return the claim form quickly with any estimates you need. Try and obtain the name and address of at least one witness.

When filling in a claim form, details of the incident should be as comprehensive and accurate as possible. A sketch of the incident will also be required, together with a brief description of what happened at the time.

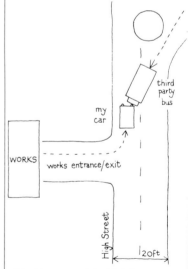

'I had just entered the High Street from my works when a bus coming from the opposite direction came across on to the wrong side of the road and collided with my car. It was not possible for me to take avoiding action.

The driver of the car behind me came forward as a witness'.

Buying and selling Useful information

Buying a new car

The very wide choice of new car models available means that everyone should be able to find the most suitable car for themselves. It also increases the chances of making the wrong choice.

The ingredients which make up the choice are as follows:

Suitability Identify what sort of car you need, but also check that you are not buying a car which is bigger (and therefore more expensive) than you really need. Examine each car critically from this point of view, and test drive it.

Purchase price Examine whether this includes car tax, VAT, seat belts, delivery, number plates and road tax. Also see whether you can obtain a discount from the dealer.

Running costs When making your choice compare the road test reports (e.g. from *Drive* magazine) for different models. Look at fuel consumption figures under different driving conditions. Also examine the costs of servicing, spares, and insurance.

Safety Increasing regard is being paid to the safety features built into new cars. Are seat belts effective and convenient? Does it have an energy-absorbing steering column? Are the doors crash-proof and child-proof? Examine road test reports for answers to these questions.

Servicing Make sure you get good service after buying the car. It may be best to buy from a local dealer who has trained personnel for servicing and maintenance and a good stock of spare parts.

Warranties Look carefully at the warranties of the various makes being offered and other warranties that are available. See that both parts and labour are warrantied and check the period of time.

Condition When the new car is delivered be sure to inspect its condition thoroughly and test drive it before accepting it.

Secondhand cars

Secondhand cars can be bought and sold through dealers, privately or at auctions. Check current advertisements and published price guides to make sure you are paying or charging the right price.

Dealers

When comparing dealers you need to look for one of good local reputation with good repair facilities. It is always a good idea to shop around, however, particularly when selling a car.

Buying In choosing which car to buy you need to follow the same general guidelines which apply when buying a new car. In addition there are specific considerations which apply to the assessment of a secondhand car, and these are explained on the facing page. Reputable dealers will frequently offer a warranty with a secondhand car. Study it carefully to find out exactly what is included. If you do not feel fully competent to assess properly the car you are interested in, either take a friend with you who can advise you or obtain an engineer's report (from your motoring organisation, for example).

Selling When selling your car to a dealer shop around to obtain the best price. Offers can vary a great deal. In many cases, however, the sale of your car will be tied, in part-exchange, to the purchase of another.

Private sale

There are greater risks in buying and selling privately, but for many it is a convenient form of transaction. A private seller is not governed by the Sale of Goods Act, however.

Buying All the checks of a car's condition are especially important when buying privately because no warranty will be supplied. Another important aspect, as the vendor will probably be unknown, is to make as sure as possible that he actually owns the car and is entitled to sell it. Unfortunately the log-book is not proof of ownership. The car may also be the subject of unpaid hire purchase, causing complications.

Selling Selling a car privately may be a slow business but it will probably realise the best price. The purchaser will almost certainly wish to bargain, so choose the selling price with care, using the published price guides, and comparable advertisements. The facing page shows the points which a purchaser will examine, so pay attention to these when preparing your car for sale. Offer a test drive, provided the potential buyer has a licence and the car is insured. If the payment is by cheque retain both the car and the log book until the cheque has been cleared.

Auction

It is possible to obtain a bargain at an auction, but it is important to know exactly what you are doing.

Buying You bid for a car without hearing it run or driving it. After you have bought it you have only a few hours to discover any undeclared faults.

Selling Put on a sensible reserve price and be sure to declare any known faults.

Raising the money

There are several ways of raising the money to buy a car.

Hire purchase The car remains the property of the hire purchase company until all the repayments have been made. Normally one-third of the purchase price is required as a deposit and the rest is paid over two years.

Credit agreement You own the car right away and tax relief is available on the interest. If payments lapse, the finance house can sue for the whole amount to be paid immediately.

Personal loan These are available from finance houses. You own the car right away and tax relief is available on the interest. A personal loan may also be available from your bank.

Overdraft This depends entirely on your bank manager and the amount you may borrow is a matter for his discretion. The interest rate is determined by the prevailing minimum lending rate and is not fixed.

Assessment of the car

Bodywork Should be clean, bright and free from rust. All fittings should be clean, secure and straight. Check for signs of respraying.

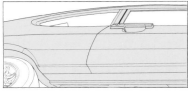

Interior Seats should be clean and firm, roof linings and carpets free from wear and tears. Check for signs of rust in the floor, and hard wear in pedals and steering.

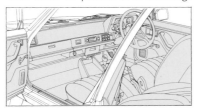

Suspension Push the car down firmly at each corner. The body should bounce once then return to a stable position.

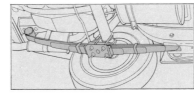

Engine Look for a clean engine that starts properly from cold. Check engine and chassis numbers against the log book. Examine hoses and electrics for signs of wear or neglect.

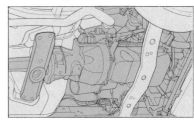

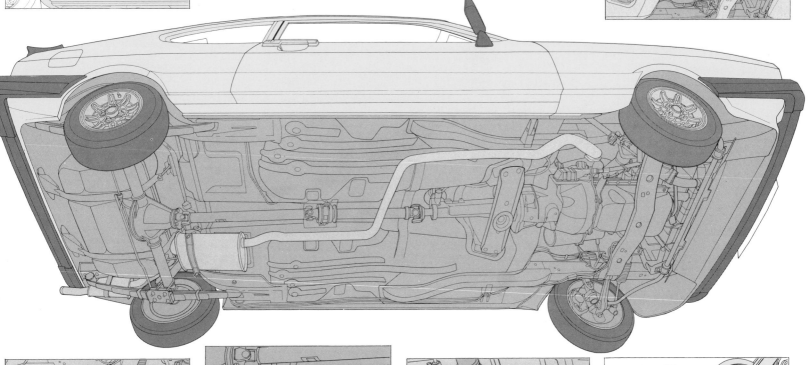

Wheels Check for wear in the king pins or bearings. Also examine brakes for leaks and rust. Also look at the tyres (including the spare) for wear and tread depth.

Exhaust Carefully examine the exhaust system for signs of leaks or loose mountings.

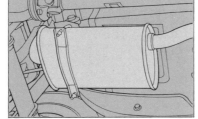

Leaks Look for leaks before and after a test drive, particularly from the back axle and around the gearbox.

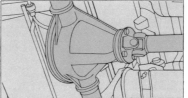

Test drive Always take the car for a test drive. Make sure all the controls work properly and listen for unusual noises from the engine, gear box or rear axle.

Books and films Useful information

A wealth of further information is available for those interested in driving. This is published in a variety of forms, books, magazines and films. Many will be available in local libraries, and the films can all be readily obtained. Everyone whose interest in driving has been aroused or developed by this work will find much of interest in the materials described here.

Books

Advanced Driver
Joe Kells.
Published by David and Charles.

Advanced Motoring
Institute of Advanced Motorists.
Published by Macdonald and Jane's.

Are You a Skilful Driver?
Norman Sullivan.
Published by Charles Letts.

Attention All Drivers
Jock Taylor.
Published by The Order of the Road.

Book of the Car
Published by Drive Publications.

Car Driving in Two Weeks
Lawrence Nathan, revised by Andrew M Hunt.
Published by Elliot Right Way Books.

Drivecraft
Geoffrey Godwin.
Published by Barrie and Rockliffe.

Driver Training for Young People
Ministry of Transport.
Published by HMSO.

Driving
Department of Transport.
Published by HMSO.

Driving Instructor's Handbook
T&E Wilson. Published by Elliot Right Way Books.

Driving Made Easy
Ken Jolly. Published by Macmillan and Penguin (paperback).

Driving Today. The BSM Way
Tom Wisdom and Ronald Priestly.
Published by Peter Davies.

Expert Driving The Police Way
John Miles.
Published by Peter Davies and Sphere Books (paperback).

Fitness for the Motorist
Dennis Chambers.
Published by Charles Letts.

Guide to Law for the Motorist
Peter Hughman and David Lewis.
Published by Aidfairs.

Highway Code
Published by HMSO.

Highway Code Questions and Answers
John Humphreys.
Published by Elliot Right Way Books.

How to Drive Safely
John Eldred Howard.
Penguin Books.

Know Your Traffic Signs
Published by the Department of Transport.

Lawyer in Your Car
Anthony Brigden and Stewart Patterson. Published by Temco.

Lucas make the 'L' Test Easy
Roy Johnstone.
Published by W Foulsham.

Money Saving Motoring
Published by Drive Publications.

Motoring Law A to Z
J L Thomas.
Published by Elliot Right Way Books.

Parking Law
Charles Brandreth.
Published by David and Charles.

Road Accidents. What would you do?
Dennis Chambers.
Published by Charles Letts.

Roadcraft
Published by HMSO.

Road Research—Driver Instruction
Published by the Organisation for Economic Co-operation and Development.

Road Safety Research
Published by Salford University.

An evaluation of the effectiveness of driver and traffic education in reducing road accidents among adolescents. S. Raymond and others.
An examination of the problems of continuous assessment in driver education. A M Risk.
An examination of the relevance of current educational research for driver education. A M Risk.
Notes for the course of driver education used in the Salford Road Safety Experiment. K W Jolly.
The use of accidents and traffic offences as criteria for evaluating courses in driver education. Jean Shaoul.
The use of driving tests as alternative criteria to accidents for evaluating driver education. Jean Shaoul.
The use of scholastic tests of driving knowledge and the national licensing test as criteria for evaluating the effects of driver education. Jean Shaoul.

The use of a test of driving knowledge and driving practices as criteria for evaluating the effectiveness of driver education. Jean Shaoul.

Road Test
Norman Sullivan.
Published by Fontana.

Save Money on Your Car
Stuart Bladon.
Published by Stanley Paul.

Sensible Driving
M J Hosken.
Published by David and Charles.

Skilful Driver
James S Blair.
Published by Temple Press.

Sportsmanlike Driving
American Automobile Association.
Published by McGraw Hill.

Steering Clear
E Hambert.
Published by Neville Spearman.

Very Advanced Driving
A Tom Topper.
Published by Elliot Right Way Books.

Your Driving Test and How To Pass
Published by the Department of Transport.

Magazines

The following is a selected list of motoring magazines which regularly carry articles on driving.
Autocar
Care on the Road
Drive
Milestones
Motor
Popular Motoring
Practical Motorist
Trail

Films

Driver's Eye View
Produced by TRRL.
Demonstrates the movements a driver's eye makes at the wheel.

Winter Driving
Produced by Shell.
Shows how motorists can ensure that their cars and driving methods can cope with winter conditions and the resultant hazards.

Night Driving
Produced by Sorel Films and sponsored by 3M.
Techniques and precautions of night driving.

Skid Sense
Produced by RHR Productions for Dunlop Rubber Company.
Skid-pan demonstrations plus sequences to explain differences in tyre construction.

Is This Your Life?
Produced by Avon Rubber in cooperation with RoSPA.
Michael Bentine introduces a humourous look at the care and maintenance of tyres.

The Law and Your Tyres
Produced for India Tyres.
New regulations on tyres explained.

Out of Sight—Out of Mind
Produced by the Shock Absorber Manufacturers' Association.
The dangers of driving on worn shock absorbers.

Worn Shock Absorbers are Dangerous
Produced by the European Shock Absorber Manufacturers' Association.
The effects of driving a car with worn shock absorbers in wet conditions.

Drivers—Turning right
Produced by Gulf Oil in co-operation with RoSPA. A Norman Hemsley production.
Ten per cent of accidents occur when turning right. This film demonstrates the correct drill for this manoeuvre.

Think Ahead
Produced by Gulf Oil in co-operation with RoSPA. A Norman Hemsley production.
Emphasises the need to think ahead and maintain sufficient distance between vehicles.

Nothing to Chance
Produced by Gulf Oil in co-operation with RoSPA. A Norman Hemsley production.
Demonstrates that good maintenance and good driving go hand-in-hand. Braking in articulated heavy vehicles demonstrated.

Turn to Better Driving
Produced for RoSPA in co-operation with Avon Tyres. A Norman Hemsley production.
Dick Emery (a one-time driving instructor) demonstrates with the help of models the right and wrong way of dealing with a number of driving hazards.

Road Sense
Produced by RHR Productions for the Dunlop Rubber Company.
Illustrates the right approach to everyday driving situations. Demonstrated by a police driving instructor.

Motoring Practice
Produced by Shell for the Institute of Advanced Motorists. (Sole distribution via RoSPA film library).
Every driver needs to practise. This film covers a wide range of motoring techniques.

Six Candles
Produced for the British Insurance Association.
The last two days in the life of John Smith, an insurance inspector. Although normally a good driver he meets his death through a moment's carelessness.

Ride in a car
Produced for Shell Mex and B.P. Ltd.
A family is looking for a country house by car. The film demonstrates their principles of good driving and shows children playing the 'Traffic Game'.

Motor Mania
Produced by Walt Disney Productions Ltd.
This cartoon shows that many people who behave normally as pedestrians become selfish and thoughtless behind the wheel.

Freeway Phobia (Parts I and II)
Produced by Walt Disney Productions Ltd.
Animated characters illustrate errors in motorway driving.

Defensive Driving
Produced by the Post Office.
A split second is all it takes to end a man's life.

A Testing Job
Produced by the Central Office of Information for the Ministry of Transport.
Describes the how and why of the driving test and the purpose behind the examiner's approach.

A Moment's Reflection
Produced by the Central Office of Information for the Ministry of Transport.
The importance of continuous, defensive driving and the danger of loss of concentration are shown.

Too Close For Comfort
Produced by the Central Office of Information for the Department of the Environment.
Reg Varney commentates while a Driving Instructor demonstrates how space can be preserved in normal driving conditions.

L For Logic
Produced by the Central Office of Information for the Department of the Environment.
The film illustrates that there is a reason for everything asked of a candidate who takes the driving test.

Without Due Care
Produced by the Metropolitan Police.
A twenty-four hour tour of duty by Metropolitan Police traffic officers is like a mobile chess game.

Drive Carefully, Darling
Produced by the Central Office of Information for the Department of the Environment.
A science fiction account of the consequences of ignoring the rules of safe driving. The 'action' takes place inside the driver's head.

The Motorway File
Produced by the Central Office of Information for the Department of the Environment.
A dramatised story of a fatal motorway accident and the events preceding it.

Night Call
Produced by the Central Office of Information for the Department of Transport.
The story of a motoring correspondent's search for the perfect driver. It deals with all aspects of motorway driving procedure, particularly at night or in bad weather conditions.

Know the law Useful information

The law affecting drivers is far from straightforward. Nevertheless, every driver should have a general knowledge of what he can and cannot do, as well as what his rights and obligations are. These pages contain a summary, arranged alphabetically, of the main aspects of the law which should concern the driver. The details given here relate to the law as it affects car drivers in England and Wales, and reflects the law as it stands at 14 September 1979.

Accidents

1 If in any case, owing to the presence of a motor vehicle on a road, an accident occurs whereby personal injury is caused to a person other than the driver of that motor vehicle, or damage is caused to a vehicle other than that motor vehicle or trailer drawn thereby, or damage is caused to an animal other than an animal in or on that vehicle or a trailer drawn thereby or to any other property constructed on, fixed to, growing in or otherwise forming part of the land on which the road in question is situated or land adjacent thereto, the driver of the motor vehicle shall stop and, if required to do so by any person having reasonable grounds for so requiring, give his/her name and address, the name and address of the owner and the identification mark of the vehicle.
2 If, in any such accident the driver of the motor vehicle for any reason does not give his/her name and address to any person so requiring them, he/she should report the accident at a police station or to a police constable as soon as reasonably practicable and, in any case, within twenty-four hours.

Where personal injury to another person is involved, section 166 of the Road Traffic Act 1972 requires the driver, in addition, to produce a Certificate of Insurance to any person having reasonable grounds for wishing to see it. If no such request is made at the time of the accident the driver(s) must report to the police forthwith and certainly within twenty-four hours. In addition the Certificate of Insurance mentioned in this section must be produced then, or within five days of the accident.

The original requirement was that the driver must produce within five days the Certificate of Insurance himself but this is no longer necessary. It must be produced but this can be done by any person. The driver will be at risk if the Certificate of Insurance is not produced but he is no longer personally required to do so.

There is no requirement upon the police to give a notice of intended prosecution if at the time of the alleged offence or immediately thereafter an accident occurs owing to the presence on a road of the vehicle in respect of which this offence was committed.

Age of drivers

It is an offence to drive a motor car on a public road, or to permit another person to do so, under the age of 17. There is no maximum age limit.

Alcohol

It is an offence to drive, attempt to drive or be in charge of a motor vehicle on a public highway if one's ability to drive properly is for the time being impaired by reason of drink and a police officer may arrest without warrant any person who is committing such an offence.

It is also an offence to drive, attempt to drive or be in charge of a motor vehicle on a public highway if the proportion of alcohol in your blood exceeds 80 milligrammes of alcohol in 100 millilitres of blood or 107 milligrammes of alcohol in 100 millilitres of urine.

You may be required by a police officer in uniform to undergo a breath test on the spot if there has been an accident in which he suspects you were involved when driving, or attempting to drive, with alcohol in your body (special provisions apply in the case of hospital patients).

A police officer in uniform may require any person driving or attempting to drive a motor vehicle on a road or other public place to take a breathalyser test if he has reasonable cause to suspect him of having alcohol in his body or if he suspects him of having committed a moving traffic offence.

It is an offence to refuse the request for a breath test without reasonable excuse and you may be arrested if you do so. The phrase 'without reasonable excuse' has been narrowly interpreted and you should always co-operate with the request unless, for example, it is physically impossible for you to do so.

If the breath test shows that the maximum level of alcohol in your blood has been exceeded, you can be arrested and be taken to a police station and there you will be given the opportunity of taking another breath test.

If this second test is positive, or you

refuse to take one, the police will then ask you to have a blood sample taken. If you refuse this, you will be asked to give two urine samples within one hour. It is an offence for you to refuse to give either a blood sample or a urine sample and the penalties are the same as for the main offence under the Act.

Brakes

With some exceptions relating to ancient cars and certain vintage cars, a car must either have one braking system with two means of operation, or two braking systems, each with a separate means of operation. Most modern cars comply with the latter by having a handbrake and a footbrake.

The systems must be made so that in the event of failure of any part (except a fixed member or a brakeshoe anchor pin) through which the braking force is transmitted, the driver is still able to apply the brakes to at least two wheels and so be able to stop within a reasonable distance. This is usually done by the handbrake.

The application of one system must not affect the operation of the other system. Cars first used on or after 1 April 1938 must not have a braking system rendered ineffective by the non-rotation of the engine. It must be capable of being applied by direct mechanical action without any hydraulic, electrical or pneumatic device.

Every part of each braking system must be in good working order at all times and be properly adjusted.

Careless driving

This term covers the offences of (a)

driving without due care and attention and (b) driving without reasonable consideration for other road users. (See *Reckless driving*).

Driver licensing

You may drive a motor vehicle on a public road if you hold, or are renewing, an appropriate driving licence issued in Great Britain. Special rules apply to holders of licences issued abroad.

A full licence runs until your 70th birthday or for three years, whichever is the longer. Licences can be renewed after your 70th birthday and will run for three years or less, with the possibility of further renewals after that.

In order to obtain a full licence it is necessary for first-time drivers to pass a driving test. With a view to passing this test, a person can apply for a provisional driving licence. Conditions attached to a provisional licence are that the driver must not drive unless under the supervision of a qualified driver, no trailer is drawn and 'L' plates are displayed.

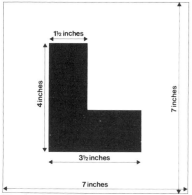

To obtain a driving test a completed form (available from post offices or the Traffic Area Office) must be

sent to the latter with the correct fee. On the day of the test, and at the specified location, you must provide a suitable vehicle, your provisional driving licence and you must also sign the examiner's attendance sheet.

To pass the test you must prove that you are:
1 Fully conversant with the Highway Code;
2 Competent to drive without danger to and with due consideration for other road users;
3 Able to comply with the requirements listed in the relevant Regulations. These requirements concern the ability to carry out certain driving manoeuvres and the ability to see properly.

If you pass the test you may immediately drive any vehicle in the group printed on your driving licence. If you fail, the examiner will hand you a statement listing the reasons why; and one month must elapse before you may retake the test.

Drugs

In relation to motoring offences, drugs include those obtained by a doctor's prescription as well as illegal drugs. It is an offence to drive or be in charge of a motor vehicle whilst 'unfit' through the taking of drugs, which means your ability to drive is impaired as a result of the influence of drugs consumed. If you are charged with driving under the influence of drugs, the procedure with the police is somewhat similar to that for alcohol.

Eyesight

It is an offence for a driver to be unable to read a registration mark,

in good daylight, with $3\frac{1}{2}$ inches high letters and figures at a distance of 75 feet (67 feet if the letters are $3\frac{1}{8}$ inches high). It is also an offence to refuse a policeman's request to undergo such a test.
Note You may wear glasses while taking this test and they must then always be worn for driving.

Horn

An audible warning device must be fitted to all motor vehicles. Only certain motor vehicles are permitted to have a bell, a gong, a siren or a two-tone horn.

The horn must not be sounded:
1 on a stationary vehicle, except as a warning to a moving vehicle;
2 between 11.30pm and 7.00am on a restricted road.

Restricted road means one with a system of street lamps placed not more than 200 yards apart or one which is subject to a 30mph speed limit.

Insurance

It is an offence to use, or allow the use of, a motor vehicle on a public road unless there is in existence a current, valid insurance policy relating to that vehicle and its use at the time. Insurance companies will issue a cover note, which is temporary insurance cover, whilst the policy and certificate are being prepared, thus enabling you to drive legally immediately insurance cover is requested.

Lights

The contravention of any lighting provision is an offence but the most common is allowing a vehicle to be on a public road during the

hours of darkness without showing the required lights. Even during the day a car must be equipped with the necessary lights in proper working order. However, it is a defence to show that contravention in respect of use on a road by day arose from a defect in the lights or reflectors which occurred in the course of the journey during which the contravention occurred, or that the contravention arose from a defect in the lights or reflectors and that before the contravention occurred steps had been taken to have the defect remedied with all reasonable expedition.

Direction indicators

With certain limited exceptions (mainly covering old vehicles) all cars must have direction indicators and there are detailed regulations governing their design, use and position. Cars first used before 1 September 1965 may have direction indicators of either the electrically operated semaphore arm type or flashing light type. After that date direction indicators must be of the flashing light type. A flashing light indicator must flash at between 60 and 120 flashes per minute.

Indicators showing to the front only must be amber or white, to the rear only amber or red, to both front and rear, amber. All indicators on the same side must be worked by the same switch and there must be an audible or visible device to show when an indicator is operating. Drivers failing to cancel their indicators have been convicted of careless driving. When a car is stationary direction indicators may be used simultaneously to show an accident, breakdown or other emergency has occurred.

Know the law Useful information

Fog lights (front)

At night, in conditions of fog or falling snow, the law permits you to use two front fog lights or a front fog and a head light instead of head lights. In order to comply with the law's requirements, the lights must be symmetrically placed and must meet prescribed positional requirements. You are also permitted to use the aforementioned lights during daytime in conditions of poor visibility (see *Poor visibility*). With the exception noted below, no front light with a wattage of over 7 watts may be positioned with the highest part of the lit area above 1200mm or with the lowest part below 500mm. It is permissible to mount such a light below 500mm only if its use is confined to fog and falling snow.

Fog lights (rear)

These are obligatory for cars made on or after 1 October 1979 and first used on or after 1 April, 1980. Either a single light marked with an approval mark or two lights each marked with an approval mark will be permitted. If a single light is fitted it will have to be positioned on the offside of the vehicle, and if two are fitted these will have to be fitted symmetrically. In all cases the lit surface of the lights must not be less than 250mm nor more than l metre from the ground. Rear fog lights must meet certain wiring conditions. In the case of fog lights fitted to any vehicle on or after 1 October, 1979, they will have to be fitted so that they are at least 100mm away from a stop light and will not be capable of being illuminated when the car's brakes are applied.

Rear fog lights may only be used

during adverse weather conditions and when the vehicle is in motion, or during an enforced stoppage.

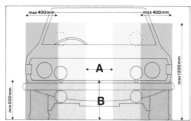

*Fog light positioning, Note **A** Cars registered before 31 December, 1970, may fix their lights not less than 350 mm apart rather than 400 mm from the outside edge of the vehicle.*
*Note **B** Lights sited less than 500 mm from the ground may only be used in fog or falling snow.*

Headlights

A car must have two matched headlights that can show together either main beams, or dipped beams, or two or more matched pairs of headlights so arranged that when the outermost lamps are dipped, the main beams shown by the others go out. The highest part of the lit area must not be more than 1200mm from the ground and the lowest part of the lit area may not be less than 500mm from the ground. In each matched pair, headlights must be at the same height, have the same shape and area, give the same coloured beams and go on and off together. A dipped beam means a beam deflected down, or down and to the left, so as not to dazzle others, technically anyone more than 25ft 3 inches (7·7 metres) away whose eyes are at least 3ft 6 inches (1·1 metres) from the ground.

Headlights must be switched on:
a when a car is in motion on a road during the hours of darkness (half an hour after sunset and half an hour before sunrise), except when the road has street lights not more than 200 yards apart

b in poor daytime visibility. Headlights must be switched off when a car is stationary, except in traffic stops.

Parking lights

There are now standard regulations regarding parking lights which apply all over the country.

Cars parked at night must show two white lights to the front, two red lights and reflectors to the rear, and the rear number plate must be illuminated. They must always be parked with the nearside against the edge of the road.

Cars may stand unlighted if:
a on a road with a speed limit not exceeding 30mph; and
b no part of the vehicle is within 15yds of any part of a junction; and
c facing the correct way, with its nearside as close as possible and parallel to the left hand side of the road (either side when parked in a one-way street).

Rear lights

All cars must have two red matched rear lights visible from a reasonable distance. The lights must be fitted each side of the centre line of the car not more than 16 inches (406mm) from the outermost side of the car and not more than 30 inches (762mm) from the rearmost part of the car. The maximum height from the ground of the highest part of the lit area must not exceed 3ft 6 inches (1060mm), and the minimum height from the ground of the lowest part of this lit area must be at least 15 inches (381mm).

As an alternative the lights may be fitted symmetrically each side of the centre line of the car not more

than 400mm from the outermost side of the car. The maximum height from the ground of the highest part of the lit area must not exceed 1500mm and the minimum height from the ground of the lowest part of such area must be not less than 350mm.

Reflectors

Every car must have two rear facing reflector lights at least 21 inches apart on each side of the centre line of the car. The other positional requirements are the same as for rear lights. Each reflecting area must be vertical and face squarely to the rear.

As an alternative to the above positional requirements you may have rear reflectors fitted symmetrically at least 600mm apart on each side of the centre line of the car and not more than 400mm from its outermost side. The highest part of the reflecting surface must not be further than 900mm from the ground and the lowest part not nearer than 350mm.

Reversing lights

These are not compulsory, but if fitted the maximum number is two and they must only be used for reversing. To use them otherwise will constitute an offence. The lights must be electric, not over 24 watts, and the beam emitted must be incapable of dazzling an observer at least 25ft 3 inches (7·7 metres) away whose eye level is at least 3ft 6 inches (1·1 metres).

The lights may be switched on either automatically when engaging reverse gear, or by operating a switch which serves no other purpose and has a visible device indicating the light is on.

Side lights

During the hours of darkness all cars must carry two lights showing a white light to the front. Yellow is permitted in certain circumstances. The rated wattage of these lights should not exceed 7 watts (otherwise they will have to be capable of being dipped like headlights) and the wattage must be marked on them. In the case of cars first used on or after 1 January, 1972 these lights must have an approval mark. The lights must be on opposite sides of the car at the same height —the highest part of the lit area not more than 5ft 7 inches (1700 mm) from the ground and not more than 1ft 3¾ inches (400mm) from the outermost edge of the car.

Stop lights

Every car first used on or after January 1, 1971 must have two rear red stop lights of not less than 15 and not more than 36 watts. They must be symmetrically positioned on each side of the vehicle. The lit areas must be at least 600mm apart and between 400–500mm above the ground. They must be individually wired, both must be operated automatically when the foot brakes are applied and show a steady red light easily visible from the rear. Stop lights fitted after 1 January, 1974 must be marked with the prescribed 'E' approval mark.

Mascots

It is illegal to carry a mascot on a vehicle in any position where it is likely to cause injury to a person in the event of a collision.

Mirrors

All cars must be fitted with at least one rear-view mirror which may be inside or outside. Passenger vehicles able to carry more than seven people, and goods vehicles, must have at least two mirrors, one externally on the offside the second either inside or externally on the nearside. All cars made on or after 1 December, 1977 and first used on or after 1 June, 1978 must be fitted with two mirrors— one inside, the other mounted on the exterior offside.

Motorways

Restrictions Private cars:
1 must not contravene traffic signs or reverse or be driven on any part which is not a carriageway.
2 must not stop on a carriageway;
3 must not stop on verges or the hard shoulder except in emergencies (note—tiredness is rarely considered an emergency);
4 must not be driven on the central reservation;
5 drawing a trailer must not use the outside lane of a three-lane carriageway;
6 must not be driven by a learner driver.
No-one may walk on a motorway unless absolutely necessary due to an emergency.

Speed limits

Most cars drawing a trailer if the latter has less than four wheels or is a close-coupled four-wheeler— 50mph. Close-coupled means that the distance between the centres of the wheels on one side of the trailer is not over 33 inches.

The maximum speed limit for motor cars is 70mph.

Further requirements

Outside lane is for overtaking only

Overtake only on the right
Never use the hard shoulder for overtaking
When amber warning lights are flashing keep below 30mph.
When red warning lights are flashing, stop.

Noise

Subject to certain exceptions it is illegal to use a motor vehicle which creates noise greater than the permitted sound level as measured by a 'noise-meter'. It is also illegal to use a motor vehicle in such a manner as to cause excessive noise that could reasonably be avoided. In this context, it should be noted, that it is also an offence not to stop the engine of a vehicle when it is stationary (except owing to traffic conditions or repairs). Finally it is an offence to use any motor vehicle or trailer which causes excessive noise. In this latter case, you have a defence if you can show that the noise was due to a temporary or accidental cause which could not reasonably have been avoided or that it was caused by a defect in design or construction or that it was caused by someone else who failed to keep the vehicle in good condition or to correctly pack any load.

Number plates

A car's registration number must be clearly shown at the front and rear either on a flat plate or on a flat, unbroken area on the surface of the car. The letters and figures must be white, silver or grey on a black background; or, on reflective plates, black on a white background at the front and on a yellow background at the rear. All cars first registered after 1972 must have reflective plates. Rear number plates must

be lit at night (but see exceptions described under *Parking lights*). A car may be driven on a public road without a number only if it is on its way to be registered. (See also *Trailers*).

Obstruction

It is an offence to allow a motor vehicle to cause an unnecessary obstruction to others on a public road. No-one has a right, including residents, to leave a vehicle on the roadway except on authorised parking areas. The absence of prohibitory signs does not necessarily imply a right to park, because the rights of road users are limited to a right to pass and repass along a road. A more serious offence is allowing a parked vehicle to cause actual danger e.g. by the place or manner of parking to other road users, which is dependent on prevailing traffic conditions. (See also *Parking*).

One-way streets

It is an offence to drive along a one-way street the wrong way.

Opening doors

Opening a vehicle door on a road in a manner which may cause injury or danger to another person is an offence.

Parking

Controlled zones

Some towns prohibit street parking over a specific area and all points of entry into this area are marked by a sign, although the hours may vary from town to town. Throughout the zone the streets are marked with yellow lines unless signs indicate that parking is permitted. (See *Road markings*). A complication in some controlled areas is that the 'No waiting' restrictions apply for a longer period than that shown on the Controlled Zone signs, and in some streets parking may be prohibited all the time. It is therefore important to read all the relevant signs carefully.

Disc parking zones

Street parking is restricted in zones in the same way as Controlled Zones but 'Disc' replaces 'Controlled' on the zone perimeter signs and disc parking places are marked in certain streets. The disc is set at the time of arrival and this automatically shows the time limit for departure. It is an offence to set the disc ahead of the time the car was actually first parked, to alter it during the time the car is parked or to park for longer than the limited period shown.

Parking meter zones

Street parking in these zones is restricted as explained under Controlled Zones but the street parking places are regulated by meters here. 'Meter' replaces 'Controlled' on the zone perimeter signs. The procedure for parking at meters is:
1 Park in a meter bay and insert the appropriate amount of money, as specified, for the period you wish to park. The maximum lengths of stay vary.

2 A yellow flag appears on the meter when your time has expired and you must remove your car before this happens. You are not allowed to 'feed' the meter by inserting more money for another period of time. If you do not move your car at this stage you become liable to an excess charge which is payable to the local authority within fourteen days.

3 If you leave your car parked at a meter for an excess period of more than that allowed, you have committed an offence.

4 You are not allowed to park again at the same group of meters for at least an hour.

Under another system, generally for off-street parking, you obtain a ticket from a machine and place it conspicuously on your car and the above procedure then applies.

Parking meter offences are usually dealt with under the fixed penalty system whereby a parking ticket is issued and provided the offender pays the penalty specified therein no further proceedings are taken.

Residents' parking

Some urban streets reserve parking places solely for the use of residents of that street. Payment is made to the local council for this privilege and a card of some sort is displayed on the car.

Pedestrian crossings

Two types of crossing exist:

Pelican crossings

These consist of a combination of normal traffic light signals for vehicular traffic and red and green lights for pedestrians. Vehicles must obey the traffic light signals in the usual way but when a flashing amber light is shown, if a pedestrian is on the crossing before the vehicle, he must be given precedence.

The road markings at Pelican Crossings include two lines of studs placed in front of the actual crossing. Vehicles may only stop between the studs and the crossing in complying with the light signals. This is subject to exceptions, e.g. stopping to avoid an accident or being prevented from proceeding by circumstances beyond the driver's control.

Vehicles may not stop on the crossing itself unless either of the above exceptions apply.

Zebra crossings

These are the traditional type of crossing. The motorist must not stop on the crossing itself. He must give precedence to pedestrians unless his vehicle has entered the crossing before the pedestrian. Where there is a central road island, each side of the crossing is regarded as a separate crossing. The motorist must not stop in the 'Zebra controlled area' (indicated by a line of Give Way studs and at least two rows of white zig-zag lines either side of the crossing) except to give precedence to a pedestrian. Nor may he overtake within the Zebra controlled area marked by the zig-zag lines.

Poor visibility

This term includes such conditions adversely affecting visibility (weather consisting of or including fog, smoke, heavy rain or spray, snow, dense cloud or any similar condition), which seriously reduce the ability of the driver (after the appropriate use by him of the windscreen wipers and washer) to see other vehicles or persons on the road or reduces the ability of other users of the road to see the vehicle.

The significance of the definition of poor visibility lies in the fact that you are now required to use either a pair of dipped headlights or a headlight and a front fog light meeting certain requirements, or two front fog lights meeting similar requirements during such weather conditions. In addition, you are also permitted to switch on your rear fog light or lights if fitted to the car.

Reckless driving

Sections 1 and 2 of the Road Traffic Act 1972 as amended read as follows:—
1 A person who causes the death of another person by driving a motor vehicle recklessly shall be guilty of an offence.

2 A person who drives a motor vehicle on a road recklessly shall be guilty of an offence.

A Magistrate's Court during or immediately after hearing a reckless driving charge it considers not proved, can direct or allow a charge of careless driving to be preferred forthwith and may proceed on it by informing the accused (or his representative) of this and giving him opportunity to answer to the new charge.

Registration

All vehicles used on a public road must be registered first. A registration document is issued by the Driver and Vehicle Licensing Centre and must be returned if any of the particulars on the document change or the vehicle is destroyed or permanently exported. It is an offence to mutilate a registration document, obliterate any part of it or make an unauthorised addition.

Reversing

Every vehicle weighing over 410kg must be able to travel backwards. Vehicles must not be reversed for a greater distance or time than may be requisite for the safety or reasonable convenience of the occupants of that vehicle or of other traffic on the road. Negligent reversing can be categorised as careless or dangerous driving and you can be charged accordingly.

Road markings

White lines

It is an offence to cross or straddle continuous double white lines or to stop on a road marked with them except in order to get in and out of premises or a side road, or in order to avoid a stationary obstruction, or in compliance with a direction of a policeman or a traffic warden.

Overtaking is permitted only if the white line on the same side of the road as you are is broken. It is an offence to stop on a road thus marked and to cross the white lines if the continuous line is on the same side of the road as you are (subject to the exceptions above).

The long white dashes which form a hazard warning line should not be crossed until a clear view arises.

Yellow lines

All three markings impose the same restriction, i.e. No Waiting except for loading or unloading and boarding and alighting. However, each marking signifies different periods during which this restriction applies.

2 continuous lines—during every working day and additional times
1 continuous line—during every working day
1 broken line—during any other periods as specified
Always accompanying these road markings are small, yellow, oblong plates on nearby posts showing exactly when parking is prohibited.

Kerb markings

These prohibit loading and unloading during every working day (2), during every working day and additional times (3), and during any other periods as specified (1). Here again the exact periods are shown on nearby signs.

Box junction

This box must not be entered unless the exit from it is clear, except if you intend turning right and are waiting for a gap in the traffic.

School crossing patrols

When a school crossing patrol is exhibiting a 'Stop—Children' sign it is compulsory to stop clear of the crossing and not move forward.

Seat belts

It is compulsory for cars to be fitted with seat belts for the driver and front seat passenger. Cars made before June 30, 1964 are exempt from this ruling as are those registered before January 1, 1965. Regulations control the requirements which must be met by all seat belts including any additional non-compulsory seat belts fitted in the car.

Selling a vehicle

The registered owner of the car in question should tear off the Notification of Sale and Transfer section of the registration document and send it completed to Swansea. The remainder of the document should be handed over to the new owner.

Smoke

It is an offence to use a motor vehicle emitting smoke, vapour or sparks which may cause damage to property or injury to any person on the road.

Speeding

Speed limits are only legal if they are made pursuant to an Act of Parliament and in compliance therewith or as a result of an Order made by a Highway Authority under and in compliance with its statutory powers.

The speed at which a vehicle is driven is restricted either:
1 by the overall speed limit or
2 because of the type of road or
3 by the class of vehicle itself.
Where two or more speed limits apply, the vehicle must be driven at the lowest speed.

Roads which are subject to speed limits must have the correct signs at the commencement and end of the restriction and sometimes at intervals in between.

You cannot be convicted of exceeding any speed limit solely on the opinion of one person—even a policeman—unless the latter can substantiate his evidence with speedometer readings or has used radar detection.

Generally a person who is charged with speeding must:
1 be warned at the time

2 within 14 days have been served with a summons
3 within 14 days have been served with a Notice of Intended Prosecution

It should be noted if you are involved in an accident while speeding the above does not apply.

Alerting a speeding motorist to the presence of a police operated speed trap can risk incurring prosecution on a charge of obstructing the police.

Television

If a television set is installed in a vehicle, it is an offence for the driver to be able to see the screen or a reflection of it. He must not have the controls other than the main switch and volume control within his reach.

Test certificate

Cars more than 3 years old must be covered by an MoT Test Certificate issued within the last 12 months otherwise an offence will be committed. You do not need a current test certificate if you are driving either to or from a previously arranged test nor is a current test certificate required during a previously arranged test. Notwithstanding this exemption the car must be roadworthy. A vehicle may be tested up to one month before the test certificate is due for renewal and the new certificate will run from the expiry date of the old one. Anyone dissatisfied with the result of a test can appeal within 14 days to the Department of the Environment who will re-test the car and may direct a refund of all or part of the appeal fee if the complaint is valid.

Know the law Useful information

Trailers

A trailer is 'a vehicle drawn by a motor vehicle' and this includes caravans and broken-down vehicles. When being towed a trailer must have another person in attendance in addition to the driver unless a) it has only two wheels or b) it has four wheels with two close-coupled wheels on each side or c) it has both automatic overrun and parking brakes.

The maximum overall width generally permitted is 2.3 m and the length must not exceed 7 m unless it has four wheels with a wheel base not less than three fifths its overall length, and is drawn by a vehicle weighing at least 2030 kg, in which case the maximum length is 12 m.

Brakes

Generally, every trailer exceeding 102 kg must be equipped with an efficient braking system, whose requirements vary according to the date of the trailer's manufacture. Unless the brakes automatically operate on the overrun a trailer weighing more than 102 kg unladen, manufactured after 1967, must have a braking system so made that when the trailer is being drawn a) the brakes can be applied to all its wheels by the car driver and b) if any part of the car's braking system fails, the brakes can still be applied to at least two wheels of the trailer.

The braking system must be so constructed that when the trailer is stationary the brakes can be applied to at least two wheels and be released by a person standing on the ground. The operation should be carried out using a device fitted to the trailer,

such that it can be operated by mechanical action alone and the braking force can hold the trailer stationary on a gradient of at least 1 in 6.25.

Note The foregoing does not apply to broken-down vehicles when being towed.

Trailer closets

It is illegal to allow the contents of any closet, urinal, lavatory basin or sink to be discharged on to the road surface.

Indicator lights

Trailers must in general have flashing amber indicators optically separated from other lights. These must be displayed unless the car's indicators are visible at 6 m from behind the rear of the trailer.

Note The foregoing does not apply to broken-down vehicles when being towed.

Trailer lights

It is compulsory to have two red lights, two triangular red reflectors and an illuminated number plate at the rear of a trailer. Front side lights must also be carried if the sides of the trailer extend more than 12 inches beyond the outermost point of the side lights of the towing car and they must indicate the width of the trailer and its load. If the front of the trailer is more than 5 feet from the car drawing it, the towing car must also show rear lights and the trailer must show front side lights.

Registration mark

A trailer and a broken-down vehicle towed must show at the rear the same registration mark as the towing car.

Tow ropes

The rope or chain between the two vehicles concerned must not exceed 5 m and if it extends to over 1·5 m in length must be rendered easily distinguishable.

Traffic lights

It is an offence not to stop at the red light of any traffic signals. It is also an offence not to stop when amber alone is shown except when to do so would be unsafe. If, when the lights are in your favour, the front part of your vehicle travels over the 'stop' line and you then have to stop owing to traffic conditions, you are not allowed to continue travelling forward when the lights turn to red and must wait until green shows again. A policeman's 'stop' signal overrides a traffic light 'go' signal to cross a junction.

Traffic wardens

When so required to do so by a Chief Officer of Police, traffic wardens are authorised to perform certain police traffic duties (but not from a moving vehicle) and have similar powers, including requiring your name and address for offences regarding lighting, obstruction, no waiting, disobeying signs and signals, road parking, licensing and registration.

Tyres

Pneumatic tyres must be fitted to all cars weighing over 1020 kg and those first used after 2nd January, 1933. Tyres must not be used which are either unsuitable in themselves or in combination with other tyres, i.e. you may not mix different types of tyre such as cross ply and radials; are not

properly inflated; have a break in the fabric; have a cut more than 25 mm long or 10% of the section width, whichever is the greater; have a lump or bulge caused by separation or partial failure of their structure; have any part of the ply or cord structure exposed; or have a tread pattern less than 1 mm deep for at least three-quarters of the tread's width all round the tyre. It is permissible to use one of the new varieties of tyre which are designed to be used even when flat.

Vehicle licence (tax)

It is illegal (with certain exceptions) to use or keep a vehicle on a public road without a licence. Once it is proved that the vehicle was on the road it is up to the accused to prove that it was licensed. A person is not usually prosecuted (but can be) for using an unlicensed vehicle within 14 days of the expiry of the old licence, provided he obtains a new licence within that time.

It is also an offence to:
1 Fail to exhibit a current licence
2 Fail to display a licence on the nearside of the car's windscreen
3 Alter, deface or mutilate a licence
4 Exhibit a licence on which the details have become illegible or the colour has changed
5 Exhibit anything which could be mistaken for a licence

Windscreen wipers and washers

Windscreens must be fitted with one or more efficient automatic wipers capable of clearing the screen so that the driver has an adequate view of the road in front of the vehicle and in front of the near and off sides of the vehicle. There must also be windscreen washers which work in conjunction with the wipers.

Index

Entries printed in bold type, eg **18**, refer to the page where the main discussion of the topic takes place.

Entries printed in italic type, eg *218*, refer to the section of the book directed at those learning to drive.

A

B

C

D

Index

E

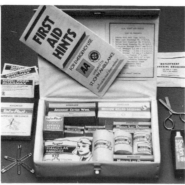

F

G

H

I

J

K

Karting **189**
Keep fit exercises **154**

L

M

N

O

P

Index

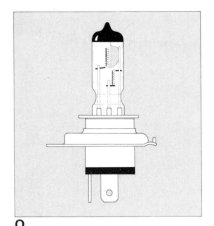

Q

R

S

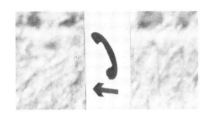

U

V

W

Y

Z

The publishers wish to thank the following individuals and organisations for their assistance in the preparation of this book:

F Ashton Limited
Autocar
Autosafe Limited
Berkshire Caravans
Robert Bosch Limited
Britax
British School of Motoring Limited
Britover (Continental) Limited
Brown Brothers Limited
Burmah Castrol Limited
C B S Limited
Jim Clark Foundation
Cobra Automotive Products Limited
L Dennis
Department of Transport
Desmo Limited
Dollond & Aitchison Limited
Ebley Tyre Services
W Edwards
Firesnow Limited
Ford Motor Company Limited
Freeline Limited
Harrow Driving Centre
Hertfordshire County Council
Dennis Hunter Limited
Institute of Advanced Motorists
Kangol Magnet Limited
Kemble Skid Training School
K L Automotive Products Limited
Leicestershire Constabulary
Magnatex Limited
Medic-Alert Foundation
The Metropolitan Police
Motor Schools Association
Panasonic Limited
Radiomobile Limited
Romark
Royal Society for the Prevention of Accidents
Jim Russell International Racing Drivers' School
Schukra
SOS Talisman Company Limited
Transport and Road Research Laboratory
Voxson Audio Limited
Waso Security Systems Limited
Wilmot Breeden Limited
Wiltshire County Council
Wolfrace Wheels Limited
Wood & Pickett Limited